Readings from the
Ancient Near East

Encountering Biblical Studies
Walter A. Elwell, General Editor and New Testament Editor
Eugene H. Merrill, Old Testament Editor

Encountering the Old Testament: A Christian Survey
Bill T. Arnold and Bryan E. Beyer

Readings from the Ancient Near East: Primary Sources for Old Testament Study
Bill T. Arnold and Bryan E. Beyer, editors

Encountering the New Testament: A Historical and Theological Survey
Walter A. Elwell and Robert W. Yarbrough

Readings from the First-Century World: Primary Sources for New Testament Study
Walter A. Elwell and Robert W. Yarbrough, editors

Encountering the Book of Genesis: A Study of Its Content and Issues
Bill T. Arnold

Encountering the Book of Psalms: A Literary and Theological Introduction
C. Hassell Bullock

Encountering the Book of Isaiah
Bryan E. Beyer

Encountering John: The Gospel in Historical, Literary, and Theological Perspective
Andreas J. Köstenberger

Encountering the Book of Romans: A Theological Survey
Douglas J. Moo

Encountering the Book of Hebrews: An Exposition
Donald A. Hagner

Readings from the Ancient Near East

Primary Sources for Old Testament Study

Edited by

**Bill T. Arnold
and Bryan E. Beyer**

Baker Academic
Grand Rapids, Michigan

Published by Baker Academic
a division of Baker Publishing Group
P.O. Box 6287, Grand Rapids, MI 49516-6287
www.bakeracademic.com

Fourth printing, October 2006

Printed in the United States of America

Library of Congress Cataloging-in-Publication Data
Readings from the ancient Near East : primary sources for Old Testament study / edited by Bill T. Arnold and Bryan E. Beyer.
     p.   cm. — (Encountering biblical studies)
   Includes bibliographical references and index.
   ISBN 10: 0-8010-2292-4 (pbk.)
   ISBN 978-0-8010-2292-0 (pbk.)
    1. Middle East—Religion—History—Sources. 2. Bible. O.T.—History of contemporary events—Sources. I. Arnold, Bill T. II. Beyer, Bryan. III. Series.
BL1060 .R42 2002
221.9′5—dc21

2002023957

Contents

Readings

Acknowledgments

The publisher and editors wish to thank the following for granting permission to reprint, in a slightly modified form, material from their works.

A. K. Grayson

A. K. Grayson, *Assyrian Royal Inscriptions* (Harrassowitz, 1972–76).

American Oriental Society

J. J. Finkelstein, "An Old Babylonian Herding Contract and Genesis 31:38f," *Journal of the American Oriental Society* (1968).

S. N. Kramer, "The 'Babel of Tongues': A Sumerian Version," *Journal of the American Oriental Society* (1968).

American Schools of Oriental Research

M. Held, "Philological Notes on the Mari Covenant Rituals," *Bulletin of the American Schools of Oriental Research* (1970).

B. Lewis, *The Sargon Legend: A Study of the Akkadian Text and the Tale of the Hero Who Was Exposed at Birth* (1980).

E. A. Speiser, "New Kirkuk Documents Relating to Family Laws," *Annual of the American Schools of Oriental Research* (1930).

Biblical Archaeology Society

P. K. McCarter Jr., *Ancient Inscriptions: Voices from the Biblical World* (1996). Used by permission of the Biblical Archaeology Society.

D. I. Block

D. I. Block, *The Gods of the Nations: Studies in Ancient Near Eastern National Theology* (Evangelical Theological Society, 1988).

Eisenbrauns

W. G. Lambert and A. R. Millard, *Atra-ḫasīs: The Babylonian Story of the Flood* (1969).

B. T. Arnold, "The Weidner Chronicle and the Idea of History in Israel and Mesopotamia," in *Faith, Tradition, and History: Old Testament Historiography in Its Near Eastern Context* (1994).

E. J. Brill

W. W. Hallo and K. L. Younger Jr., eds., *The Context of Scripture*, vol. 1: *Canonical Compositions from the Biblical World* (1997).

Helsinki University Press

S. Parpola and K. Watanabe, *Neo-Assyrian Treaties and Loyalty Oaths* (1988).

Hermann Hunger and Stephen A. Kaufman

H. Hunger and S. A. Kaufman, "A New Akkadian Prophecy Text," *Journal of the American Oriental Society* (1975).

Israel Exploration Society, Jerusalem

A. Biran and J. Naveh, "The Tel Dan Inscription: A New Fragment," *Israel Exploration Journal* (1995).

J. J. Augustin

A. K. Grayson, *Assyrian and Babylonian Chronicles* (1975).

Johns Hopkins University Press

W. L. Moran, *The Amarna Letters*. Pp. 326–32. © 1992. Johns Hopkins University Press.

Oxford University Press

R. O. Faulkner, *The Ancient Egyptian Pyramid Texts* (1969), 246–47. Reprinted by permission of Oxford University Press.

J. C. L. Gibson, *Textbook of Syrian Semitic Inscriptions*, volume 1 (1971), 2, 53, 75–77. Reprinted by permission of Oxford University Press.

J. C. L. Gibson, *Textbook of Syrian Semitic Inscriptions*, volume 2 (1975), 9–13. Reprinted by permission of Oxford University Press.

J. C. L. Gibson, *Textbook of Syrian Semitic Inscriptions*, volume 3 (1982), 47–55. Reprinted by permission of Oxford University Press.

Pontifical Biblical Institute Press

J. A. Fitzmyer, *The Aramaic Inscriptions of Sefire* (Editrice Pontificio Istituto Biblico, Roma, 1967).

D. J. McCarthy, *Treaty and Covenant: A Study in Form in the Ancient Oriental Documents and in the Old Testament* (Editrice Pontificio Istituto Biblico, Roma, 1978).

W. L. Moran, "New Evidence from Mari on the History of Prophecy." *Biblica* (Editrice Pontificio Istituto Biblico, Roma, 1969).

Princeton University Press

J. B. Pritchard, ed., *Ancient Near Eastern Texts Relating to the Old Testament.* Copyright © 1950, 1955, 1969 renewed 1978 by Princeton University Press. Reprinted by permission of Princeton University Press.

SCM Press

W. Beyerlin, ed., *Near Eastern Religious Texts Relating to the Old Testament*, translated by John Bowden, Old Testament Library (1975). Used by permission of SCM Press.

Semitic Museum, Harvard University

J. A. Hackett, *The Balaam Text from Deir 'Alla* (1980). Reprinted by permission of the Semitic Museum, Harvard University.

Society of Biblical Literature

H. A. Hoffner Jr., *Hittite Myths*, edited by G. M. Beckman (1990). Reprinted by permission of the Society of Biblical Literature.

M. T. Roth, *Law Collections from Mesopotamia and Asia Minor*, edited by P. Michalowski (1995). Reprinted by permission of the Society of Biblical Literature.

T & T Clark

K. A. D. Smelik, *Writings from Ancient Israel: A Handbook of Historical and Religious Documents*, translated by G. I. Davies (1991).

Thomas Nelson

D. W. Thomas, ed., *Documents from Old Testament Times* (1958).

Toronto University Press

A. K. Grayson, *Assyrian Rulers of the Early First Millennium B.C. (858–745 B.C.)* (1996). Reprinted by permission of Toronto University Press.

Tyndale House

R. S. Hess, "Yahweh and His Asherah? Epigraphic Evidence for Religious Pluralism in Old Testament Times," in *One God, One Lord in a World of Religious Pluralism* (1991).

University of California Press

M. Lichtheim, *Ancient Egyptian Literature: A Book of Readings* (1973–80).

Westminster John Knox Press

M. D. Coogan, *Stories from Ancient Canaan.* ©1978 The Westminster Press. Used by permission of Westminster John Knox Press.

W. Beyerlin, ed., *Near Eastern Religious Texts Relating to the Old Testament*, translated by John Bowden, Old Testament Library (1975). Used by permission of Westminster John Knox Press.

Yale University Press

T. Jacobsen, *The Harps That Once . . . : Sumerian Poetry in Translation* (1987).

The authors and publisher have made every effort to ascertain the copyright status of every reading in this book. Any failure to give proper credit that is brought to the publisher's attention will be amended in subsequent printings of the book.

Introduction

The present volume complements *Encountering the Old Testament* and likewise targets an undergraduate audience. The book's goal is to provide college students with a basic collection of the ancient Near Eastern texts that most closely parallel or complement the biblical text. We want our readers to understand that the Bible was written in a certain historical, political, social, and cultural context, and we trust that these texts will help provide some of that context.

The texts are arranged according to the canonical order of the English Bible. While some texts have relevance to several different parts of the Old Testament, we have tried to place them at the point of closest correspondence. We have also included a limited number of pictures for illustrative purposes.

The anthologizing of ninety texts from various monographs and journals provided special challenges. When possible, we maintained standard scholarly practice, but to promote better student understanding, we removed archaic English language and brought consistency to spelling and punctuation. In addition, we standardized and simplified diacritical markings and applied the following symbols and typographic conventions:

italic type	sense-completing words (that is, material added for clarification)
SMALL CAPS	foreign words
[ ]	gap in the text; translator made educated/logical guess
. . .	short gap in the text; translator uncertain about what went there
(gap)	long gap in the text; translator uncertain about what went there
(?)	uncertain translation

Our goal is to give our readers a basic knowledge of the ancient voices, not to retranslate these texts. We acknowledge the careful scholarship of those who have gone before us, and any responsibility for errors in smoothing translations must remain our own.

We wish to thank Brian Bolger of Baker Book House for working with us to produce a quality volume. Elizabeth Eremic, a Columbia International University student, provided valuable support by proofing the manuscript and also assisted in the English translation of the SHURPU and MAQLU incantation texts (readings 88 and 89). A special note of thanks is due to Dr. Avraham Biran, Director of the Nelson Glueck School of Biblical Archaeology at the Hebrew Union College–Jewish Institute of Religion in Jerusalem, for his gracious permission to use the photo of the Tel Dan inscription on the cover of the volume. We are also grateful to Ms. Hanni Hirsch, Dr. Biran's assistant, for working out the details. As Hebrew Union College alumni, we feel especially honored to have this text adorn the cover of our book.

It is our hope and prayer that many students will come to a better understanding of the biblical text in its historical, political, social, and cultural context through reading this volume.

Part
1

Pentateuch

1 Creation and the Flood

Every human society attempts to explain the origins of the universe. In the nineteenth century, scholars began to recover and decipher literary texts from the ancient Near East. The great civilizations of Mesopotamia, Egypt, and Asia Minor had their own cosmogonies and cosmologies, which scholars quickly compared to Genesis. The Bible's accounts of the creation of the world, the creation of humankind, and the flood were not borrowed from these, but neither are they unique in every respect. These parallel myths and epics from the ancient Near East illustrate that Israel was part of a larger world community and offered an alternative perception on reality.

#1: Eridu Genesis
(Jacobsen, *Harps That Once*, 145–50)[1]

Several versions of a Sumerian creation account from approximately 1600 B.C. have been preserved in fragmentary form. "Eridu Genesis" contains several parallels with the opening chapters of Genesis, but is particularly interesting because of the similar way in which it structures the stories of the creation of humankind, the institution of kingship, the first cities, and a great flood. The hero of the Sumerian flood story is named Ziusudra.

[Nintur] was paying [attention]:
Let me bethink myself of my
    humankind,
all forgotten as they are;
and [mindful] of mine, Nintur's,
    creatures
let me bring them back,
let me lead the people back from their
    trails.
May they come and build cities and cult
    places,

that I may cool myself in their shade;
may they lay the bricks for the cult cities
in pure spots, and
may they found places for divination
in pure spots!
She gave directions for purification, and
    cries for clemency,
the things that cool *divine* wrath,
perfected the divine service and the
    august offices,
said to the *surrounding* regions: Let me
    institute peace there!
When An, Enlil, Enki, and Ninhursaga
fashioned the dark-headed *people*,
they had made the small animals *that*
    come up from *out of* the earth
come from the earth in abundance
and had let there be, as befits *it*, gazelles,
wild donkeys and four-footed beasts in
    the desert.
And let me have *him* advise;
let me have *him* oversee their [labor],
and let *him* [teach] the nation to follow
    along
unerringly like [cattle]!
When the royal [scepter] was [coming]
    down from heaven,
the august [crown] and the royal
    [throne] being already
down from heaven,
he *the king* [regularly] performed to
    perfection
the august divine services and offices,
laid [the bricks] of those cities [in pure
    spots].
They were named by name and [allotted
    half]-bushel baskets.
The firstling of those cities, Eridu,
she gave to the leader Nudimmud,
the second, Bad-Tibira, she gave to the
    prince and the sacred one

the third, Larak, she gave to Pabilsag,
the fourth, Sippar, she gave to the
　　gallant, Utu.
the fifth, Shuruppak, she gave to
　　Ansud.
These cities, which had been named by
　　names,
and had been allotted half-bushel
　　baskets,
dredged the canals, which were blocked
　　with purplish
wind-borne clay, and they carried water.
Their cleaning of the smaller canals
established abundant growth.

　　(gap)

That day [Nintur] wept over her
　　creatures
and holy Inanna [was full] of grief over
　　their people;
but Enki [took] counsel with his own
　　heart.
An, Enlil, Enki, and Ninhursaga
had the gods of heaven and earth
　　[swear]
by the names An and Enlil.
At that time Ziusudra was king
and priest of purification.
He fashioned, being a seer,
the god of giddiness
and [stood] in awe beside it, wording
　　his wishes humbly.
[As he] stood there regularly day after
　　day
something that was not a dream was
　　appearing:
[conversation]
a swearing *of* oaths by heaven and earth,
[a touching of throats]
and the gods [bringing their thwarts] *up*
　　to Kiur.
And as Ziusudra stood there beside it,
　　he [went on hearing]:
Step up to the wall to my left and listen!
Let me speak a word to you at the wall
[and may you grasp] what *I* say:
May you [heed] my advice!
By our hand a flood will sweep over
the cities of the half-bushel [baskets, and
　　the country;

the decision] that humankind is to be
　　destroyed,
has been made.
a verdict, a command of the [assembly,
cannot be revoked],
an order of An and [Enlil is not known
ever to have been countermanded],
their kingship, their term, [has been
　　uprooted
they must bethink themselves of that]
Now . . .
What I [have to say to you] . . .
All the evil winds, all stormy winds
　　gathered into one
and with them, then, the Flood was
　　sweeping over *the cities of*
the half-bushel baskets
for seven days and seven nights.
After the flood had swept over the
　　country,
after the evil wind had tossed the big
　　boat
about on the great waters,
the sun came out spreading light
over heaven and earth.
Ziusudra then drilled an opening in the
　　big boat.
and the gallant Utu sent his light
into the interior of the big boat.
Ziusudra, being the king,
stepped up before Utu kissing the
　　ground *before him.*
The king was butchering oxen, was
　　being lavish with the sheep
[barley cakes], crescents together with
　　. . .
. . . he was crumbling for him

　　(gap)

[juniper, the pure plant of the
mountains] he filled [on the fire]
and with a . . . clasped to
[the beast he] . . .
You here have sworn
by the life's breath of heaven
the life's breath of earth
that he truly is allied with you yourself;
you there, An and Enlil,
have sworn by the life's breath of
　　heaven,
the life's breath of earth,

that he is allied with all of you.
He will disembark the small animals
that come up from the earth!
Ziusudra, being king,
stepped up before An and Enlil
kissing the ground,
And An and Enlil after [honoring him]
were granting him life like a god's,
were making lasting breath of life, like a
    god's,
descend into him.
That day they made Ziusudra,
preserver, as king, of the name of the
    small
animals and the seed of humankind,
live toward the east over the mountains
in Mount Dilmun.

#2: Enki and Ninhursag
(*ANET* 37–41)[2]

"Enki and Ninhursag" is a Sumerian myth about the loss of paradise. Some scholars believe it parallels the loss of the garden of Eden.[3] Dilmun, the paradisaical location of the action, is a clean and pure place with neither sickness nor death. The gods inhabit the land peacefully until the Sumerian water-god, Enki, eats eight plants in Dilmun. The date of composition is unknown, although our copies are from the first half of the second millennium B.C.

[The place] is [pure] . . . ,
. . . [the land] Dilmun is pure;
[the land Dilmun is pure] . . . ,
. . . the [land Dilmun] is pure;
the land Dilmun is pure, the land
    Dilmun is clean;
the land Dilmun is clean, the land
    Dilmun is most bright.
Who had lain by himself in Dilmun—
the place, after Enki had lain with his
    wife,
that place is clean, that place is most
    bright;
who had lain by himself *in Dilmun*—
the place, *after* Enki *had lain* by
    Ninsikilla,
that place is clean, *that place is bright*.
In Dilmun the raven utters no cries,
the ITTIDU bird utters not the cry of the
    ITTIDU bird,
the lion kills not,

the wolf snatches not the lamb,
unknown is the kid-devouring [wild
    dog],
unknown is the grand-devouring . . . ,
[unknown] is the . . . widow,
the bird on high . . . not its . . . ,
the dove [droops] not the head,
the sick-eyed says not, I am sick-eyed,
the sick-headed *says* not, I am sick-
    headed,
its old woman *says* not, I am an old
    woman,
its old man *says* not, I am an old man,
unbathed is the maid, no sparkling
    water is poured in the city,
who crosses the river utters no . . . ,
[the wailing priest walks not round
    about him],
the singer utters no [wail],
by the side of the city he *utters* no
    [lament].
Ninsikilla says to her father Enki:
The city you have given, the city you
    have given, your . . . ,
Dilmun, the city you have given, the city
    you have given, your . . . ,
has not . . . [of] the river;
Dilmun, the city you have given, the city
    you have given, your . . . ,

    (gap)

[Father Enki answers Ninsikilla, his
    daughter:
Let Utu standing in heaven,
from the . . . , the breast of his . . . ,
from the . . . of Nanna,
the mouth from which issues the water
    of the earth,
bring you sweet water from the earth];
let him bring up the water into your
    large . . . ,
let him make your city drink from it the
    waters of abundance,
let him make Dilmun *drink from it* the
    waters of [abundance],
let your well of bitter water become a
    well of sweet water,
[Let your furrowed fields and farms
    bear you grain],
let your city become the [bank-quay]
    house of the land,

now Utu is a . . .
Utu [standing] in heaven,
from the . . . , the [breast] of his . . . ,
from the . . . of Nanna,
the mouth from which issues the water
    of the earth,
brought her sweet water from the earth;
he brings up the water into her large
    . . . ,
makes her city drink from it the waters
    of abundance,
makes Dilmun *drink from it* the waters of
    [abundance],
her well of bitter water, truly it is
    become a well of sweet water,
her [furrowed] fields *and* farms [bore]
    her grain,
her city, truly it is become the [bank-
    quay] house of the land
Dilmun, *truly it is become* the [bank-
    quay] house *of the land*,
now Utu is . . . ; truly it was so.
Who is alone, [before] the wise Nintu,
    the mother of the land,
Enki [before] the wise Nintu, *the mother
    of the land*,
[causes his penis to water] the dikes,
[causes his penis to submerge] the reeds,
truly [causes his penis to] . . .
Thereupon he said: [Let] no one walk in
    the marshland.
Thereupon Enki said: *Let no one walk in
    the marshland*,
he swore by the life of Anu.
[His . . . of] the marshland, . . . [of] the
    marshland,
Enki . . . [his] semen of Damgalnunna,
poured the semen in the womb of
    Ninhursag.
She took the semen into the womb, the
    semen of Enki.
One day being her one month,
two days being her two months,
three days being her three months,
four days being her four months,
five days *being her five months*,
six days *being her six months*,
seven days *being her seven months*,
eight [days] *being her eight months*,
nine [days] being her nine months, the
    months of womanhood,

[like . . . fat], like . . . fat, like good
    princely fat,
[Nintu], the mother of the land, like . . .
    [fat], *like . . . fat, like good princely fat*,
gave birth to [Ninmu].
Ninmu . . . [at] the bank of the river,
Enki in the marshland [looks about,
    looks about],
he says to his messenger Isimud:
Shall I not kiss the young one, the fair?
Shall I not kiss Ninmu, the fair?
His messenger Isimud answers him:
Kiss the young one, the fair,
kiss Ninmu, the fair,
for my king I shall [blow up a mighty
    wind], I shall [blow up a mighty
    wind].
[First] he set his foot in the boat,
[then] he set it on [dry land],
he embraced her, he kissed her,
Enki poured the semen into the womb,
she took the semen into the womb, the
    semen of Enki,
one day being her one month,
two days being her two months,
nine days being her nine months, the
    months of womanhood,
[like] . . . fat, like . . . [fat], like good
    princely fat,
[Ninmu], *like . . .* [fat], *like . . . fat, like
    good princely fat*,
gave birth to [Ninkurra].
Ninkurra . . . [at] the bank of the river,
Enki in the marshland [looks about,
    looks about],
he [says] to his messenger Isimud:
Shall I not [kiss] the young one, the fair?
Shall I not kiss Ninkurra, the fair?
His messenger Isimud answers him:
Kiss the young one, the fair,
kiss Ninkurra, the fair.
For my king I shall [blow up a mighty
    wind], I shall [blow up a mighty
    wind].
[First] he set his foot in the boat,
[then] he set it on [dry land],
he embraced her, he kissed her,
Enki poured the semen into the womb,
She took the semen into the womb, the
    semen of Enki,
one day being her one month,

nine days being her nine months, the
    months [of] womanhood,
like . . . fat, like . . . fat, like good,
    princely fat,
Ninkurra, *like . . . fat, like . . . fat, like good,*
    princely fat,
gave birth to Uttu, the [fair] lady.
Nintu says [to] Uttu, [the fair lady]:
Instruction I offer you, [take] my
    instruction,
a word I speak to you, [take] my word.
Someone in the marshland [looks about,
    looks about],
Enki in the marshland [looks about,
    looks about],
[the eye] . . .

    (gap)

. . . Uttu, the fair lady . . . ,

    (gap)

. . . [in his] . . . ,
. . . [heart] . . .
[bring the cucumbers in their] . . . ,
[bring the apples] in their . . . ,
[bring] the grapes in their . . . ,
in the house may he take hold of my
    leash,
may Enki there take hold of my leash.
A second time while he was filling with
    water,
he filled the dikes with water,
he filled the ditches with water,
he filled the uncultivated places with
    water.
The gardener [in the dust] in his joy . . . ,
he [embraces] him.
Who are you who . . . [my] garden?
Enki [answers] the gardener:

    (gap)

[Bring me the cucumbers in their . . . ,
bring me the apples in their . . . ,
bring me the grapes in their . . .
He] brought him the cucumbers in their
    . . . ,
he brought him the apples in their . . . ,
he brought him the grapes in their . . . ,
    he heaped them on his lap.
Enki, his face turned green, he gripped
    the staff,

to Uttu Enki directed his step.
Who . . . in her house, open.
You, who are you?
I, the gardener, would give you
    cucumbers, apples, and grapes as a
    "so be it."
Uttu with joyful heart opened the door
    of the house.
Enki to Uttu, the fair lady,
gives the cucumbers in their . . . ,
gives the apples in their . . . ,
gives the grapes in their . . .
Uttu, the fair lady . . . the . . . for him, . . .
    the . . . for him.
Enki took his joy of Uttu,
he embraced her, lay in her lap,
he . . . the thighs, he touches the . . . ,
he embraced her, lay in her lap,
with the young one he cohabited, he
    kissed her.
Enki poured the semen into the womb,
she took the semen into the womb, the
    semen of Enki.
Uttu, the fair lady . . . ,
Ninhursag . . . the [semen from the
    thighs],
[the tree plant sprouted,
the honey plant sprouted,
the roadweed plant sprouted,
the . . . plant sprouted,
the thorn sprouted,
the caper plant sprouted,
the . . . plant sprouted,
the cassia plant sprouted].
Enki in the marshland [looks about,
    looks about],
he says to his messenger Isimud:
Of the plants, their fate . . . ,
What, pray is this? What, pray is this?
His messenger Isimud answers him:
My [king], the tree plant, he says to him;
he cuts it down for him, he eats it.
My king, the honey plant, he says to him;
he plucks it for him, he eats it.
My king, the [roadweed] plant, he *says to*
    him,
he cuts it down for him, he *eats it.*

    (gap)

My king, the . . . plant, he *says to him;*
[he plucks it for him, he eats it.

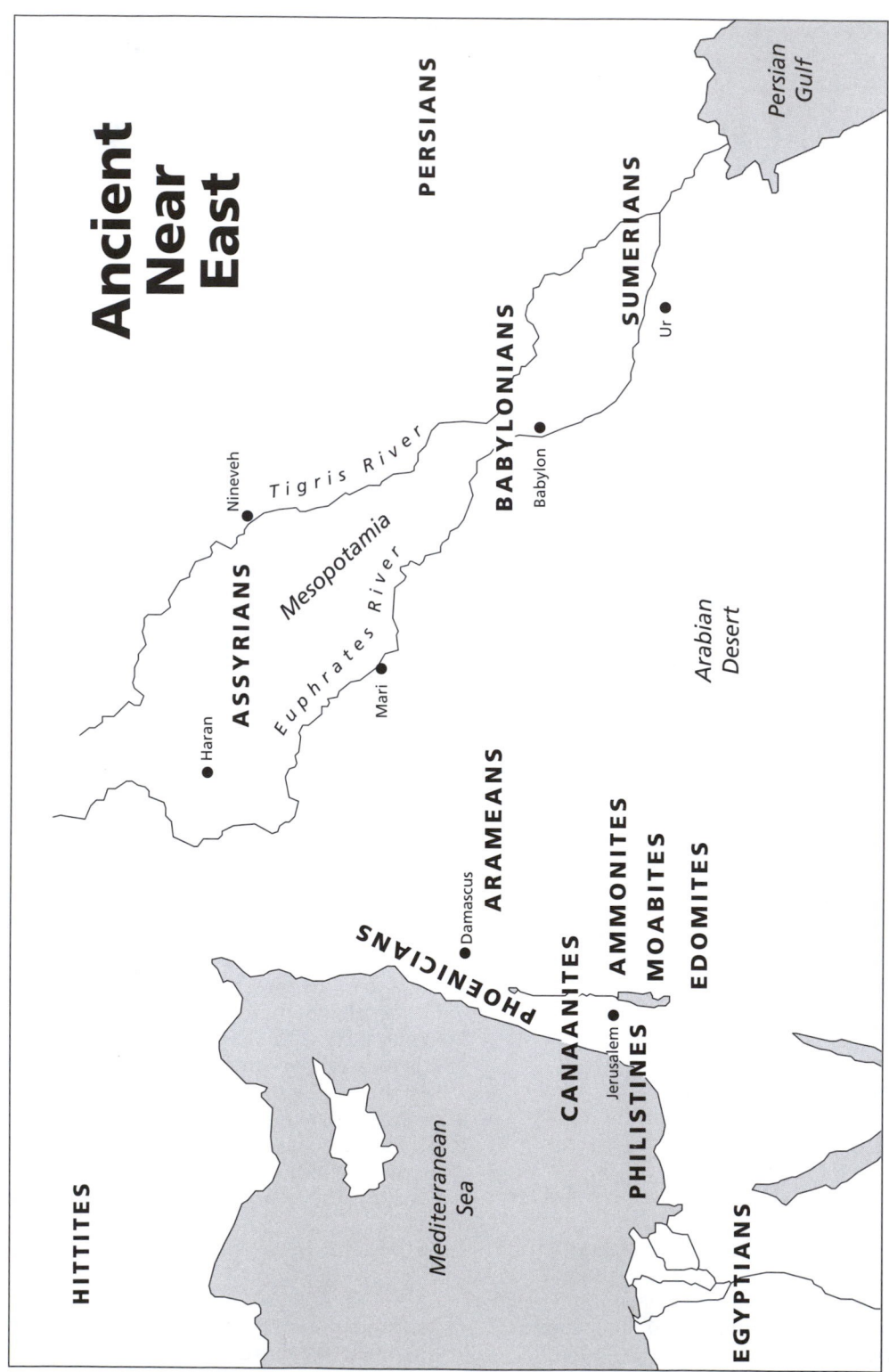

The ancient Near East forms the backdrop for the texts in this book as well as for the Bible.

My king, the thorn] plant, he *says to him*;
[he cuts it down for him], he *eats it*.
[My king, the caper plant], he *says to him*,
[he plucks it for him, he eats it.
My king, the . . . plant, he says to him;
he cuts it down for him], he *eats it*.
My king, the cassia plant, he says to him;
[he plucks it for him], he eats it.
Of the plants, [Enki] decreed their fate,
    [knew] their heart.
Thereupon Ninhursag cursed Enki's
    name:
Until he is dead I shall not look upon him
    with the eye of life.
The Anunnaki sat in the dust,
when up speaks the fox to Enlil:
If I bring Ninhursag before you, what
    shall be my reward?
Enlil answers the fox:
If you will bring Ninhursag before me,
in my city I will [plant] trees [and fields]
    for you, truly your name will be
    uttered.
The fox, [as one . . . his skin,
as one, loosened his . . . ,
as one], painted his face.

    (gap)

[To Nippur] I shall go, Enlil . . . ,
[to Ur] I shall go, Nanna . . . ,
[to Larsa] I shall go, Utu . . . ,
[to Erech] I shall go, Inanna . . . ,
. . . [is, my name . . . bring.
Enlil] . . .
Ninhursag . . .

    (gap)

. . . [stood by him].
Ninhursag . . . ,
The Anunnaki seized her garments,
[made] . . . ,
decreed the fate,
[interpreted] the . . . ,
Ninhursag seated Enki by her vulva.
My brother, what hurts you? My . . .
    hurts me.
Abu I have caused to be born for you.
My brother, what hurts you? My [jaw]
    hurts me.
Nintulla I have caused to be born for
    you.

My brother, what hurts you? My tooth
    hurts me.
Ninsutu I have caused to be born for you.
My brother, what hurts you? My mouth
    hurts me.
Ninkasi I have [caused] to be [born] for
    you.
My brother what hurts you? My . . .
    [hurts me].
Nazi I have caused to be [born] for you.
My brother, what hurts you? [My] arm
    [hurts me].
Azimua I have [caused] to be [born] for
    you.
My brother, what hurts you? [My] rib
    [hurts me].
Ninti I have caused to be [born] for you.
My brother, what hurts you? My . . .
    [hurts me].
Enshag I have caused to be [born] for
    you.
For the little ones that I have caused to be
    born . . .
Let Abu be the king of the plants,
let Nintulla be the lord of Magan,
let Ninsutu marry Ninazu,
let Ninkasi be she who [sates the desires],
let Nazi marry [Nindara],
let [Azimua] marry [Ningishzida],
let [Ninti] be the [queen of the months],
let [Enshag] be the lord of Dilmun.
[O father Enki], praise!

#3: Enki and the Ordering of the World
(Beyerlin, *Near Eastern Religious Texts*, 78–80)[4]

A badly damaged text composed around 2000 B.C., "Enki and the Ordering of the World" tells of the creative role of the Sumerian god of wisdom, Enki. In cooperation with Enlil, the creator-god who made the general plans, Enki organized the earth and instituted the essential cultural ingredients of human civilization. The selections included here illustrate the Sumerian hymnic creation traditions and are vaguely reminiscent of the Old Testament creation psalms (compare Psalms 8, 19, 104).

Enki determined *Sumer's* destiny:
Sumer, great mountain, land of heaven
    and earth,

filled with a fearful gleam that has given
the *whole* land
divine powers from dawn to dusk,
your divine powers are supreme,
unassailable.
Your purpose is deep, impossible to
fathom . . .
he summoned the two winds *and* the
water of the heaven,
he made them approach like two clouds,
made their life-giving breath go to the
horizon,
changed the barren hills into fields.
The one who ushers in the heavy
weather, who strikes with lightning,
who puts the sacred bolt in the midst of
heaven—
the son of An, the water-master of
heaven and earth,
Ishkur, the good, the son of An,
was put in charge of this by Enki.
He instituted plow, yoke, *and* span,
the exalted prince Enki made the . . .
oxen go in straight lines *when plowing*,
opened the holy furrows,
so that the good ground could make
barley shoot.
The lord who wears the diadem, the
adornment of the high steppe,
the strong armed, Enlil's countryman,
Enkimdu, the lord of digging and
canals,
was put in charge of this by Enki . . .
He drew the line, arranged the
foundations,
he built the house beside the council
and arranged the rites of purification,
the great ruler laid the foundation walls
and set the bricks on them.
The one whose foundation walls set in
the earth will never shift,
whose well-built house will never totter,
whose well-established roof reaches like
the rainbow to heaven—
Mushdama, Enlil's great master builder,
was put in charge of this by Enki . . .
He set up the hurdles, accomplished the
rites of purification,
erected sheepfolds, made fat and milk to
be at their best,

bestowed luxuriance on the place where
the gods feed,
made the steppe flourish, where grass
and herbs grow.
The king, the just protector of Eanna, the
friend of An,
the beloved son-in-law of the strong
Suen, the holy consort of Inanna,
the queen of heaven, the mistress of the
majestic divine powers,
the one who brings about meetings . . .
on the streets of Kullaba,
Dumuzi, the dragon of heaven, the
friend of An,
was put in charge of this by Enki.

#4: Enki, Ninmakh, and the Creation of Humankind
(Jacobsen, *Harps That Once*, 155–57)[5]

"Enki, Ninmakh, and the Creation of Humankind,"
a Sumerian myth, explains why humankind owes
so much to Enki, the deity who thought of a way
for humans to be born. Prior to the events in the
reading included here, the gods themselves had
to farm for their food. They cleaned rivers and
canals, and the hard work put them in a rebellious mood—a standard motif in Mesopotamian
creation accounts. Enki devised a plan based on
the way he himself was created by "the fathering clay from the Apsu." This probably refers to
clay from water under the earth's surface (that is,
groundwater).[6] With the help of Namma (his
mother), Ninmakh (the midwife goddess), and
other minor goddesses, his plan was carried out
and humankind was fashioned from moistened
clay, which is reminiscent of Genesis 2:7.

Enki,
at his mother Namma's word,
rose from his bed,
in Halankug,
his room for pondering,
he smote the thigh,
The ingenious and wise one,
skillful custodian
of heaven and earth,
creator and constructor
of everything,
had Imma-en and Imma-shar
come out.
Enki reached out
his arm toward them,

and a fetus
was getting big there,
and for Enki it was awakening
to consciousness in the heart
thoughts of his own
creator and constructor.
To his mother Namma
he called out:
O mother mine, since the sire
who was once
provided with heir
by you
is still there,
have the god's birth-chair
put together!
When you have drenched
even the core
of the Apsu's
fathering clay
Imma-en and Imma-shar
can make the fetus bigger,
and when you have
put limbs on it
may Ninmah act
as your midwife,
and may Ninimma, Shuzidanna
Ninmada, Ninshara, Ninbara
Ninmug, Dududuh, and Ereshguna
   assist you
at your giving birth.
O mother mine,
when you have determined
its mode of being
may Ninmah put together
the birth-chair
and when,
[without any male],
you have built it up in it,
[may you give birth]
to [humankind]!
[Without] the sperm
of a [male]
she gave [birth]
to [offspring],
to the [embryo]
of humankind.
[When she had broadened
its shoulders],
she made [a hole] in the head
for the mouth
she . . .

and [enclosed] its body
in an amnion,

   (gap)

Enki tied wool for swathing
around it
and its heart rejoiced.

#5: Epic of Atra-khasis
(Lambert and Millard, *Atra-ḫasīs*, 43–105)[7]

Composed probably in the early second millennium B.C., the "Epic of Atra-khasis" presents in historical sequence both the creation of humanity and its near extinction in the flood. It naturally therefore evokes comparisons with Genesis.[8] Before humankind existed, the high gods forced the rest of the deities to perform manual labor. The lesser gods rebelled against this arrangement, and when one of their number was killed the high gods created humankind from his remains. Humankind was thus created in order to perform undesirable physical work and to provide for the gods. Eventually, however, humans also became vexatious to the high gods, and they decided to destroy humankind in a massive flood. One human was warned in advance of the flood, and he survived in a boat. This man, Atra-khasis (whose name means "ultrawise"), is the hero of the epic. Many editions of the "Epic of Atra-khasis" are extant from various periods of Mesopotamian history. The following selections are taken from a reconstruction of the epic based on the best-preserved edition: three tablets from the Old Babylonian period copied by the scribe Ku-Aya.[9] These selections may seem repetitious because of pieces inserted from other editions and because of missing text.

When the gods like men
bore the work and suffered the toil—
the toil of the gods was great,
the work was heavy, the distress was
   much—
the Seven great Anunnaki
were making the IGIGI suffer the work.
Anu, their father, was the king;
their counselor was the warrior Enlil;
their chamberlain was Ninurta;
and their sheriff Ennugi.
The gods had clasped hands together,
had cast lots and had divided.
Anu had gone up to heaven,

. . . the earth to his subjects.
[The bolt], the bar of the sea,
[they had given] to Enki, the prince.
[After Anu] had gone up to heaven
[and Enki] had gone down to the Apsu,

(gap)

. . . all the mountains,
[they counted the years] of the toil.
. . . the great marsh,
[they] counted [the years] of the toil.
Excessive . . . for forty years
. . . they suffered the work night and
day.
They [were complaining], backbiting,
grumbling in the excavation:
Let us confront our . . . , the
chamberlain,
That he may relieve us of our heavy
work.
. . . the counselor of the gods, the hero,
come, let us unnerve him in his
dwelling!
[Enlil], counselor of the gods, the hero,
come, let us unnerve him in his
dwelling!
. . . opened his mouth
[and addressed] the gods, his brothers,
. . . the chamberlain of old time

(gap)

. . . let us kill [him]
. . . let us break the yoke!
. . . opened [his mouth
and addressed] the gods his brothers,
. . . the chamberlain of old time
the counselor of the gods, the hero,
come, let us unnerve him in his
dwelling!
Enlil, counselor of the gods, the hero,
come, let us unnerve him in his
dwelling!
Now, proclaim war,
let us mingle hostilities and battle.
The gods heeded his words:
they set fire to their tools,
fire to their spades they put
and flame to their hods.
They held them as they went
to the gate of the shrine of the hero Enlil.
It was night, halfway through the watch,

the temple was surrounded, but the god
did not know.
It was night, halfway through the watch,
Ekur was surrounded, but Enlil did not
know.
Kalkal observed it and was disturbed.
He slid the bolt and watched . . .
Kalkal roused [Nusku],
and they listened to the noise of . . .
Nusku roused [his] lord,
he got [him] out of his bed:
My lord, [your] temple is surrounded,
battle has come right up [to your gate].
Enlil, your temple is surrounded,
battle has come right up to your gate.
Enlil . . . to his dwelling.
Enlil opened his mouth
and addressed the vizier Nusku:
Nusku, bar your gate,
take your weapons and stand before me.
Nusku barred his gate,
took his weapons and stood before Enlil.
Nusku opened his mouth
and addressed the hero Enlil:
My lord, sons are your . . .
why do you fear your own sons?
Enlil, sons are your . . .
why do you fear your own sons?
Send that Anu be fetched down
and that Enki be brought to your
presence.
He sent and Anu was fetched down,
Enki was brought also to his presence.
Anu, king of heaven, was present,
king of the Apsu, Enki, was in
attendance.
With the great Anunnaki present
Enlil arose . . .
Enlil opened his mouth
and addressed the great [gods]:
Is it against me that it is being done?
must I engage in hostilities . . . ?
What did my very own eyes see?
That battle has come right up to my
gate!
Anu opened his mouth
and addressed the hero Enlil:
Let Nusku go out and [ascertain]
the reason why the IGIGI have
surrounded your gate.
A command . . .

to [your] sons . . .
Enlil opened his mouth
and addressed [vizier Nusku]:
Nusku, open [your gate],
take your weapons . . .
In the assembly of [all the gods]
bow down, stand up, [and repeat to
    them] our [words]:
Anu, [your father],
your counselor, [the warrior] Enlil,
your chamberlain Ninurta,
and your sheriff Ennugi, have sent me *to
    say*:
Who is [the instigator of] battle?
Who is [the provoker of] hostilities?
Who [declared] war
[and . . . battle?
In . . .
Bring] . . . Enlil.
[Nusku went to the assembly of] all the
    gods,
. . . he explained:
Anu, your father,
[your counselor, the] warrior Enlil,
[your chamberlain] Ninurta,
and [your sheriff] Ennugi [have sent me
    to say]:
Who is [the instigator of] battle?
Who is [the provoker of] hostilities?
Who [declared] war
[and] . . . battle?
In . . .
Bring . . . Enlil.
Every single [one of us gods has
    declared] war;
we have . . . our . . . in the [excavation.
Excessive] toil [has killed us,
our] work was heavy, [the distress
    much].
Now, every single [one of us gods]
has spoken in favor of . . . with Enlil.
Nusku took [his weapons . . .
He went, he . . .
My lord to the . . . [you sent] me
I went . . .
I explained . . . great . . .

    (gap)

[Every single one of us] gods has
    declared war;
we [have] . . . our . . . in the excavation.

Excessive [toil] has killed us;
our work [was heavy], the distress
    much.
[Now, every] single one of us gods
has spoken in favor of . . . with Enlil.
When Enlil heard that speech
his tears flowed.
Enlil . . . his words
and addressed the warrior Anu:
Noble one, carry your authority
with you to heaven, take your power,
while the Anunnaki are present before
    you,
summon one god and have him done to
    death.
Anu opened his mouth
and addressed the gods his brothers:
What are we accusing them of?
Their work was heavy, their distress was
    much!
[Every day] . . .
[the lamentation was] heavy, [we could]
    hear the noise.
. . . to do
. . . assigned] tasks
you . . .
Take . . .
[While the Anunnaki] are present
    [before you],
and while Belet-ili, [the birth-goddess],
    is present,
summon one and do [him to death].
Anu opened his mouth to speak,
    addressing . . .
Nusku, open your gate, [take] your
    weapons . . .
in the assembly of the great gods bow
    down . . .
Speak to them . . .
Anu [your father] has sent me,
also your counselor, [the warrior Enlil].
Ea [opened] his mouth
and addressed the gods [his brothers]:
What are we [accusing] them of?
Their work was heavy, [the distress was
    much]!
Every day . . .
The lamentation was heavy . . .
There is/was . . .
While [Belet-ili, the birth-goddess, is
    present],

23

Let her create humanity.
let him bear the yoke . . .
Let him bear the yoke . . .
[let man carry the] toil of the gods.
While Belet-ili, the birth-goddess, is
    present,
let the birth-goddess [create] humanity.
[Let man carry] the toil of the gods,
let her create humanity.
Let him bear the yoke . . .
Let him bear the yoke . . .
While [Belet-ili, the birth-goddess], is
    present,
let the birth-goddess create offspring,
and let man bear the toil of the gods.
They summoned and asked the
    goddess,
the midwife of the gods, wise Mami,
You are the birth-goddess, creator of
    humankind,
create humanity that he may bear the
    yoke,
let him bear the yoke assigned by Enlil,
let man carry the toil of the gods.
Nintu opened her mouth
and addressed the great gods:
It is not possible for me to make things,
skill lies with Enki.
Since he can cleanse everything
let him give me the clay so that I can
    make it.
Enki opened his mouth
and addressed the great gods:
On the first, seventh, and fifteenth day
    of the month
I will make a purifying bath.
Let one god be slaughtered
So that all the gods may be cleansed in a
    dipping.
From his flesh and blood
let Nintu mix clay,
that god and man
may be thoroughly mixed in the clay,
let there be a spirit from the god's flesh
so that we may hear the drum for the
    rest of time.
Let it proclaim living *man* as its sign,
so that this be not forgotten let there be
    a spirit.
And the assembly answered Yes.

The great Anunnaki, who administer
    destinies.
On the first, seventh, and fifteenth day
    of the month
he made a purifying bath.
We-ila, who had personality,
they slaughtered in their assembly.
From his flesh and blood
Nintu mixed clay.
For the rest [of time they heard the
    drum],
from the flesh of the god [there was] a
    spirit.
It proclaimed living *man* as its sign,
and so that this was not forgotten [there
    was] a spirit.
After she had mixed that clay
she summoned the Anunnaki, the great
    gods.
The IGIGI, the great gods,
spat upon the clay.
Mami opened her mouth
and addressed the great gods:
You commanded me a task, I have
    completed it;
you have slaughtered a god together
    with his personality.
I have removed your heavy work,
I have imposed your toil on man.
You raised a cry for humankind,
I have loosed the yoke, I have
    established freedom.
They heard this speech of hers,
they ran together and kissed her feet,
    saying:
Formerly we used to call you Mami,
now let your name be Mistress-of-All-
    the-Gods.
They entered the house of destiny
did prince Ea and the wise Mami.
With the birth-goddesses assembled
he trod the clay in her presence.
She kept reciting the incantation,
Ea, seated before her, was prompting
    her.
After she had finished her incantation
she nipped off fourteen pieces of clay.
Seven she put on the right,
seven on the left.
Between them she placed the brick
. . . the umbilical cord . . .

[Prince] Ea spoke
. . . he was prompting her
. . . she] recited the incantation
after she had recited her incantation
[she] put [her hand out] to her clay.
She nipped off [fourteen] pieces of clay,
seven she put on the right,
[seven] she put on the left,
Between them she placed the brick . . .
the cutter of the umbilical cord.
The wise and learned
twice seven birth-goddesses had
    assembled,
seven produced males,
[seven] produced females.
The birth-goddess, creator of destiny—
they completed them in pairs,
they completed them in pairs in her
    presence,
since Mami conceived the regulations
    for the human race.
In the house of the pregnant woman in
    confinement
let the brick be in place for seven days,
that Belet-ili, the wise Mami, may be
    honored.
Let the midwife rejoice in the house of
    the woman in confinement,
and when the pregnant woman gives
    birth
let the mother of the babe sever herself.
The man to [the young lady]

(gap)

. . . her breasts
. . . beard
. . . the cheek of the young man
. . . open air shrine and street
. . . wife and her husband.
The birth-goddesses were assembled
and Nintu [sat] counting the months.
[At the] destined [moment] the tenth
    month was summoned.
The tenth month arrived
and the elapse of the period opened the
    womb.
With a beaming, joyful face
and covered head she performed the
    midwifery.
She girded her loins as she pronounced
    the blessing,

she drew a pattern in meal and placed
    the brick.
I have created, my hands have made it.
Let the midwife rejoice in the
    prostitute's house.
Where the pregnant woman gives birth
and the mother of the babe severs
    herself,
let the brick be in place for nine days,
that Nintu, the birth-goddess, may be
    honored.
Without ceasing proclaim Mami their
    . . .
Without ceasing praise the birth-
    goddess, praise Kesh!
When . . . the bed is laid
let the wife and her husband lie
    together.
When, to institute marriage,
they heed Ishtar in the house of [the
    father-in-law],
let there be rejoicing for nine days,
let them call Ishtar Ishhara.
. . . at the destined moment

(gap)

A man . . .
Cleanse the dwelling (?) . . .
The son to [his] father . . .

(gap)

They sat and . . .
he was carrying . . .
he saw and . . .
Enlil . . .
Were becoming stiff . . .
With picks and spades they built the
    shrines,
they built the big canal banks.
For food for the peoples, for the
    sustenance of [the gods]

(gap)

Twelve hundred years [had not yet
    passed
when the land extended] and the
    peoples multiplied.
The [land] was bellowing [like a bull],
the god got disturbed with [their uproar.
Enlil heard] their noise
[and addressed] the great gods:

The noise of humankind [has become
   too intense for me,
with their uproar] I am deprived of
   sleep.
. . . let there be plague

   (gap)

Now [Atra-khasis]
was informing his god Enki.
He spoke [with his god]
and his god [spoke] with him.
Atra-khasis [opened] his mouth
and addressed [his] lord:
So long as . . .
will they impose disease on us
   [forever]?
Enki opened his mouth
and addressed his slave:
The elders . . .
. . . counsel in the house,
[command] that heralds proclaim,
and make a loud noise in the land,
do not reverence your gods,
do not pray to your goddesses,
but seek the door of Namtara
and bring a baked *loaf* in front of it.
The offering of sesame meal may be
   pleasing to him,
then he will be put to shame by the gift
   and will lift his hand.
Atra-khasis received the command
and gathered the elders to his gate.
Atra-khasis opened his mouth
and addressed the elders:
Elders . . .
. . . counsel [in] the house,
[command] that heralds proclaim,
and make a loud [noise] in the land:
[Do not reverence] your gods,
[do not] pray to your [goddesses,
but seek] the door of [Namtara,
and bring a baked loaf] in front of it.
The offering of sesame meal may be
   pleasing to him,
then he will be put to shame by the gift
   and will lift his hand.
The elders hearkened to [his] words.
They built a temple for Namtara in the
   city.
They commanded and [heralds]
   proclaimed,

they made a loud noise [in the land],
they did [not] reverence their gods,
they did [not] pray to [their goddesses],
but they sought [the door] of Namtara
and [brought] a baked *loaf* in front of [it].
The offering of sesame meal was
   pleasing to him.
[He was put to shame] by the gift and
   lifted his hand.
[Plague] left them
. . . they returned.

   (gap)

Twelve hundred years had not yet
   passed
when the land extended and the peoples
   multiplied.
The land was bellowing like a bull,
the god got disturbed with their uproar.
Enlil heard their noise
and addressed the great gods:
The noise of humankind has become too
   intense for me,
with their uproar I am deprived of
   sleep.
Cut off supplies for the peoples,
let there be a scarcity of plant life to
   satisfy their hunger.
Adad should withhold his rain,
And below, the flood should not come
   up from the abyss.
Let the wind blow and parch the
   ground,
let the clouds thicken but not release a
   downpour,
let the fields diminish their yields,
let Nisaba stop up her breast.
There must be no rejoicing among them,
. . . must be suppressed.
May there not . . .

   (gap)

. . . left
. . . to go
. . . his lord
. . . to disappear
. . . their work

   (gap)

. . . I shouted

   (gap)

. . . assembly
. . . oath
. . . [elders]
. . . counsel [in the house.
Command that] heralds [proclaim,
and make a loud] noise in the land:
Do not reverence your gods,
do not pray to your [goddesses],
but seek [the door of] Adad
and bring a baked *loaf* [in front of it.
The offering of sesame meal] may be
    pleasing to him,
then he will be put to shame [by the] gift
    and will lift his hand.
He may rain down a mist in the
    morning
and may furtively rain down a dew in
    the night,
so that the fields will furtively bear
    grain.
They built a temple for Adad in the city.
They commanded, and the heralds
    proclaimed
and made a loud noise in the land.
They did not reverence their gods,
they did [not] pray to their goddesses,
but they [sought] the door [of Adad,
and brought] a baked *loaf* in front of it.
The offering of sesame meal was
    pleasing to him,
he was put to shame by the gift and
    lifted his hand.
In the morning he rained down a mist,
and furtively rained down a dew in the
    night.
[The fields] furtively bore grain,
. . . the famine] left them.
. . . their prosperity . . . returned.

    (gap)

. . . of his god
. . . he set his foot.
Every day he wept,
bringing offerings in the morning.
He swore by . . . of the god,
giving [attention] to dreams.
He swore by . . . of Enki,
giving [attention] to dreams.
. . . the temple of his god
. . . seated, he wept.
. . . put

. . . seated, he wept.
. . . was still
in . . . finished
. . . seen
addressed . . . of the river:
Let the river take . . . and bear away,
let it . . .
to . . . my . . .
May he see . . .
May he . . .
In the night I . . .
After he . . .
facing the river . . .
on the bank . . .
To the Apsu he . . .
Enki heard [his words]
and [instructed] the water monsters:
The man who . . .
Let this being . . .
go, the order . . .
Ask . . .

    (gap)

Above . . .
Below, the flood did not [rise] from the
    abyss.
The womb of earth did not bear,
vegetation did not sprout . . .
People were not seen . . .
The black fields became white,
the broad plain was choked with salt.
For one year they ate couch grass;
for the second year they suffered the
    itch.
The third year came
[and] their features [were altered] by
    hunger.
[Their faces] were encrusted, like malt,
[and they were living] on the verge of
    death.
[Their] faces appeared green,
they walked hunched [in the street].
Their broad shoulders [became narrow],
their long legs [became short].
The command that they received . . .
before . . .
They were present and . . .
The decree . . .
before . . .

    (gap)

He was filled with anger [at the IGIGI.
All we] great Anunnaki
decided together [on a rule].
Anu and [Adad] guarded [the upper
regions],
I guarded the [lower] earth.
Where Enki [went]
he loosed the yoke [and established
freedom].
He let loose [abundance for the
peoples],
he established . . . [in/from the . . . of the
sun].
Enlil [opened] his mouth
[and addressed] the vizier Nusku:
Let them bring [to me] . . .
Let them [send] them into [my]
presence.
They brought [to him] . . .
and the warrior [Enlil] addressed them:
[All we] great Anunnaki
decided together on a rule.
Anu and Adad guarded the upper
[regions],
I guarded the lower earth.
Where you [went
you loosed the yoke and established
freedom.
You let loose abundance for the peoples,
you established . . . in /from the . . . of
the sun].

(gap)

Adad [sent down] his rain
. . . filled the fields
[and] the clouds covered . . .
[Do not] feed his peoples,
[and do not] supply corn rations, on
which the peoples thrive.
[The god] got fed up with sitting,
[in] the assembly of the gods laughter
overcame him.
[Enki] got fed up with sitting,
[in] the assembly of the gods laughter
overcame him.
. . . slander in his hand

(gap)

. . . of the gods . . .
. . . Enki and Enlil:
[All we great Anunnaki

decided] together [on a rule].
Anu and Adad guarded the upper
regions,
I guarded the lower earth.
Where you went
[you] loosed the yoke and established
freedom.
[You] let loose abundance for the
peoples
[you established] . . . in/from the . . . of
the sun.

(gap)

. . . the warrior Enlil

(gap)

[She imposed] your toil [on man,
you] raised a cry [for humankind],
you slaughtered [a god] together with
[his personality,
you] sat and . . .
. . . bring . . .
You determined on a [rule . . .
Let it turn to . . .
Let us bind prince Enki . . . by an oath.
Enki opened his mouth
and addressed the gods [his brothers]:
Why will you bind me with an oath . . . ?
Am I to lay my hands on [my own
peoples]?
The flood that you are commanding
[me],
who is it? I [do not know].
Am I to give birth to [a flood]?
That is the task of [Enlil].
Let him [and] . . . choose,
let Shullat and [Hanish] go [in front],
let Errakal [tear up] the mooring poles,
let [Ninurta] go and make [the dikes]
overflow.

(gap)

The assembly . . .
do not obey . . .
The gods commanded total destruction,
Enlil did an evil deed on the peoples.
Atra-khasis opened his mouth
and addressed his lord,
Atra-khasis opened his mouth
and addressed his lord,

(gap)

Atra-khasis opened his mouth
and addressed his lord:
Teach me the meaning [of the dream],
... that I may seek its outcome.
[Enki] opened his mouth
and addressed his slave:
You say: What am I to seek?
Observe the message that I will speak to
    you:
Wall, listen to me!
Reed wall, observe all my words!
Destroy your house, build a boat,
abandon property and save life.
The boat that you build
... be equal ...

(gap)

Roof it over like the Apsu.
So that the sun shall not see inside it
let it be roofed over above and below.
The tackle should be very strong,
let the pitch be tough, and so give *the
    boat* strength.
I will rain down upon you here
an abundance of birds, a profusion of
    fishes.
He opened the water clock and filled it;
he announced to him the coming of the
    flood for the seventh night.
Atra-khasis received the command,
he assembled the elders to his gate.
Atra-khasis opened his mouth
and addressed the elders:
My god [does not agree] with your god,
Enki and [Enlil] are angry with one
    another.
They have expelled me from [my
    house],
since I revere [Enki,
he told me] of this matter.
I [cannot] live in [your] ...,
I cannot [set my feet on] the earth of
    Enlil.
With the gods ...
[This] is what he told me ...

(gap)

The elders ...
The carpenter [carried his ax],
the reed worker [carried his stone.
The child carried] the pitch,

the poor man [brought what was
    needed].

(gap)

He/they ...

(gap)

Atra-khasis ...

(gap)

Bringing ...
whatever he [had ...
whatever he had ...
Clean *animals* ...
fat *animals* ...
he caught [and put on board]
The winged [birds of] the heavens.
The cattle (?) ...
The wild [creatures (?) ...
... he put on board
... the moon disappeared.
... he invited his people
... to a banquet.
... he sent his family on board,
They ate and they drank.
But he was in and out: he could not sit,
    could not crouch,
for his heart was broken and he was
    vomiting gall.
The appearance of the weather changed,
Adad roared in the clouds.
As soon as he heard Adad's voice
pitch was brought for him to close his
    door.
After he had bolted his door
Adad was roaring in the clouds,
the winds became savage as he arose,
he severed the mooring line and set the
    boat adrift.

(gap)

... the storm
... were yoked
[Zu with] his talons [rent] the heavens.
[He] ... the land
and shattered its noise [like a pot].
... the flood [set out],
its might came upon the peoples [like a
    battle array].
One person did [not] see another,

they were [not] recognizable in the
　destruction.
[The flood] bellowed like a bull,
[like] a whinnying wild ass the winds
　[howled].
The darkness [was dense], there was no
　sun
. . . like . . .
. . . of the flood

(gap)

. . . the noise of the [flood]
It was trying . . . of the gods.
[Enki] was beside himself,
[seeing that] his sons were thrown down
　before him.
Nintu, the great lady,
her lips were covered with feverishness.
The Anunnaki, the great gods,
were sitting in thirst and hunger.
The goddess saw it as she wept,
the midwife of the gods, the wise Mami.
She spoke: Let the day become dark,
let it become gloom again.
In the assembly of the gods
How did I, with them, command total
　destruction?
Enlil has had enough of bringing about
　an evil command,
like that Tiruru, he uttered abominable
　evil.
As a result of my own choice
and to my own hurt I have listened to
　their noise.
My offspring—cut off from me—have
　become like flies!
And as for me, like the occupant of a
　house of lamentation
my cry has died away.
Shall I go up to heaven
as if I were to live in a treasure house?
Where has Anu the president gone,
whose divine sons obeyed his
　command?
He who did not consider but brought
　about a flood
and consigned the peoples to
　destruction?

(gap)

Nintu was wailing . . .

What? Have they given birth to the
　[rolling] sea?
They have filled the river like dragon
　flies!
Like a raft they have put in to the edge,
like a raft . . . they have put in to the
　bank!
I have seen and wept over them;
I have ended my lamentation for them.
She wept and eased her feelings;
Nintu wailed and spent her emotion.
The gods wept with her for the land,
she was surfeited with grief and thirsted
　for beer.
Where she sat, they sat weeping,
like sheep, they filled the trough.
Their lips were feverishly thirsty,
they were suffering cramps from
　hunger.
For seven days and seven nights
came the deluge, the storm, [the flood].
Where it . . .
Was thrown down . . .

(gap)

To the [four] winds . . .
he put . . .
providing food . . .

(gap)

[The gods sniffed] the smell,
they gathered [like flies] over the
　offering.
[After] they had eaten the offering
Nintu arose to complain against all of
　them:
Where has Anu the president gone?
Has Enlil come to the incense?
They, who did not consider but brought
　about a flood
and consigned the peoples to
　destruction?
You decided on total destruction,
now their clean faces have become dark.
Then she approached the big flies
that Anu had made (?) and was
　carrying,
she said: His grief is mine! Now
　determine my destiny!
Let him get me out of this distress and
　relieve (?) me.

Truly . . .
In . . .
Let [these] flies be the lapis lazuli
    around my neck
that I may remember it [every] day [and
    forever.
The warrior Enlil] saw the vessel
and was filled with anger at the IGIGI:
All we great Anunnaki
decided together on an oath.
Where did life escape?
How did man survive in the
    destruction?
Anu opened his mouth
and addressed the warrior Enlil:
Who but Enki could do this?
. . . I did not reveal the command.
[Enki] opened his mouth
[and addressed] the great gods:
I did it [indeed] in front of you!
[I am responsible] for saving life . . .
. . . gods . . .
. . . the flood

    (gap)

. . . your heart
. . . and relax
Impose your penalty [on the criminal
and] whoever disregards your
    command
. . . the assembly . . .

    (gap)

. . . her/it
. . . he/she/they put
[I have] eased my feelings.
[Enlil] opened his mouth
and addressed Enki the prince:
[Come], summon Nintu, the birth-
    goddess,
[you] and she, confer in the assembly.
[Enki] opened his mouth
and [addressed] Nintu, the birth-
    goddess:
[You], birth-goddess, creator of destinies
. . . for the peoples

    (gap)

. . . let there be

    (gap)

In addition let there be a third category
    among the peoples,
let there be among the peoples women
    who bear and women who do not
    bear.
Let there be among the peoples the
    PASHITTU demon
to snatch the baby from the lap of her
    who bore it.
Establish UGBABTU women, ENTU women,
    and IGITSITU women,
and let them be taboo and so stop
    childbirth.

    (gap)

. . . and life (?)

    (gap)

Oil . . .
Regulations for the human race . . .
the male . . .
to the young lady . . .
the young lady . . .
the young man to the young [lady . . .
let the young [lady] take . . .

    (gap)

That we brought about [the flood],
but man survived [the destruction].
You, the counselor of the [great] gods,
at [your] decree I set battle in motion.
For your praise let the IGIGI hear
this song and extol your greatness to
    one another.
I have sung of the flood to all the
    peoples.
Hear it!

#6: ENUMA ELISH
(*ANET* 60–72, 501–3)[10]

Sometimes called the "Epic of Creation," this text is better known by the Akkadian words that open the composition: ENUMA ELISH ("when on high"). The text consists of seven tablets probably composed during the eleventh century B.C., and the story tells of a cosmic conflict between the leading deities. The monstrous Tiamat, mother goddess personifying the primeval ocean, was killed by the young and daring Marduk. The victorious Marduk then creates the universe (from Tiamat's carcass) and humankind (from the blood of her co-conspirator, Kingu) to do the hard physical labor, thus leaving the deities free from work. In gratitude to Marduk for rescuing them from Tiamat, the gods build the city of Babylon for him. "ENUMA ELISH" ends with the gods assembling for a great feast at Esagil, Marduk's new temple. They acknowledge him as supreme deity of the universe and enumerate his fifty honorific names. For nearly a century, scholars have extensively explored numerous similarities between Genesis and "ENUMA ELISH." Perhaps most interesting is the way Marduk splits Tiamat's corpse in order to create two spheres of water, reminiscent of the divided waters of the firmament on the second day of creation (Genesis 1:6–8; "ENUMA ELISH" 4.135–38; 5.62).[11] "ENUMA ELISH" is important for Old Testament scholarship in general because there is evidence that the battle with the dragon Ocean (i.e., Tiamat in this East Semitic, Akkadian version) is actually West Semitic in origin, and therefore, close in culture and geography to the ancient Israelites.[12]

When on high the heaven had not been
   named,
firm ground below had not been called
   by name,
there was nothing but primordial Apsu,
   their begetter,
and Mummu-Tiamat, she who bore them
   all,
their waters commingling as a single
   body;
no reed hut had been matted, nor marsh
   land had appeared,
when no gods whatever had been
   brought into being,
uncalled by name, their destinies
   undetermined—
then it was that the gods were formed
   within them.
Lahmu and Lahamu were brought forth,
   by name they were called.
Before they had grown in age and
   stature,
Anshar and Kishar were formed,
   surpassing the others.
They prolonged the days, added on the
   years.
Anu was their heir, the rival of his
   fathers;
indeed, Anshar's firstborn, Anu, was his
   equal.
Anu begot in his image Nudimmud.

This Nudimmud was the master of his
   fathers;
being of broad wisdom, understanding,
   mighty in strength,
mightier by far than his grandfather,
   Anshar.
He had no rival among the gods, his
   brothers.
The divine brothers banded together,
they disturbed Tiamat [as they surged
   back and forth],
indeed, they troubled the mood of
   Tiamat
in the Abode of Heaven by their
   [hilarity].
Apsu could not lessen their clamor
and Tiamat was speechless at their
   [ways].
Their doings were loathsome unto . . .
unsavory were their ways; they were
   [overbearing].
Then Apsu, the begetter of the great
   gods,
cried out, addressing Mummu, his
   vizier:
O Mummu, my vizier, who rejoices my
   spirit,
come here and let us go to Tiamat!
They went and sat down before Tiamat,
exchanging counsel about the gods,
   their firstborn.
Apsu, opening his mouth,
said unto [resplendent] Tiamat:
Their ways are truly loathsome unto me.
By day I find no relief, nor repose by
   night.
I will destroy, I will wreck their ways,
that quiet may be restored. Let us have
   rest!
As soon as Tiamat heard this,
she was greatly angered and called out
   to her husband.
She cried out aggrieved, as she raged all
   alone,
injecting woe into her mood:
What? Should we destroy what we have
   built?
Their ways indeed are most
   troublesome, but let us treat them
   kindly!

Then answered Mummu, giving counsel
to Apsu;
[ill wishing] and ungracious was
Mummu's advice:
Do destroy, my father, the mutinous
ways.
Then shall you have relief by day and
rest by night!
When Apsu heard this, his face grew
radiant
because of the evil he planned against
the gods, his sons.
As for Mummu, he embraced him by
the neck
as *that one* sat down on his knees to kiss
him.
Now whatever they had plotted between
them,
was repeated unto the gods, their
firstborn.
When the gods heard *this*, they were
stirred up at first,
then lapsed into silence and remained
speechless.
Surpassing in wisdom, accomplished,
resourceful,
Ea, the all wise, saw through their
scheme.
A master design against it he devised
and set up,
making his spell artful against it,
surpassing and holy.
He recited it and made it subsist in the
deep,
as he poured sleep upon him. Sound
asleep he lay.
When he had made Apsu prone,
drenched with sleep,
Mummu, the adviser, was powerless to
stir.
He loosened his band, tore off his tiara,
removed Apsu's halo *and* put it on
himself.
Having fettered Apsu, he slew him.
Mummu he bound and left behind lock.
Having established his dwelling upon
Apsu in that manner,
he laid hold on Mummu, holding him
by the nose-rope.
After Ea had vanquished and trodden
down his foes,

had secured his triumph over his
enemies,
in his sacred chamber in profound peace
had rested,
he named it Apsu, for shrines he
assigned *it*.
In that same place his cult hut he
founded.
Ea and Damkina, his wife, dwelled *there*
in splendor.
In the chamber of fates, the abode of
destinies,
a god was engendered, most able and
wisest of gods.
In the heart of Apsu was Marduk
created,
in the heart of holy Apsu was Marduk
created.
He who begot him was Ea, his father;
she who bore him was Damkina, his
mother.
The breast of goddesses he did suck.
The nurse that nursed him filled him
with awesomeness.
Alluring was his figure, sparkling the
lift of his eyes.
Lordly was his gait, commanding from
of old.
When Ea saw him, the father who begot
him,
he exulted and glowed, his heart filled
with gladness.
He rendered him perfect and endowed
him with a double godhead.
Greatly exalted was he above them,
exceeding throughout.
Perfect were his members beyond
comprehension,
unsuited for understanding, difficult to
perceive.
Four were his eyes, four were his ears;
when he moved his lips, fire blazed
forth.
Large were all four hearing organs,
and the eyes, in like number, scanned all
things.
He was the loftiest of the gods,
surpassing was his stature;
his members were enormous, he was
exceeding tall.
My little son, my little son!

My son, the sun! Sun of the heavens!
Clothed with the halo of ten gods, he
was strong to the utmost,
as their awesome flashes were heaped
upon him.
Anu brought forth and begot the
fourfold wind
consigning to its power the [leader of
the host].
He fashioned . . . , [stationed] the
whirlwind,
he produced streams to disturb Tiamat.
The gods, given no rest, [suffer in] the
storm.
Their hearts having plotted evil,
to Tiamat, their mother, he said:
When they slew Apsu, your consort,
you did not aid him but remained still.
When the dread fourfold wind he
created,
your vitals were diluted and so we can
have no rest.
Let Apsu, your consort, be in your mind
and Mummu, who has been
vanquished! You are left alone!
. . . you pace about distraught,
. . . without cease]. You do not love us!
. . . pinched are our eyes,
. . . without cease. Let us have rest!
. . . [to battle]. Do you avenge them!
. . . and render *them* as the wind!
[When] Tiamat [heard] *these* words, she
was pleased:
. . . you have given. Let us make
[monsters],
. . . and the gods in the [midst] . . .
. . . let us do] battle and against the gods
. . . !
They thronged and marched at the side
of Tiamat.
Enraged, they plot without cease night
and day,
they are set for combat, growling,
raging,
they form a council to prepare for the
fight.
Mother Hubur, she who fashions all
things,
added matchless weapons, bore monster
serpents,
sharp of tooth, unsparing of [fang].

[With venom] for blood she has filled
their bodies.
Roaring dragons she has clothed with
terror,
has crowned them with haloes, making
them like gods,
so that he who beholds them shall
perish abjectly,
and that, with their bodies reared up,
none might turn [them back].
She set up the Viper, the Dragon, and
the [Sphinx],
the Great Lion, the Mad Dog, and the
Scorpion Man,
mighty Lion Demons, the Dragonfly, the
Centaur—
bearing weapons that spare not, fearless
in battle.
Firm were her decrees, past
withstanding were they.
Using these, she brought [forth] eleven
of this kind.
From among the gods, her firstborn,
who formed [her assembly],
she elevated Kingu, made him chief
among them.
Giving him leadership of the ranks,
command of the assembly,
the raising of weapons for the
encounter, advancing to combat,
in battle the command-in-chief—
These to his hand she entrusted as she
seated him in the council:
I have cast for you the spell, exalting
you in the assembly of the gods.
I have given you full power to counsel
all the gods.
Truly, you are supreme, my only consort
you are!
Your utterance shall prevail over all the
Anunnaki!
She gave him the Tablet of Destinies,
and fastened on his breast:
As for you, your command shall be
unchangeable, [your word] shall
endure!
As soon as Kingu was elevated,
possessed of [the rank of Anu],
for the gods, his sons, [they decreed] the
fate:
Your word shall make the first subside,

shall humble the Power-Weapon, so
potent in *its* [sweep]!
When Tiamat had lent import to her
handiwork in that way,
she prepared for battle against the gods,
her offspring.
To avenge Apsu, Tiamat wrought evil.
That she was girding for battle, was
divulged to Ea.
As soon as Ea heard of this matter,
he lapsed into dark silence and sat right
still.
Then, on further thought, his anger
subsided,
to Anshar, his *fore*father he betook
himself.
When he came before his grandfather,
Anshar,
he repeated all that Tiamat had plotted
to him:
My faith, Tiamat, she who bore us,
detests us.
She has set up the assembly and is
furious with rage.
All the gods have rallied to her;
even those whom you brought forth
march at her side.
They throng and march at the side of
Tiamat,
enraged, they plot without ceasing night
and day.
They are set for combat, growling,
raging,
they have formed a council to prepare
for the fight.
Mother Hubur, she who fashions all
things,
has added matchless weapons, has born
monster serpents,
sharp of tooth, unsparing of [fang].
With venom for blood she has filled
their bodies.
Roaring dragons she has clothed with
terror,
has crowned them with haloes, making
them like gods,
so that he who beholds them shall
perish abjectly,
and that, with their bodies reared up,
none might turn them back.

She has set up the Viper, the Dragon,
and the [Sphinx],
the Great Lion, the Mad Dog, and the
Scorpion Man,
mighty Lion Demons, the Dragonfly, the
Centaur—
bearing weapons that spare not, fearless
in battle.
Firm are her decrees, past withstanding
are they.
Using these, she has brought forth
eleven of this kind.
From among the gods, her firstborn,
who formed her assembly,
she has elevated Kingu, has made him
chief among them.
Giving him leadership of the ranks,
command of the assembly,
the raising of weapons for the
encounter, advancing to combat,
in battle the command-in-chief—
these to his hands [she entrusted] as she
seated him in the council:
[I have cast the spell] for you, exalting
you in the assembly of the gods.
[I have given you] full power [to counsel
all the] gods.
[Truly, you are supreme, my only
consort] are you!
[Your utterance shall prevail over all the
Anunnaki!
She has given him the Tablet of
Destinies, and fastened on his breast:
As for you, your command shall be
unchangeable], Your word shall
endure!
[As soon as Kingu was elevated],
possessed of the rank of Anu,
[for the gods, her sons, they decreed the
fate:
[Your word] shall make the fire subside,
shall humble the Power-Weapon, [so
potent in its sweep]!
When Anshar heard that Tiamat] was
sorely troubled,
[he smote his loins and] bit his lips.
[Gloomy was his heart], restless his
mood.
[He covered] his [mouth] to stifle his
outcry:
. . . battle.

[The weapon you have made], bear it up!
[For, Mummu and] Apsu you did slay.
[Now, slay Kingu], who marches before her.
. . . wisdom.
[Answered the counselor of] the gods, Nudimmud.

(gap—Ea-Nudimmud's reply is lost; when the text resumes, Anshar is addressing Anu)

[To Anu], his son, [a word] he addressed:
. . . this, the most powerful of heroes,
whose strength [is outstanding], past resisting his onslaught.
[Go] and stand up to Tiamat,
that her mood [be calmed], that her heart expand.
[If] she will not listen to your word,
then tell her our [word], that she might be calmed.
When [he heard] the command of his father, Anshar,
[he made straight] for her way, following the road to her.
[But when Anu was near enough] to see the plan of Tiamat,
[he was not able to face her and] he turned back.
[He came abjectly to his father], Anshar.
[As though he were Tiamat thus he] addressed him:
My hand is not sufficient to subdue you.
Speechless was Anshar as he stared at the ground,
hair on edge, shaking his head at Ea.
All the Anunnaki gathered at that place;
their lips closed tight, [they sat] in silence.
No god, *thought they*, can go [to battle and],
facing Tiamat, escape [with his life].
Lord Anshar, father of the gods, [rose up] in grandeur,
and having pondered in his heart, he [said to the Anunnaki]:
He whose [strength] is potent shall be [our] avenger,

he who is [keen] in battle: Marduk, the hero!
Ea called [Marduk] to his place of seclusion.
[Giving] counsel, he told him what was in his heart:
O Marduk, consider my advice. Hearken to your father,
for you are my son who comforts his heart.
When facing Anshar, approach as though in combat;
stand up as you speak; seeing you, he will grow restful.
The lord rejoiced at the word of his father;
he approached and stood up facing Anshar.
When Anshar saw him, his heart filled with joy.
He kissed his lips, his *own* gloom dispelled.
[Anshar], be not muted; open wide your lips.
I will go and attain your heart's desire.
[Anshar], be not muted; open wide your lips.
I will go and attain your heart's desire!
What male is it who had pressed his fight against you?
[It is but] Tiamat, a woman, that flies at you with weapons!
[O my father]-creator, be glad and rejoice;
you shall soon tread upon the neck of Tiamat!
[O my father]-creator, be glad and rejoice;
you shall soon tread upon [the neck] of Tiamat!
My son, *you* who know all wisdom,
calm [Tiamat] with your holy spell.
On the storm-[chariot] proceed with all speed.
From her [presence] they shall not drive *you*! Turn *them* back!
The lord [rejoiced] at the word of his father.
His heart exulting, he said to his father:
Creator of the gods, destiny of the great gods,

if I indeed, as your avenger,
Am to vanquish Tiamat and save your
lives,
set up the assembly, proclaim supreme
my destiny!
When jointly in Ubshukinna you have
sat down rejoicing,
let my word, instead of you, determine
the fates.
What I may bring into being shall be
unalterable;
neither shall the command of my lips be
recalled nor changed.
Anshar opened his mouth and
to Gaga, his vizier, a word he addressed:
O Gaga, my vizier, who brings gladness
to my spirit,
to Lahmu and Lahamu I will dispatch
you.
You know discernment, and are adept at
fine talk;
produce the gods, your fathers, before
me!
Let all the gods proceed here,
let them have conversation, sit down to
a banquet,
let them eat festive bread and poured
wine;
for Marduk, their avenger, let them fix
the decrees.
Be on your way, Gaga, take the stand
before them,
and what I shall tell you repeat unto
them:
Anshar, your son, has sent me here,
charging me to give voice to [the
dictates] of his heart,
[saying]: Tiamat, she who bore us,
detests us.
She has set up the [assembly] and is
furious with rage.
All the gods have rallied to her;
even those whom you brought forth
march at her side.
They throng and march at the side of
Tiamat.
Enraged, they plot without ceasing
night and day.
They are set for combat, growling,
raging,

they have formed a council to prepare
for the fight.
Mother Hubur, she who fashions all
things,
has added matchless weapons, has born
monster serpents,
sharp of tooth, unsparing of [fang].
With venom for blood she has filled
their bodies.
Roaring dragons she has clothed with
terror,
has crowned them with haloes, making
them like gods,
so that he who beholds them shall
perish abjectly,
and that, with their bodies reared up,
none might turn them back.
She has set up the Viper, the Dragon,
and the [Sphinx],
the Great Lion, the Mad Dog, and the
Scorpion Man,
mighty Lion Demons, the Dragonfly, the
Centaur—
bearing weapons that spare not, fearless
in battle.
Firm are her decrees, past withstanding
are they.
Using these, she has brought forth
eleven of this kind.
From among the gods, her firstborn,
who formed [her assembly],
she has elevated Kingu, has made [him]
chief among them.
Giving him leadership of the ranks,
[command of the assembly],
the raising of weapons for the
encounter, [advancing to combat],
in battle the [command]-in-chief—
these to his hands [she entrusted] as she
[seated him in the council:
I have] cast the spell for you, [exalting
you] in the assembly of the gods.
[I have given you full power] to counsel
all the gods.
[Truly], you are supreme, my [only
consort are you]!
Your utterance shall prevail over all the
[Anunnaki]!
She has given him the Tablet of
Destinies, [fastened on his] breast:

As for you, your command shall be
  unchangeable, your word shall
  endure!
As soon as Kingu was elevated,
  possessed of the rank of Anu,
for the gods, her sons, they decreed the
  fate:
Your word shall make the fire subside,
shall humble the Power-Weapon, so
  potent in [its sweep]!
I sent forth Anu; he could not face her.
Nudimmud was afraid and turned back.
Forth came Marduk, the wisest of gods,
  your son,
his heart having prompted him to set
  out to face Tiamat.
He opened his mouth, saying unto me:
If I indeed, as your avenger,
am to vanquish Tiamat and save your
  lives,
set up the assembly, proclaim supreme
  my destiny!
When jointly in Ubshukinna you have
  sat down rejoicing,
let my word, instead of you, determine
  the fates.
What I may bring into being shall be
  unalterable;
neither shall the command of my lips be
  recalled nor changed!
Now hasten here and promptly fix for
  him your decrees,
that he may go forth to face your mighty
  foe!
Gaga departed, proceeding on his way.
Before Lahmu and Lahamu, the gods,
  his fathers,
he made obeisance, kissing the ground
  at their feet.
He bowed low as he took his place to
  address them:
It was Anshar, your son, who has sent
  me here,
charging me to give voice to the dictates
  of his heart,
saying: Tiamat, she who bore us, detests
  us.
She has set up the assembly and is
  furious with rage.
All the gods have rallied to her,

even those whom you brought forth
  march at her side.
They throng and march at the side of
  Tiamat.
Enraged, they plot without cease night
  and day.
They are set for combat, growling,
  raging,
they have formed a council to prepare
  for the fight.
Mother Hubur, she who fashions all
  things,
has added matchless weapons, has born
  monster serpents.
Sharp of tooth, unsparing of [fang].
With venom for blood she has filled
  their bodies.
Roaring dragons she has clothed with
  terror,
has crowned them with haloes, making
  them like gods,
so that he who beholds them shall
  perish abjectly,
and that, with their bodies reared up,
  none might turn them back.
She has set up Vipers, Dragons, and
  [Sphinxes],
Great Lions, Mad Dogs, and Scorpion
  Men,
mighty Lion Demons, Dragonflies, and
  Centaurs—
bearing weapons that spare not, fearless
  in battle.
Firm are decrees, past withstanding are
  they.
Using these she has brought forth
  eleven of this kind.
From among the gods, her firstborn,
  who formed her assembly,
she has elevated Kingu, has made him
  chief among them.
Giving him leadership of the ranks,
  command of the assembly,
the raising of weapons for the
  encounter, advancing to combat,
in battle the command-in-chief—
these to his hands she has entrusted as
  she seated him in the council:
I have cast the spell for you, exalting
  you in the assembly of the gods.

I have given you full power to counsel
    all the gods.
Truly, you are supreme, my only consort
    are you!
Your utterance shall prevail over all the
    Anunnaki!
She has given him the Tablet of
    Destinies, [fastened on his breast]:
As for you, your command shall be
    [unchangeable, your word shall
    endure]!
As soon as Kingu was elevated,
    [possessed of the rank of Anu],
for the gods, her sons, [they decreed the
    fate]:
Your word shall make the fire subside,
[shall humble the Power]-Weapon, so
    potent in *its* [sweep]!
I sent forth Anu; he could not [face her].
Nudimmud was afraid [and turned
    back].
Forth came Marduk, the wisest [of gods,
    your son,
his heart having prompted him to set
    out] to face Tiamat.
He opened his mouth, [saying unto me]:
If I indeed, [as your avenger],
am to vanquish Tiamat [and save your
    lives],
set up the assembly, [proclaim supreme
    my destiny]!
When in Ubshukinna [jointly you sit
    down rejoicing],
let my word, instead of [you, determine
    the fates].
What *I* may bring into being shall be
    unalterable;
neither shall the command [of my lips]
    be recalled nor changed!
Now hasten here and promptly [fix for
    him] your decrees,
that he may go forth to face your mighty
    foe!
When Lahmu and Lahamu heard this,
    they cried out aloud,
all the IGIGI wailed in distress:
How strange that they should have
    made [this] decision!
We cannot fathom the doings of Tiamat!
They made ready to leave on their
    journey,

all the great gods who decree the fates.
They entered before Anshar, filling
    [Ubshukinna].
They kissed one another in the
    assembly.
They had conversation as they [sat
    down] to the banquet.
They ate festive bread and poured [the
    wine],
they wetted their drinking tubes with
    sweet intoxicant.
As they drank the strong drink, [their]
    bodies swelled.
They became very languid as their
    spirits rose.
For Marduk, their avenger, they fixed
    the decrees.
They erected for him a princely throne.
Facing his fathers, he sat down,
    presiding.
You are the most honored of the great
    gods,
your decree is unrivaled, your
    command is Anu.
You, Marduk, are the most honored of
    the great gods,
your decree is unrivaled, your word is
    Anu.
From this day *forth* your pronouncement
    shall be unchangeable.
To raise or bring low—these shall be *in*
    your hand.
Your utterance shall be true, your
    command shall be unimpeachable.
No one among the gods shall transgress
    your bounds!
Adornment being wanted for the seats
    of the gods,
let the place of their shrines ever be in
    your place.
O Marduk, you are indeed our avenger.
We have granted you kingship over the
    entire universe.
When you sit in assembly, your word
    shall be supreme.
Your weapons shall not fail; they shall
    smash your foes!
O lord, spare the life of him who trusts
    you,
but pour out the life of the god who
    seized evil.

Having placed in their midst the
   constellation,
they addressed themselves to Marduk,
   their firstborn:
Lord, truly your decree is first among
   gods.
Say but to wreck or create; it shall be.
Open your mouth: the constellation will
   vanish!
Speak again, and the constellation shall
   be whole!
At the word of his mouth the
   constellation vanished.
He spoke again, and the constellation
   was restored.
When the gods, his fathers, saw the fruit
   of his word,
joyfully they did homage: Marduk is
   king!
They conferred on him scepter, throne,
   and [vestment];
they gave him matchless weapons that
   ward off the foes:
Go and cut off the life of Tiamat.
May the winds bear her blood to places
   undisclosed.
Bel's destiny thus fixed, the gods, his
   fathers,
caused him to go the way of success and
   attainment.
He constructed a bow, marked it as his
   weapon,
and fitted an arrow to the bowstring.
He raised the mace, made his right hand
   grasp it;
bow and quiver he hung at his side.
In front of him he set the lightning,
with a blazing flame he filled his body.
He then made a net with which to
   enfold Tiamat.
The four winds he stationed that
   nothing of her might escape,
the south wind, the north wind, the east
   wind, *and* the west wind.
Close to his side he held the net, the gift
   of his father, Anu.
He brought forth Imhullu the Evil Wind,
   the Whirlwind, the Hurricane,
the Fourfold Wind, the Sevenfold Wind,
   the Cyclone, *and* the Matchless Wind;

then he sent forth the winds he had
   brought forth, the seven of them.
They rose up behind him to stir up the
   inside of Tiamat.
Then the lord raised up the floodstorm,
   his mighty weapon.
He mounted the irresistible [and]
   terrifying storm-chariot.
He harnessed *and* yoked to it a team of
   four,
the Killer, the Relentless, the Trampler,
   and the Swift.
Their lips were parted, their teeth bore
   poison.
They were tireless and skilled in
   destruction.
On his right he posted the [Smiter],
   fearsome in battle,
on the left the Combat, which repels all
   the zealous.
For a cloak he was wrapped in an armor
   of terror;
with his fearsome halo his head was
   turbaned.
The lord went forth and followed his
   course,
toward the raging Tiamat he set his face.
In his lips he held a spell;
a plant to put out poison was grasped in
   his hand.
Then they milled about him, the gods
   milled about him,
the gods, his fathers, milled about him,
   the gods milled about him.
The lord approached to scan the inside
   of Tiamat,
and to perceive the scheme of Kingu, her
   consort.
As he looks on, his course becomes
   upset,
his will is distracted and his doings are
   confused.
And when the gods, his helpers, who
   marched at his side,
saw the valiant hero, their vision
   became blurred.
Tiamat emitted [a cry], without turning
   her neck,
framing savage defiance in her lips:
You are too [important for] the lord of
   the gods to rise up against you!

Is it in their place that they have
gathered, *or in yours?*
Thereupon the lord, having [raised] the
floodstorm, his mighty weapon,
sent the following word [to] Tiamat,
saying:
[Why] have you risen up and haughtily
exalted yourself,
[you have] charged your own heart to
stir up conflict,
. . . sons reject their own fathers,
While you, who have born them, have
forsworn love!
You have appointed Kingu as your
consort,
conferring upon him the rank of Anu,
which is not rightfully his.
Against Anshar, king of the gods, you
seek evil;
[against] the gods, my fathers, you have
confirmed your wickedness.
[Although] your forces are drawn up
and your weapons girded,
stand up, so that you and I might meet
in single combat!
When Tiamat heard this,
she was like one possessed; she took
leave of her senses.
In fury Tiamat cried out aloud.
To the roots her legs shook together.
She recites a charm, keeps casting her
spell,
while the gods of battle sharpen their
weapons.
Then Tiamat and Marduk, wisest of
gods, joined issue.
They strove in single combat, locked in
battle.
The lord spread out his net to enfold her,
he let loose the Evil Wind, which
followed behind, in her face.
When Tiamat opened her mouth to
consume him,
he drove in the Evil Wind that she could
not close her lips.
As the fierce winds charged her belly,
her body was distended and her mouth
was wide open.
He released the arrow, it tore her belly,
it cut through her insides, splitting the
heart.

Having thus subdued her, he
extinguished her life.
He cast down her carcass to stand upon
it.
After he had slain Tiamat, the leader,
her band was shattered, her troupe
broken up;
and the gods, her helpers who marched
at her side,
trembling with terror, turned their backs
about,
in order to save and preserve their lives.
Tightly encircled, they could not escape.
He made them captives and he smashed
their weapons.
Thrown into the net, they found
themselves ensnared;
placed in cells, they were filled with
wailing;
bearing his wrath, they were held
imprisoned.
And the eleven creatures that she had
charged with awe,
the whole band of demons that marched
on her right,
he cast into fetters, their hands he
bound.
[For] all their resistance, he trampled
them underfoot.
And Kingu, who had been made chief
among them,
he bound and accounted him to Uggae.
He took from him the Tablet of
Destinies, not rightfully his,
sealed *them* with a seal and fastened
them on his breast.
When he had vanquished and subdued
his adversaries,
had . . . the vainglorious foe,
had wholly established Anshar's
triumph over the foe,
Nudimmud's desire had achieved,
valiant Marduk
strengthened his hold on the
vanquished gods,
and turned back to Tiamat whom he
had bound.
The lord trod on the legs of Tiamat,
with his unsparing mace he crushed her
skull.

When he had severed the arteries of her
blood,
the north wind bore *it* to places
undisclosed.
On seeing this, his fathers were joyful
and jubilant,
they brought gifts of homage to him.
Then the lord paused to view her dead
body,
that he might divide the monster and do
artful works.
He split her like a shellfish into two
parts:
half of her he set up and ceiled it as sky,
pulled down the bar and posted guards.
He bade them to not allow her waters to
escape.
He crossed the heavens and surveyed
the regions.
He squared Apsu's quarter, the abode of
Nudimmud,
as the lord measured the dimensions of
Apsu.
The Great Abode, its likeness, he fixed
as Esharra,
the Great Abode, Esharra, which he
made as the firmament.
Anu, Enlil, and Ea he made occupy their
places.
He constructed stations for the great
gods,
fixing their astral likenesses as the
Images.
He determined the year by designating
the zones:
he set up three constellations for each of
the twelve months.
After defining the days of the year [by
means] of *heavenly* figures,
he founded the station of Nebiru to
determine their *heavenly* bands,
that none might transgress or fall short.
Alongside it he set up the stations of
Enlil and Ea.
Having opened up the gates on both
sides,
he strengthened the locks to the left and
the right.
In her belly he established the zenith.
The moon he caused to shine, entrusting
the night *to him*.

He appointed him a creature of the
night to signify the days:
Monthly, without cease, form designs
with a crown.
At the month's very start, rising over the
land,
you shall have luminous horns to
signify six days,
on the seventh day reaching a [half]-
crown.
At full moon stand in opposition in mid-
month.
When the sun [overtakes] you at the
base of heaven,
[diminish your crown] and retrogress in
light.
At the time [of disappearance] approach
the course of the sun,
and [on the thirtieth] day you shall
again stand in opposition to the sun.
When Marduk hears the words of the
gods,
his heart prompts *him* to fashion artful
works.
Opening his mouth, he addresses Ea
to impart the plan he had conceived in
his heart:
Blood I will mass and cause bones to be.
I will establish a savage, Man shall be
his name.
Truly, savage man I will create.
He shall be charged with the service of
the gods that they might be at ease!
The ways of the gods I will artfully alter.
Although they will be revered alike,
they shall be divided into two *groups*.
Ea answered him, speaking a word to
him,
giving him another plan for the relief of
the gods:
Let but one of their brothers be handed
over;
he alone shall perish that humankind
may be fashioned.
Let the great gods be here in assembly,
let the guilty be handed over that they
may endure.
Marduk summoned the great gods to
assembly;
Presiding graciously, he issues
instructions.

The gods pay heed to his utterance.
The king addresses a word to the
    Anunnaki:
If your former statement was true,
declare the truth to me now, under oath.
Who was it that contrived the uprising,
and made Tiamat rebel, and joined
    battle?
Let him be handed over who contrived
    the uprising.
His guilt I will make him bear. You shall
    dwell in peace!
The IGIGI, the great gods, replied to him,
to Lugaldimmerankia, counselor of the
    gods, their lord:
It was Kingu who contrived the
    uprising,
and made Tiamat rebel, and joined
    battle.
They bound him, holding him before Ea.
They imposed on him his guilt and
    severed his blood *vessels*.
Out of his blood they fashioned
    humankind.
He imposed the service and let free the
    gods.
After Ea, the wise, had created
    humankind,
had imposed upon it the service of the
    gods—
that work was beyond comprehension;
as artfully planned by Marduk, did
    Nudimmud create it—
Marduk, king of the gods, divided
all the Anunnaki above and below.
He assigned *them* to Anu to guard his
    instructions.
Three hundred in the heavens he
    stationed as a guard.
In like manner he defined the ways of
    the earth.
In heaven and on earth he settled six
    hundred *thus*.
After he had ordered all the instructions,
to the Anunnaki of heaven and earth
    had allotted their portions,
the Anunnaki opened their mouths
and said to Marduk, their lord:
Now, O lord, you who have caused our
    deliverance,
what shall be our homage to you?

Let us build a shrine whose name shall
    be called
Lo, a Chamber for Our Nightly Rest; let
    us repose in it!
Let us build a throne, a recess for his
    abode!
On the day that we arrive we shall
    repose in it.
When Marduk heard this,
his features glowed brightly, like the
    day:
Construct Babylon, whose building you
    have requested,
let its brickwork be fashioned. You shall
    name it the Sanctuary.
The Anunnaki applied the implement;
for one whole year they molded bricks.
When the second year arrived,
they raised high the head of Esagila
    equaling Apsu.
Having built a stage tower [as high as]
    Apsu,
they set up [in it] an abode for Marduk,
    Enlil, *and* Ea.
In their presence he was seated in
    grandeur.
To the base of Esharra its horns look
    down.
After they had achieved the building of
    Esagila,
all the Anunnaki erected their shrines.
The three hundred IGIGI . . . all of them
    gathered,
the lord being on the lofty dais that they
    had built as his abode,
the gods, his fathers, he seated at his
    banquet:
This is Babylon, the place that is your
    home!
Make merry in its precincts, occupy its
    broad [places].
The great gods took their seats,
they set up festive drink, sat down to a
    banquet.
After they had made merry within it,
in Esagila, the [splendid], had
    performed their rites,
the norms had been fixed *and* [all their]
    portents,
all the gods apportioned the stations of
    heaven and earth.

43

The fifty great gods took their seats.

The seven gods of destiny set up the three hundred [in heaven].

Enlil raised the bow, his weapon, and laid *it* before them.

The gods, his fathers, saw the net he had made.

When they beheld the bow, how skillful its shape,

his fathers praised the work he had wrought.

Raising *it*, Anu spoke up in the assembly of the gods,

as he kissed the bow: This is my daughter!

He named the names of the bow as follows:

Longwood is the first, the second is Accurate;

its third name is Bow Star, *for* I have made it shine in heaven.

(gap)

Most exalted be the son, our avenger;

let his sovereignty be surpassing, having no rival.

May he shepherd the black-headed ones, his creatures.

To the end of days, without forgetting, let them acclaim his ways.

May he establish for his fathers the great food offerings;

their support they shall furnish, shall tend their sanctuaries.

May he cause incense to be smelled, . . . their spells,

make a likeness on earth of what he has wrought in heaven.

May he order the black-headed to revere him,

may the subjects ever bear in mind to speak of their god,

and may they at his word pay heed to the goddess.

May food offerings be borne for their gods and goddesses.

Without fail let them support their gods!

Their lands let them improve, build their shrines,

let the black-headed wait on their gods.

As for us, by however many names we pronounce, he is our god!

Let us then proclaim his fifty names:

He whose ways are glorious, whose deeds are likewise,

Marduk, as Anu, his father, called him from his birth;

who provides grazing and drinking places, enriches their stalls,

who with the floodstorm, his weapon, vanquished the detractors,

and who the gods, his fathers, rescued from distress.

Truly, the son of the sun, most radiant of gods is he.

In his brilliant light may they walk forever!

On the people he brought forth, endowed with [life],

he imposed the service of the gods that these may have ease.

Creation, destruction, deliverance, grace—

shall be by his command. They shall look up to him!

Truly Marukka is the god, creator of all,

who gladdens the heart of the Anunnaki, appeases the IGIGI.

Truly Marutukku is the refuge of his land, city, and people.

Unto him shall the people give praise forever.

Barashakushu stood up and took hold of its reins;

wide is his heart, warm his sympathy.

Lugaldimmerankia is his name that we proclaimed in our assembly.

His commands we have exalted above the gods, his fathers.

Truly, he is lord of all the gods of heaven and underworld,

the king at whose discipline the gods above and below are in mourning.

Nari-Lugaldimmerankia is the name of him

whom we have called the monitor of the gods;

who in heaven and on earth found for us retreats in trouble,

and who allots stations to the IGIGI and Anunnaki.

At his name the gods shall tremble and
quake in retreat.
Asaruludu is that name of his
that Anu, his father, proclaimed for him.
He is truly the light of the gods, the
mighty leader,
who, as the protecting deities of gods
and land,
in fierce single combat saved our
retreats in distress.
Asaruludu, second, they have named
Namtillaku, the god who maintains
life,
who restored the lost gods, as though
his own creation;
the lord who revives the dead gods by
his pure incantation,
who destroys the wayward foes. Let us
praise his prowess!
Asaruludu, whose name was, third,
called Namru,
the shining god who illumines our
ways.
Three each of his names have Anshar,
Lahmu, and Lahamu proclaimed;
they did utter them unto the gods, their
sons:
We have proclaimed three each of his
names.
Like us, do you utter his names!
Joyfully the gods did heed their
command,
as in Ubshukinna they exchanged
counsels:
Of the heroic son, our avenger,
of our supporter we will exalt the name!
They sat down in their assembly to
fashion destinies,
all of them uttering his names in the
sanctuary.
Asaru, bestower of cultivation, who
established [water levels];
creator of grain and herbs, who causes
vegetation to sprout.
Asarualim, who is honored in the place
of counsel, who excels in counsel;
to whom the gods hope, not being
possessed of fear.
Asarulimnunna, the gracious, light of
the father, [his] begetter,

who directs the decrees of Anu, Enlil, Ea
and Ninigiku.
He is their provider who assigns their
portions,
whose horned cap is plenty,
[multiplying] . . .
Tutu is he, who effects their restoration.
Let him purify their shrines that they
may have ease.
Let him devise the spell that the gods
may be at rest.
Should they rise in anger, let them turn
[back].
Truly, he is supreme in the assembly of
the gods;
no one among the gods is his [equal].
Tutu is Ziukkinna, life of the host of [the
gods],
who established for the gods the holy
heavens;
who keeps a hold on their ways,
determines [their courses];
he shall not be forgotten by the
beclouded. Let them [remember] his
deeds!
Tutu they, third, called Ziku, who
establishes holiness,
the god of the benign breath, the lord
who hearkens and accedes;
who produces riches and treasures,
establishes abundance;
who has turned all our wants to plenty;
whose benign breath we smelled in sore
distress.
Let them speak, let them exalt, let them
sing his praises!
Tutu, fourth, let the people magnify as
Agaku,
the lord of the holy charm, who revives
the dead;
who had mercy on the vanquished gods,
who removed the yoke imposed on the
gods, his enemies,
and who, to redeem them, created
humankind;
the merciful, in whose power it lies to
grant life.
May his words endure, not to be
forgotten,
in the mouth of the black-headed, whom
his hands have created.

Tutu, fifth, is Tuku, whose holy spell
    their mouths shall murmur;
who with his holy charm has uprooted
    all the evil ones.
Shazu, who knows the heart of the gods,
    who examines the inside;
from whom the evildoer cannot escape;
who sets up the assembly of the gods,
    gladdens their hearts;
who subdues the unsubmissive; their
    widespread [protection];
who directs justice, roots [out] crooked
    talk,
who keeps wrong and right apart in his
    place.
Shazu may they, second, exalt as Zisi,
    who silences the insurgent;
who banishes consternation from the
    body of the gods, his fathers.
Shazu is, third, Suhrim, who with the
    weapon roots out all enemies,
who frustrates their plans, scatters *them*
    to the winds;
who blots out all the wicked ones who
    [tremble] before him.
Let the gods exult in assembly!
Shazu is, fourth, Suhgurim, who insures
    a hearing for the gods, his fathers,
creator of the gods, his fathers,
who roots out the enemies, destroys
    their progeny;
who frustrates their doings, leaving
    nothing of them.
May his name be evoked and spoken in
    the land!
Shazu, fifth, they shall praise as Zahrim,
    [the lord of the living],
who destroys all adversaries, all the
    disobedient; [pursues] the evil;
who all the fugitive gods brought home
    to their shrines.
May this his name endure!
To Shazu, moreover, they shall, sixth,
    render all honor as Zahgurim,
who all the foes destroyed as though in
    battle.
Enbilulu, the lord who makes them
    flourish, is he;
the mighty one who named them, who
    instituted roast offerings;

who ever regulates for the land the
    grazing and watering places;
who opened the wells, apportioning
    waters of abundance.
Enbilulu, second, they shall glorify as
    Epadun,
the lord who sprinkles the [field],
irrigator of heaven and earth, who
    establishes seed rows,
who forms fine plow land in the steppe,
dam and ditch regulates, who delimits
    the furrow;
Enbilulu, third, they shall praise as
    Enbilulu-Gugal,
the irrigator of the plantations of the
    gods;
lord of abundance, opulence, [and] of
    ample crops,
who provides wealth, enriches all
    dwellings,
who furnishes millet, causes barley to
    appear.
Enbilulu is Hegal, who heaps up
    abundance for the people's
    [consumption];
who causes rich rains over the wide
    earth, provides vegetation.
Sirsir, who heaped up a mountain over
    [her], Tiamat,
who carried off the corpse of Tiamat
    with [his] weapon;
who directs the land—their faithful
    shepherd;
whose [hair] is a grain field, his horned
    cap furrows;
who vaults the wide-spreading Sea in
    his wrath,
crossing *her* like a bridge at the place of
    single combat.
Sirsir, second, they named Malah—and
    so forth—
Tiamat is his vessel and he the rider.
Gil, who stores up grain heaps—
    massive mounds—
who brings forth barley and millet,
    furnishes the seed of the land.
Gilma, who makes lasting the lofty
    abode of the gods,
creator of security,
the hoop that holds the barrel together,
    who presents good things.

Agilma, the exalted one, who tears off
the crown from the wrong position,
who creates the clouds above the
waters, makes them to endure aloft.
Zulum, who designates the fields for the
gods, allots the creation,
who grants portions and food offerings,
tends the shrines.
Mummu, creator of heaven and earth,
who directs . . .
the god who sanctifies heaven and earth
is, second, Zulummar,
whom no other among the gods can
match in strength.
Gishnumunab, creator of all people,
who made the *world* regions,
destroyer of the gods of Tiamat; who
made men out of their substance.
Lugalabdubur, the king who frustrated
the work of Tiamat,
rooted out her weapons;
whose foundation is firm in front and in
the rear.
Pagalguenna, the foremost of all the
lords, whose strength is outstanding;
who is preeminent in the royal abode,
most exalted of the gods.
Lugaldurmah, the king, bond of the
gods, lord of the Durmah,
who is preeminent in the abode of the
gods, most exalted of the gods.
Aranunna, counselor of Ea, creator of
the gods, his fathers,
whose princely ways no god whatever
can equal.
Dumuduku, whose pure dwelling is
renewed in Duku;
Dumuduku, without whom
Lugalkuduga makes no decision.
Lugallanna, the king whose strength is
outstanding among the gods.
The lord, strength of Anu, who became
supreme [at the call] of Anshar.
Lugalugga, who carried off all of them
amidst the struggle,
who all wisdom encompasses, *and is*
broad in perception.
Irkingu, who carried off Kingu in the
[thick] of the battle,
who conveys guidance for all,
establishes rulership.

Kinma, who directs all the gods, the
giver of counsel,
at whose name the gods quake in fear,
as at the storm.
Esizkur shall sit aloft in the house of
prayer;
may the gods bring their presents before
him,
that *from him* they may receive their
assignments;
none can create artful works without
him.
Four black-headed ones are among his
creatures;
aside from him no god [knows] the
answer as to their days.
Gibil, who maintains the [sharp point]
of the weapon,
who creates artful works in the battle
with Tiamat;
who has broad wisdom, is accomplished
in insight,
whose mind is so vast that the gods, all
of them, cannot fathom *it.*
Addu be his name, the whole sky may
he cover.
May his beneficent roar ever hover over
the earth;
may he, as Mummu, diminish the
clouds;
below, may he furnish sustenance for
the people.
Asharu, who, as is his name, guided the
gods of destiny;
all of the people are truly in his charge.
Nebiru shall hold the crossings of
heaven and earth,
so that they *the gods* cannot cross above
and below,
they must wait upon him.
Nebiru is the star that in the skies is
brilliant.
Truly he holds the central position, they
shall bow down to him,
saying: He who the midst of the Sea
restlessly crosses,
let Crossing be his name, who controls
its midst.
May they uphold the course of the stars
of heaven;
may he shepherd all the gods like sheep.

May he vanquish Tiamat; may her life
    be strait and short!
Into the future of humankind, when
    days have grown old,
may she recede without cease and stay
    away forever.
Because he created the spaces and
    fashioned the firm ground,
father Enlil called his name lord of the
    lands.
When all the names that the IGIGI
    proclaimed,
Ea had heard, his spirit rejoiced,
thus: He whose names his fathers have
    glorified,
he is indeed even as I; his name shall be
    Ea.
All my combined rites he shall
    administer;
all my instructions he shall carry out!
With the title Fifty, the great gods
proclaimed him whose names are fifty
    and made his way supreme.
Let them be kept *in mind* and let the
    leader explain them.
Let the wise and the knowing discuss
    them together.
Let the father recite *them* and impart to
    his son.
Let the ears of shepherd and herdsman
    be opened.
Let him rejoice in Marduk, the Enlil of
    the gods,
that his land may be fertile and that he
    may prosper.
Firm in his order, his command
    unalterable,
no god shall change the utterance of his
    mouth.
When he looks he does not turn away
    his neck;
when he is angry, no god can withstand
    his wrath.
Vast is his mind, broad his sympathy,
sinner and transgressor may come
    before him.
I [have appointed] a sign, follow its
    path,
. . . approach and give judgment.

    (gap)

After he [had appointed] the days [to
    Shamash,
and had established] the precincts of
    night and [day,
taking] the spittle of [Tiamat]
Marduk created . . .
He formed the [clouds] and filled *them*
    with [water].
The raising of winds, the bringing of
    rain *and* cold,
making the mist smoke, piling up her
    poison:
These he appointed to himself, took into
    his own charge.
Putting her head into position, he
    formed [the mountains on it],
opening the deep *that* was in flood,
he caused to flow from her eyes the
    [Euphrates and Tigris],
stopping her nostrils he left . . . ,
he formed at her udder the lofty
    [mountains],
therein he drilled springs for the wells to
    carry off *the water.*
Twisting her tail he bound it to Durmah,
. . . Apsu at his foot,
. . . her crotch, she was fastened to the
    heavens,
thus he covered [the heavens] *and*
    established the earth.
. . . in the midst of Tiamat he made flow,
. . . his net he completely let out,
so he [created] heaven and earth . . . ,
. . . their bounds . . . established.
When he had designed his rules *and*
    fashioned [his] ordinances,
he founded [the shrines] *and* handed
    them over to Ea.
[The Tablet of] Destinies that he had
    taken from Kingu he carried,
he brought *it* as the first gift of greeting,
    he gave *it* to Anu.
[The gods] who had [done battle] *and*
    been scattered,
he led [bound] into the presence of his
    fathers.
Now the eleven creatures that Tiamat
    had made . . . ,
whose weapons he had shattered, which
    he had tied to his foot:

[Of these] he made statues and set *them* up [at the Gate of] Apsu *saying*:

Let it be a token that this may never be forgotten!

When [the gods] saw *this* they were exceedingly glad,

[Lahmu], Lahamu, and all of his fathers [crossed] over to him, and Anshar, the king, made manifest his greeting,

[Anu], Enlil, and Ea presented to him gifts.

[With a gift] Damkina, his mother, made him joyous,

she sent offerings, his face brightened.

[To] Usmi who brought her gift to a secret place

[he entrusted] the chancellorship of Apsu *and* the stewardship of the shrines.

Being [assembled], all the IGIGI bowed down,

while everyone of the Anunnaki kissed his feet,

. . . their assembly to do obeisance,

they stood [before him], bowed *and said*: He is the king!

[After] the gods, his fathers, were satiated with his charms.

(gap)

Ea and Damkina . . . ,

They opened their mouths to [speak to the great gods], the IGIGI:

Formerly [Marduk] was *merely* our beloved son,

now he is your king, proclaim his title!

A second *speech* they made, they all spoke:

His name shall be Lugaldimmerankia, trust in him!

When they had given the sovereignty to Marduk,

they declared for him a [formula] of good fortune and success:

Henceforth you will be the patron of our sanctuaries,

whatever you command we will do.

Marduk opened his mouth to speak,

to say a word to the gods, his fathers:

Above the Apsu where you have resided,

the counterpart of Esharra that I have built over you,

below I have hardened the ground for a building site,

I will build a house, it will be my luxurious abode.

I will found therein its temple,

I will establish my sovereignty.

When you come up from the Apsu for assembly,

you will spend the night therein, *it is there* to receive all of you.

When you [descend] from heaven [for assembly],

you will spend the night [therein] *it is there* to receive all of you.

I will call [its] name [Babylon], *which means* the Houses of the Great Gods,

I shall build it [with] the skill of craftsmen.

[When the gods], his fathers, [heard] this [speech] of his,

[they put] the following question [to Marduk, their firstborn]:

Over all that your hands have created,

who will have your [authority]?

Over the ground that your hands have created,

who will have your [power]?

Babylon, which you gave a fine name,

[therein] establish our [abode] forever!

. . . , let them bring our daily ration,

. . . our . . . ,

let no one [usurp] our tasks that we [previously performed],

therein . . . its labor . . .

Marduk rejoiced [when he heard this and]

he [answered] those gods [who had questioned] him,

he that [slew Tiamat showed] them light,

he opened [his mouth], his [speech] was noble:

. . . them . . . ,

. . . will be entrusted to you.

The gods bowed down before him, they spoke [to him],

they said to Lugaldimmerankia:

Formerly the lord [was merely our beloved] son,

49

now he is our king, [proclaim his title]!
He whose pure incantation gave us life,
[he is the lord of splendor], mace, and
  scepter.
[Ea who knows the skill] of all crafts,
let him prepare the plans, we [will be
  the workers].
He fixed its position with the gods its
  brothers.
After Anu had decreed the fate of the
  bow,
and had placed the [lofty] royal throne
  before the gods,
Anu placed it in the assembly of the
  gods.
When the great gods had assembled,
they extolled the destiny of Marduk,
  they bowed down,
they pronounced among themselves a
  curse,
swearing by water and oil to place life in
  jeopardy.
When they had granted him the exercise
  of kingship of the gods,
when they had given him dominion
  over the gods of heaven and
  underworld,
Anshar pronounced supreme his name
  Asarluhi *saying*:
Let us do obeisance at the mention of his
  name,
to his utterance let the gods give heed,
let his command be supreme above and
  below!
He wrote down and *thereby* preserved *it*
  for the future.
The [dwelling] of Marduk that the gods,
  the IGIGI, had made,
. . . let them speak.
. . . the song of Marduk,
[who] vanquished [Tiamat] and
  achieved the kingship.

#7: Baal Cycle
(Coogan, *Stories from Ancient Canaan*,
86–115)[13]

Scholars have often speculated about the West
Semitic origins of "ENUMA ELISH" (reading 6), a
Babylonian conflict myth in which the young up-
start deity defeats the dragon Ocean.[14] In the
early 1930s, archeologists retrieved and deci-
phered numerous tablets in a cuneiform alphabetic language used at the Mediterranean port
city of Ugarit. Six of these tablets contain just such
a conflict myth, in which the young Baal defeats
Yam, the impetuous and dangerous god of the
sea. This account was committed to writing in
the first half of the fourteenth century B.C. and is
now recognized as one of the great classics of
ancient Near Eastern literature. A colophon at the
end of the final tablet names Ilimilku as the scribe
responsible for preserving the myth and Niqmaddu
as the Ugaritic king in power at the time. The six
tablets of the "Baal Cycle" tell of Baal's struggle
for supremacy in the West Semitic pantheon.[15]
The major deities of the story represent different
realms of the universe: Baal the storm-god, Yam
the sea-god, and Mot the underworld-god. At
stake in the struggle is cosmic domination and
the right to succeed El as the chief deity of the
pantheon.[16] Although technically not a cos-
mogonic myth, the cycle establishes the kingship
of Baal in the cosmological order, and the entire
myth must have done for West Semitic society
what "ENUMA ELISH" did for Mesopotamia. Furthermore, since its discovery and decipherment,
scholars have compared many of its religious ideas
with those of the Old Testament.[17]

Sea sent two messengers . . .
Leave, lads, do not turn back;
now head toward the assembly in
  council,
at the center of the mountain of night.
Do not fall at El's feet,
do not prostrate yourselves before the
  assembly in council;
still standing speak your speech,
repeat your message;
and address the bull, my father El,
repeat to the assembly in council:
Message of Sea, your master,
your lord, Judge River:
El, give up the one you are hiding,
the one the masses are hiding;
give up Baal and his powers,
the son of Dagan: I will assume his
  inheritance.
The lads left; they did not turn back;
they headed toward the center of the
  mountain of night,
the assembly in council.
There the gods had sat down to eat,
the holy ones to a meal;

Baal was standing by El.
As soon as the gods saw them,
saw the messengers of Sea,
the mission of Judge River,
the gods lowered their heads
to the top of their knees,
and onto their princely seats.
Baal rebuked them:
Gods, why have you lowered your
    heads
to the top of your knees,
and onto your princely seats?
I see, gods, that you are stricken
with fear of the messengers of Sea,
the mission of Judge River.
Gods, raise your heads
from the top of your knees,
from your princely seats.
For I will reply to the messengers of Sea,
the mission of Judge River.
The gods raised their heads
from the top of their knees,
from their princely seats.
Then the messengers of Sea arrived,
the mission of Judge River.
They did not fall at El's feet,
they did not prostrate themselves before
    the assembly in council;
still standing they spoke their speech,
they repeated their message.
They seemed like one fire, or two;
their tongues were sharpened swords.
They addressed the bull, his father El:
Message of Sea, your master,
your lord, Judge River:
El, give up the one you are hiding,
the one the masses are hiding;
give up Baal and his powers,
the son of Dagan: I will assume his
    inheritance.
And the bull, his father El, replied:
Sea, Baal is your servant;
River, Baal is your servant,
the son of Dagan your prisoner.
He will be brought as your tribute,
when the gods bring you payment,
and the holy ones gifts.
Then Baal will be gentle . . .

    (gap)

The mighty will fall to the ground,

the powerful into the Slime.
These words had just come from her
    mouth,
this speech from her lips,
she had just spoken,
when he groaned from under Prince
    Sea's throne.
And Kothar-wa-khasis replied:
Let me tell you, Prince Baal,
let me repeat, Rider on the Clouds:
behold, your enemy, Baal,
behold, you will kill your enemy,
behold, you will annihilate your foes.
You will take your eternal kingship,
your dominion forever and ever.
Kothar brought down two clubs,
and he pronounced their names:
As for you, your name is Driver;
Driver, drive Sea,
drive Sea from his throne,
River from the seat of his dominion.
Dance in Baal's hands,
like a vulture from his fingers.
Strike Prince Sea on the shoulder,
Judge River between the arms.
The club danced in Baal's hands,
like a vulture from his fingers.
It struck Prince Sea on the shoulder,
Judge River between the arms.
Sea was strong; he did not sink;
his joints did not shake;
his frame did not collapse.
Kothar brought down two clubs,
and he pronounced their names:
As for you, your name is Chaser;
Chaser, chase Sea,
chase Sea from his throne,
River from the seat of his dominion.
Dance in Baal's hands,
like a vulture from his fingers.
Strike Prince Sea on the skull,
Judge River between the eyes.
Sea will stumble,
he will fall to the ground.
And the club danced in Baal's hands,
like a vulture from his fingers.
It struck Prince Sea on the skull,
Judge River between the eyes.
Sea stumbled;
he fell to the ground;
his joints shook;

his frame collapsed.
Baal captured and drank Sea;
he finished off Judge River.
Astarte shouted Baal's name:
Hail, Baal the Conqueror!
hail, Rider on the Clouds!
For Prince Sea is our captive,
Judge River is our captive.
He served Baal the Conqueror,
he honored the prince, the lord of the
    earth:
he arose, prepared food, and gave it to
    him to eat;
he carved a breast before him,
with a sharp knife the loin of a fatling;
he got up, made ready the feast, and
    gave him drinks;
he put a cup in his hand,
a goblet in both his hands,
a large beaker, manifestly great,
a jar to astound a mortal,
a holy cup that women should not see,
a goblet that Asherah must not set her
    eye on;
he took a thousand jugs of wine,
he mixed ten thousand in the mixing
    bowl.
He arose, he sang a song;
there were cymbals in the minstrel's
    hands;
the Hero sang with a sweet voice
of Baal on the peaks of Zaphon.
Baal looked at his daughters,
he set his eye on Pidray, maid of light,
also on Tallay, maid of rain.

(gap)

The gates of Anat's house were shut,
and the lads met the lady of the
    mountain.
And then Anat went to battle in the
    valley,
she fought between the two cities:
she killed the people of the coast,
she annihilated the men of the east.
Heads rolled under her like balls,
hands flew over her like locusts,
the warriors' hands like swarms of
    grasshoppers.
She fastened the heads to her back,
she tied the hands to her belt.

She plunged knee deep into the soldiers'
    blood,
up to her thighs in the warriors' gore;
with a staff she drove off her enemies,
with the string of her bow her
    opponents.
And then Anat arrived at her house,
the goddess reached her palace;
there, not satisfied with her battling in
    the valley,
her fighting between the two cities,
she made the chairs into warriors,
she made the tables into an army,
the stools into heroes.
She battled violently, and looked,
Anat fought, and saw:
her soul swelled with laughter,
her heart was filled with joy,
Anat's soul was exuberant,
as she plunged knee deep into the
    soldiers' blood,
up to her thighs in the warriors' gore,
until she was satisfied with her battling
    in the house,
her fighting between the tables.
The soldiers' blood was wiped from the
    house,
oil of peace was poured from a bowl.
The virgin Anat washed her hands,
the Mistress of the Peoples her fingers;
she washed the soldiers' blood from her
    hands,
the warriors' gore from her fingers.
She made the chairs chairs again,
the tables tables;
she made the stools stools.
She drew water and washed,
the heaven's dew, the earth's oil,
the rain of the Rider on the Clouds,
dew that the heavens pour,
rain that is poured from the stars.

(gap)

For the love of Baal the Conqueror,
the love of Pidray, maid of light,
the desire of Tallay, maid of rain,
the love of Arsay, maid of the floods.
So then, lads, enter:
at Anat's feet bow down and adore,
prostrate yourselves, worship her,
and say to the virgin Anat,

repeat to the Mistress of the Peoples:
Message of Baal the Conqueror,
the word of the Conqueror of Warriors:
Remove war from the earth,
set love in the ground,
pour peace into the heart of the earth,
rain down love on the heart of the fields.
Hasten! hurry! rush!
Run to me with your feet,
race to me with your legs;
for I have a word to tell you,
a story to recount to you:
the word of the tree and the charm of
    the stone,
the whisper of the heavens to the earth,
of the seas to the stars.
I understand the lightning that the
    heavens do not know,
the word that men do not know,
and earth's masses cannot understand.
Come, and I will reveal it:
in the midst of my mountain, the divine
    Zaphon,
in the sanctuary, in the mountain of my
    inheritance,
in the pleasant place, in the hill I have
    conquered.
As soon as Anat saw the gods,
her feet shook,
her back was as though shattered,
her face broke out in sweat,
her joints trembled,
her vertebras became weak.
She raised her voice and shouted:
Why have Gapn and Ugar come?
What enemy has risen against Baal,
what foe against the Rider on the
    Clouds?
Didn't I demolish El's Darling, Sea?
Didn't I finish off the divine river,
    Rabbim?
Didn't I snare the Dragon?
I enveloped him,
I demolished the Twisting Serpent,
the seven-headed monster.
I demolished El's Darling, Desire,
I annihilated the divine calf, the Rebel;
I demolished El's dog, Fire,
I finished off El's daughter, Zebub.
I battled for the silver,
I took possession of the gold.

Has Baal been driven from the heights
    of Zaphon?
Have they driven him from his royal
    chair,
from his dais, from the seat of his
    dominion?
What enemy has risen against Baal,
what foe against the Rider on the
    Clouds?
Then the lads replied as follows:
No enemy has risen against Baal,
no foe against the Rider on the Clouds.
Message of Baal the Conqueror,
the word of the Conqueror of Warriors:
Remove war from the earth,
set love in the ground,
pour peace into the heart of the earth,
rain down love on the heart of the fields.
Hasten! hurry! rush!
Run to me with your feet,
race to me with your legs;
for I have a word to tell you,
a story to recount to you:
the word of the tree and the charm of
    the stone,
the word that men do not know,
and earth's masses cannot understand:
the whisper of the heavens to the earth,
of the seas to the stars.
I understand the lightning that the
    heavens do not know.
Come, and I will reveal it:
in the midst of my mountain, the divine
    Zaphon,
in the sanctuary, in the mountain of my
    inheritance.
And the virgin Anat replied,
the Mistress of the Peoples answered:
I will remove war from the earth,
I will set love in the ground,
I will pour peace into the heart of the
    earth,
I will rain down love on the heart of the
    fields . . .
I will remove war from the earth,
I will set love in the ground,
I will pour peace into the heart of the
    earth,
I will rain down love on the heart of the
    fields.
And I have something else to tell you:

Go, go, divine powers;
you are slow, but I am swift.
Is not my mountain far from El,
my cave far from the gods?
Two fathoms under the earth's springs,
three rods under the caves.
Then she headed toward Baal on the
    heights of Zaphon,
a thousand fields, ten thousand acres at
    each step.
Baal saw his sister coming,
his father's daughter approaching;
he dismissed his wives from his
    presence.
He put an ox before her,
a fatling in front of her.
She drew water and washed,
the heaven's dew, the earth's oil,
dew that the heavens pour,
rain that is poured from the stars . . .

   (gap)

But Baal has no house like the other
    gods,
no court like Asherah's sons':
El's home, his son's shelter,
lady Asherah-of-the-Sea's home,
the home of Pidray, maid of light,
the shelter of Tallay, maid of rain,
the home of Arsay, maid of the floods,
the home of the beautiful brides.
And the virgin Anat replied:
My father, El the Bull, will answer me,
he'll answer me . . . or else
I'll push him to the ground like a lamb,
I'll make his gray hair run with blood,
his gray beard with gore,
unless he gives Baal a house like the
    other gods,
and courts like Asherah's sons.
She stamped her feet and left the earth;
then she headed toward El,
at the source of the two rivers,
in the midst of the two seas' pools;
she opened El's tent and entered
the shrine of the king, the father of time
    . . .
And the virgin Anat spoke:
Don't rejoice in your well-built house,
in your well-built house, El,

don't rejoice in the height of your
    palace:
don't rely on them!
I'll smash your head,
I'll make your gray hair run with blood,
your gray beard with gore.
El replied from the seven rooms,
from the eight enclosures:
I know you, daughter, how gentle you
    can be;
but there is no restraint among
    goddesses.
What do you want, virgin Anat?
And the virgin Anat replied:
Your decree is wise, El,
your wisdom is eternal,
a lucky life is your decree.
But our king is Baal the Conqueror,
our judge, higher than all:
all of us must bear his chalice,
all of us must bear his cup.
The bull El, her father, shouted loudly,
El the king who brought her into being;
Asherah and her sons shouted,
the goddess and her pride of lions:
But Baal has no house like the other
    gods,
no court like Asherah's sons':
El's home, his son's shelter,
lady Asherah-of-the-Sea's home,
the home of Pidray, maid of light,
the shelter of Tallay, maid of rain,
the home of Arsay, maid of the floods,
the home of the beautiful brides.

   (gap)

Cross Byblos, cross Qaal,
cross the islands on the far horizon;
proceed, Asherah's fisherman;
advance, holy and most blessed one;
then head toward Egypt,
the god of it all—
Kaphtor is his royal house,
Egypt is the land of his inheritance—
a thousand fields, ten thousand acres at
    each step.
At Kothar's feet bow down and adore,
prostrate yourself and worship him;
and speak to Kothar-wa-khasis,
repeat to the Clever Craftsman:
Message of Baal the Conqueror . . .

(gap)

The bull El, her father, shouted loudly,
El the king, who brought her into being;
Asherah and her sons shouted,
the goddess and her pride of lions:
But Baal has no house like the other
      gods,
no court like Asherah's sons':
El's home, his son's shelter,
lady Asherah-of-the-Sea's home,
the home of the beautiful brides,
the home of Pidray, maid of light,
the shelter of Tallay, maid of rain,
the home of Arsay, maid of the floods.
But I have something else to tell you:
give gifts to lady Asherah-of-the-Sea,
presents to the mother of the gods.
Have the clever one go up to the
      bellows,
have *Kothar-wa*-khasis take the tongs in
      his hands;
have him cast silver, have him pour
      gold:
have him cast a thousand bars of silver,
have him cast ten thousand bars of gold.
Have him cast a canopy and a reclining
      couch,
a divine dais worth twenty thousand,
a divine dais decorated with silver,
laminated with a layer of gold;
a divine seat set on top of it;
a divine stool covered with electrum;
divine sandals with straps
that he has plated with gold;
a divine table filled with everything
yielded by the earth's foundations;
a divine bowl with a handle shaped like
      a lamb,
with a base like the land of Yaman,
where there are tens of thousands of
      wild oxen.

      (gap)

She took her spindle in her hand,
she raised her spindle in her right hand;
she tore off the garment that covered her
      flesh;
she threw her robe into the sea,
her two garments into the river;
she put a pot on the fire,
a caldron on top of the coals.

She implored the bull, El the
      Compassionate,
she entreated the Creator of All.
Then she raised her eyes and looked:
Asherah saw Baal coming,
the virgin Anat coming,
the Mistress of the Peoples approaching.
Her feet shook,
her back was as though shattered,
her face broke out in sweat,
her joints trembled,
her vertebras became weak.
She raised her voice and shouted:
Why has Baal the Conqueror arrived?
Why has the virgin Anat arrived?
Have my enemies killed my sons?
Have they finished off my pride of
      lions?
But when Asherah saw the gleam of the
      silver,
the gleam of the silver and the shine of
      the gold,
lady Asherah-of-the-Sea was glad;
she called to her lad:
Look at the marvelous gifts,
lady Asherah-of-the-Sea's fisherman:
take your net in your hand . . .

      (gap)

Baal the Conqueror answered,
the Rider on the Clouds replied:
. . . He arose and spat at me
in the midst of the assembly of the gods.
Filth has been set on my table,
bilge in my drinking cup.
Baal hates two kinds of banquets,
the Rider on the Clouds hates three:
a shameful banquet,
a degrading banquet,
a banquet with wanton women.
But here there is shameful behavior,
and here there are wanton women.
After Baal the Conqueror had arrived,
the virgin Anat arrived;
she gave her gifts to lady Asherah-of-
      the-Sea,
she gave her presents to the mother of
      the gods.
But lady Asherah-of-the-Sea said:
Why do you give gifts to lady Asherah-
      of-the-Sea,

presents to the mother of the gods?
You should give gifts to the bull, El the
    Compassionate,
and presents to the Creator of All.
But the virgin Anat replied:
We give gifts to you, lady Asherah-of-
    the-Sea,
presents to the mother of the gods . . .

(gap)

And lady Asherah-of-the-Sea replied:
Listen, holy and most blessed one,
lady Asherah-of-the-Sea's fisherman:
saddle an ass, harness a donkey,
attach the silver reins, the golden bridle,
fasten the reins to my she-ass.
The holy and most blessed one obeyed;
he saddled the ass, he harnessed the
    donkey,
he attached the silver reins, the golden
    bridle,
he fastened the reins to the she-ass.
The holy and most blessed one lifted her
    in his arms,
he put Asherah on the ass's back,
on the splendid back of the donkey.
The holy one began to lead,
the most blessed one like a guiding star.
The virgin Anat followed her,
as Baal left for the heights of Zaphon.
Then Asherah headed toward El,
at the source of the two rivers,
in the midst of the two seas' pools.
She opened El's tent and entered
the shrine of the king, the father of time.
At El's feet she bowed down and
    adored;
she prostrated herself and worshiped
    him.
As soon as El saw her,
he opened his mouth and laughed;
he put his feet on a stool,
his fingers danced with excitement;
he raised his voice and shouted:
Why has lady Asherah-of-the-Sea
    arrived?
Why has the mother of the gods come?
Are you hungry . . .
or thirsty . . . ?
Have something to eat or drink:
eat some food from the table,

drink some wine from the goblet,
blood of the vine from the golden cup.
Or does El the king's passion excite
    you?
Does the love of the bull arouse you?
But lady Asherah-of-the-Sea replied:
Your decree is wise, El,
your wisdom is eternal,
a lucky life is your decree.
But Baal the Conqueror is our king,
our judge, higher than all.
All of us must bear his chalice,
all of us must bear his cup.
The bull El, her father, shouted loudly,
El the king, who brought her into being;
Asherah and her sons shouted,
the goddess and her pride of lions:
But Baal has no house like the other
    gods' *houses*,
no court like Asherah's sons':
El's home, his son's shelter,
lady Asherah-of-the-Sea's home,
the home of the beautiful brides,
the home of Pidray, maid of light,
the shelter of Tallay, maid of rain,
the home of Arsay, maid of the floods.
But El the Kind, the Compassionate,
    replied:
Am I a servant, a power of Asherah?
Am I a servant, holding a trowel,
or Asherah's brickmaker?
Let a house like the other gods' *houses* be
    built for Baal,
a court like Asherah's sons'.
And lady Asherah-of-the-Sea replied:
You are great, El, you are truly wise;
your gray beard truly instructs you . . .
Now Baal will begin the rainy season,
the season of wadis in flood;
and he will sound his voice in the
    clouds,
flash his lightning to the earth.
Let him complete his house of cedar!
let him construct his house of bricks!
Let Baal the Conqueror be commanded:
Call a caravan into your house,
a wagon train within your palace;
the mountains will bring you much
    silver,
the hills fine gold in abundance;
the camels will bring you jewels.

And build a house of silver and gold,
a house of purest lapis lazuli.
The virgin Anat was glad;
she stamped her feet and left the earth;
then she headed toward Baal on the
    heights of Zaphon,
a thousand fields, ten thousand acres at
    each step.
The virgin Anat laughed;
she raised her voice and shouted:
I have good news for you, Baal:
a house like your brothers' will be built
    for you,
and a court like your cousins';
call a caravan into your house,
a wagon train within your palace;
the mountains will bring you much
    silver,
the hills fine gold in abundance;
and build a house of silver and gold,
a house of purest lapis lazuli.
Baal the Conqueror was glad;
he called a caravan into his house,
a wagon train within his palace;
the mountains brought him much silver,
the hills fine gold in abundance;
the camels brought him jewels.
He sent messengers to Kothar-wa-
    khasis.
After Kothar-wa-khasis had arrived,
Baal put an ox before him,
a fatling in front of him.
A chair was brought, and he was seated
to the right of Baal the Conqueror.
When the god had eaten and drunk,
Baal the Conqueror spoke,
the Rider on the Clouds said:
Kothar, hurry, build a house;
hurry, erect a palace;
hurry, build a house;
hurry, raise a palace
among the peaks of Zaphon.
Let the house extend over a thousand
    fields,
the palace over ten thousand acres.
And Kothar-wa-khasis replied:
Listen, Baal the Conqueror,
pay attention, Rider on the Clouds:
I should put a casement in the house,
a window within the palace.
But Baal the Conqueror replied:

Don't put a casement in the house,
a window within the palace . . .
But Kothar-wa-khasis replied:
You'll recall my words, Baal.
And Kothar-wa-khasis repeated:
Listen, Baal the Conqueror:
I should put a casement in the house,
a window within the palace.
But Baal the Conqueror replied:
Don't put a casement in the house,
a window within the palace . . .
But Kothar-wa-khasis replied:
You'll recall my words, Baal.
They built his house,
they erected his palace;
they went to the Lebanon for wood,
to Sirion for the finest cedar;
they went to the Lebanon for wood,
to Sirion for the finest cedar.
They set fire to the house,
they inflamed the palace.
One day passed, then two:
the fire ate the house,
the flames consumed the palace.
Three days passed, then four:
the fire ate the house,
the flames consumed the palace.
Five days passed, then six:
the fire ate the house,
the flames consumed the palace.
Then, on the seventh day,
the fire died down in the house,
the flames died down in the palace:
the silver had turned into blocks,
the gold had become bricks.
Baal the Conqueror was glad:
I have built my house of silver,
my palace of gold.
Baal prepared the house,
Hadad made preparations within his
    palace:
he slaughtered oxen,
he killed sheep,
bulls, fatling rams,
yearling calves;
he strangled lambs and kids.
He invited his brothers into his house,
his cousins within his palace;
he invited Asherah's seventy sons.
He gave the gods lambs;
he gave the gods ewes;

he gave the gods oxen;
he gave the gods cows;
he gave the gods seats;
he gave the gods thrones;
he gave the gods a jar of wine;
he gave the goddesses a cask of wine.
Until the gods had eaten and drunk
    their fill,
he gave them sucklings to eat,
with a sharp knife carved the breast of a
    fatling.
They drank wine from goblets,
blood of the vine from golden cups.

   (gap)

Baal captured sixty-six cities,
seventy-seven towns;
Baal sacked eighty,
Baal sacked ninety;
then Baal returned to his house.
And Baal the Conqueror said:
I will do it, Kothar, Sea's son,
Kothar, son of the assembly:
let a window be opened in the house,
a casement within the palace;
then a slit can be opened in the clouds,
as Kothar-wa-khasis said.
Kothar-wa-khasis laughed;
he raised his voice and shouted:
Baal the Conqueror, didn't I tell you:
You'll recall my words, Baal?
He opened a window in the house,
a casement within the palace.
Then Baal opened a slit in the clouds,
Baal sounded his holy voice,
Baal thundered from his lips . . .
the earth's high places shook.
Baal's enemies fled to the woods,
Hadad's haters took to the mountains.
And Baal the Conqueror said:
Hadad's enemies, why are you quaking?
Why are you quaking, assailants of the
    valiant one?
Baal's eye guided his hand,
as he swung a cedar in his right hand.
So Baal was enthroned in his house.
No other king or non-king
shall set his power over the earth.
I will send no tribute to El's son Death,
no homage to El's Darling, the Hero.
Let Death cry to himself,

let the Darling grumble in his heart;
for I alone will rule over the gods;
I alone will fatten gods and men;
I alone will satisfy earth's masses.
Baal called to his lads:
Look, Gapn and Ugar, sons of Galmat
   . . .

   (gap)

Then head toward Mount Targuziza,
toward Mount Tharumagi,
toward the mounds that block the way
    to the underworld.
Raise the mountain with your hands,
the hill on top of your palms;
then go down to the sanatorium of the
    underworld;
you will be counted among those who
    go down into the earth.
Then head toward the midst of his city,
    the Swamp,
Muck, his royal house,
Phlegm, the land of his inheritance.
But, divine powers, be on your guard:
don't approach El's son, Death,
lest he put you in his mouth like a lamb,
crush you like a kid in his jaws.
Sun, the gods' torch, burns,
the heavens shimmer under the sway of
    El's Darling, Death.
A thousand fields, ten thousand acres at
    each step;
at Death's feet bow down and adore,
prostrate yourselves and worship him;
and speak to El's son, Death,
repeat to El's Darling, the Hero:
Message of Baal the Conqueror,
the word of the Conqueror of Warriors:
I have built my house of silver,
my palace of gold . . .
When you killed Lotan, the Fleeing
    Serpent,
finished off the Twisting Serpent,
the seven-headed monster,
the heavens withered and drooped
like the folds of your robes . . .
Now you will surely descend into the
    throat of El's son, Death,
into the watery depths of El's Darling,
    the Hero.
The gods left; they did not turn back;

they headed toward Baal on the heights
　of Zaphon;
then Gapn and Ugar spoke:
Message of El's son, Death,
the word of El's Darling, the Hero:
My appetite is like that of a lioness,
or the desire of a dolphin in the sea;
my pool seizes the wild oxen,
my well grabs the deer;
when I have the appetite for an ass,
then I eat with both my hands . . .

(gap)

One lip to the earth, one lip to the
　heavens;
he will stretch his tongue to the stars.
Baal must enter inside him;
he must go down into his mouth,
like an olive cake,
the earth's produce,
the fruit of the trees.
Baal the Conqueror became afraid;
the Rider on the Clouds was terrified:
Leave me; speak to El's son Death,
repeat to El's Darling, the Hero:
Message of Baal the Conqueror,
the word of the Conqueror of Warriors:
Hail, El's son Death!
I am your servant, I am yours forever.
They left; they did not turn back;
then they headed toward El's son Death,
to the midst of his city, the Swamp,
Muck, his royal house,
Phlegm, the land of his inheritance.
They raised their voices and shouted:
Message of Baal the Conqueror,
the word of the Conqueror of Warriors:
Hail, El's son Death!
I am your servant, I am yours forever.
El's son Death was glad . . .

(gap)

. . . I will put him into the hole of the
　gods of the earth.
As for you, take your clouds,
your wind, your bolts, your rain;
take with you your seven lads,
your eight noble boars;
take with you Pidray, maid of light;
take with you Tallay, maid of rain;
then head toward Mount Kankaniya:

raise the mountain with your hands,
the hill on top of your palms;
then go down to the sanatorium of the
　underworld;
you will be counted among those who
　go down into the earth.
And the gods will know that you have
　died.
Baal the Conqueror obeyed.
He fell in love with a heifer in the desert
　pasture,
a young cow in the fields on Death's
　shore:
he slept with her seventy-seven times,
he mounted her eighty-eight times;
and she became pregnant,
and she bore him the lord.

(gap)

We arrived at the pleasant place, the
　desert pasture,
at the lovely fields on Death's shore.
We came upon Baal:
he had fallen to the ground.
Baal the Conqueror has died;
the prince, the lord of the earth, has
　perished.
Then El the Kind, the Compassionate,
came down from his throne,
sat on his stool,
and coming down from his stool he sat
　on the ground.
He poured earth on his head as a sign of
　mourning,
on his skull the dust in which he rolled;
he covered his loins with sackcloth.
He cut his skin with a knife,
he made incisions with a razor;
he cut his cheeks and chin,
he raked his arms with a reed,
he plowed his chest like a garden,
he raked his back like a valley.
He raised his voice and shouted:
Baal is dead: what will happen to the
　peoples?
Dagan's son: what will happen to the
　masses?
I will go down into the earth in Baal's
　place.
Anat also was taking a walk and
　wandering

on every mountain in the heart of the
    earth,
on every hill in the heart of the fields.
She arrived at the pleasant place, the
    desert pasture,
the lovely fields on Death's shore.
She came upon Baal:
he had fallen to the ground.
She covered her loins with sackcloth.
She cut her skin with a knife,
she made incisions with a razor;
she cut her cheeks and chin,
she raked her arms with a reed,
she plowed her chest like a garden,
she raked her back like a valley.
Baal is dead: what will happen to the
    peoples?
Dagan's son: what will happen to the
    masses?
Let us go down into the earth in Baal's
    place.
Sun, the gods' torch, went down with
    her.
When she had finished weeping,
had drunk her tears like wine,
she called to Sun, the gods' torch:
Lift Baal the Conqueror onto me!
Sun, the gods' torch, obeyed;
she lifted up Baal the Conqueror;
she put him on Anat's shoulders.
She brought him up to the peaks of
    Zaphon;
she wept for him and buried him;
she put him into the hole of the gods of
    the earth.
She slaughtered seventy wild oxen
as an oblation for Baal the Conqueror.
She slaughtered seventy plow oxen
as an oblation for Baal the Conqueror.
She slaughtered seventy sheep
as an oblation for Baal the Conqueror.
She slaughtered seventy deer
as an oblation for Baal the Conqueror.
She slaughtered seventy mountain goats
as an oblation for Baal the Conqueror.
She slaughtered seventy asses
as an oblation for Baal the Conqueror . . .
Then she headed toward El
at the source of the two rivers,
in the midst of the two seas' pools.
She opened El's tent and entered

the shrine of the king, the father of time.
At El's feet she bowed down and
    adored,
she prostrated herself and worshiped
    him.
She raised her voice and shouted:
Now let Asherah and her sons rejoice,
the goddess and her pride of lions:
for Baal the Conqueror has died,
the prince, the lord of the earth, has
    perished.
El called to lady Asherah-of-the-Sea:
Listen, lady Asherah-of-the-Sea:
give me one of your sons;
I'll make him king.
And lady Asherah-of-the-Sea replied:
Why not make Yadi-Yalhan king?
But El the Kind, the Compassionate,
    replied:
He's much too weak to race,
to compete in spear throwing with Baal,
with Dagan's son in contest.
And lady Asherah-of-the-Sea replied:
Can't we make Athtar the Awesome
    king?
Let Athtar the Awesome be king!
Then Athtar the Awesome
went up to the peaks of Zaphon;
he sat on Baal the Conqueror's throne:
his feet did not reach the footstool,
his head did not reach the headrest.
And Athtar the Awesome spoke:
I can't be king on the peaks of Zaphon.
Athtar the Awesome descended,
he descended from Baal the
    Conqueror's throne,
and he became king of the underworld,
    the god of it all.

(gap)

One day passed, then two;
and the Maiden Anat approached him.
Like the heart of a cow for her calf,
like the heart of a ewe for her lamb,
so was Anat's heart for Baal.
She seized Death by the edge of his
    clothes,
she grabbed him by the hem of his
    garments;
she raised her voice and shouted:
Come, Death, give me my brother!

And El's son Death replied:
What do you want, virgin Anat?
I was taking a walk and wandering
on every mountain in the heart of the
    earth,
on every hill in the heart of the fields;
I felt a desire for human beings,
a desire for earth's masses.
I arrived at my pleasant place, the desert
    pasture,
the lovely fields on Death's shore.
I approached Baal the Conqueror;
I put him in my mouth like a lamb,
he was crushed like a kid in my jaws.
Sun, the gods' torch, burned;
the heavens shimmered under the sway
    of El's son Death.
One day passed, then two;
the days became months.
The Maiden Anat approached him.
Like the heart of a cow for her calf,
like the heart of a ewe for her lamb,
so was Anat's heart for Baal.
She seized El's son Death:
with a sword she split him;
with a sieve she winnowed him;
with fire she burned him;
with a hand mill she ground him;
in the fields she sowed him.
May the birds not eat his remains,
may the fowl not consume his parts:
let flesh cry out to flesh!

  (gap)

And if Baal the Conqueror lives,
if the prince, the lord of the earth, has
    revived,
in a dream of El the Kind, the
    Compassionate,
in a vision of the Creator of All,
let the heavens rain down oil,
let the wadis run with honey;
then I will know that Baal the
    Conqueror lives,
that the prince, the lord of the earth, has
    revived.
In a dream of El the Kind, the
    Compassionate,
in a vision of the Creator of All,
the heavens rained down oil,
the wadis ran with honey.

El the Kind, the Compassionate, was
    glad:
he put his feet on a stool,
he opened his mouth and laughed;
he raised his voice and shouted:
Now I can sit back and relax;
my heart inside me can relax;
for Baal the Conqueror lives,
the prince, the lord of the earth, has
    revived.
El called to the virgin Anat:
Listen, virgin Anat—
speak to Sun, the gods' torch:
Sun, the furrows in the fields have
    dried,
the furrows in El's fields have dried;
Baal has neglected the furrows of his
    plow land.
Where is Baal the Conqueror?
where is the prince, the lord of the
    earth?
The virgin Anat left;
she headed toward Sun, the gods' torch;
she raised her voice and shouted:
Message of the bull, El your father,
the word of the kind one, your parent:
Sun, the furrows in the fields have
    dried,
the furrows in El's fields have dried;
Baal has neglected the furrows of his
    plow land.
Where is Baal the Conqueror?
where is the prince, the lord of the
    earth?
And Sun, the gods' torch, replied:
Pour sparkling wine from its container,
bring a garland for your relative;
and I will look for Baal the Conqueror.
And the virgin Anat replied:
Wherever you go, Sun,
wherever you go, may El protect you.

  (gap)

Baal seized Asherah's sons;
he struck Rabbim on the shoulder;
he struck the Waves with his club;
he pushed sallow Death to the ground.
Baal returned to his royal chair,
to his dais, the seat of his dominion.
The days became months,
the months became years.

Then, in the seventh year,
El's son Death spoke to Baal the
    Conqueror;
he raised his voice and shouted:
Baal, because of you I suffered shame;
because of you I suffered splitting with a
    sword;
because of you I suffered burning with
    fire;
because of you I suffered grinding with
    a hand mill;
because of you I suffered winnowing
    with a sieve;
because of you I suffered scattering in
    the fields;
because of you I suffered sowing in the
    sea.
Give me one of your brothers,
so that I may sit down and eat . . .

   (gap)

Let Baal give his little brothers for me to
    eat,
his mother's sons for me to consume.
He returned to Baal on the peaks of
    Zaphon;
he raised his voice and shouted:
Let Baal give his little brothers for me to
    eat,
his mother's sons for me to consume.
They butted each other like camels—
Death was strong, Baal was strong.
They gored each other like wild oxen—
Death was strong, Baal was strong.
They bit each other like serpents—
Death was strong, Baal was strong.
They kicked each other like stallions—
Death fell, Baal fell.
Sun shouted from above:
Listen, El's son Death:
How can you battle with Baal the
    Conqueror?
How can you keep the bull, El your
    father, from hearing you?
He will surely undermine the
    foundations of your throne;
he will surely overturn your royal chair;
he will surely smash your scepter of
    judgment.
El's son Death became fearful;
El's Darling, the Hero, was terrified;

Death was afraid of her voice.

   (gap)

But you will eat the sacrificial meal,
you will drink the offertory wine.
Sun judged the healers,
Sun judged the divine ones:
Gods, Death is yours;
Kothar, your friend, is yours,
and your acquaintance Khasis.
In Sea—Desire and the Dragon—
Kothar-wa-khasis wandered,
Kothar-wa-khasis roamed.
The scribe was Ilimilku from Shubbani;
the reciter was Attanu-Purlianni, the
    chief priest, the chief herdsman;
the sponsor was King Niqmaddu of
    Ugarit, master of Yargub, lord of
    Tharumani.

#8: Heliopolis Pyramid Text
(Faulkner, *Ancient Egyptian Pyramid Texts*, 246–47)[18]

Egyptian speculation concerning the beginning of the cosmos is marked by diverse views in the leading religious centers of the country. In time, there was a tendency to harmonize and reconcile these different theologies. The cosmogony that provided the basis for later speculations was developed at Heliopolis and is known from a pyramid text that recalls the original creation. The creator-god, Atum, rose up on the primeval hill from the undifferentiated watery chaos called Nun. He then created the other deities, and creation began. The purpose of this text is to call upon Atum to bless the pharaoh of the new pyramid.

O Atum-Khoprer, you became high on the height, you rose up as the BENBEN stone in the mansion of the phoenix in On, you spat out Shu, you coughed up Tefenet, and you set your arms about them as the arms of a KA symbol, that your essence might be in them. O Atum, set your arms about the king, about this construction, and about this pyramid as the arms of a KA symbol, that the king's essence may be in it, enduring forever.

O Atum, set your protection over this king, over this pyramid of his, and over this construction of the king, prevent anything evil from happening against it forever, just as your protection was set over Shu and Tefenet.

One of Egypt's great pyramids with the Sphinx in the foreground. (Jim Yancey)

O you great Ennead that is on On, *namely* Atum, Shu, Tefenet, Geb, Nut, Osiris, Isis, Seth, and Nephthys; O you children of Atum, extend his goodwill to his child in your name of Nine Bows.

Let his back be turned from you toward Atum, that he may protect this king, that he may protect this pyramid of the king and protect this construction of his from all the gods and from all the dead and prevent anything evil from happening against it forever.

#9: Memphis Creation Story
(*ANET* 4–6)[19]

The clearest ancient Near Eastern parallels with biblical concepts of creation are the Mesopotamian readings presented above (readings 1–6). But these texts provide few parallels to God's spoken decree—the principal tool of creation in Genesis 1. On the six successive days of creation, God created by divine order or command: "Let there be light," "Let there be an expanse between the waters," etc. This is traditionally known as the divine decree or *fiat* (Latin: "let it be done"). This feature of Genesis 1 is particularly reminiscent of Egyptian speculation concerning the beginning of the universe, as illustrated by the Memphite theology.[20]

Live the Horus: who prospers the Two Lands; the Two Goddesses: who prospers the Two Lands; the Horus of gold: who prospers the Two Lands; the king of Upper and Lower Egypt: Nefer-ka-Re; the son of Re: Sha-[ba-ka], beloved of Ptah-South-of-His-Wall, living like Re forever. His majesty copied this text anew in the house of his father Ptah-South-of-His-Wall. Now his majesty had found *it* as *something* that the ancestors had made but that was worm eaten. It was unknown from beginning to end. Then [his majesty] copied [it] anew, *so that* it is better than its former state, in order that his name might endure and his memorial be made to last in the house of his father Ptah-South-of-His-Wall in the course of eternity, through that which the son of Re [Sha-ba-ka] did for his father Ptah-tenen, so that he might be given life forever . . .

The Ennead gathered themselves to him, and he judged Horus and Seth. He prevented them from quarreling *further*, and he made Seth the king of Upper Egypt in the land of Upper Egypt, at the place where he was *born*, [Su]. Then Geb made Horus the king of Lower Egypt in the land of Lower Egypt, at the place where his father was drowned, Pezshet-Tawi. Thus Horus stood in *one* place, and Seth stood in *another* place, and they were reconciled about the Two Lands . . .

Words spoken *by* Geb *to* Seth: Go to the place in which you were born. Seth—Upper Egypt.

Words spoken *by* Geb *to* Horus: Go to the place in which your father was drowned. Horus—Lower Egypt.

Words spoken *by* Geb *to* Horus and Seth: I have judged you. Lower and Upper Egypt.

But then it became ill in the heart of Geb that the portion of Horus was *only* equal to the portion of Seth. So Geb gave his *entire* inheritance to Horus, that is, the son of his son, his firstborn . . . *Thus* Horus stood over the *entire* land. Thus this land was united, proclaimed with the great name Ta-tenen, South-of-His-Wall, the lord of eternity. The two Great Sorceresses grew upon his head. So it was that Horus appeared as king of Upper and Lower Egypt, who united the Two Lands in Wall Nome, in the place in which the Two Lands are united.

It happened that reed and papyrus were set at the great double door of the house of Ptah. That means Horus and Seth, who were reconciled and united, so that they associated and their quarreling ceased in the place that they [reached], being joined in the house of Ptah, the balance of the Two Lands, in which Upper and Lower Egypt have been weighed . . .

The gods who came into being as
    Ptah:—
Ptah who is upon the great throne . . . ;
Ptah-Nun, the father who [begot] Atum;
Ptah-Naunet, the mother who bore
    Atum;
Ptah the Great, that is, the heart and
    tongue of the Ennead;
[Ptah] . . . who gave birth to the gods;
    . . .

There came into being as the heart and there came into being as the tongue *something* in the form of Atum. The mighty great one is Ptah, who transmitted [life to all gods], as well as *to* their KA, through this heart, by which Horus became Ptah, and through this tongue, by which Thoth became Ptah.

Thus it happened that the heart and tongue gained control over [every] *other* member of the body, by teaching that he is in every body and in every mouth of all gods, all men, [all] cattle, all creeping things, and *everything* that lives, by thinking and commanding everything that he wishes.

His Ennead is before him in *the form of* teeth and lips. That is *the equivalent of* the semen and hands of Atum. Whereas the Ennead of Atum came into being by his semen and his fingers, the Ennead *of Ptah*, however, is the teeth and lips in this mouth, which pronounced the name of everything, from which Shu and Tefnut came forth, and which was the fashioner of the Ennead.

The sight of the eyes, the hearing of the ears, and the smelling the air by the nose, they report to the heart. It is this that causes every completed *concept* to come forth, and it is the tongue that announces what the heart thinks.

Thus all the gods were formed and his Ennead was completed. Indeed, all the divine order really came into being through what the heart thought and the tongue commanded. Thus the KA spirits were made and the HEM-SUT spirits were appointed, they who make all provisions and all nourishment, by this speech. *Thus justice was given to* him who does what is liked, *and injustice to* him who does what is disliked. Thus life was given to him who has peace and death was given to him who has sin. Thus were made all work and all crafts, the action of the arms, the movement of the legs, and the activity of every member, in conformance with *this* command that the heart thought, that came forth through the tongue, and that gives value to everything.

Thus it happened that it was said of Ptah: He who made all and brought the gods into being. He is indeed Ta-tenen, who brought forth the gods, for everything came forth from him, nourishment and provisions, the offerings of the gods, and every good thing. Thus it was discovered and understood that his strength is greater than *that of the other* gods. And so Ptah was satisfied, after all he had made everything, as well as all the divine order. He had formed the gods, he had made cities, he had founded nomes, he had put the gods in their shrines, he had established their offerings, he had founded their shrines, and he had made their bodies like that *with which* their hearts were satisfied. So the gods entered into their bodies of every *kind of* wood, of every *kind of* stone, of every *kind of* clay, or anything that might grow upon him, in which they had taken form. So all the gods, as well as their KA gathered themselves to him, content and associated with the lord of the Two Lands.

The great seat, which [rejoices] the heart of the gods, which is in the house of Ptah, [the mistress of all life], is the granary of the god, through which the sustenance of the Two Lands is prepared, because of the fact that Osiris drowned in his water, while Isis and Nephthys watched. They saw him and they [were distressed at] him. Horus commanded Isis and Nephthys [repeatedly] that they lay hold on Osiris and prevent his drowning. They turned *their* heads in time. So they brought him to land. He entered the mysterious portals in the glory of the lords of eternity, in the steps of him who shines forth on the horizon, on the ways of Re in the Great Seat. He joined with the court and associated with the gods of Ta-tenen Ptah, the lord of years.

Thus Osiris came to be in the land in the house of the sovereign on the north side of this land, which he had reached. His son Horus appeared as king of Upper Egypt and appeared as king of Lower Egypt, in the embrace of his father Osiris, together with the gods who were in front of him and who were behind him.

#10: Instruction of Merikare
(Lichtheim, *Ancient Egyptian Literature*, 1.106)[21]

An Egyptian text about the creation of humankind mentions their receiving the breath of life from the gods. These details are reminiscent of the Bible's references to the "image of God" and "breath of life" (Genesis 1:26–27; 2:7).

Well tended is humankind—god's cattle,
he made sky and earth for their sake,
he subdued the water monster,
he made breath for their noses to live.

They are his images, who came from his body,
he shines in the sky for their sake;
he made for them plants and cattle,
fowl and fish to feed them.

#11: Song of Ullikummi
(Hoffner, *Hittite Myths*, 59)[22]

The deity Kumarbi was a central figure in a series of Hurrian mythological tales preserved by the later Hittites. The theme of the entire cycle of Hurrian myths is the competition between Kumarbi and Teshub, the storm-god, for royal supremacy over the gods.[23] Kumarbi seeks to depose Teshub by means of a series of malevolent offspring. In this text, Ullikummi is a monstrous stone offspring resulting from a union between Kumarbi and a mountain thought of in female form. The reading presented here shows the building of heaven and earth and their separation with a copper cutting tool at some time in the obscure primeval past. The "Song of Ullikummi" mentions this ancient event because it is a model for the way in which Teshub establishes his supremacy over the gods.

When Ea [finished speaking] the words, [he went] to Ubelluri . . . Ubelluri [lifted] his eyes [and saw Ea]. Ubelluri [spoke words] to Ea: May you live long, O Ea! [Ea stood] up [and spoke] a greeting to Ubelluri: [May you] live, [Ubelluri, you] on whom the heaven and earth are built!

Ea spoke to Ubelluri: Don't you know, Ubelluri? Has no one brought you word? Do you not know the swiftly rising god whom Kumarbi created against the gods, and that Kumarbi is . . . planning death against Teshub, and is creating against him a supplanter? Do you not know the Basalt that grew in the water? It is lifted up like a . . . It has blocked heaven, the holy temples, and Hebat. Is it because you, Ubelluri, are remote from the Dark Earth, that you are unaware of this swiftly rising god?

Ubelluri spoke to Ea: When they built heaven and earth upon me, I was aware of nothing. And when they came and cut heaven and earth apart with a copper cutting tool, I was even unaware of that. But now something makes my right shoulder hurt, and I don't know who this god is.

When Ea heard those words, he went around Ubelluri's right shoulder, and *there* the Basalt stood on Ubelluri's right shoulder like a shaft.

Ea spoke to the primeval gods: Hear my words, O primeval gods, who know the primeval words. Open again the old, fatherly, grandfatherly storehouses. Let them bring forth the seal of the primeval fathers and with it reseal them. Let them bring forth the primeval copper cutting tool with which they cut apart heaven and earth. We will cut off Ullikummi, the Basalt, under his feet, him whom Kumarbi raised against the gods as a supplanter *of Teshub.*

#12: Epic of Gilgamesh
(*ANET* 93–95)[24]

The "Epic of Gilgamesh" is arguably the greatest literary piece to come from Babylonian soil. It narrates the touching account of how Gilgamesh, an ancient king of Uruk, rebelled against death when he lost his friend Enkidu. On the eleventh tablet, Gilgamesh (probably a historical figure from around 2600 B.C.) meets Utnapishtim, who has been called the "Babylonian Noah." Utnapishtim relates how he achieved immortality when he was forewarned of a divine plan to flood the world, which allowed him to survive the flood in a large reed boat accompanied by his family and pairs of all animals. Since, however, this event was nonrepeatable, it gave Gilgamesh little hope for immortality. He himself fails three tests by which he could have received immortality, but in defeat he resigns himself to the inevitability of death and takes comfort in his achievements. Based on Sumerian stories, the Babylonian text of the "Epic of Gilgamesh" is a composite from early in the second millennium B.C.[25] The famous flood story in tablet eleven appears to be dependent on the "Epic of Atrakhasis"[26] (reading number 5) and bears many obvious similarities with the Genesis flood account. The following reading from tablet eleven contains Utnapishtim's description of the flood as an explanation of his own immortality.

Gilgamesh said to him, to Utnapishtim
    the Faraway:
As I look upon you, Utnapishtim,
your features are not strange; even as I
    you are.
You are not strange at all; even as I you
    are.

My heart had regarded you as resolved
    to do battle,
[yet] you lie in an indolent way upon
    your back!
[Tell me], how did you join the assembly
    of the gods,
in your quest of life?
Utnapishtim said to him, to Gilgamesh:
I will reveal to you, Gilgamesh, a hidden
    matter
and a secret of the gods will I tell you:
Shurippak—a city that you know,
[and that is situated on Euphrates'
    banks]—
that city was ancient, *as were* the gods
    within it,
when their heart led the great gods to
    produce the flood.
There were Anu, their father,
valiant Enlil, their counselor,
Ninurta, their assistant,
Ennuge, their irrigator.
Ninigiku-Ea was also present with
    them;
their words he repeats to the reed hut:
Reed hut, reed hut! Wall, wall!
Reed hut, hearken! Wall, reflect!
Man of Shuruppak, son of Ubar-Tutu,
tear down *this* house, build a ship!
Give up possessions, seek life.
Forswear *worldly* goods and keep the
    soul alive!
Take the seed of all living things aboard
    the ship.
The ship that you shall build,
her dimensions shall be to measure.
Equal shall be her width and her length.
Like the Apsu you shall ceil her.
I understood, and I said to Ea, my lord:
[Behold], my lord, what you have thus
    ordered,
I will be honored to carry out.
[But what] shall I answer the city, the
    people and elders?
Ea opened his mouth to speak,
saying to me, his servant:
You shall then speak unto them in this
    way:
I have learned that Enlil is hostile to me,
so that I cannot reside in your city,
nor set my [foot] in Enlil's territory.

The eleventh tablet of the Epic of Gilgamesh, which records the account of an ancient universal flood. (© Copyright The British Museum)

Therefore I will go down to the Deep,
to dwell with my lord Ea.
[But upon] you he will shower down abundance,
[the choicest] birds, the [rarest] fishes.
[The land shall have its fill] of harvest riches.
[He who at dusk orders] the husk greens,
will shower down upon you a rain of wheat.
With the first glow of dawn,
the land was gathered [about me].

(gap)

The little ones [carried] bitumen,
while the grown ones brought [all else] that was needful.
On the fifth day I laid her framework.
One *whole* acre was her floor space,
ten dozen cubits the height of each of her walls,
ten dozen cubits each edge of the square deck.

I laid out the contours *and* joined her
    together.
I provided her with six decks,
dividing her *thus* into seven parts.
Her floor plan I divided into nine parts.
I hammered water plugs into her.
I saw to the punting poles and laid in
    supplies.
Six sar *measures* of bitumen I poured into
    the furnace,
three sar of asphalt [I also] poured
    inside.
Three sar of oil the basket bearers
    carried,
aside from the one sar of oil that the
    [caulking] consumed,
and the two sar of oil [that] the boatman
    stowed away.
Bullocks I slaughtered for the [people],
and I killed sheep every day.
Must, red wine, oil, and white wine
[I gave the] workmen [to drink], as
    though river water,
that they might feast as on New Year's
    Day.
I [opened] . . . ointment, applying *it* to
    my hand.
[On the seventh day] the ship was
    completed.
[The launching] was very difficult,
so that they had to shift the floor planks
    above and below,
[until] two-thirds of [the structure had
    gone into the water.
Whatever I had] I laded upon her:
whatever I had of silver I laded upon
    her;
whatever I [had] of gold I laded upon
    her;
whatever I had of all the living beings I
    [laded] upon her.
All my family and kin I made go aboard
    the ship.
The beasts of the field, the wild
    creatures of the field,
all the craftsmen I made go aboard.
Shamash had set for me a stated time:
When he who orders unease at night,
will shower down a rain of blight,
board the ship and batten up the
    entrance!

That stated time had arrived:
He who orders unease at night, showers
    down a rain of blight.
I watched the appearance of the
    weather.
The weather was awesome to behold.
I boarded the ship and battened up the
    entrance.
To batten down the *whole* ship, to Puzur-
    Amurri, the boatman,
I handed over the floating palace with
    its contents.
With the first glow of dawn,
a black cloud rose up from the horizon.
Inside it Adad thunders,
while Shullat and Hanish go in front,
moving as heralds over hill and plain.
Erragal tears out the posts;
forth comes Ninurta and causes the
    dikes to follow.
The Anunnaki lift up the torches,
setting the land ablaze with their glare.
Consternation over Adad reaches to the
    heavens,
who turned to blackness all that had
    been light.
[The wide] land was shattered like [a
    pot]!
For one day the south storm [blew],
gathering speed as it blew, [submerging
    the mountains],
overtaking the [people] like a battle.
No one can see his fellow,
nor can the people be recognized from
    heaven.
The gods were frightened by the deluge,
and, shrinking back, they ascended to
    the heaven of Anu.
The gods cowered like dogs
crouched against the outer wall.
Ishtar cried out like a woman in travail,
the sweet-voiced mistress of the [gods]
    moans aloud:
The olden days are alas turned to clay,
because I bespoke evil in the assembly
    of the gods
how could I bespeak evil in the
    assembly of the gods,
ordering battle for the destruction of my
    people,

when it is I myself who give birth to my
people!
Like the spawn of the fishes they fill the
sea!
The Anunnaki gods weep with her,
the gods, all humbled, sit and weep,
their lips [drawn tight], . . . one and all.
Six days and [six] nights
blows the flood wind, as the south
storm sweeps the land.
When the seventh day arrived,
the flood-carrying south storm subsided
in the battle,
which it had fought like an army.
The sea grew quiet, the tempest was
still, the flood ceased.
I looked at the weather: stillness had set
in,
and all of humankind had returned to
clay.
The landscape was as level as a flat roof.
I opened a hatch, and light fell upon my
face.
Bowing low, I sat and wept,
tears running down on my face.
I looked about for coast lines in the
expanse of the sea:
in each of fourteen *regions*
there emerged a *mountain* region.
On Mount Nisir the ship came to a halt.
Mount Nisir held the ship fast,
allowing no motion.
One day, a second day, Mount Nisir held
the ship fast,
allowing no motion.
A third day, a fourth day, Mount Nisir
held the ship fast,
allowing no motion.
A fifth, and a sixth *day*, Mount Nisir
held the ship fast,
allowing no motion.
When the seventh day arrived,
I sent forth and set free a dove.
The dove went forth, but came back;
since no resting place for it was visible,
she turned round.
Then I sent forth and set free a swallow.
The swallow went forth, but came back;
since no resting place for it was visible,
she turned round.
Then I sent forth and set free a raven.

The raven went forth and, seeing that
the waters had diminished,
he eats, circles, caws, and turns not
round.
Then I let out *all* to the four winds
and offered a sacrifice.
I poured out a libation on the top of the
mountain.
Seven and seven cult vessels I set up,
upon their pot stands I heaped cane,
cedar wood, and myrtle.
The gods smelled the savor,
the gods smelled the sweet savor,
the gods crowded like flies about the
sacrificer.
When at length as the great goddess
arrived,
she lifted up the great jewels that Anu
had fashioned to her liking:
Ye gods here, as surely as this lapis
upon my neck I shall not forget,
I shall be mindful of these days,
forgetting *them* never.
Let the gods come to the offering;
but let not Enlil come to the offering,
for he, unreasoning, brought on the
deluge
and my people consigned to
destruction.
When at length as Enlil arrived,
and saw the ship, Enlil was angry,
he was filled with wrath over the IGIGI
gods:
Has some living soul escaped?
No man was to survive the destruction!
Ninurta opened his mouth to speak,
saying to valiant Enlil:
Who, other than Ea, can devise plans?
It is Ea alone who knows every matter.
Ea opened his mouth to speak,
saying to valiant Enlil:
You, O wisest of gods, you, O hero,
how could you, unreasoning, bring on
the deluge?
On the sinner impose his sin,
on the transgressor impose his
transgression!
Yet be lenient, lest he be cut off,
be patient, lest he be [dislodged]!
Instead of your bringing on the deluge,

would that a lion had risen up to
   diminish humankind!
Instead of your bringing on the deluge,
would that a wolf had risen up to
   diminish humankind!
Instead of your bringing on the deluge,
would that a famine had risen up to [lay
   low] humankind!
Instead of your bringing on the deluge,
would that pestilence had risen up to
   [smite down] humankind!
It was not I who disclosed the secret of
   the great gods.
I let Atra-khasis see a dream,
and he perceived the secret of the gods.
Now then take counsel in regard to him!

There upon Enlil went aboard the ship.
Holding me by the hand, he took me
   aboard.
He took my wife aboard and made *her*
   kneel by my side.
Standing between us, he touched our
   foreheads to bless us:
Hitherto Utnapishtim has been but
   human.
Henceforth Utnapishtim and his wife
   shall be like unto us gods.
Utnapishtim shall reside far away, at the
   mouth of the rivers!
Thus they took me and made me reside
   far away,
at the mouth of the rivers.

2 Tower of Babel

Where did the world's many languages originate? Genesis 11:1–9 records the account of the tower of Babel, in part to answer this question. The sole text in this chapter represents a Sumerian answer to why so many languages exist.

#13: Confusion of Tongues
(Kramer, "Babel of Tongues," 109–11)[1]

The Sumerian epic "Enmerkar and the Lord of Aratta" contains an interesting incantation pronounced by Enmerkar that may offer a parallel to the Tower of Babel in Genesis 11:1–9. This is far from certain since the translation of the key phrase *harmony-tongued Sumer* has been called into question.[2]

Once upon a time there was no snake,
    there was no scorpion,
there was no hyena, there was no lion,
there was no wild dog, no wolf,
there was no fear, no terror,
man had no rival.
In those days, the lands Shunbur *and*
    Hamazi,
harmony-tongued Sumer, the great land
    of the decrees of princeship,
Uri, the land having all that is
    appropriate,
the land Martu, resting in security,
the whole universe, the people in
    unison,
to Enlil in one tongue . . .
Then A-DA the lord, A-DA the prince,
    A-DA the king,
Enki A-DA the lord, A-DA the prince, A-DA
    the king,
A-DA the lord, A-DA the prince, A-DA the
    king . . .
Then A-DA the lord, A-DA the prince,
    A-DA the king,
Enki A-DA the lord, A-DA the prince, A-DA
    the king,
A-DA the lord, A-DA the prince, A-DA the
    king,
Enki, the lord of abundance, *whose*
    commands are trustworthy,
the lord of wisdom, who understands
    the land,
the leader of the gods,
endowed with wisdom, the [lord] of
    Eridu,
changed the speech in their mouths,
    [brought] contention into it,
into the speech of man that *until then*
    had been one.

3 Ancestral Customs

The ancestral narratives of Genesis 12–50 contain many references to the day-to-day activities of Israel's ancestors, especially financial dealings (for example, inheritance rights, employment, and land purchase) and personal institutions (for example, marriage and adoption). Archeological research at Nuzi in the heartland of Mesopotamia yielded personal, family archives from the fifteenth and fourteenth centuries B.C. and give many potential parallels to ancestral customs. Since the Nuzi customs often reflect Old Babylonian culture in general in the middle of the second millennium B.C., it should not be surprising that legal texts from Nuzi illuminate the customs of Israel's ancestors. In addition, important archives from other cities in Mesopotamia and Syria-Palestine (Mari, Emar, Alalakh, and perhaps Ebla) continue to shed light on the social and cultural customs of the ancestral period.

In the enthusiasm to find parallels with the Bible, scholars sometimes made claims for the Nuzi texts that proved to be untenable upon later scrutiny. Against earlier claims, it can no longer be maintained that the Nuzi texts (or other texts from the Old Babylonian period) authenticate the ancestral narratives as genuine early second-millennium traditions. Recent studies, however, balance the comparative approach to the Nuzi materials and show that several parallels are still valid, while some of the initial claims have to be abandoned.[1] Although we are left with few direct parallels to the biblical ancestors, such comparisons nevertheless illustrate that the ancestral families as portrayed in Genesis were part and parcel of the ancient Near Eastern world of the early second millennium B.C.

#14: Adoption of Shennima
(Speiser, "New Kirkuk Documents," 32–33)[2]

A legal adoption contract from Nuzi illustrates three conventional practices of the mid-second millennium B.C. First, a man could be contractually prohibited from marrying additional wives, which is reminiscent of Laban's restriction on Jacob in Genesis 31:50. Second, it was customary to give a handmaid to one's daughter at the time of her marriage, as with Rebekah, Rachel, and Leah. Third, it was not unusual to provide a second wife or concubine in cases of barrenness, as Sarah provided Hagar for Abraham.[3]

Tablet of adoption belonging to [Zigi] son of Akkuya; his son [Shennima] as son to [Shurihil he has given]. And [Shurihil], as far as Shennima is concerned, all *these* lands, his earnings, whatever their description, one *portion* of it all to Shennima he has given. If Shurihil has a son *of his own*, firstborn *he shall be*; a double share he shall take. Shennima shall then be second and according to his allotment his inheritance share he shall take. As long as Shurihil is alive, Shennima shall serve him. When Shurihil [dies], Shennima shall become [heir]. Further, Gilimninu as wife to Shennima has been given. If Gilimninu bears *children*, Shennima shall not take another wife; and if Gilimninu does not bear, Gilimninu a woman of the Lulla as wife for Shennima shall take. As for *the concubine's* offspring, Gilimninu shall [not] send *them* away. Any sons that out of the womb of Gilimninu [to Shennima] may be [born, all the] lands, buildings, [whatever their description], to *these* sons are given. [In case] she does not bear [a son], then the daughter of [Gilimninu of] the lands and buildings one portion shall take. As for Shurihil, another son in addition to Shennima he shall not adopt.

Whoever among them breaks [the contract] shall furnish one mina of silver and one mina of gold.

Moreover, Yalampa as handmaid to Gilimninu has been given, and Shatimninu for supervision has been assigned. As long as *Yalampa* is alive, she shall [serve her]; and Shatimninu . . . shall not annul.

If Gilimninu bears *children* and Shennima takes another wife, her bundle she shall *pick up* and she shall leave.

ten witnesses

The remaining sons of Zigi shall not interfere with the lands and buildings of the property.

The tablet was written after the proclamation.

eight seals

#15: Old Babylonian Shepherding Contract
(Finkelstein, "Old Babylonian Herding Contract," 31)

The agreement between Jacob and Laban in Genesis 31:38–40 is illuminated by an Old Babylonian shepherding contract, which explains the responsibilities of the sheep owner and the shepherd to one another. The shepherd was paid for his work by receiving a portion of the newborn animals.[4]

92 ewes, 20 rams, 22 breeding lambs, 24 [spring] lambs, 33 she-goats, 4 male goats, 27 kids—total: 158 sheep; total: 64 goats, which Sinshamuh has entrusted to Dada the shepherd. *Dada* assumes liability *therefore* and will replace any lost *animals*. Should Nidnatum, *Dada's* shepherd boy, absent himself, *Nidnatum* will bear responsibility for any *consequent* loss, *and* Dada will measure out five kor of barley.

Three witnesses; date: Samsuiluna year one, fourth month, sixteenth day.

#16: Turpunna's Bride-Price
(Speiser, "New Kirkuk Documents," 65)

A Nuzi marriage agreement illustrates the proper distribution of the bride-price. The father could give a portion to the bride herself or retain it on her behalf in case her husband died or abandoned her. This practice sheds light on the complaint of Laban's daughters that Laban had used the money and reduced their marriages to sales transactions. Since Laban could no longer provide their financial security, they had no hesitation about leaving with Jacob (Genesis 31:14–16).[5]

Sheep and goats were important commodities in many parts of the ancient world. (Jim Yancey)

Thus *says* Arinturi daughter of Pakkaya: My daughter Turpunna placed my husband for me *at my disposal*. And I have sold Turpunna as wife; I have received the money for her from her husband. And the daughter of Turpunna, Eluanza, is living as a servant. Now I have given Eluanza as my daughter-in-law to Matkashar; and Matkashar shall sell Eluanza to a man as wife and she shall receive and use forty shekels of silver for her from her husband.

Thus *says* Arinturi: My father gave me one imer of land as dowry; and now I have given to the same Matkashar. And Matkashar in accordance with the other tablet to their [*sic*] sons shall give it: to a stranger she shall not give it.

Thus further *says* Arinturi: The money for Kanzu I have received and used; and the remaining money of Kanzu, belonging to Matkashar, I have given *to her*.

six witnesses; five seals

4 Epic Literature

The ancient Near East produced epics that are instructive when compared with the pentateuchal narratives. The ancestral narratives of Genesis, for example, appear in many ways to be unique in the literature of the ancient world, but the recovery of ancient Near East epics yielded several parallels with the biblical narratives. These epics were about supposedly historical individuals, although to what extent they relate historical details accurately is much in debate. Some are written in an elevated prose not unlike the biblical ancestral narratives, while others are in an epic poetic form popular in the ancient Near East.

#17: Autobiography of Sargon
(Lewis, *Sargon Legend*, 24–29)[1]

The Akkadian document known as the "Autobiography of Sargon" is a birth legend dating from the first millennium B.C.[2] It gives an explanation for the rapid and unexpected rise of the first great Semitic ruler of Mesopotamia, Sargon I of Akkad (2334–2279 B.C.). Some argue that the document was actually composed later in the court of King Sargon II of Assyria (721–705 B.C.). It is impossible to be confident about either position, although it seems likely that the text already had a rather long written history by the early first millennium. Written in the first person, the account explains that Sargon is an illegitimate son of a priestess who abandoned the baby because her calling did not permit her to bear children. The themes of untimely pregnancy, concealed birth, abandonment of a newborn to river waters, rescue, and adoption are most familiar to Bible readers from the narrative concerning Moses (Exodus 2:1–10).

Sargon, strong king, king of Agade, am I.
My mother was a high priestess, my
    father I do not know.
My paternal kin inhabit the mountain
    region.
My city *of birth* is Azupiranu, which lies
    on the bank of the Euphrates.
My mother, a high priestess, conceived
    me, in secret she bore me.
She placed me in a reed basket, with
    bitumen she caulked my hatch.
She abandoned me to the river from
    which I could not escape.
The river carried me along; to Aqqi, the
    water drawer, it brought me.
Aqqi, the water drawer, when
    immersing his bucket lifted me up.
Aqqi, the water drawer, raised me as his
    adopted son.
Aqqi, the water drawer, set me to his
    garden work.
During my garden work, Ishtar loved
    me *so that*
fifty-five years I ruled as king.
The black-headed people I took over *and*
    governed.
Difficult mountains I [passed through
    (?)] using copper picks.
The upper ranges I climbed again and
    again.
The lower ranges I jumped over again
    and again.
The sea [land (?)] I besieged three times.
I conquered Tilmun . . .
To greater Der I went up, I . . .
[Kazallu (?)] I destroyed . . .
Whatever king may arise after me,
[let him rule as king fifty-five years (?)
Let him take over and govern] the black-
    headed people.
[Let him pass through (?)] difficult
    mountains using [copper picks].
Let him climb the upper ranges again
    and again.

[Let him jump over the lower ranges
    again and again].
Let him besiege the sea [land (?)] three
    times.
[Let him conquer Tilmun . . .
Let him go up to greater Der and . . .
. . . from my city Agade

    (gap)

To . . .
and the HUQU [bird (?)] . . .
and the ewe ran about in the steppe,
    why not . . .
and the gazelle, the . . . of the wind, the
    stag . . .
The QATA bird that was crying out
in its continuous crying, what did it
    achieve?
The wind blew . . .
The wild ass ran about, what . . .
The wind blows from the steppe
the wild ass ran about, he spent the
    night in the steppe.
The . . . runs . . .
of a swift onager what . . .
The wolf did not escape the blood . . .
The devouring lion the blood . . .
. . . the spiller of blood . . .
. . . the smearer of blood . . .
It ran about from the judgment of
    Shamash to
the wind blew the house of men
. . . tears the temple of
. . . turns into wasteland.

#18: Tale of Sinuhe
(Lichtheim, *Ancient Egyptian Literature*, 1.222–35)[3]

The "Tale of Sinuhe" narrates how Sinuhe, an Egyptian court official, is forced to flee Egypt for political reasons. He finds refuge and lives with a seminomadic chieftain in Canaan around the time of Israel's early ancestors. The tale is set in the mid-twentieth century B.C., and our oldest copies are from approximately 1800 B.C., illustrating that narratives could be created and preserved in the early second millennium B.C. If this story is historical (a question in dispute), it also demonstrates that such historical narratives could be produced within a century or so of the events they describe. The tale is a literary masterpiece that became a classic in ancient Egypt and offers an example of

Egyptian Scribe. (Egyptian Museum, Cairo)

ancient elevated prose similar to the ancestral narratives and other pentateuchal narratives concerning Moses.

The prince, count, governor of the domains of the sovereign in the lands of the Asiatics, true and beloved friend of the king, the attendant Sinuhe, says:

I was an attendant who attended his lord, a servant of the royal harem, waiting on the princess, the highly praised royal wife of King Sesostris in Khenemsut, the daughter of King Amenemhet in Kanefru, Nefru, the revered.

Year thirty, third month of the inundation, day seven: the god ascended to his horizon. The king of Upper and Lower Egypt, Sehetepibre, flew to heaven and united with the sun disk, the divine body merging with its maker. Then the residence was hushed; hearts grieved; the great portals were shut; the courtiers were head-on-knee; the people moaned.

His majesty, however, had despatched an army to the land of the Tjemeh, with his eldest son as its commander, the good god Sesostris. He had been sent to smite the foreign lands and to punish those of Tjehenu.

Now he was returning, bringing captives of the Tjehenu and cattle of all kinds beyond number. The officials of the palace sent to the western border to let the king's son know the event that had occurred at the court. The messengers met him on the road, reaching him at night. Not a moment did he delay. The falcon flew with his attendants, without letting his army know it.

But the royal sons who had been with him on this expedition had also been sent for. One of them was summoned while I was standing *there*. I heard his voice, as he spoke, while I was in the near distance. My heart fluttered, my arms spread out, a trembling befell all my limbs. I removed myself in leaps, to seek a hiding place. I put myself between two bushes, so as to leave the road to its traveler.

I set out southward. I did not plan to go to the residence. I believed there would be turmoil and did not expect to survive it. I crossed Maaty near Sycamore; I reached Isle-of-Snefru. I spent the day there at the edge of the cultivation. Departing at dawn I encountered a man who stood on the road. He saluted me while I was afraid of him. At dinner time I reached Cattle-Quay. I crossed in a barge without a rudder, by the force of the west wind. I passed to the east of the quarry, at the height of Mistress of the Red Mountain. Then I made my way northward. I reached the Walls of the Ruler, which were made to repel the Asiatics and to crush the Sand-farers. I crouched in a bush for fear of being seen by the guard on duty upon the wall.

I set out at night. At dawn I reached Peten. I halted at Isle-of-Kem-Wer. An attack of thirst overtook me; I was parched, my throat burned. I said: This is the taste of death. I raised my heart and collected myself when I heard the lowing sound of cattle and saw Asiatics. One of their leaders, who had been in Egypt, recognized me. He gave me water and boiled milk for me. I went with him to his tribe. What they did for me was good.

Land gave me to land. I traveled to Byblos; I returned to Qedem. I spent a year and a half there. Then Ammunenshi, the ruler of Upper Retenu, took me to him, saying to me: You will be happy with me; you will hear the language of Egypt. He said this because he knew my character and had heard of my skill, Egyptians who were with him having borne witness for me. He said to me: Why have you come here? Has something happened at the residence? I said to him: King Sehetepibre departed to the horizon, and one did not know the circumstances. But I spoke in half-truths: When I returned from the expedition to the land of the Tjemeh, it was reported to me and my heart grew faint. It carried me away on the path of flight, although I had not been talked about; no one had spat in my face; I had not heard a reproach; my name had not been heard in the mouth of the herald. I do not know what brought me to this country; it is as if planned by god. As if a Delta-man saw himself in Yebu, a marsh-man in Nubia.

Then he said to me: How then is that land without that excellent god, fear of whom was throughout the lands like Sakhmet in a year of plague? I said to him in reply: Of course his son has entered into the palace, having taken his father's heritage.

He is a god without peer,
no other comes before him;
he is lord of knowledge, wise planner,
    skilled leader,
one goes and comes by his will.
He was the smiter of foreign lands,
while his father stayed in the palace,
he reported to him on commands
    carried out.
He is a champion who acts with his arm,
a fighter who has no equal,
when seen engaged in archery,
when joining the melee.
Horn-curber who makes hands turn
    weak,
his foes can not close ranks;
keen-sighted he smashes foreheads,
none can withstand his presence.
Wide-striding he smites the fleeing,
no retreat for him who turns him his
    back;
steadfast in time of attack,
he makes turn back and turns not his
    back.
Stouthearted when he sees the mass,
he lets not slackness fill his heart;
eager at the sight of combat,

joyful when he works his bow.
Clasping his shield he treads under foot,
no second blow needed to kill;
none can escape his arrow,
none turn aside his bow.
The bowmen flee before him,
as before the might of the goddess;
as he fights he plans the goal,
unconcerned about all else.
Lord of grace, rich in kindness,
he has conquered through affection;
his city loves him more than itself,
acclaims him more than its own god.
Men outdo women in hailing him,
now that he is king;
victor while yet unborn,
set to be ruler since his birth.
Augmenter of those born with him,
he is unique, god given;
happy the land that he rules!
Enlarger of frontiers
he will conquer southern lands,
while ignoring northern lands,
though made to smite Asiatics and tread
   on Sand-farers!

Send to him! Let him know your name as one who inquires while being far from his majesty. He will not fail to do good to a land that will be loyal to him.

He said to me: Well then, Egypt is happy knowing that he is strong. But you are here. You shall stay with me. What I shall do for you is good.

He set me at the head of his children. He married me to his eldest daughter. He let me choose for myself of his land, of the best that was his, on his border with another land. It was a good land called Yaa. Figs were in it and grapes. It had more wine than water. Abundant was its honey, plentiful its oil. All kinds of fruit were on its trees. Barley was there and emmer, and no end of cattle of all kinds. Much also came to me because of the love for me; for he had made me chief of a tribe in the best part of his land. Loaves were made for me daily, and wine as daily fare, cooked meat, roast fowl, as well as desert game. For they snared for me and laid it before me, in addition to the catch of my hounds.

Many sweets were made for me, and milk dishes of all kinds.

I passed many years, my children becoming strong men, each a master of his tribe. The envoy who came north or went south to the residence stayed with me. I let everyone stay with me. I gave water to the thirsty; I showed the way to him who had strayed; I rescued him who had been robbed. When Asiatics conspired to attack the rulers of hill countries, I opposed their movements. For this the ruler of Retenu made me carry out numerous missions as commander of his troops. Every hill tribe against which I marched I vanquished, so that it was driven from the pasture of its wells. I plundered its cattle, carried off its families, seized their food, and killed people by my strong arm, by my bow, by my movements and my skillful plans. I won his heart and he loved me, for he recognized my valor. He set me at the head of his children, for he saw the strength of my arms.

There came a hero of Retenu,
to challenge me in my tent.
A champion was he without peer,
he had subdued it all.
He said he would fight with me,
he planned to plunder me,
he meant to seize my cattle
at the behest of his tribe.

The ruler conferred with me and I said: I do not know him; I am not his ally, that I could walk about in his camp. Have I ever opened his back rooms or climbed over his fence? It is envy, because he sees me doing your commissions. I am indeed like a stray bull in a strange herd, whom the bull of the herd charges, whom the longhorn attacks. Is an inferior beloved when he becomes a superior? No Asiatic makes friends with a Delta-man. And what would make papyrus cleave to the mountain? If a bull loves combat, should a champion bull retreat for fear of being equaled? If he wishes to fight, let him declare his wish. Is there a god who does not know what he has ordained, and a man who knows how it will be?

At night I strung my bow, sorted my arrows, practiced with my dagger, polished my weapons. When it dawned Retenu came. He had assembled his tribes; he had gathered his neighboring peoples; he was intent on this combat.

He came toward me while I waited, having placed myself near him. Every heart burned for me; the women jabbered. All hearts ached for me thinking: Is there another champion who could fight him? He raised his battle-ax and shield, while his armful of missiles fell toward me. When I had made his weapons attack me, I let his arrows pass me by without effect, one following the other. Then, when he charged me, I shot him, my arrow sticking in his neck. He screamed; he fell on his nose; I slew him with his ax. I raised my war cry over his back, while every Asiatic shouted. I gave praise to Mont, while his people mourned him. The ruler Ammunenshi took me in his arms.

Then I carried off his goods; I plundered his cattle. What he had meant to do to me I did to him. I took what was in his tent; I stripped his camp. Thus I became great, wealthy in goods, rich in herds. It was the god who acted, so as to show mercy to one with whom he had been angry, whom he had made stray abroad. For today his heart is appeased.

A fugitive fled his surroundings—
I am famed at home.
A laggard lagged from hunger—
I give bread to my neighbor.
A man left his land in nakedness—
I have bright clothes, fine linen.
A man ran for lack of one to send—
I am rich in servants.
My house is fine, my dwelling
    spacious—
my thoughts are at the palace!

Whichever god decreed this flight, have mercy, bring me home! Surely you will let me see the place in which my heart dwells! What is more important than that my corpse be buried in the land in which I was born! Come to my aid! What if the happy event should occur! May god pity me! May he act so as to make happy the end of one whom he punished! May his heart ache for one whom he forced to live abroad! If he is truly appeased

today, may he hearken to the prayer of one far away! May he return one whom he made roam the earth to the place from which he carried him off!

May Egypt's king have mercy on me, that I may live by his mercy! May I greet the mistress of the land who is in the palace! May I hear the commands of her children! Would that my body were young again! For old age has come; feebleness has overtaken me. My eyes are heavy, my arms weak; my legs fail to follow. The heart is weary; death is near. May I be conducted to the city of eternity! May I serve the mistress of all! May she speak well of me to her children; may she spend eternity above me!

Now when the majesty of King Kheperkare was told of the condition in which I was, his majesty sent word to me with royal gifts, in order to gladden the heart of this servant like that of a foreign ruler. And the royal children who were in his palace sent me their messages. Copy of the decree brought to this servant concerning his return to Egypt:

Horus: living in births; the Two Ladies: living in births; the king of Upper and Lower Egypt: Kheperkare; the son of Re: Sesostris, who lives forever. Royal decree to the attendant Sinuhe:

This decree of the king if brought to you to let you know: That you circled the foreign countries, going from Qedem to Retenu, land giving you to land, was the counsel of your own heart. What had you done that one should act against you? You had not cursed, so that your speech would be reproved. You had not spoken against the counsel of the nobles, that your words should have been rejected. This matter—it carried away your heart. It was not in my heart against you. This your heaven in the palace lives and prospers to this day. Her head is adorned with the kingship of the land; her children are in the palace. You will store riches that they give you; you will live on their bounty. Come back to Egypt! See the residence in which you lived! Kiss the ground at the great portals, mingle with the courtiers! For today you have begun to age. You have lost a man's strength. Think of the day of burial, the passing into reveredness.

A night is made for you with ointments and wrappings from the hand of Tait. A funeral procession is made for you on the day of burial; the mummy case is of gold, its head of lapis lazuli. The sky is above you as you lie in the hearse, oxen drawing you, musicians going before you. The dance of the MWW dancers is done at the door of your tomb; the offering list is read to you; sacrifice is made before your offering stone. Your tomb pillars, made of white stone, are among *those of* the royal children. You shall not die abroad! No Asiatics shall inter you. You shall not be wrapped in the skin of a ram to serve as your coffin. Too long a roaming of the earth! Think of your corpse, come back!

This decree reached me while I was standing in the midst of my tribe. When it had been read to me, I threw myself on my belly. Having touched the soil, I spread it on my chest. I strode around my camp shouting: What compares with this that is done to a servant whom his heart led astray to alien lands? Truly good is the kindness that saves me from death! Your KA will grant me to reach my end, my body being at home!

Copy of the reply to this decree:

The servant of the palace, Sinuhe, says: In very good peace! Regarding the matter of this flight that this servant did in his ignorance. It is your KA, O good god, lord of the Two Lands, which Re loves and which Mont lord of Thebes favors; and Amon lord of thrones of the Two Lands, and Sobk-Re lord of Sumenu, and Horus, Hathor, Atum with his Ennead, and Sopdu-Neferbau-Semseru the eastern Horus, and the lady of Yemet—may she enfold your head—and the conclave upon the flood, and Min-Horus of the hill countries, and Wereret lady of Punt, Nut, Haroeris-Re, and all the gods of Egypt and the isles of the sea—may they give life and joy to your nostrils, may they endue you with their bounty, may they give you eternity without limit, infinity without bounds! May the fear of you resound in lowlands and highlands, for you have subdued all that the sun encircles! This is the prayer of this servant for his lord who saves from the west.

The lord of knowledge who knows people knew in the majesty of the palace that this servant was afraid to say it. It is like a thing too great to repeat. The great god, the peer of Re, knows the heart of one who has served him willingly. This servant is in the hand of one who thinks about him. He is placed under his care. Your majesty is the conquering Horus; your arms vanquish all lands. May then your majesty command to have brought to you the prince of Meki from Qedem, the mountain chiefs from Keshu, and the prince of Menus from the lands of the Fenkhu. They are rulers of renown who have grown up in the love of you. I do not mention Retenu—it belongs to you like your hounds.

Lo, this flight that the servant made—I did not plan it. It was not in my heart; I did not devise it. I do not know what removed me from my place. It was like a dream. As if a Delta-man saw himself in Yebu, a marsh-man in Nubia. I was not afraid; no one ran after me. I had not heard a reproach; my name was not heard in the mouth of the herald. Yet my flesh crept, my feet hurried, my heart drove me; the god who had willed this flight dragged me away. Nor am I a haughty man. He who knows his land respects me. Re has set the fear of you throughout the land, the dread of you in every foreign country. Whether I am at the residence, whether I am in this place, it is you who covers this horizon. The sun rises at your pleasure. The water in the river is drunk when you wish. The air of heaven is breathed at your bidding. This servant will hand over to the brood that this servant begot in this place. This servant has been sent for! Your majesty will do as he wishes! One lives by the breath that you give. As Re, Horus, and Hathor love your august nose, may Mont lord of Thebes wish it to live forever!

I was allowed to spend one more day in Yaa, handing over my possessions to my children, my eldest son taking charge of my tribe; all my possessions became his—my serfs, my herds, my fruit, my fruit trees. This servant departed southward. I halted at Horus-ways. The commander in charge of the garrison sent a message to the residence to let it be known. Then his majesty sent a trusted overseer of the royal domains with whom were loaded ships, bearing royal gifts for the Asiatics who had come with me to escort me to Horus-ways. I called each one by his name, while every butler was at his task. When I had started and set sail, there was kneading and straining beside me, until I reached the city of Itj-tawy.

When it dawned, very early, they came to summon me. Ten men came and ten men went to usher me into the palace. My forehead touched the ground between the sphinxes, and the royal children stood in the gateway to meet me. The courtiers who usher through the forecourt set me on the way to the audience hall. I found his majesty on the great throne in a kiosk of gold. Stretched out on my belly, I did not know myself before him, while this god greeted me pleasantly. I was like a man seized by darkness. My BA was gone, my limbs trembled; my heart was not in my body, I did not know life from death.

His majesty said to one of the courtiers: Lift him up, let him speak to me. Then his majesty said: Now you have come, after having roamed foreign lands. Flight has taken its toll of you. You have aged, have reached old age. It is no small matter that your corpse will be interred without being escorted by Bowmen. But don't act thus, don't act thus, speechless though your name was called! Fearful of punishment I answered with the answer of a frightened man: What has my lord said to me, that I might answer it? It is not disrespect to the god! It is the terror that is in my body, like that which caused the fateful flight! Here I am before you. Life is yours. May your majesty do as he wishes!

Then the royal daughters were brought in, and his majesty said to the queen: Here is Sinuhe, come as an Asiatic, a product of nomads! She uttered a very great cry, and the royal daughters shrieked all together. They said to his majesty: Is it really he, O king, our lord? Said his majesty: It is really he! Now having brought with them their necklaces and rattles, they held them out to his majesty:

Your hands upon the radiance, eternal king,
  jewels of heaven's mistress!
The gold gives life to your nostrils,
the lady of stars enfolds you!

Southcrown fared north, northcrown
  south,
joined, united by your majesty's word.
While the cobra decks your brow,
you deliver the poor from harm.
Peace to you from Re, lord of lands!
Hail to you and the mistress of all!
Slacken your bow, lay down your arrow,
give breath to him who gasps for breath!
Give us our good gift on this good day,
grant us the son of north wind, bowman
  born in Egypt!
He made the flight in fear of you,
he left the land in dread of you!
A face that sees you shall not pale,
eyes that see you shall not fear!

His majesty said: He shall not fear, he shall not dread! He shall be a companion among the nobles. He shall be among the courtiers. Proceed to the robing room to wait on him!

I left the audience hall, the royal daughters giving me their hands. We went through the great portals, and I was put in the house of a prince. In it were luxuries: a bathroom and mirrors. In it were riches from the treasury; clothes of royal linen, myrrh, and the choice perfume of the king and of his favorite courtiers were in every room. Every servant was at his task. Years were removed from my body. I was shaved; my hair was combed. Thus was my squalor returned to the foreign land, my dress to the Sand-farers. I was clothed in fine linen; I was anointed with fine oil. I slept on a bed. I had returned the sand to those who dwell in it, the tree oil to those who grease themselves with it.

I was given a house and garden that had belonged to a courtier. Many craftsmen rebuilt it, and all its woodwork was made anew. Meals were brought to me from the palace three times, four times a day, apart from what the royal children gave without a moment's pause.

A stone pyramid was built for me in the midst of the pyramids. The masons who build tombs constructed it. A master draftsman designed in it. A master sculptor carved in it. The overseers of construction in the necropolis busied themselves with it. All the equipment that is placed in a tomb shaft was supplied. Mortuary priests were given me. A funerary domain was made for me. It had fields and a garden in the right place, as is done for a Companion of the first rank. My statue was overlaid with gold, its skirt with electrum. It was his majesty who ordered it made. There is no commoner for whom the like has been done. I was in the favor of the king, until the day of landing came.

Colophon: It is done from beginning to end as it was found in writing.

#19: Tale of Aqhat
(Coogan, *Stories from Ancient Canaan*, 32–47)[4]

The "Tale of Aqhat" is an Ugaritic narrative from approximately the mid-fourteenth century B.C. and contains themes of barrenness familiar from the Abrahamic narrative and elsewhere in the Old Testament. The story is about a certain Canaanite king named Danel[5] who has no son and heir. When he appeals to the deities for a son, Baal grants his petition, and a son, Aqhat, is born. Unfortunately, the lad meets an untimely death. Although the narrative may have originally recounted his resurrection, the conclusion of the story is now lost.

Then Danel, the healer's man,
the Hero, the man of the god of
    Harnam,
made an offering for the gods to eat,
made an offering for the holy ones to
    drink.
Then he climbed onto his mat and lay
    down,
onto his pallet, where he spent the night.
One day had ended, and on the second
Danel made an offering to the gods,
an offering for the gods to eat,
an offering for the holy ones to drink.
Three days had ended, and on the
    fourth
Danel made an offering to the gods,
an offering for the gods to eat,
an offering for the holy ones to drink.
Five days had ended, and on the sixth
Danel made an offering to the gods,
an offering for the gods to eat,
an offering for the holy ones to drink.
Danel climbed onto his mat,
he climbed onto his mat and lay down,

onto his pallet, where he spent the night.
Then, on the seventh day,
Baal approached the assembly with his
    plea:
Danel, the healer's man, is unhappy;
the Hero, the man of the god of
    Harnam, sighs:
he has no son, but his brothers do,
no heir, like his cousins;
unlike his brothers, he has no son,
nor an heir, like his cousins.
Yet he has made an offering for the gods
    to eat,
an offering for the holy ones to drink.
So, my father, El the Bull, won't you
    bless him?
Creator of All, won't you show him
    your favor?
Let him have a son in his house,
a descendant inside his palace,
to set up a stela for his divine ancestor,
a family shrine in the sanctuary;
to free his spirit from the earth,
guard his footsteps from the Slime;
to crush those who rebel against him,
drive off his oppressors;
to hold his hand when he is drunk,
support him when he is full of wine;
to eat his offering in the temple of Baal,
his portion in the temple of El;
to patch his roof when it leaks,
wash his clothes when they are dirty.
El took care of his servant,
he blessed Danel, the healer's man,
he showed favor to the hero, the man of
    the god of Harnam:
Let the passion of Danel, the healer's
    man, revive,
the desire of the hero, the man of the
    god of Harnam.
Let him go up to his bed:
when he kisses his wife she'll become
    pregnant;
when he embraces her she'll conceive:
she will become pregnant, she will give
    birth, she will conceive;
and there will be a son in his house,
an heir inside his palace,
to set up a stela for his divine ancestor,
a family shrine in the sanctuary;
to free his spirit from the earth,

guard his footsteps from the Slime;
to crush those who rebel against him,
drive off his oppressors . . .

   (gap)

. . . a family shrine in the sanctuary;
to free your spirit from the earth,
guard your footsteps from the Slime;
to crush those who rebel against you,
drive off your oppressors;
to eat your offering in the temple of
   Baal,
your portion in the temple of El;
to hold your hand when you are drunk,
support you when you are full of wine;
to patch your roof when it leaks,
wash your clothes when they are dirty.
Danel's face was glad,
and above his brow shone.
He opened his mouth and laughed,
put his feet on a stool,
raised his voice and shouted:
Now I can sit back and relax;
my heart inside me can relax;
for a son will be born to me, like my
   brothers,
an heir, like my cousins,
who will set up a stela for my divine
   ancestor,
a family shrine in the sanctuary;
who will free my spirit from the earth,
guard my footsteps from the slime;
who will crush those who rebel against
   me,
drive off my oppressors;
who will hold my hand when I am
   drunk,
support me when I am full of wine;
who will eat my offering in the temple
   of Baal,
my portion in the temple of El;
who will patch my roof when it leaks,
wash my clothes when they are dirty.
Danel arrived at his house,
Danel reached his palace.
The wise women entered his house,
the singers, the swallows.
Then Danel, the healer's man,
the hero, the man of the god of Harnam,
slaughtered an ox for the wise women,
he gave food to the wise women,

drink to the singers, the swallows.
One day had ended, and on the second
he gave food to the wise women,
drink to the singers, the swallows.
Three days had ended, and on the
   fourth
he gave food to the wise women,
drink to the singers, the swallows.
Five days had ended, and on the sixth
he gave food to the wise women,
drink to the singers, the swallows.
Then, on the seventh day,
the wise women left his house,
the singers, the swallows . . .
. . . the pleasures of bed,
. . . the delights of bed . . .
Danel sat and counted the months.

   (gap)

I'll bring a bow there,
I'll provide the arrows.
And then, on the seventh day,
Danel, the healer's man,
the Hero, the man of the god of
   Harnam,
got up and sat at the entrance to the
   gate,
next to the granary on the threshing
   floor.
He judged the cases of widows,
presided over orphans' hearings.
Then he raised his eyes and looked:
a thousand fields, ten thousand acres at
   each step,
he saw Kothar coming,
he saw Khasis approaching;
not only was he bringing a bow,
he had also provided arrows.
Then Danel, the healer's man,
the Hero, the man of the god of
   Harnam,
called to his wife:
Listen, lady Danataya:
prepare a lamb from the flock
for Kothar-wa-khasis's appetite,
for the desire of the Clever Craftsman.
Give food and drink to the god;
serve and honor him,
the lord of Egypt, the god of it all.
Lady Danataya obeyed;
she prepared a lamb from the flock

for Kothar-wa-khasis's appetite,
for the desire of the Clever Craftsman.
After Kothar-wa-khasis had arrived,
he put the bow in Danel's hands,
he set the arrows on his knees.
Then lady Danataya gave food and
    drink to the god;
she served and honored him,
the lord of Egypt, the god of it all.
Kothar left for his tent,
the clever one for his divine home.

   (gap)

Anat poured her cup on the ground,
she raised her voice and shouted:
Listen, Aqhat the Hero:
if you want silver, I'll give it to you,
or gold—I'll make it yours.
But give your bow to Anat,
let the Mistress of the Peoples have your
    arrows.
But Aqhat the Hero replied:
I'll donate wood from the Lebanon,
I'll donate tendons from wild oxen,
I'll donate horns from mountain goats,
sinews from the hocks of a bull,
I'll donate reeds from the vast marshes;
give them to Kothar-wa-khasis:
he'll make a bow for Anat,
arrows for the Mistress of the Peoples.
But the virgin Anat replied:
If you want eternal life, Aqhat the Hero,
even if you want eternal life, I'll give it
    to you,
immortality—I'll make it yours.
You'll be able to match years with Baal,
months with the sons of El.
For when Baal gives life, he makes a
    feast,
makes a feast for the life-given and
    gives him drinks;
he sings a song in his honor,
a pleasant refrain for him.
So will I give life to Aqhat the Hero.
But Aqhat the Hero replied:
Don't lie to me, virgin,
for with a hero your lies are wasted.
A mortal—what does he get in the end?
What does a mortal finally get?
Plaster poured on his head,
lime on top of his skull.

As every man dies, I will die;
yes, I too will surely die.
And I have something else to tell you:
bows are for men!
Do women ever hunt?
Anat laughed, but not in her heart;
she replied:
Listen to me, Aqhat the Hero,
listen to me while I speak:
I'll surely meet you on the path of
    rebellion,
on the proud path I'll make you fall
under my feet, pretty-boy, he-man.
She stamped her feet and left the earth;
then she headed toward El,
at the source of the two rivers,
in the midst of the two seas' pools;
she opened El's tent and entered
the shrine of the king, the father of time.
At El's feet she bowed down and
    adored,
she prostrated herself and worshiped
    him.
Then she maligned Aqhat the Hero,
she slandered the child of Danel, the
    healer's man.

   (gap)

And the virgin Anat replied:
Don't rejoice in your well-built house,
in your well-built house, El,
don't rejoice in the height of your
    palace:
don't rely on them!
I'll smash your head,
I'll make your gray hair run with blood,
your gray beard with gore;
then you may call to Aqhat—he can
    save you;
to the son of Danel—he can save you
from the hand of the virgin Anat!
But El the Kind, the Compassionate,
    replied:
I know you, daughter, how gentle you
    can be;
but there is no restraint among
    goddesses.
Leave, my unscrupulous daughter;
you will store it up in your heart,
and then whatever you desire you will
    do,

whatever you wish;
whoever slanders you will be crushed.
The virgin Anat left;
she headed toward Aqhat the Hero,
a thousand fields, ten thousand acres at
each step.
And the virgin Anat laughed;
she raised her voice and shouted:
Listen, Aqhat the Hero:
you are my brother and I am your sister
. . .

(gap)

The virgin Anat left,
she headed for Yatpan, the lady's man.
She raised her voice and shouted:
Pay attention, Yatpan:
Aqhat is now in the city of Abiluma,
Abiluma, the city of Prince Moon . . .
But Yatpan, the lady's man, replied:
Listen, virgin Anat:
will you really kill him for his bow,
kill him for his arrows,
not let him live?
Pretty-boy, the Hero, has fixed a meal;
he is all alone in the pavilion.
But the virgin Anat replied:
Pay attention, Yatpan, and I'll give the
orders.
I'll put you in my pouch like a vulture,
in my bag like a bird.
When Aqhat sits down to eat,
the son of Danel to his meal,
vultures will swoop over him,
a flock of birds will soar above.
I'll be swooping among the vultures,
I'll set you over Aqhat:
strike him twice on the skull,
three times over the ear;
make his blood run like a slaughterer,
run to his knees like a butcher.
His breath will leave him like wind,
his spirit like a breeze,
like smoke from his nostrils;
his strength will leave his nostrils.
I won't let him live!
She took Yatpan, the lady's man,
she put him in her pouch like a vulture,
in her bag like a bird.
When Aqhat sat down to eat,
the son of Danel to his meal,

vultures swooped over him,
a flock of birds soared above.
Among the vultures swooped Anat;
she set him over Aqhat.
He struck him twice on the skull,
three times over the ear;
he made his blood run like a slaughterer,
run to his knees like a butcher.
His breath left him like wind,
his spirit like a breeze,
like smoke from his nostrils . . .
And she wept.

(gap)

. . . into the water it fell . . .
the bow was broken.

(gap)

I killed him only for his bow,
I killed him for his arrows;
I did not let him live,
but his bow has not become mine.
And because of his death
the first fruits of summer have withered,
the ear in its husk.

(gap)

Then Danel, the healer's man,
the Hero, the man of the god of
Harnam,
got up and sat at the entrance to the
gate,
next to the granary on the threshing
floor.
He judged the cases of widows,
presided over orphans' hearings . . .
Pagat raised her eyes and looked:
on the threshing floor the greenery had
dried,
it drooped, it had withered.
Over her father's house vultures were
swooping,
a flock of birds soared above,
Pagat wept in her heart,
she cried inwardly.
She tore the clothes of Danel, the
healer's man,
the garments of the Hero, the man of the
god of Harnam.
Then Danel, the healer's man,
cursed the clouds in the still heat,

the rain of the clouds that falls in
    summer,
the dew that drops on the grapes:
For seven years let Baal fail,
eight, the Rider on the Clouds:
no dew, no showers,
no surging of the two seas,
no benefit of Baal's voice.
For the clothes of Danel, the healer's
    man, have been torn,
the garments of the Hero, the man of the
    god of Harnam.
Danel called to his daughter:
Listen, Pagat,
you get up early to draw water,
you brush the dew from the barley,
you know the course of the stars.
Saddle an ass, harness a donkey;
attach my silver reins, my golden bridle.
Pagat obeyed,
she who got up early to draw water,
who brushed the dew from the barley,
who knew the course of the stars;
in tears she saddled the ass,
in tears she harnessed the donkey,
in tears she lifted her father,
she put him on the ass's back,
on the splendid back of the donkey.
Danel made a tour of inspection in his
    fields;
he saw a stalk in the fields,
he saw a stalk in the plots;
he embraced the stalk and kissed it:
If only the stalk could grow,
in the fields the stalk grow,
in the plots the plant,
the hand of Aqhat the Hero would
    harvest you,
place you in the granary.
He made a tour of inspection in his
    plots;
he saw an ear growing in the plots,
an ear growing in the scorched fields.
He embraced the ear and kissed it:
If only the ear could grow,
in the plots the ear grow,
in the scorched fields the plant,
the hand of Aqhat the Hero would
    harvest you,
place you in the granary.

These words had just come from his
    mouth,
this speech from his lips,
when she raised her eyes and looked:
two lads were coming . . .
He was struck twice on the skull,
three times over the ear . . .
Tears poured like quarter-shekels . . .
We have news for you, Danel . . .
She made his breath leave him like
    wind,
his spirit like a breeze,
like smoke from his nostrils.
They arrived; they raised their voices
    and shouted:
Listen, Danel, the healer's man:
Aqhat the Hero is dead.
The virgin Anat made his breath leave
    him like wind,
his spirit like a breeze.
His feet shook,
his face broke out in sweat,
his back was as though shattered,
his joints trembled,
his vertebras weakened.

    (gap)

When he raised his eyes and looked,
he saw vultures in the clouds.
He raised his voice and shouted:
May Baal shatter the vultures' wings,
may Baal shatter their pinions;
let them fall at my feet.
I will split their gizzards and look;
if there is fat, if there is bone,
I will weep and I will bury him,
I will put him into the hole of the gods
    of the earth.
These words had just come from his
    mouth,
this speech from his lips,
when Baal shattered the vultures' wings,
Baal shattered their pinions,
and they fell at his feet.
He split their gizzards and looked;
there was no fat, there was no bone.
He raised his voice and shouted:
May Baal rebuild the vultures' wings,
may Baal rebuild their pinions;
vultures, up, and fly away!
When he raised his eyes and looked,

he saw Hirgab, the father of vultures.
He raised his voice and shouted:
May Baal shatter Hirgab's wings,
may Baal shatter his pinions:
let him fall at my feet.
I will split his gizzard and look;
if there is fat, if there is bone,
I will weep and I will bury him,
I will put him into the hole of the gods
    of the earth.
These words had just come from his
    mouth,
this speech from his lips,
when Baal shattered Hirgab's wings,
Baal shattered his pinions,
and he fell at his feet.
He split his gizzard and looked;
there was no fat, there was no bone.
He raised his voice and shouted:
May Baal rebuild Hirgab's wings,
may Baal rebuild his pinions;
Hirgab, up, and fly away!
When he raised his eyes and looked,
he saw Samal, the mother of vultures.
He raised his voice and shouted:
May Baal shatter Samal's wings,
may Baal shatter her pinions;
let her fall at my feet.
I will split her gizzard and look;
if there is fat, if there is bone,
I will weep and I will bury him,
I will put him into the hole of the gods
    of the earth.
These words had just come from his
    mouth,
this speech from his lips,
when Baal shattered Samal's wings,
Baal shattered her pinions,
she fell at his feet.
He split her gizzard and looked:
there was fat, there was bone.
From them he took Aqhat . . .
he wept and he buried him,
he buried him in a grave, in an urn.
Then he raised his voice and shouted:
May Baal shatter the vultures' wings,
may Baal shatter their pinions,
if they fly over my son's grave
and wake him from his sleep.
The king cursed Qor-maym:
Woe to you, Qor-maym,

for near you Aqhat the Hero was killed,
the young lion of El's house met his end.
Now flee forever,
from now on and forevermore.
Then he destroyed his royal scepter.
He arrived at Mararat-tagullal-banir;
he raised his voice and shouted:
Woe to you, Mararat-tagullal-banir,
for near you Aqhat the Hero was killed.
May your root not rise from the ground,
your head droop because you have been
    plucked.
Now flee forever,
from now on and forevermore.
Then he destroyed his royal scepter.
He arrived at the city of Abiluma,
Abiluma, the city of Prince Moon.
He raised his voice and shouted:
Woe to you, city of Abiluma,
for near you Aqhat the Hero was killed.
May Baal make you blind, now and
    forever,
from now on and forevermore.
Then he destroyed his royal scepter.
Danel arrived at his house,
Danel reached his palace.
The keeners entered his palace,
the mourners his court;
those who gash their skin wept,
they shed tears for Aqhat the Hero,
the child of Danel, the healer's man.
The days became months,
the months became years;
for seven years they wept for Aqhat the
    Hero,
they shed tears for the child of Danel,
    the healer's man.
Then, in the seventh year, Danel, the
    healer's man, spoke;
the Hero, the man of the god of
    Harnam, raised his voice and
    shouted:
Leave my house, keeners;
leave my palace, mourners,
leave my court, you who gash your skin.
He made a sacrifice to the gods,
he sent an offering up to heaven,
an offering for the god of Harnam to the
    stars . . .
Pagat who got up early to draw water
    spoke:

My father, you have made a sacrifice to
the gods,
you have sent an offering up to heaven,
an offering for the god of Harnam to the
stars.
Now bless me, that I may go with your
blessing;
favor me, that I may go with your favor.
I will kill my brother's killer,
put an end to whoever put an end to my
mother's son.
Danel, the healer's man, replied:
Pagat, you will restore my life,
you who get up early to draw water,
who brush the dew from the barley,
who know the course of the stars;
I will truly live again
when you have killed your brother's
killer,
put an end to whoever put an end to
your mother's son.
She washed in the sea,
using a sea dye she put on rouge,
applied special cosmetics from the sea.
She put on a hero's clothes,
she placed a knife in her sheath,
she placed a sword in her scabbard;
and over all this she put on women's
clothes.
As Sun, the gods' torch, went in,
Pagat entered the fields;
as Sun, the gods' torch, set,
Pagat arrived at the tents.
Word was brought to Yatpan:
Our mistress has come to your pavilion,
Pagat has come to the tents.
And Yatpan, the lady's man, replied:
Receive her: she'll give me wine to
drink;
she'll take the cup from my hand,
the mug from my right hand.
Pagat was received; she gave him a
drink;
she took the cup from his hand,
the mug from his right hand.
Then Yatpan, the lady's man, said:
. . . The hand that killed Aqhat the Hero
can kill a thousand enemies . . .
Twice she gave him wine to drink,
she gave him wine to drink.

#20: Legend of King Kirta
(Coogan, *Stories from Ancient Canaan*, 58–74)[6]

The "Legend of King Kirta," an Ugaritic narrative cycle from the mid-fourteenth century B.C., describes how King Kirta (perhaps pronounced Keret) survived three threats to his reign. The first threat was the death of his family, leaving him without an heir. In this, the Kirta cycle resembles the "Tale of Aqhat" (reading 19) and again reflects the ancestral theme of barrenness. The second and third threats are illness and a son's attempt to remove Kirta from the throne. The "Legend of King Kirta" provides parallels to the succession themes in the so-called "court history" of the Davidic narratives (otherwise known as the succession narrative [2 Samuel 9–20; 1 Kings 1–2]) and the tragic suffering of Job and is also informative about the centrality of kingship as an ancient Canaanite institution.

Ruined was the house of the king
who once had seven brothers,
eight sons of one mother.
Kirta our patriarch was destroyed,
Kirta's dynasty was finished.
His legal wife went away,
his lawful spouse:
the woman he married left him.
He had had descendants,
but one-third died in childbirth,
one-fourth of disease,
one-fifth Resheph gathered to himself,
one-sixth were lost at sea,
one-seventh fell in battle.
Kirta saw his offspring,
he saw his offspring destroyed,
his royal house completely finished.
His line was utterly ruined,
and he had no heir in his household.
He entered his room and wept,
he repeated his words and shed tears;
his tears poured
like shekels to the ground,
like fifth-shekels onto his bed.
As he wept he fell asleep,
as he shed tears he had a dream;
sleep overpowered him and he lay
down,
but his dream made him restless.
For in his dream El came down,
in his vision the father of men.

He approached and asked Kirta:
Why are you weeping, Kirta?
Why does the gracious one, the lad of
   El, shed tears?
Does he want to rule like the bull, his
   father,
or to have power like the father of men?

   (gap)

Why should I want silver and gleaming
   gold,
a controlling share in a mine,
perpetual slaves, three horses,
a chariot from the stable, servants?
Let me have sons,
let me produce descendants!
And the bull, his father El, replied:
No more weeping, Kirta,
nor tears, gracious one, lad of El.
Wash yourself and put on rouge,
wash your arm to the elbow,
from your fingers to your shoulder.
Enter the shade of your tent,
take a lamb in your hand,
a sacrificial lamb in your right hand,
a young animal in both your hands,
all the food that accompanies the
   libation.
Take the proper sacrificial bird,
pour wine from a silver goblet,
honey from a golden bowl,
and go up to the top of the tower,
climb to the height of the wall;
raise your hands to heaven,
sacrifice to the bull, your father El;
serve Baal with your sacrifice,
the son of Dagan with your provisions.
Then let Kirta come down from the roof,
let him prepare food for the city,
grain for Bit-Hubur;
let him bake enough bread for five
   months,
enough food for six.
Let the populace be supplied and come
   out,
let the special forces be supplied
and the populace come out.
Your army will be powerful indeed,
three hundred thousand strong,
serfs beyond counting,
archers beyond reckoning.

The infantry will advance in thousands,
and in ten thousands, like the early rain;
they will advance two by two,
three by three, all together.
The bachelor will close his house;
the widow will hire a substitute;
the sick man will carry his bed;
the blind man will be assigned a station;
even the new husband will come out:
he will entrust his wife to another,
his love to a stranger.
Like the locusts that live in the fields,
like grasshoppers at the edge of the
   desert,
advance one day, and a second,
three days, then four,
five days, then six.
Then, at sunset on the seventh day,
you will arrive at Udm the great,
Udm the well watered;
and attack the cities,
raid the towns;
drive the woodcutters from the fields,
the gatherers of straw from the
   threshing floors;
drive the water carriers from the well,
the women filling their jars from the
   spring.
Wait one day, and a second,
three days, then four,
five days, then six.
Don't shoot your arrows at the city,
your sling stones at the fortress.
Then, by sunset on the seventh day,
King Pabil will be unable to sleep
because of the sound of his horses
   neighing,
because of the noise of his asses braying,
because of the lowing of his plow oxen,
because of the howl of his sheepdog.
And he will send messengers to you,
to Kirta his peer:
Message of King Pabil:
take silver and gleaming gold,
a controlling share in a mine,
perpetual slaves, three horses,
a chariot from the stable, servants;
Kirta, take these as peace offerings,
and leave my house, king,
go away from my court, Kirta.
Do not lay siege to Udm the great,

Udm the well watered:
for Udm is El's gift,
and a present from the father of men.
Then you will send messengers back to
     him:
Why should I want silver and gleaming
     gold,
a controlling share in a mine,
perpetual slaves, three horses,
a chariot from the stable, servants?
Give me rather what is not in my house:
give me the lady Hurriya,
the fairest of your firstborn:
her fairness is like Anat's,
her beauty is like Astarte's,
her eyebrows are lapis lazuli,
her eyes are jeweled bowls . . .
I will rest in the gaze of her eyes.
This in my dream El granted,
in my vision the father of men;
she will bear offspring for Kirta,
a body for El's servant.
Kirta looked, and it was a dream:
El's servant had had a vision.
He washed himself and put on rouge,
he washed his arm to the elbow,
from his fingers to his shoulder.
He entered the shade of the tent,
he took a lamb in his hand,
a sacrificial lamb in his right hand,
a young animal in both his hands,
all the food that accompanies the
     libation.
He took the proper sacrificial bird,
he poured wine from a silver goblet,
honey from a golden bowl,
and he went up to the top of the tower,
he climbed to the height of the wall;
he raised his hands to heaven,
he sacrificed to the bull, his father El;
he served Baal with his sacrifice,
the son of Dagan with his provisions.
Kirta came down from the roof,
he prepared food for the city,
grain for Bit-Hubur;
he baked enough bread for five months,
enough food for six.
The populace was supplied and came
     out,
the special forces were supplied
and the populace came out.

His army was powerful indeed,
three hundred thousand strong.
The infantry advanced in thousands,
and in ten thousands, like the early rain;
they advanced two by two,
three by three, all together.
The bachelor closed his house;
the widow hired a substitute,
the sick man carried his bed,
the blind man was assigned a station;
even the new husband came out:
he entrusted his wife to another,
his love to a stranger.
Like the locusts that live in the fields,
like grasshoppers at the edge of the
     desert,
they advanced one day, and a second;
then, at sunset on the third day,
they arrived at the shrine of Asherah of
     Tyre,
and of the goddess of Sidon.
There Kirta the Noble made a vow:
As Asherah of Tyre lives,
and the goddess of Sidon,
if I take Hurriya to my house,
if I bring the maiden to my court,
then I will give double her price in
     silver,
and triple her price in gold.
They advanced one day, and a second,
three days, then four;
after sunset on the fourth day
they arrived at Udm the great,
Udm the well watered.
They attacked the cities,
they raided the towns;
they drove the woodcutters from the
     fields,
and the gatherers of straw from the
     threshing floors;
they drove the water carriers from the
     well,
and the women filling their jars from the
     spring.
He waited one day, then a second,
three days, then four,
five days, then six;
then, by sunset on the seventh day,
King Pabil was unable to sleep
because of the sound of his horses
     neighing,

because of the noise of his asses braying,
because of the lowing of his plow oxen,
because of the howl of his sheepdog.
Then King Pabil called to his wife . . .

(gap)

Then head toward Kirta, my peer,
and say to Kirta the Noble:
Message of King Pabil:
take silver and gleaming gold,
a controlling share in a mine,
perpetual slaves, three horses,
a chariot from the stable, servants;
Kirta, take these as peace offerings;
do not lay siege to Udm the great,
Udm the well watered:
for Udm is El's gift,
and a present from the father of men.
Go away from my house, king,
leave my court, Kirta . . .
The two messengers left; they did not
    turn back;
they headed toward Kirta, his peer;
they raised their voices and shouted:
Message of King Pabil:
take silver and gleaming gold,
a controlling share in a mine,
perpetual slaves, three horses,
a chariot from the stable, servants;
Kirta, take these as peace offerings;
do not lay siege to Udm the great,
Udm the well watered:
for Udm is El's gift,
a present from the father of men.
Go away from my house, king,
leave my court, Kirta.
And Kirta the Noble replied:
Why should I want silver and gleaming
    gold,
a controlling share in a mine,
and perpetual slaves, three horses,
a chariot from the stable, servants?
Give me rather what is not in my house:
give me the lady Hurriya,
the fairest of your firstborn:
her fairness is like Anat's,
her beauty is like Astarte's,
her eyebrows are lapis lazuli,
her eyes are jeweled bowls.
This in my dream El granted,
in my vision the father of men;

she will bear offspring for Kirta,
a boy for El's servant.
The two messengers left; they did not
    turn back;
they headed toward King Pabil;
they raised their voices and shouted:
Message of Kirta the Noble,
the word of the gracious one, the lad of
    El.

(gap)

She leads the hungry by the hand,
she leads the thirsty by the hand . . .
to Kirta, his peer.
As the cow lows for her calf,
as recruits long for their mothers,
so Udm will sigh.
And Kirta the Noble answered . . .

(gap)

. . . the bull,
. . . Baal the Conqueror,
. . . Prince Moon,
. . . Kothar-wa-khasis,
. . . the Maiden, Prince Resheph,
and the assembly of the gods in
    procession . . .
The assembly of the gods arrived,
and Baal the Conqueror said:
Come now, El the Kind, the
    Compassionate:
bless Kirta the Noble,
show your favor to the gracious one, the
    lad of El.
El took a cup in his hand,
a goblet in his right hand;
he pronounced a blessing over his
    servant,
El blessed Kirta the Noble,
he showed his favor to the gracious one,
    the lad of El:
Kirta, you have taken a wife,
you have taken a wife into your house,
you have brought a maiden into your
    court.
She will bear you seven sons,
she will produce eight for you;
she will bear Yassib the Lad,
who will drink the milk of Asherah,
suck the breasts of the virgin Anat,
the two wet nurses of the gods.

(gap)

May Kirta be highly praised,
in the midst of the healers of the earth,
in the assembly of the gatherers of
    Ditan.
She will soon bear you daughters:
she will bear the girl . . .
she will bear the girl . . .
she will bear the girl . . .
she will bear the girl . . .
she will bear the girl . . .
she will bear the girl . . .
May Kirta be highly praised,
in the midst of the healers of the earth,
in the assembly of the gatherers of
    Ditan;
to the youngest I will give a firstborn's
    rights.
The gods pronounced their blessing and
    went,
the gods went to their tents,
the council of El to their divine homes.
And she soon bore him sons,
and she soon bore him daughters.
Then, after seven years,
the sons of Kirta were as many as had
    been promised;
so too were the daughters of Hurriya.
And Asherah remembered his vow,
the goddess recalled his pledge;
and she raised her voice and shouted:
Look now, has Kirta changed his vow?
I will break . . .

(gap)

He called to his wife:
Listen, lady Hurriya:
slaughter your fattest animal;
open a jar of wine;
call my seventy noble bulls,
my eighty noble gazelles,
the noble bulls of Hubur the great,
of Hubur the well watered . . .
Lady Hurriya obeyed;
she slaughtered her fattest animal;
she opened a jar of wine;
she invited the noble bulls into her
    presence,
she invited the noble gazelles into her
    presence,
the noble bulls of Hubur the great,

of Hubur the well watered.
They came to Kirta's house,
to his home . . .
She extended her hand to the bowl,
she put her knife to the meat,
and the lady Hurriya said:
I have called you to eat and drink
at the banquet of Kirta your master.

(gap)

She extended her hand to the bowl,
she put her knife to the meat,
and the lady Hurriya said:
I have called you to eat and drink . . .
They wept for Kirta,
the noble bulls spoke,
they wept as though he were dead . . .
At sunset Kirta will surely arrive,
at sundown our master will rule . . .

(gap)

And the lady Hurriya said:
I have called you to eat and drink
at the banquet of Kirta your lord.
They came to Kirta,
their words were like the words of noble
    bulls.
In a vision . . . Kirta . . .

(gap)

As a dog is removed from your house,
a hound from your court,
so you too, father, must die like a
    mortal,
and your court become a place of
    mourning,
controlled by women, beloved father.
Baal's mountain, father, will weep for
    you,
Zaphon, the holy stronghold,
the holy stronghold will lament,
the stronghold wide and broad:
Is not Kirta El's son,
an offspring of the kind and holy one?
He entered his father's presence;
he wept and gnashed his teeth;
he spoke through his tears:
Our father, we were glad while you
    seemed to live forever,
we rejoiced at your immortality;

but as a dog is removed from your
    house,
a hound from your court,
so you too, father, must die like a
    mortal,
and your court become a place of
    mourning,
controlled by women, beloved father.
How can it be said that Kirta is El's son,
an offspring of the kind and holy one?
Or do the gods die?
Will the kind one's offspring not live on?
But Kirta the Noble replied:
My son, don't weep,
don't grieve for me;
my son, don't drain the well of your
    eyes,
your head's springs of tears.
Call your sister Titmanit,
a maiden whose ardor is strong:
she will weep and grieve for me . . .
Speak to your sister . . .
I know how loving she is:
she will make her cry heard in the fields,
her spirit's outpourings in the sky.
. . . the setting of lady Sun,
and the light of the Ten Thousand
    shines.
Then say to your sister Titmanit:
Our Kirta has prepared a banquet,
the king has ordered a feast.
Take your drum in your hand,
your lyre in your right hand;
go stand by your lord's singers . . .
Then the Hero Ilihu
took his spear in his hand,
his lance in his right hand,
and he approached at a run.
As he arrived, it grew dark;
his sister was coming out to draw water.
He put his spear on the hill,
he went to meet her at the gate.
As soon as she saw her brother,
her back was as though shattered on the
    ground;
when she saw her brother, she wept.
Is the king sick?
Is Kirta your lord ill?
And the Hero Ilihu replied:
The king is not sick;
Kirta your lord is not ill.

But he has prepared a banquet,
the king has ordered a feast . . .

    (gap)

She approached her brother and
    shouted:
Why did you deceive me, my brother?
How many months has he been sick?
How long has he been ill?
And the Hero Ilihu replied:
He has been sick for three months,
Kirta has been ill for four.
His end is at hand:
prepare a grave,
prepare a grave,
make ready a tomb . . .
She prepared a grave . . .
she wept and gnashed her teeth;
she spoke through her tears:
Our father, we were glad while you
    seemed to live forever,
we rejoiced at your immortality;
but as a dog is removed from your
    house,
a hound from your court,
so you too, father, must die like a
    mortal,
and your court become a place of
    mourning,
controlled by women, beloved father.
Or do the gods die?
Will the kind one's offspring not live on?
Baal's mountain, father, will weep for
    you,
Zaphon, the holy stronghold,
the holy stronghold will lament,
the stronghold wide and broad:
Is not Kirta El's son,
an offspring of the kind and holy one?

    (gap)

. . . Baal's rain for the earth,
and the rain of the Most High for the
    fields;
for Baal's rain benefits the earth,
and the rain of the Most High the fields,
benefits the wheat in the furrow,
the spelt in the tilled ground . . .
The plowmen lifted their heads,
the sowers of grain their backs:
gone was the food from their bins,

gone was the wine from their skins,
gone was the oil from their vats.

(gap)

El has heard your speech:
look—you are wise, like El,
like the bull, the kind one;
call to Ilisha, the carpenter god,
Ilisha, the carpenter of Baal's house,
and his wives, the carpenter goddesses
. . .

He called to Ilisha, the carpenter god,
Ilisha, the carpenter of Baal's house,
and his wives, the carpenter goddesses.
And El the Kind, the Compassionate,
    replied:
Listen, Ilisha, carpenter god,
Ilisha, the carpenter of Baal's house,
and your wives, the carpenter
    goddesses:
go up to the height of the building . . .

(gap)

And El the Kind, the Compassionate,
    replied:
Who among the gods can expel the
    sickness,
drive out the disease?
But none of the gods answered him.
He spoke a second, then a third time:
Who among the gods can expel the
    sickness,
drive out the disease?
But none of the gods answered him.
He spoke a fourth, then a fifth time:
Who among the gods can expel the
    sickness,
drive out the disease?
But none of the gods answered him.
He spoke a sixth, then a seventh time:
Who among the gods can expel the
    sickness,
drive out the disease?
But none of the gods answered him.
Then El the Kind, the Compassionate,
    replied:
My sons, sit down upon your thrones,
upon your princely seats.
I will work magic,
I will bring relief:
I will expel the sickness,

I will drive out the disease.

(gap)

Death—be broken!
Shataqat—be strong!
And Shataqat left;
she came to Kirta's house:
in tears she entered and went in,
in sobs she went inside.
She flew over cities . . .
she flew over villages . . .
. . . the sickness on its head.
She returned, she washed off his sweat;
she restored his appetite for food,
his desire for a meal.
Death was broken—
Shataqat was strong!
Then Kirta the Noble gave a command;
he raised his voice and shouted:
Listen, lady Hurriya:
slaughter a lamb so that I may eat,
some mutton for my meal.
Lady Hurriya obeyed:
she slaughtered a lamb and he ate,
some mutton for his meal.
One day had ended, and on the second
Kirta sat on his throne,
he sat on his royal chair,
on his dais, on the seat of dominion.
Now Yassib too lived in the palace,
and his heart instructed him:
Go to your father, Yassib,
go to your father and speak,
repeat to Kirta your lord:
Listen closely and pay attention:
as though raiders had raided, you will
    be driven out,
and forced to live in the mountains.
Weakness has stayed your hand:
you do not judge the cases of widows,
you do not preside over the hearings of
    the oppressed;
the sickbed has become your brother,
the stretcher your close friend.
Come down from the kingship—let me
    be king,
from your power—let me sit on the
    throne.
Yassib the Lad left;
he entered his father's presence;
he raised his voice and shouted:

Listen, Kirta the Noble,
listen closely and pay attention:
as though raiders had raided, you will
    be driven out,
and forced to live in the mountains.
Weakness has stayed your hand:
you do not judge the cases of widows,
you do not preside over the hearings of
    the oppressed;
you do not drive out those who plunder
    the poor,
you do not feed the orphan before you,
the widow behind your back.

The sickbed has become your brother,
the stretcher your close friend.
Come down from the kingship—let me
    be king,
from your power—let me sit on the
    throne.
But Kirta the Noble replied:
My son, may Horon smash,
may Horon smash your head,
Astarte, Baal's other self, your skull.
May you fall at the prime of your life . . .
The scribe was Ilimilku the Noble.

5 Covenants and Treaties

The covenant—a binding agreement between two parties—is an important concept in the Bible. Political treaties and covenants from ancient Near Eastern literature offer many points of comparison with covenants in ancient Israel. These treaties have historical interest because the Bible contains examples of agreements between individuals in early Israel (Genesis 21:27; 26:28; 31:44). And they are of literary interest because several sections of the Old Testament appear to be intentionally structured on the analogy of such political treaties (Exodus 20–24; Deuteronomy; Joshua 24).

#21: Mari Covenant Ritual
(Held, "Philological Notes on the Mari Covenant Rituals," 33)[1]

> Treaties were often concluded by means of symbolic acts. At ancient Mari, the purely West Semitic expression HA(YA)RUM QATALUM ("to slaughter a donkey foal") indicates one such symbol. In the reading presented here, a possible ploy introduced other animals into the ritual. In the peace treaty between the Haneans and the land of Idamarats, a Mari official reports that he refused to allow a dog and a goat to be substituted in the ritual. This text has often been compared to Genesis 15:9–10 and Jeremiah 34:18–20.

I went to Ashlakka and they brought to me a young dog and a she-goat in order to conclude a covenant between the Haneans and the land of Idamarats. But, in deference to my lord, I did not permit *the use of* the young dog and the she-goat, but *instead* had a donkey foal, the young of a she-donkey, killed, and thus established a reconciliation between the Haneans and the land of Idamarats.

#22: Treaty between Abban and Yarimlim
(McCarthy, *Treaty and Covenant*, 307–8)

> The ancient city of Alalakh was located near the modern Syria-Turkey border. Among other important discoveries from Alalakh, archeologists have found cuneiform tablets from the first half of the second millennium B.C. written in the Old Babylonian script. The reading presented here describes an oath and ritual reminiscent of Genesis 15.[2] This selection is important because it preserves a covenant-making ceremony between Abban and King Yarimlim of Alalakh from roughly the time of Abraham in a West Semitic culture related to Abraham's family.[3] After towns and villages were exchanged, presumably as part of widespread reorganization of northern Syria, the agreement was sealed by solemn oath and the slaying of a sheep.

The city of Imar along with its fields, the city of Zar . . . at, the city of . . . na, the city of Nashtarbi, the city of Zabunap, the city of Kazkuwa, the city of Ammakki, *and* the city of Parre in exchange for the city of Uwiya; the city of Adrate in exchange for the territory that is . . . [were given].

The city of Amame, the city of Aushun, the city of Zikir, the city of Murar, the city of Iriddi: Yarimlim [held them].

Zitraddu, the mayor of [Iriddi] turned against Yarimlim *and* led the [robber] MUSNADDU. He let *the robber band* enter Iriddi; his city and all its land he turned away from Abba-AN, king . . . With . . . and the mighty weapon . . . with silver, gold, lapis lazuli, *crystal* and the mighty [weapon] of Addu he captured and destroyed Iriddi, and he captured the MUSNADDU, his enemy. He returned safely to Aleppo *and said*: Can I give my brother a pile of ruins? In exchange for Iriddi [that] rebelled [against] him [and that I captured] and [destroyed, I shall give Yarimlim] the city of Alalakh, and the city of Murar over and above his portion I shall add to it.

Abba-AN is under oath to Yarimlim, and also he cut the neck of a lamb. *He swore*: I shall never take back what I gave you.

If in days to come Yarimlim sins against Abba-AN, [if] he repeats anything Abba-AN says to him and reveals *it* to another king, if he lets go of the hem of Abba-AN's robe and takes hold of another king's robe, he [shall forfeit] his cities and territories. Further, if a successor of Yarimlim sins against Abba-AN or a successor of Abba-AN, if he lets go of the hem of Abba-AN's robe or the hem of the robe of a successor of Abba-AN and takes hold of the hem of another king's robe, he shall forfeit his city and his territories.

If successors of Yarimlim wish to sell one of his cities, then their older brother shall buy *it*; he may sell it only to a successor of Abba-AN, *but* to another king he may not sell it.

If [there is] no successor to Yarimlim, *but* [there is] a successor to Abba-AN, if . . . his cities . . .

[Akhi-saduq] son of . . .

[Irpadda] . . .

[Niqmaddu] . . .

(*gap*)

. . . made Yarimlim swear by the gods.

#23: Treaty between Suppiluliuma and Mattiwaza
(*ANET* 205–6)

Hittite political treaties from the fourteenth and thirteenth centuries B.C. present the most important parallels to the covenant structure of Exodus 20–24, Deuteronomy, and Joshua 24. Hittite treaties between unequal parties (known as suzerainty treaties) are remarkably similar in form and structure to Israelite covenants and suggest that the Bible's claim to have used such a literary structure in the second millennium B.C. is plausible.[4] The treaty presented here was between Suppiluliuma, powerful king of the Hittites (approximately 1380–1345 B.C.), and Mattiwaza of Mitanni and preserves the god list and the blessings and curses of the treaty.

A duplicate of this tablet has been deposited before the sun-goddess of Arinna, because the sun-goddess of Arinna regulates kingship and queenship.

In the Mitanni land *a duplicate* has been deposited before Teshub, the lord of the KURINNU of Kahat. At regular [intervals] shall they read it in the presence of the king of the Mitanni land and in the presence of the sons of the Hurri country. Whoever will remove this tablet from before Teshub, the lord of the KURINNU of Kahat, and put it in a hidden place, if he breaks it or causes anyone else to change the wording of the tablet—at the conclusion of this treaty we have called the gods to be assembled and the gods of the contracting parties to be present, to listen and to serve as witnesses: The sun-goddess of Arinna who regulates kingship and queenship in Hatti land, the sun-god, the lord of heaven, the storm-god, the lord of Hatti land, Seris *and* Hurris, the mountains Nanni *and* Hazzi, the storm-god, the lord of the KI.LAM, the storm-god, the lord of the encampment, the storm-god, the lord of aid, the storm-god of Betti-yarik, the storm-god of Nerik, the storm-god, the lord of the mounds, the storm-god of Halab, the storm-god of Lihzina, the storm-god of Samuha, the storm-god of Hurma, the storm-god of Saressa, the storm-god of Sapinuwa, the storm-god of Hissashapa, the storm-god of Tahaya, the storm-god of . . . , the storm-god of Kizzuwatna, the storm-god of Uda, the Hattian patron-god of Karahna, Zithariyas, Karzis, Hapantalliyas, the patron-god of the field, the patron-god of the shield, Leliwanis, Ea and Damkina, Telepinus of Tawiniya, Telepinus of Durmitta, Telepinus of Hanhana, the warlike Ishtar, Askasipa, Halkis, the moon-god lord of the oath, Ishara queen of the oath, Hebat queen of heaven, Hebat of Halba, Hebat of Uda, Hebat of Kizzuwatna, the warrior-god, the Hattian warrior-god, the warrior-god of Ellaya, the warrior-god of Arziya, Yarris, Zappanas, Hasammelis, Hantidassus of Hurma, Abaras of Samuha, Katahhas of Ankuwa, Katahhas of Katapa, Mammas of Tahurpa, Hallaras of Dunna, Huwassanas of Hupisna, the lady of Landa, Kunniyawannis of Landa, the Lulahhi gods *and* the Hapiri gods, all the gods and goddesses of Hatti land, the gods and goddesses of the country of Kizzuwatna, Ereskigal, Nara,

Namsara, Minku, Amminku, Tussi, Ammizadu, Alalu, Anu, Antu, Ellil, Ninlil, Belat-Ekalli, the mountains, the rivers, the Tigris *and* the Euphrates, heaven and earth, the winds *and* the clouds.

Teshub, the lord of heaven and earth, Kusuh and Simigi, the Harranian moon-god of heaven and earth, Teshub lord of the KURINNU of Kahat, the . . . of Gurta, Teshub lord of Uhusuman, Ea-sarru lord of wisdom, Anu and Antu, Ellil and Ninlil, the twin gods Mitra and Uruwana, Indar, the Nassatiyana gods, ELLAT, Samaminuhi, Teshub lord of Wassukkanni, Teshub lord of the KAMARI of Irrite, Partahi of Suta, Nabarbi, Suruhi, Ashur star, Sala, Belat-Ekalli, Damkina, Ishara, the mountains and the rivers, the gods of heaven and the gods of the earth—at the conclusion of the words of this treaty let them be present, let them listen and let them serve as witnesses. If you, Mattiwaza, the prince, and *you* the sons of the Hurri country do not fulfill the words of this treaty, may the gods, the lords of the oath, blot you out, *you* Mattiwaza and *you* the Hurri men together with your country, your wives and all that you have. May they draw you like malt from its hull. Just as one does not obtain a plant from BUBUWAHI, even so may you Mattiwaza with a second wife that you may take, and *you* the Hurri men with your wives, your sons and your country have no seed. These gods of the contracting parties may bring misery and poverty over you. May they overturn your throne, *yours*, of Mattiwaza. May the oaths sworn in the presence of these gods break you like reeds, you, Mattiwaza, together with your country. May they exterminate from the earth your name and your seed *born* from a second wife that you may take. Much as you may seek [uninterrupted] peace for your country, from the midst of the Hurrians may that be banned. May the earth be coldness so that you fall down slipping. May the soil of your country be a hardened quagmire so that you break in, but never get across. May you, Mattiwaza, and *you*, the Hurrians, be hateful to the thousand gods, may they pursue you.

If *on the other hand* you, Mattiwaza, the prince, and *you*, the Hurrians, fulfill this treaty and *this* oath, may these gods protect you, Mattiwaza, together with your wife, the daughter of Hatti land, her children and her children's children, and also *you*, the Hurrians, together with your wives, your children, and your children's children and together with your country. May the Mitanni country return to the place that it occupied before, may it thrive and expand. May you, Mattiwaza, your sons and your sons' sons *descended* from the daughter of the great king of Hatti land, and *you*, the Hurrians, exercise kingship forever. May the throne of your father persist, may the Mitanni country persist.

#24: Treaty between Mursilis and Duppi-Teshub
(*ANET* 203–5)[5]

> The son of Suppiluliuma, Mursilis III, entered an agreement with Duppi-Teshub, establishing him as king of Amurru and binding the population to him by oath.

These are the words of the Sun Mursilis, the great king, the king of Hatti land, the valiant, the favorite of the storm-god, the son of Suppiluliumas, the great king, the king of Hatti land, the valiant.

Aziras was the grandfather of you, Duppi-Teshub. He rebelled against my father, but submitted again to my father. When the kings of Nuhasse land and the kings of Kinza rebelled against my father, Aziras did not rebel. As he was bound by treaty, he remained bound by treaty. As my father fought against his enemies, in the same manner fought Aziras. Aziras remained loyal toward my father and did not incite my father's anger. My father was loyal toward Aziras and his country; he did not undertake any unjust action against him or incite his or his country's anger in any way. Three hundred *shekels of* refined and first-class gold, the tribute that my father had imposed upon your father, he brought year for year; he never refused it.

When my father became god and I seated myself on the throne of my father, Aziras behaved toward me just as he had behaved toward my father. It happened that the Nuhasse kings and the king of Kinza rebelled a second time against me. But Aziras, your grandfather, and DU-Teshub, your father, [did not take their side]; they remained loyal to me as their lord. [When he grew too old] and could no longer go to war and fight, DU-Teshub fought against the enemy with the foot soldiers and the charioteers of the Amurru land just as he had fought with foot soldiers and charioteers against the enemy. And the Sun destroyed them.

(gap)

. . . [When I die, accept my son] Duppi-Teshub as your vassal.

When your father died, in accordance with your father's word I did not drop you. Since your father had mentioned to me your name [with great praise], I sought after you. To be sure, you were sick and ailing, but although you were ailing, I, the Sun, put you in the place of your father and took your brothers *and* sisters and the Amurru land in oath for you.

When I, the Sun, sought after you in accordance with your father's word and put you in your father's place, I took you in oath for the king of Hatti land, Hatti land, and for my sons and grandsons. So honor the oath *of loyalty* to the king and the king's [kin]! And I, the king, will be loyal toward you, Duppi-Teshub. When you take a wife, and when you beget an heir, he shall be king in the Amurru land likewise. And just as I shall be loyal toward you, even so shall I be loyal toward your son. But you, Duppi-Teshub, remain loyal toward the king of Hatti land, Hatti land, my sons *and* my grandsons forever! The tribute that was imposed upon your grandfather and your father—they presented three hundred shekels of good, refined first-class gold weighed with standard weights—you shall present them likewise. Do not turn your eyes to anyone else! Your fathers presented tribute to Egypt; you [shall not do that]!

With my friend you shall be friend, and with my enemy you shall be enemy. If the king of Hatti land is either in the Hurri land, or in the land of Egypt, or in the country of Astata, or in the country of Alse—any country coming in contact with the territory of your country that is friendly with the king of Hatti land—*or in* any country coming in contact with the territory of your country that is friendly with the king of Hatti land—*as* the country of Mukis, the country of Halba *and* the country of Kinza—but turns around and becomes inimical toward the king of Hatti land while the king of Hatti land is on a marauding campaign—if then you, Duppi-Teshub, do not remain loyal together with your foot soldiers and your charioteers and if you do not fight wholeheartedly; or if I should send out a prince *or* a high officer with foot soldiers and charioteers to reinforce you, Duppi-Teshub, *for the purpose of* going out to maraud in another [country—if then you, Duppi-Teshub, do not fight wholeheartedly] *that* enemy with [your army and your charioteers] and speak as follows: I am under an oath of loyalty, but [how am I to know] whether they will beat the enemy, or the enemy will beat them?; or if you even send a man to that enemy and inform him as follows: An army and charioteers of Hatti land are on their way; be on your guard! *If you do such things* you act in disregard of your oath.

As I, the Sun, am loyal toward you, extend military help to the Sun and Hatti land. If an evil rumor originates in Hatti land that someone is to rise in revolt against the Sun and you hear it, leave with your foot soldiers and your charioteers and go immediately to the aid of the king of Hatti land! But if you are not able to leave yourself, dispatch either your son or your brother together with your foot soldiers *and* your charioteers to the aid of the king of Hatti land! If you do not dispatch your son *or* your brother with your foot soldiers *and* your charioteers to the aid of the king of Hatti land, you act in disregard of the gods of the oath.

If anyone should press you hard, Duppi-Teshub, or if anyone should revolt against you, *if* you then write to the king of Hatti land, and the king of Hatti land dispatches foot soldiers and charioteers to your aid—if you treat them in an unfair manner, you act in disregard of the gods of the oath.

If they take Hittites—foot soldiers and charioteers—through Duppi-Teshub's territory and Duppi-Teshub provides them with food and drink while passing through *his* towns—if *that army* engages in any misconduct—pilfering in his country or his towns or in an attempt at deposing Duppi-Teshub from his kingship—it acts in disregard of the oath.

If anyone of the deportees from the Nuhasse land or of the deportees from the country of Kinza whom my father removed and myself removed escapes and comes to you, *if* you do not seize him and turn him back to the king of Hatti land, and even tell him as follows: Go! Where you are going to, I do not want to know; you act in disregard of your oath.

If anyone utters words unfriendly toward the king or Hatti land before you, Duppi-Teshub, you shall not withhold his name from the king. Or if the Sun gives you an order in secrecy *saying*: Do this or that! *if* that order cannot be executed, petition about it on the spot *stating*: This order I cannot execute and will not execute; and the king will [reconsider] it then and there. But if you do not execute an order that can *well* be executed and deceive the king, or *if* you do not keep to yourself the word that the king told you in secrecy, you act in disregard of the oath.

If a country or a fugitive takes to the road and while betaking themselves to Hatti land pass through your territory, put them on the right way, show them the way to Hatti land and speak friendly words to them! Do not send them to anyone else! If you do not put them on the right way, *if* you do not guide them on the right way to Hatti land, but direct them into the mountains or speak unfriendly words before them, you act in disregard of the oath.

Or if the king of Hatti land is getting the better of a country and puts them to flight, and they come to your country, if then you desire to take anything from them, ask the king of Hatti land for it! You shall not take it on your own! If you lay hand on it by yourself or conceal it, *you act in disregard of the oath.*

Furthermore, if a fugitive comes to your country, seize him! . . .

[The sun-god of Heaven, the sun-goddess of Arinna, the storm-god of Heaven, the Hattian storm-god, Seris and Hurris, Mount Nanni and Mount Hazzi, the storm-god of . . . , the storm-god of Halab, the storm-god of Zippalanda, the storm-god of Nerik, the storm-god of Lihzina, the storm-god of Hissashapa, the storm-god of Sabina, the storm-god of Tahaya, the storm-god of Bettiyarik, the storm-god of Samuha, the storm-god of Hurma, the storm-god of Saressa, the storm-god of . . . , the storm-god of Uda, the storm-god of Kizzuwatna, the storm-god of Ishupitta, the storm-god of Nuhasse; the patron-god, the Hattian patron-god, Zithariyas, Hapantalliyas, the patron-god of Karahna, the patron-god of the shield, Ea, Allatum, Telepinus of Durmitta, Telepinus of Tawiniya, Telepinus of Hanhana, Ishtar the Mighty, Askasepas; Sin lord of the oath, Ishara queen of the oath, Hebat queen of heaven, Ishtar, Ishtar of the battlefield, Ishtar of Nineveh, Ishtar of Hattarina, Ninatta and] Kulitta, the Hattian warrior-god, the warrior-god of Ellaya, the warrior-god of Arziya, Yarris, Zampanas; Hantidassus of Hurma, Abaras of Samuhas, Katahhas of Ankuwa, the queen of Katapa, Ammammas of Tahurpa, Hallaras of Dunna, Huwassanas of Hupisna, Tapisuwa of Ishupitta, the lady of Landa, Kunniyawannis of Landa, NIN.PISAN.PISAN of Kinza, Mount Lablana, Mount Sariyana, Mount Pisaisa, the Lulahhi gods *and* the Hapiri gods, Ereskigal, the gods and goddesses of Hatti land, the gods and goddesses of Amurru land, all the olden gods, Naras, Napsaras, Minki, Tuhusi, Ammunki, Ammizadu, Allalu, Anu, Antu, Apantu, Ellil, Ninlil, the mountains, the rivers, the springs, the great Sea, heaven and earth, the winds *and* the clouds—let these be witnesses to this treaty and to the oath.

The words of the treaty and the oath that are inscribed on this tablet—should Duppi-Teshub not honor these words of the treaty and the oath, may these gods of the oath destroy Duppi-Teshub together with his person, his wife, his son, his grandson, his house, his land and together with everything that he owns.

But if Duppi-Teshub honors these words of the treaty and the oath that are inscribed on this tablet, may these gods of the oath protect him together with his person, his wife, his son, his grandson, his house *and* his country.

#25: Treaty between Ashurnirari V and Mati'-ilu
(Parpola and Watanabe, *Neo-Assyrian Treaties*, 8–9)[6]

The first millennium B.C. provides Neo-Assyrian treaties that are similar to the previous examples (readings 22–24). Unlike earlier treaties, however, these often contain a rite of substitution in which the slain animal becomes an illustration of what awaits the individual who breaks the treaty. It is not at all clear that this substitutionary element is present in Genesis 15, and the reading included here may in fact have more in common with Jeremiah 34:18–20.[7] This reading presents a few of the curses against Mati'-ilu should he break the agreement.

[. . . may Mati'-ilu], his sons and daughters, his mag[nates and the people of his land become] altogether like [. . .], may his land [be reduced] to wasteland, may only an area of the size of a brick (be left) for [him to stand upon], may nothing be left for his sons, [his daughters, his magnates and the peo]ple of his land to stand upon. May Mati'-ilu [together with his sons], daughters, magnates and the people of his land [. . .] like limestone, and may he, together with the people of his land, be cru[shed] like gypsum.

This spring lamb has not been brought out of its fold for sacrifice, nor for a banquet, nor for a purchase, nor for (divination concerning) a sick man, nor to be slaughtered for [. . .]: it has been brought to conclude the treaty of Aššur-nerari, king of Assyria with Mati'-ilu. If Mati'-ilu [sins] against th[is] sworn treaty, then, just as this spring lamb has been brought from its fold and will not return to its fold and [not behold] its fold again, (in like manner) may, alas, Mati'-ilu, together with his sons, daughters, [magnates] and the people of his land [be ousted] from his country, not return to his country, and not [behold] his country again.

This head is not the head of a spring lamb, it is the head of Mati'-ilu, it is the head of his sons, his magnates and the people of [his la]nd. If Mati'-ilu [should sin] against this treaty, so may, just as the head of this spring lamb is c[ut] off, and its knuckle placed in its mouth, [. . .] the head of Mati'-ilu be cut off,

and his sons [and magnates] be th[rown] into [. . .]

This shoulder is not the shoulder of a spring lamb, it is the shoulder of Mati'-ilu, it is the shoulder of his so[ns, his magnates, and the people of his land. If Mati'-ilu] should sin against this [treaty], so may, just as the shou[lder of this spring lamb] is torn out and [placed in . . .], the shoulder of Mati'-ilu, of his sons, [his magnates] and the people of his land be torn out and [placed] in [. . .]

#26: Treaty between Mati'el and Bar-ga'yah
(Fitzmyer, *Aramaic Inscriptions of Sefîre*, 13–21)[8]

Similar to the Assyrian treaty between Ashurnirari V and Mati'-ilu (reading 25), an Aramaic treaty from the mid-eighth century reflects the widespread use of the treaty structure across northern Syria. Unlike second-millennium Hittite treaties, these Assyrian and Aramaic treaties contain no historical prologue, an integral component in the Hittite and Israelite forms.[9] The treaty presented here involves Mati'el of Arpad (who is the same person as Mati'-ilu in reading 25; Mati'el being the Aramaic spelling and Mati'-ilu the Akkadian) and Bar-ga'yah, another powerful Mesopotamian overlord. This text probably predates reading 25 by only a few years.

The treaty of King Bar-ga'yah of KTK, with Mati'el son of Attarsamak, the king [of Arpad; and the treaty] of the sons of Bar-ga'yah with the sons of Mati'el; and the treaty of the grandsons of Bar-[ga'yah and] his [offspring] with the offspring of Mati'el son of Attarsamak, king of Arpad; and the treaty of KTK with [the treaty of] Arpad; and the treaty of the lords of KTK with the treaty of the lords of Arpad; and the treaty of the [union of] . . . with all Aram and with the king of Mutsr and with his sons who will come after [him], and [with the kings of] all Upper Aram and Lower Aram and with all who enter the royal palace.

And the [stele with this inscription] he has set up, as well as this treaty. Now *it is* this treaty that Bar-[ga'yah] has concluded [in the presence of] . . . and *Mullesh*, in the presence of Marduk and Zarpanit, in the presence of Nabu and [Tashmet, in the presence of Ir and Nusk], in the presence of Nergal and Lats, in the presence of Shamash and Nur, in the presence of [Sin and Nikkal, in the presence] of Nikkar and Kadi'ah, in the presence of all the gods of Rahbah and Adam in the presence of Hadad of Aleppo], in the presence of Sibitti, in the presence of El and Elyan, in the presence of [Heaven and Earth, in the presence of the Abyss] and *the* Springs, and in the presence of Day and Night—all the [gods of KTK and the gods of Arpad] *are* witnesses *to it*. Open your eyes *O gods* to gaze upon the treaty of Bar-ga'yah [with King Mati'el of Arpad].

Now if Mati'el son of Attarsamak, the [king of Arpad], should be false [to King Bar-ga'yah of KTK, and if] the offspring of Mati'el should be false [to the offspring of Bar-ga'yah] . . . and if the Bene-[Gush should be false . . . from YM . . . and should seven rams cover] a ewe, may she not conceive; [and should seven nurses] anoint [their breasts and] nurse a young boy, may he not have his fill; and should seven mares suckle a colt, may it not be [sated; and should seven] cows give suck to a calf, may it not have its fill; and should seven ewes suckle a lamb, [may it not be sated]; and should seven *hens* go looking for food, may they not *kill anything*! And if [Mati'el] should be false to Bar-ga'yah [and to] his son and to his offspring, may his kingdom become like a kingdom of sand, a kingdom of sand, as long as *Ashur* rules! And [may Hadad pour over it] every sort of evil *that exists* on earth and in heaven and every sort of trouble; and may he shower upon Arpad [hailstones]! For seven years may the locust devour *Arpad*, and for seven years may the worm eat, and for seven [years may] TWY come up upon the face of its land! May the grass not come forth so that no green may be seen; and may its vegetation not be [seen]! Nor may the sound of the lyre be heard in Arpad; but among its people *let there rather be* the din of *affliction* and [the noise of crying] and lamentation! May the gods send every sort of devourer against Arpad and against its people! [May the mouth] of a snake [eat], the mouth of a scorpion, the mouth of *a bear*, the mouth of a panther! And may a moth and a louse and a . . . [become] to it a serpent's throat! May its vegetation be destroyed unto desolation! And may Arpad become a mound

to [house the desert animal]: the gazelle and the fox and the hare and the wildcat and the owl and the . . . and the magpie! May [this city] not be mentioned *any more*, [nor] MDR nor MRBH nor MZH nor MBLH nor Sharun nor Tu'im nor Bethel nor BYNN nor . . . [nor Arneh] nor Hazaz nor Adam!

Just as this wax is burned by fire, so may Arpad be burned and [her great daughter-cities]! May Hadad sow in them salt and *weeds*, and may it not be mentioned *again*! This GNB and . . . *are* Mati'el; it is his person. Just as this wax is burned by fire, so may [Mati'el, be burned by fire]! Just as *this* bow and these arrows are broken, so may Inurta and Hadad break [the bow of Mati'el], and the bow of his nobles! And just as a man of wax is blinded, so may [Mati'el] be blinded! [Just as] this calf is cut in two, so may Mati'el be cut in two, and may his nobles be cut in two! [And just as] a [harlot is stripped naked], so may the wives of Mati'el be stripped naked, and the wives of his offspring and the wives of [his nobles! And just as this wax woman is taken] and one strikes her on the face, so may the [wives of Mati'el be taken] and . . .

[The treaty of King Bar-ga'yah of KTK, with Mati'el son of Attarsamak, king of Arpad]; and the treaty of the son of Bar-ga'yah with the sons of Mati'el; and the treaty of the [grandson of Bar]-ga'yah with the offspring of Mati'el and with the offspring of any king who [will come up and rule] in his place, and with the Bene-Gush and with Bet-SLL and with [all Aram; and the treaty] of KTK with the treaty of Arpad; and the treaty of the lords of KTK with the [treaty of the lords of Arpad] and with its people and the treaty of the gods of KTK with the treaty of the [gods of Arpad; for] this is the treaty of gods, which gods have concluded *happy* forever *be the reign of* [Bar-ga'yah], a great king, and *from* this treaty . . . and heaven. [All the gods] will guard [this] treaty. Let not one of the words of this inscription be silent [but let them be heard from] Arqu to [Ya'di and] BZ, from Lebanon to Yabrud, from Damascus] to *Aru* and . . . , [and from] the valley to KTK . . . [in Bet]-Gush and its people with their *sanctuary* this treaty . . . YTH HSHK.HW . . . in Mutsr and MRBH . . . DSH . . . TM to Mati'el son [of Attarsamak.

. . . to your house. And *if* Mati'el will not obey [and if his sons will not obey, and *if* his people will not obey, and if] all the kings who will rule over Arpad [will not obey] the . . . LMNYN, you will have been false to all the gods of the treaty [that is in this inscription. But if you obey and fulfill] this treaty and say: *I* am an ally, [I shall not be able to raise a hand] against you; nor will my son be able to raise a hand against [your] son, nor my offspring against [your offspring. And if] one of *the* kings [should speak a word] against me or one of my enemies *should so speak* and you say to any king: What are you [going to do? and he should raise a hand against] my son and kill him and raise his hand to take some of my land or some of my possessions, you will have been [false to the treaty] that is in this inscription. If one of *the* kings comes and surrounds me, [your army] must come [to me with] every [archer] and every sort [of weapon], and you must *surround those who surround me* and you must *draw* for me . . . and *I shall pile* corpse upon corpse in [Arpad] . . . some king L'WYN WMWT . . . and if on a day when *the* gods . . . MRHY, you do not come with your army and *if* [you do not] come with your armies to strengthen my house and [if your offspring does not] come to strengthen [my] offspring, [you will have been false to] the gods of the treaty that is in this inscription. And *when* . . . Y'PN with me, I shall be able [to

drink] water [of the well of] . . . ; whoever *lives around* that well will not be able to *destroy it* or raise a hand against the water of [the well. And the king] who will enter and take LBKH or . . . , who will take . . . [to] destroy NGD . . . MLHM . . . in the town of YM'M. And if *you do* not *do* so, you will have been [false to the treaty] that is in this inscription. And if . . . , you shall send . . . , and if you do not give *me* my provisions, [or] deduct provisions from me, and do not deliver *them*, you will have been false to this treaty . . .

Thus have we spoken [and thus have we written]. What I, [Mati'el], have written *is to act* as a reminder for my son [and] my [grandson] who will come [after] me. May they make good relations [beneath] the sun [for the sake of my royal house] that no [evil may be done against] the house of [Mati'el and his son and] his [grandson forever].

May *the* gods keep [all evils] away from his day and from his house.

Whoever will not observe the words of the inscription that is on this stela or will say: I shall efface some of his (its) words, or I shall upset the good relations and turn *them* [to] evil, on any day on which he will do so, may the gods overturn [that man] and his house and all that *is* in it; and may they make its lower part its upper part! May his scion *inherit* no name!

6 Law Codes

Various types of legal materials have survived from the ancient Near East. This chapter deals only with codified laws, which provide interesting comparisons with biblical law. Laws codes[1] have not been found in Canaan, although this may be an accident of archeology. Egypt also preserves very little legal material, but for a different reason. Because of the veneration of the pharaoh as semidivine, his word was divine decree; there was, therefore, no need for a legal code that approved him before the gods and validated his performance as king—which was the function of such codes in Mesopotamia.

The Mesopotamian and Hittite cuneiform law codes presented here show striking comparisons with Israelite law. Cuneiform and biblical law both contain a significant amount of criminal law (murder, adultery, theft, etc.). Cuneiform law focused on civil law (marriage, inheritance, property, slaves, etc.); biblical law emphasized cultic law (types of sacrifices, purification rites, modes of worship, etc.).[2] Based on the impressive similarities in content and form, the biblical material is likely dependent on ancient Near Eastern antecedents. On the other hand, Israelite law transformed the legal codes with its religious applications. In Mesopotamia, an offense was viewed in terms of the good of society; in Israel, all offenses were ultimately against God. In the Bible, law is revelatory, since it is God given and prescribed for the people; in Mesopotamia, the law was approved and sanctioned by the gods, but was only descriptive of what a well-ordered society should be like.

#27: Laws of Ur-Nammu or Shulgi
(Roth, *Law Collections from Mesopotamia*, 13–22)[3]

Around 2350 B.C., King Uru-KA-gina[4] of Lagash attempted to reform the laws in current practice in Sumerian culture. His reforms limited bureaucracy and cut taxes for the general populace and served as the first attempt to standardize a legal system.[5] Over two centuries later, a law code was produced during the Ur III period of Sumerian history (approximately 2112–2004 B.C.) that should be credited to either the founder of the dynasty, Ur-Nammu, or his son and successor, Shulgi. The badly damaged text is known only from Old Babylonian copies produced in the scribal schools at Nippur and Ur two or three hundred years later (eighteenth century B.C.). Only a portion of the prologue and less than forty laws are preserved, but they illustrate the format that came to characterize Mesopotamian laws for centuries to come: prologue followed by casuistic law.

Ur-Namma, the mighty warrior, king of the city of Ur, king of the lands of Sumer and Akkad . . . he established 21,600 silas of barley, thirty sheep, thirty silas of butter, per month, as regular offerings . . . in the land.

When the gods An and Enlil turned over the kingship of the city of Ur to the god Nanna, at that time, for Ur-Namma, son born of the goddess Ninsun, for her beloved house-born slave, according to *Nanna's* justice and truth . . . gave to him . . . I promoted Namhani to be the governor of the city of Lagash. By the might of the god Nanna, my lord, I returned Nanna's Magan-boat to the quay, and made it shine in the city of Ur.

At that time, the NISKU people had control of the fields, the sea captains had control of the foreign maritime trade . . . those who appropriate [the oxen] . . . those who appropriate [the sheep] . . .

[At that time, I], Ur-Namma, [mighty warrior, lord of the city of Ur, king of the lands of Sumer and] Akkad, [by the might] of the god Nanna, my lord, [by the true command of the god Utu], I established [justice in the land].

. . . I returned. I established freedom for the Akkadians and foreigners in the lands of Sumer and Akkad, for those conducting foreign maritime trade *free from* the sea captains, for the herdsmen *free from* those who appropriate oxen, sheep, and donkeys.

At that time, by the might of Nanna, my lord, I liberated Akshak, Marad, Girkal, Kazallu, and their settlements, and for Utsarum, whatever *territories* were under the subjugation of Anshan.

I made the copper bariga-measure and standardized it at sixty silas. I made the copper seah-measure, and standardized it at ten silas. I made the normal king's copper seah-measure, and standardized it at five silas. I standardized *all* the stone weights *from* the pure one-shekel *weight* to the one-mina *weight*. I made the bronze one-sila measure and standardized it at one mina.

At that time, [I regulated] the riverboat traffic on the banks of the Tigris River, on the banks of the Euphrates River, on the banks of all rivers. [I secured safe roads for] the couriers; I [built] the *roadside* house. [I planted] the orchard, the king placed a gardener in charge of them.

I did not deliver the orphan to the rich. I did not deliver the widow to the mighty. I did not deliver the man with but one shekel to the man with one mina, *that is, sixty shekels.* I did not deliver the man with but one sheep to the man with one ox.

I settled *in independent settlements* my generals, my mothers, my brothers, and their families; I did not accept their instructions, I did not impose orders. I eliminated enmity, violence, and cries for justice. I established justice in the land.

If a man commits a homicide, they shall kill that man.

If a man acts lawlessly, they shall kill him.

If a man detains *another*, that man shall be imprisoned and he shall weigh and deliver fifteen shekels of silver.

If a male slave marries a female slave, his beloved, and that male slave *later* is given his freedom, she/he will not *be evicted from* (lit., leave) the house.

If a male slave marries a native woman, she/he shall place one male child in the service of his master; the child who is placed in the service of his master, his paternal estate, . . . the wall, the house . . . ; *any other* child of the native woman will not be owned by the master, nor will he be pressed into slavery.

If a man violates the rights of another and deflowers the virgin wife of a young man, they shall kill that male.

If the wife of a young man, on her own initiative, approaches a man and initiates sexual relations with him, they shall kill that woman; that male shall be released.

If a man acts in violation of the rights of another and deflowers the virgin slave woman of a man, he shall weigh and deliver five shekels of silver.

If a man divorces his first-ranking wife, he shall weigh and deliver sixty shekels of silver.

If he divorces a widow, he shall weigh and deliver thirty shekels of silver.

If a man has sexual relations with the widow without a formal written contract, he will not weigh and deliver any silver *as a divorce settlement.*

If . . .

(gap)

If a man accuses another man of . . . and he has him brought to the divine river ordeal but the divine river ordeal clears him, *the accuser* . . . shall weigh and deliver three shekels of silver.

If a man accuses the wife of a young man of promiscuity but the river ordeal clears her, the man who accused her shall weigh and deliver twenty shekels of silver.

If a son-in-law [enters] the household of his father-in-law but subsequently the father-in-law [gives his wife to the son-in-law's comrade], *the father-in-law* shall [weigh and deliver to the jilted son-in-law] twofold *the value of* the gifts [that the son-in-law brought when he entered the house].

If . . . , he shall weigh and deliver to him two shekels of silver.

If [a slave or (?)] a slave woman . . . ventures beyond the borders of *his or* her city and a man returns *him or* her, the slave's master shall weigh and deliver . . . shekels of silver to the man who returned *the slave.*

If [a man] cuts off the foot of [another man with] . . . , he shall weigh and deliver ten shekels of silver.

If a man shatters the . . . bone of another man with a club, he shall weigh and deliver sixty shekels of silver.

If a man cuts off the nose of another man with . . . , he shall weigh and deliver forty shekels of silver.

If [a man] cuts off [the . . . of another man] with . . . , [he shall] weigh and deliver [x shekels of silver].

If [a man knocks out another man's] tooth with . . . , he shall weigh and deliver two shekels of silver.

If . . .

(gap)

[If] . . . , he shall bring [a slave woman]; if he has no slave woman, he shall instead weigh and deliver ten shekels of silver; if he has no silver, he shall give him whatever of value he has.

If a slave woman curses someone acting with the authority of her mistress, they shall scour her mouth with one sila of salt.

If a slave woman strikes someone acting with the authority of her mistress . . .

(gap)

[If] . . .

(gap)

If a man presents himself as a witness but is demonstrated to be a perjurer, he shall weigh and deliver fifteen shekels of silver.

If a man presents himself as a witness but refuses to take the oath, he shall make compensation of whatever was the object of the case.

If a man violates the rights of another and cultivates the field of another man, and he sues *to secure the right to harvest the crop, claim-ing that the owner* neglected *the field*—that man shall forfeit his expenses.

If a man floods another man's field, he shall measure and deliver seven hundred twenty silas of grain per one hundred sars of field.

If a man gives a field to another man to cultivate but he does not cultivate it and allows it to become wasteland, he shall measure out seven hundred twenty silas of grain per one hundred sars.

If a man . . . another man . . .

(gap)

. . . he shall weigh and deliver to him.

#28: Laws of Lipit-Ishtar
(Roth, *Law Collections from Mesopotamia*, 23–35)[6]

Lipit-Ishtar was king of the city of Isin (1934–1924 B.C.). His Sumerian law code contained a prologue, perhaps as many as fifty laws (many now illegible), and an epilogue. Most extant copies are from the Old Babylonian scribal schools at Nippur.

[When] great [god An, father of the gods], and the god Enlil, [king of the lands, the lord who determines] destinies, gave a favorable reign and the kingship of the lands of Sumer and Akkad to the goddess Ninisina, child of An, pious lady, for whose reign . . . rejoicing, for whose brilliant glance . . . , in the city of Isin, her treasure house, established by the god An,

At that time, the gods An and Enlil called Lipit-Ishtar to the princeship of the land—Lipit-Ishtar, the wise shepherd, whose name has been pronounced by the god Nunamnir—in order to establish justice in the land, to eliminate cries for justice, to eradicate enmity and armed violence, to bring well-being to the lands of Sumer and Akkad.

At that time, I, Lipit-Ishtar, the pious shepherd of the city of Nippur, the faithful husbandman of the city of Ur, he who does not forsake the city of Eridu, the befitting lord of the city of Uruk, the king of the city of Isin, king of the lands of Sumer and Akkad, the heart's desire of the goddess Inanna, by the command of the god Enlil, I established justice in the lands of Sumer and Akkad.

At that time, I liberated the sons and daughters of the city of Nippur, the sons and daughters of the city of Ur, the sons and daughters of the city of Isin, the sons and daughters of the lands of Sumer and Akkad, who were subjugated [by the yoke], and I restored order.

With a . . . decree I made the father support his children, I made the child support his father. I made the father stand by his children, I made the child stand by his father.

I imposed service *equally* on the household of a living father and on the undivided household [of brothers]. I, Lipit-Ishtar son of the god Enlil obligated those in a household of a living father and in an undivided household of brothers to service for seventy *days per year*, I obligated those in a household of dependent workers to service for ten days per month . . . the wife of a man . . . the son of a man . . .

(gap)

. . . the troops, . . . the property of the paternal estate . . . the son of the governor, the son of the palace official . . .

[at that time].

If a man rents an ox for the rear of the team, he shall measure and deliver twenty-four hundred silas of grain for two years as its hire; if it is an ox for the front or middle, he shall measure and deliver eighteen hundred silas of grain *for two years* as its hire.

If a man dies without male offspring, an unmarried daughter shall be his heir.

If [a man dies] and his daughter [is married], the property of the paternal estate . . . , a younger sister, after . . . the house . . .

If . . . strikes the daughter of a man and causes her to lose her fetus, he shall weigh and deliver thirty shekels of silver.

If she dies, that male shall be killed.

If a . . . strikes the slave woman of a man and causes her to lose her fetus, he shall weigh and deliver five shekels of silver.

If . . .

(gap)

[If . . . the] boat [is lost], he shall [replace] the boat.

If a man rents a boat and an agreed route is established for him, but he violates its route and the boat . . . in that place—he has acted lawlessly; the man who rented the boat shall replace the boat and [he shall measure and deliver in grain its hire].

. . . he shall give as his gift.

If he leases his orchard to a gardener in an orchard lease, the gardener shall plant . . . for the owner of the orchard, *the gardener* shall have the use of the dates from one-tenth of the palm trees.

If a man . . .

If a man gives another man fallow land for the purpose of planting an orchard but he does not complete the planting of the orchard, they shall give the fallow land that he neglected to one who is willing to plant the orchard as his share.

If a man enters the orchard of another man and is seized there for thievery, he shall weigh and deliver ten shekels of silver.

If a man cuts down a tree in another man's orchard, he shall weigh and deliver twenty shekels of silver.

If a man—adjacent to whose house another man has neglected his fallow land—*if this* householder declares to the owner of the fallow land: Your fallow land has been neglected; someone could break into my house. Fortify your property! and it is confirmed that this formal warning was given, the owner of the fallow land shall restore to the owner of the house any of his property that is lost.

If a man's female slave or male slave flees within the city, and it is confirmed that the slave dwelled in a man's house for one month, *the one who harbored the fugitive slave* shall give slave for slave.

If he has no slave, he shall weigh and deliver fifteen shekels of silver.

If a man's slave contests his slave status against his master, and it is proven that his master has been compensated for his slavery twofold, that slave shall be freed.

If a MIQTU person is a gift of the king, he will not be appropriated.

If a MIQTU person goes *into service* to a man of his own free will, that man will not restrict him but the MIQTU shall go wherever he wishes.

If a man, without grounds, accuses another man of a matter of which he has no knowledge, and that man does not prove it, he shall bear the penalty of the matter for which he made the accusation.

If the master or mistress of an estate defaults on the taxes due from the estate and an outsider assumes the taxes, *the master* will not be evicted for three years; *but after three years of defaulting on the taxes* the man who has assumed the tax burden shall take possession of the estate and the *original* master of the estate will not make any claims.

If the master of the estate . . .

If a man rescues a child from a well, he shall [take his] feet [and seal a tablet with the size of his feet for identification].

(gap)

If a man does not raise the son whom he contracted to raise in an apprenticeship, and it is confirmed before the judges, *the child* shall be returned to his birth mother.

If a man [does not raise] the daughter whom he contracted to raise . . .

(gap)

[If] . . . marries, the *marriage* gift that is given by her/his parental estate shall be taken for her/his heir . . . [If] . . . is given to a wife, her/his brothers will not include for division *among their inheritance shares* the *marriage* gift that had been given by (?) her/his paternal estate, but . . .

If, during a father's lifetime, his daughter becomes an UGBABTU, a NADITU, or a QADISHTU, *her brothers* shall divide the estate considering her as an equal heir.

If a daughter is not given in marriage while her father is alive, her brothers shall give her in marriage.

If he takes a slave . . . he dies . . . an outsider . . . marries . . .

If a man . . .

If the second wife whom he marries bears him a child, the dowry that she brought from her paternal home shall belong only to her children; the children of the first-ranking wife and the children of the second wife shall divide the property of their father equally.

If a man marries a wife and she bears him a child and the child lives and a slave woman also bears a child to her master, the father shall free the slave woman and her children; the children of the slave woman will not divide the estate with the children of the master.

If his first-ranking wife dies and after his wife's death he marries the slave woman *who had borne him children*, the child of his first-ranking wife shall be his *primary* heir; the child whom the slave woman bore to her master is considered equal to a native freeborn son and they shall make good his *share of the* estate.

If a man's wife does not bear him a child but a prostitute from the street does bear him a child, he shall provide grain, oil, and clothing rations for the prostitute, and the child whom the prostitute bore him shall be his heir; as long as his wife is alive, the prostitute will not reside in the house with his first-ranking wife.

If a man's first-ranking wife loses her attractiveness or becomes a paralytic, she will not be evicted from the house; however, her husband may marry a healthy wife, and the second wife shall support the first-ranking wife.

If a son-in-law enters the household of his father-in-law and performs the bride-wealth presentation, but later they evict him and give his wife to his comrade, they shall restore to him twofold the bride-wealth that he brought, and his comrade will not marry his wife.

If a young married man has sexual relations with a prostitute from the street, and the judges order him not to go back to the prostitute, *and if* afterward he divorces his first-ranking wife and gives the silver of her divorce settlement to her, *still* he will not marry the prostitute.

If a father, during his lifetime, gives his favored son a gift for which he writes a sealed document, after the father has died the heirs shall divide the *remaining* paternal estate; they will not contest the share that was allotted, they will not repudiate their father's word.

If a father, during his lifetime, designates the bride-wealth for his eldest son and *the son* marries while the father is still alive, after the father has died the heirs [shall] . . . the estate . . . from the paternal estate . . . the bride-wealth they shall . . . the bride-wealth . . .

(gap)

If a man claims that another man's virgin daughter has had sexual relations but it is proven that she has not had sexual relations, he shall weigh and deliver ten shekels of silver.

If a man rents an ox and cuts the hoof tendon, he shall weigh and deliver one-third of its value *in silver*.

If a man rents an ox and destroys its eye, he shall weigh and deliver one-half of its value *in silver*.

If a man rents an ox and breaks its horn, he shall weigh and deliver one-quarter of its value *in silver*.

If a man rents an ox and breaks its tail, he shall weigh and deliver one-quarter of its value *in silver*.

[If a man] . . . , he shall weigh and deliver *in silver*.

In accordance with the true word of the god Utu, I made the lands of Sumer and Akkad hold fair judicial procedure. In accordance with the utterance of the god Enlil, I, Lipit-Ishtar son of Enlil eradicated enmity and violence. I made weeping, lamentation, shouts for justice, and suits taboo. I made right and truth shine forth, and I brought well-being to the lands of Sumer and Akkad . . .

. . . all humankind. When I established justice in the lands of Sumer and Akkad, I erected this stela. He who will not do anything evil to it, who will not damage my work, who will not efface my inscription and write his own name on it—may he be granted life and breath of long days; may he raise his neck to heaven in the Ekur temple; may the god Enlil's brilliant countenance be turned upon him from above.

But he who does anything evil to it, who damages my work, who enters the treasure room, who alters its pedestal, who effaces this inscription and writes his own name *in place of mine*, or, because of this curse, induces an outsider to remove it—that man, whether he is a king, a lord, or an ENSI ruler . . . [may he be completely obliterated] . . .

(*gap*)

May . . . [the god] . . . , primary son of the god Enlil, not approach; may the seed not enter; . . . the mighty one, the seed . . . May he

who escapes from the weapon, after he enters *the safety of* his house, may he not have [any heirs]. May [the gods] . . . , Ashnan, and Sumukan, lords of abundance, [withhold the bounty of heaven and] earth . . .

(*gap*)

May . . . the god Enlil . . . revoke the gift of the lofty Ekur temple. May the god Utu, judge of heaven and earth, remove the august word . . . its foundation bring into his house . . . May he make his cities into heaps of ruins. May the foundations of his land not be stable, may it have no king. May the god Ninurta, mighty warrior, son of the god Enlil . . .

#29: Laws of Dadusha of Eshnunna
(Roth, *Law Collections from Mesopotamia*, 62–68)[7]

A list of Babylonian laws from the city of Eshnunna is probably to be dated to the early eighteenth century B.C., perhaps to the reign of King Dadusha. Two copies of the laws recovered from Tell Harmal near modern Baghdad preserve nearly all of the legal regulations. The reading presented here illustrates laws relating to marriage, slavery, burglary, business regulations, and personal injuries.

If a man comes to claim *his bride* at the house of his father-in-law, but his father-in-law wrongs him and then gives his daughter to [another], the father of the daughter shall return twofold the bride-wealth that he received.

If a man brings the bride-wealth for the daughter of a man, but another, without the consent of her father and mother, abducts her and then deflowers her, it is indeed a capital offense—he shall die.

If a man marries the daughter of another man without the consent of her father and mother, and moreover does not conclude the nuptial feast and the contract for her father and mother, should she reside in his house for even one full year, she is not a wife.

If he concludes the contract and the nuptial feast for her father and mother and he marries her, she is indeed a wife; the day she is seized in the lap of another man, she shall die, she will not live.

If a man should be captured or abducted during a raiding expedition or while on patrol, even should he reside in a foreign land for a long time, should someone else marry his wife and even should she bear a child, whenever he returns he shall take back his wife.

If a man repudiates his city and his master and then flees, and someone else then marries his wife, whenever he returns he will have no claim to his wife.

If a man should deflower the slave woman of another man, he shall weigh and deliver twenty shekels of silver, but the slave woman remains the property of her master.

If a man gives his child for suckling and for rearing but does not give the food, oil, and clothing rations *to the caregiver* for three years, he shall weigh and deliver ten shekels of silver for the cost of the rearing of his child, and he shall take away his child.

If a slave woman acts to defraud and gives her child to a woman of the AWILU class, when he grows up should his master locate him, he shall seize him and take him away.

If a slave woman of the palace should give her son or her daughter to a commoner for rearing, the palace shall remove the son or daughter whom she gave.

However, an adopter who takes in adoption the child of a slave woman of the palace shall restore *another slave of* equal value for the palace.

If a man gives his goods to a NAPTARU for safekeeping, and the NAPTARU then allows the goods that he gave to him for safekeeping to become lost—even without evidence that the house has been broken into, the doorjamb scraped, the window forced—he shall replace his goods for him.

If the man's house has been burglarized, and the owner of the house incurs a loss along with the goods that the depositor gave to him, the owner of the house shall swear an oath to satisfy him at the gate of *the temple of* the god Tishpak: My goods have been lost along with your goods; I have not committed a fraud or misdeed; thus shall he swear an oath to satisfy him and he will have no claim against him.

If, in a partnership, one intends to sell his share and his partner wishes to buy, he shall match any outside offer.

If a man becomes impoverished and then sells his house, whenever the buyer offers it for sale, the owner of the house shall have the right to redeem it.

If a man buys a slave, a slave woman, an ox, or any other purchase, but cannot establish the identity of the seller, it is he who is a thief.

If a foreigner, a NAPTARU, or a MUDU wishes to sell his beer, the woman innkeeper shall sell the beer for him at the current rate.

If a man bites the nose of another man and thus cuts it off, he shall weigh and deliver sixty shekels of silver; an eye—sixty shekels; a tooth—thirty shekels; an ear—thirty shekels; a slap to the cheek—he shall weigh and deliver ten shekels of silver.

If a man should cut off the finger of another man, he shall weigh and deliver twenty shekels of silver.

If a man knocks down another man in the street and thereby breaks his hand, he shall weigh and deliver thirty shekels of silver.

If he should break his foot, he shall weigh and deliver thirty shekels of silver.

If a man strikes another man and thus breaks his collarbone, he shall weigh and deliver twenty shekels of silver.

If a man should inflict any other injuries on another man in the course of a fray, he shall weigh and deliver ten shekels of silver.

If a man, in the course of a brawl, should cause the death of another member of the AWILU class, he shall weigh and deliver forty shekels of silver.

And for a case involving a penalty of silver in amounts ranging from twenty shekels to sixty shekels, the judges shall determine the case against him; however, a capital case is only for the king.

If a man should be seized with a stolen slave or a stolen slave woman, a slave shall lead a slave, a slave woman shall lead a slave woman.

If a military governor, a governor of the canal system, or any person in a position of authority seizes a fugitive slave, fugitive slave woman, stray ox, or stray donkey belonging either to the palace or to a commoner, and does not lead it to Eshnunna but detains it in his house and allows more than one month to elapse, the palace shall bring a charge of theft against him.

A slave or slave woman belonging to *a resident of* Eshnunna who bears fetters, shackles, or a slave hairlock will not exit through the main city gate of Eshnunna without his owner.

A slave or slave woman who has entered the main city gate of Eshnunna in the safekeeping of only a foreign envoy shall be made to bear fetters, shackles, or a slave hairlock and thereby is kept safe for his owner.

If an ox gores another ox and thus causes its death, the two ox owners shall divide the value of the living ox and the carcass of the dead ox.

If an ox is a gorer and the ward authorities so notify its owner, but he fails to keep his ox in check and it gores a man and thus causes his death, the owner of the ox shall weigh and deliver forty shekels of silver.

If it gores a slave and thus causes his death, he shall weigh and deliver fifteen shekels of silver.

If a dog is vicious and the ward authorities so notify its owner, but he fails to control his dog and it bites a man and thus causes his death, the owner of the dog shall weigh and deliver forty shekels of silver.

If it bites a slave and thus causes his death, he shall weigh and deliver fifteen shekels of silver.

If a wall is buckling and the ward authorities so notify the owner of the wall, but he does not reinforce his wall and the wall collapses and thus causes the death of a member of the AWILU class—it is a capital case, it is decided by a royal decree.

#30: Laws of Hammurapi
(Roth, *Law Collections from Mesopotamia*, 76–81, 120–23, 128)[8]

The most famous collection of Mesopotamian laws is also the longest and best organized. It comes from the reign of the powerful sixth ruler of Babylon's first dynasty, Hammurapi (sometimes less accurately spelled Hammurabi). During his long reign (1792–1750 B.C.),[9] the city of Babylon became politically important for the first time in

Hammurapi's law code; on the top of the stele, the king receives the law from Shamash the sun god. (Copyright Réunion des Musées Nationaux/Art Resource, N.Y.)

history, serving as the center for Hammurapi's complex governmental bureaucracy. The code itself consists of an extensive prologue, 282 laws (most of which are well preserved), and an epilogue. The laws deal with nearly every possible situation in ancient Babylonian society, including criminal matters (murder, robbery, assault, bodily injuries) and civil matters (real estate sales and rentals, marriage, inheritance, adoption). This large collection of casuistic laws has many interesting parallels with biblical law, particularly in the Book of the Covenant (Exodus 21–23), the Holiness Code (Leviticus 17–26), and the legal core of Deuteronomy (Deuteronomy 12–26). The reading presented here includes the prologue (of historical and religious interest) and a few laws illustrating three personal injuries: battery (Exodus 21:15, 22–25; Leviticus 24:19–20; Deuteronomy 19:21), miscarriage (Exodus 21:22–25), and the goring ox (Exodus 21:28–32).

When the august god Anu, king of the Anunnaku deities, and the god Enlil, lord of heaven and earth, who determines the destinies of the land, allotted supreme power over all peoples to the god Marduk, the firstborn son of the god Ea, exalted him among the IGIGI deities, named the city of Babylon with its august name and made it supreme within the regions of the world, and established for him within it eternal kingship whose foundations are as fixed as heaven and earth, at that time, the gods Anu and Enlil, for the enhancement of the well-being of the people, named me by my name; Hammurapi, the pious prince, who venerates the gods, to make justice prevail in the land, to abolish the wicked and the evil, to prevent the strong from oppressing the weak, to rise like the sun-god Shamash over all humankind, to illuminate the land.

I am Hammurapi, the shepherd, selected by the god Enlil, he who heaps high abundance and plenty, who perfects every possible thing for the city Nippur, *the city known as* band-of-heaven-and-earth, the pious provider of the Ekur temple; the capable king, the restorer of the city Eridu, the purifier of the rites of the Eabzu temple; the onslaught of the four regions of the world, who magnifies the reputation of the city Babylon, who gladdens the heart of his divine lord Marduk, whose days are devoted to the Esagil temple; seed of roy-alty, he whom the god Sin created, enricher of the city of Ur, humble and talented, who provides abundance for the Egishnugal temple; discerning king, obedient to the god Shamash, the mighty one, who establishes the foundations of the city of Sippar, who drapes the sacred building of the goddess Aja with greenery, who made famous the temple of Ebabbar that is akin to the abode of heaven; the warrior, who shows mercy to the city of Larsa, who renews the Ebabbar temple for the god Shamash his ally; the lord who revitalizes the city of Uruk, who provides abundant waters for its people, who raises high the summit of the Eanna temple, who heaps up bountiful produce for the gods Anu and Ishtar; the protecting canopy of the land, who gathers together the scattered peoples of the city of Isin, who supplies abundance for the temple of Egalmah; dragon among kings, beloved brother of the gods Zababa, founder of the settlement of Kish, who surrounds the Emeteursag temple with splendor, who arranges the great rites for the goddess Ishtar, who takes charge of the temple of Hursagkalamma; the enemy-ensnaring throw-net, whose companion, the god Erra, has allowed him to obtain his heart's desire, who enlarges the city of Kutu, who augments everything for the Emeslam temple; the fierce wild bull who gores the enemy, beloved of the god Tutu, the one who makes the city of Borsippa exult, the pious one who does not fail in his duties to the Ezida temple, the dwelling of the god of kings; the one who is steeped in wisdom, who enlarges the cultivated area of the city of Dilbat, who heaps up the storage bins for the mighty god Urash; the lord, worthy recipient of the scepter and crown bestowed upon him by the wise goddess Mama, who devised the plans of the city of Kesh, who provides the pure food offerings for the goddess Nintu; the judicious one, the noble one, who allots pasturage and watering place for the cities of Lagash and Girsu, who provides plentiful food offerings for the Eninnu temple; who seizes the enemies, beloved of *the goddess Ishtar* the able one, who perfects the oracles of the city of Zabala, who gladdens the heart of the goddess Ishtar; the pure prince, whose prayers the god Adad acknowledges, appeaser of the heart of the god Adad, the hero in the city of Karkara, who installs the proper appointments throughout the Eudgalgal temple; the king who gives life to the city of Adab, who organizes the Emah temple; lord of kings, peerless warrior, who granted life to the city of Mashkanshapir, who gives waters of abundance to the Emeslam temple; wise one, the organizer, he who has mastered all wisdom, who shelters the people of the city of Malgium in the face of annihilation, who founds their settlements in abundance, who decreed eternal pure food offerings for the gods Enki and Damkina who magnify his kingship; leader of kings, who subdues the settlements along the Euphrates River by the oracular command of the god Dagan, his creator, who showed mercy to the people of the cities of Mari and Tuttul; the pious prince, who brightens the countenance of the god Tishpak, who provides pure feasts for the goddess Ninazu, who sustains his people in crisis, who secures their foundations in peace in the midst of the city of Babylon; shepherd of the people, whose deeds are pleasing to the goddess Ishtar, who establishes Ishtar in the Eulmash temple in the midst of Akkad the city; who proclaims truth, who guides the population properly, who restores its benevolent protective spirit to the city of Assur; who quells the rebellious, the king who proclaimed the rites for the goddess Ishtar in the city of Nineveh in the Emesmes temple; the pious one, who prays ceaselessly for the great gods, scion of Sumula-El, mighty heir of Sinmuballit, eternal seed of royalty, mighty king, solar disk of the city of Babylon, who spreads light over the lands of Sumer and Akkad, king who makes the four regions obedient, favored of the goddess Ishtar, am I. When the god Marduk commanded me to provide just ways for the people of the land *in order to attain* appropriate behavior, I established truth and justice as the declaration of the land, I enhanced the well-being of the people.

At that time.

If a child should strike his father, they shall cut off his hand.

If an AWILU should blind the eye of another AWILU, they shall blind his eye.

If he should break the bone of another AWILU, they shall break his bone.

If he should blind the eye of a commoner or break the bone of a commoner, he shall weigh and deliver sixty shekels of silver.

If he should blind the eye of an AWILU's slave or break the bone of an AWILU's slave, he shall weigh and deliver one-half of his value *in silver*.

If an AWILU should knock out the tooth of another AWILU of his own rank, they shall knock out his tooth.

If he should knock out the tooth of a commoner, he shall weigh and deliver twenty shekels of silver.

If an AWILU should strike the cheek of an AWILU who is of status higher than his own, he shall be flogged in the public assembly with sixty stripes of an ox whip.

If a member of the AWILU class should strike the cheek of another member of the AWILU class who is his equal, he shall weigh and deliver sixty shekels of silver.

If a commoner should strike the cheek of another commoner, he shall weigh and deliver ten shekels of silver.

If an AWILU's slave should strike the cheek of a member of the AWILU class, they shall cut off his ear.

If an AWILU should strike another AWILU during a brawl and inflict upon him a wound, that AWILU shall swear: I did not strike intentionally; and he shall satisfy the physician *by paying his fees*.

If he should die from his beating, he shall also swear: [I did not strike him intentionally]; if *the victim* is a member of the AWILU class, he shall weigh and deliver thirty shekels of silver.

If *the victim* is a member of the commoner class, he shall weigh and deliver twenty shekels of silver.

(gap)

If an AWILU strikes a woman of the AWILU class and thereby causes her to miscarry her fetus, he shall weigh and deliver ten shekels of silver for her fetus.

If that woman should die, they shall kill his daughter.

If he should cause a woman of the commoner class to miscarry her fetus by the beating, he shall weigh and deliver five shekels of silver.

If that woman should die, he shall weigh and deliver thirty shekels of silver.

If he strikes an AWILU's slave woman and thereby causes her to miscarry her fetus, he shall weigh and deliver two shekels of silver.

If that slave woman should die, he shall weigh and deliver twenty shekels of silver.

If an ox gores to death a man while it is passing through the streets, that case has no basis for a claim.

If a man's ox is a known gorer, and the authorities of his city quarter notify him that it is a known gorer, but he does not blunt its horns or control his ox, and that ox gores to death a member of the AWILU class, *the owner* shall give thirty shekels of silver.

If it is a man's slave *who is fatally gored*, he shall give twenty shekels of silver.

#31: Middle Assyrian Laws
(Roth, *Law Collections from Mesopotamia*, 155–57)[10]

From the Middle Assyrian period comes a series of tablets containing legal edicts, most of which are eleventh-century B.C. copies of fourteenth-century originals from the city of Ashur, one of the early Assyrian capitals. These laws were apparently collected by Tiglath-pileser I (1114–1076 B.C.). Rather than a single composition such as Hammurapi's law code, Tiglath-pileser's collection preserves royal edicts that treat many of the same topics known from the earlier Babylonian code. The following selections are of interest because they deal with laws in which women are victims or principal subjects.

If a woman, either a man's wife or a man's daughter, should enter into a temple and steal something from the sanctuary in the temple and either it is discovered in her possession or they prove the charges against her and find her guilty, [they shall perform] a divination, they shall inquire of the deity; they shall treat her as the deity instructs them.

If a woman, either a man's wife or a man's daughter, should speak something disgraceful or utter a blasphemy, that woman alone bears responsibility for her offense; they shall

have no claim against her husband, her sons, or her daughters.

If a man is either ill or dead, and his wife should steal something from his house and give it either to a man, or to a woman, or to anyone else, they shall kill the man's wife as well as the receivers *of the stolen goods*. And if a man's wife, whose husband is healthy, should steal from her husband's house and give it either to a man, or to a woman, or to anyone else, the man shall prove the charges against his wife and shall impose a punishment; the receiver who received *the stolen goods* from the man's wife shall hand over the stolen goods, and they shall impose a punishment on the receiver identical to what the man imposed on his wife.

If either a slave or a slave woman should receive something from a man's wife, they shall cut off the slave's or slave woman's nose and ears; they shall restore the stolen goods; the man shall cut off his own wife's ears. But if he releases his wife and does not cut off her ears, they shall not cut off *the nose and ears* of the slave or slave woman, and they shall not restore the stolen goods.

If a man's wife should steal something with a value greater than three hundred shekels of lead from the house of another man, the owner of the stolen goods shall take an oath, saying: I did not incite her, saying: Commit a theft in my house. If her husband is in agreement, *her husband* shall hand over the stolen goods and he shall ransom her; he shall cut off her ears. If her husband does not agree to her ransom, the owner of the stolen goods shall take her and he shall cut off her nose.

If a man's wife should place goods for safekeeping outside of the family, the receiver of the goods shall bear liability for stolen property.

If a woman should lay a hand upon a man and they prove the charges against her, she shall pay eighteen hundred shekels of lead; they shall strike her twenty blows with rods.

(gap)

If a man lays a hand upon a woman, attacking her like a rutting bull, and they prove the charges against him and find him guilty, they shall cut off one of his fingers. If he should kiss her, they shall draw his lower lip across the blade of an ax and cut it off.

[If either] a man or a woman enters [another man's] house and kills [either a man] or a woman, [they shall hand over] the manslayers [to the head of the household]; if he so chooses, he shall kill them, or if he chooses to come to an accommodation, he shall take [their property]; and if there is [nothing of value to give from the house] of the manslayers, either a son [or a daughter] . . .

#32: Hittite Laws
(Roth, *Law Collections from Mesopotamia*, 217–18, 228–29)[11]

> Most of the Hittite laws were composed in the early Old Hittite Kingdom (1650–1500 B.C.). But even these early laws sometimes preserve an older form of law no longer extant, indicated by the expression "Formerly they did such-and-such, but now he shall do such-and-such." In general, the laws were copied throughout the later periods of Hittite history with little attempt to revise them beyond modernizing the language of the Old Hittite copies.

[If] anyone kills [a man] or a woman in a [quarrel], he shall [bring him] for burial and shall give four persons, male or female respectively. He shall look [to his house for it.

If] anyone kills [a male] or female slave in a quarrel, he shall bring him for burial [and] shall give [two] persons (lit., heads), male or female respectively. He shall look to his house for it.

[If] anyone strikes a free [man] or woman so that he dies, but it is an accident, he shall bring him for burial and shall give two persons. He shall look to his house for it.

If anyone strikes a male or female slave so that he dies, but it is an accident, he shall bring him for burial and shall give one person. He shall look to his house for it.

If anyone kills a Hittite merchant *in a foreign land*, he shall pay four thousand shekels of silver. He shall look to his house for it. If it is in the lands of Luwiya or Pala, he shall pay the four thousand shekels of silver and also replace his goods. If it is in the land of Hatti, he shall also bring the merchant himself for burial.

If a person, man or woman, is killed in another city, the victim's heir shall deduct twelve thousand square meters from the land of the person on whose property the person was killed and shall take it for himself.

If anyone blinds a free person or knocks out his tooth, they used to pay forty shekels of silver. But now he shall pay twenty shekels of silver. He shall look to his house for it.

If anyone blinds a male or female slave or knocks out his tooth, he shall pay ten shekels of silver. He shall look to his house for it.

If anyone injures a person's head, they used to pay six shekels of silver: the injured party took three shekels of silver, and they used to take three shekels of silver for the palace. But now the king has waived the palace share, so that only the injured party takes three shekels of silver.

If anyone injures a person and temporarily incapacitates him, he shall provide medical care for him. In his place he shall provide a person to work on his estate until he recovers. When he recovers, his assailant shall pay him six shekels of silver and shall pay the physician's fee as well.

If anyone breaks a free person's arm or leg, he shall pay him twenty shekels of silver. He shall look to his house for it.

(gap)

If a free man burglarizes a house, he shall pay only according to the law. Formerly they paid forty shekels of silver as fine for the theft, but now [he shall pay] twelve shekels of silver. If he steals much, they will impose much upon him. If he steals little, they shall impose little upon him. He shall look to his house for it.

If a slave burglarizes a house, he shall pay only according to the law. He shall pay six shekels of silver for the theft. He shall disfigure the nose and ears of the slave and they will give him back to his owner. If he steals much, they will impose much upon him; if he steals little, they will impose little upon him. [If] his owner says: I will make compensation for him; then he shall make it. But [if] he refuses, he shall lose that slave.

If a free man breaks into a grain storage pit, and finds grain in the storage pit, he shall fill the storage pit with grain and pay twelve shekels of silver. He shall look to his house for it.

If a slave breaks into a grain storage pit, and finds grain in the storage pit, he shall fill the storage pit with grain and pay six shekels of silver. He shall look to his house for it.

If a free man sets fire to a house, he shall rebuild [the house]. And whatever perished in the house—whether it is persons, [cattle, or sheep], it is damage. He shall make compensation for it.

If a slave sets fire to a house, his owner shall make compensation for him, and they shall disfigure the slave's nose and ears and return him to his owner. But if the owner will not make compensation, he shall forfeit that slave.

If anyone sets fire to a shed, he shall feed *the owner's* cattle and bring them through to the following spring. He shall give back the shed. If there was no straw in it, he shall *simply* rebuild the shed.

If anyone steals a vine, a vine branch, a . . . , or an onion/garlic, formerly [they paid] one shekel of silver for one vine and one shekel of silver for a vine branch, one shekel of silver [for one KARPINA, one] shekel of silver for one clove of garlic. And they shall strike a spear on his . . . [Formerly] they proceeded so. But now if he is a free man, he shall pay six shekels [of silver]. But if he is a slave, he shall pay three shekels of silver.

#33: Neo-Babylonian Laws
(Roth, *Law Collections from Mesopotamia*, 145–49)[12]

> Preserved on a single tablet probably retrieved from Sippar and now housed in the British Museum, a collection of fifteen laws from the early part of the Neo-Babylonian period (seventh century B.C.) appears to have had no prologue or epilogue.

[A man who opens] his well to the irrigation outlet but does not reinforce it, and who thus causes a breach and thereby [floods] his neighbor's field, shall give [grain in accordance with the yields of his] neighbor [to the owner of the field].

A man who *buys* (lit., seals a tablet) a field or a house in another's name, but does not make out a contract of proxy for the matter or does not take a copy of the tablet—it is the man in whose name the tablet and sale document are written who shall take the field or house.

A man who sells a slave woman against whom a claim arises so that she is taken away—the seller shall give to the buyer the silver *of the purchase price* in its capital amount according to the sale document. Should she bear children *while in the possession of the buyer*, he shall give half a shekel of silver for each.

A woman who performs a magic act or a ritual purification against a man's field, or a boat, or an oven, or anything whatsoever—*if it is a field, then concerning* the trees among which she performs the ritual, she shall give to the owner of the field threefold its yield. If she performs the purification against a boat, or an oven, or anything else, she shall give threefold the losses caused to the property. Should she be seized [performing the purification] against the door of a man's [house], she shall be killed. Its case is not complete and is not written *here*.

A man who gives his daughter in marriage to a member of the AMELU class, and the father *of the groom* commits certain properties in his tablet and awards them to his son, and the father-in-law commits the dowry of his daughter, and they write the tablets in mutual agreement—they will not alter the commitments of their respective tablets. The father will not make any reduction to the properties as written in the tablet to his son's benefit that he showed to his in-law. Even should the father, whose wife fate carries away, then marry a second wife and should she then bear him sons, the sons of the second woman shall take one third of the balance of his estate.

A man who makes an oral promise of the dowry for his daughter, or writes it on a tablet for her, and whose estate later decreases—he shall give to his daughter a dowry in accordance with the remaining assets of his estate; the *bride's father* (lit., father-in-law) and the groom will not by mutual agreement alter the commitments.

A man who gives a dowry to his daughter, and she has no son or daughter, and fate carries her away—her dowry shall revert to her paternal estate.

[A wife who] . . . fate [carries her away] . . . to a son . . . she shall give her dowry to her husband or to whomever she wishes.

A wife whose husband takes her dowry, and who has no son or daughter, and whose husband fate carries away—a dowry equivalent to the dowry *that her husband had received* shall be given to her from her husband's estate. If her husband should award to her a marriage gift, she shall take her husband's marriage gift together with her dowry, and thus her claim is satisfied. If she has no dowry, a judge shall assess the value of her husband's estate, and shall give to her some property in accordance with the value of her husband's estate.

A man marries a wife, and she bears him sons, and later on fate carries away that man, and that woman then decides to enter another man's house—she shall take *from her first husband's estate* the dowry that she brought from her father's house and anything that her husband awarded to her, and the husband she chooses shall marry her; as long as she lives, they shall have the joint use of the properties. If she should bear sons to her *second* husband, after her death the sons of the second and first *husbands* shall have equal shares in her dowry . . .

A man who marries a wife who bears him sons, and whose wife fate carries away, and who marries a second wife who bears him sons, and later on the father goes to his fate—the sons of the first woman shall take two-thirds of the paternal estate, and the sons of the second shall take one-third. Their sisters, who are still residing in the paternal home . . .

7 Cultic Texts

Just as the ancient Israelites were interested in cultic rituals and cleansing (see especially the legal sections of the Pentateuch), so their neighbors in Egypt, Asia Minor, and Mesopotamia preserved texts on these topics. Many ancient Near Eastern texts relate to the sacred cult and often parallel the Old Testament material about the priesthood and the cult, although the Israelite concept of holiness transcends ancient Near Eastern concepts represented by the same term and makes ethical demands not attested elsewhere in the ancient world.

#34: Negative Confession of Sin
(Lichtheim, *Ancient Egyptian Literature*, 2.124–32)[1]

The Egyptian "Book of the Dead" is a New Kingdom compilation of spells intended to insure the resurrection of the deceased. It is the literary successor to the Middle Kingdom Coffin Texts and the Old Kingdom Pyramid Texts. The reading presented here from the "Book of the Dead" is the longest and most famous of these spells (no. 125) and is known variously as the "Judgment of the Dead" and the "Negative Confession of Sin." Illustrated by the dead person's heart on the scales before an assembly of gods presided over by Osiris, the spell consists of a long recitation of sins not committed by the deceased, which enables him magically to pass the judgment. The text is most useful for contrasts with Israelite views of magic and cultic rituals, although it also bears some resemblance to Deuteronomy 26:13–15 and other biblical texts.

To be said on reaching the hall of the Two Truths so as to purge N. of any sins committed and to see the face of every god:

Hail to you, great god, lord of the Two Truths!

I have come to you, my lord,
I was brought to see your beauty.
I know you, I know the names of the forty-two gods,
who are with you in the hall of the Two Truths,
who live by warding off evildoers,
who drink of their blood,
on that day of judging characters before Wennofer.
Lo, your name is He-of-Two-Daughters,
and He-of-MAAT's-Two-Eyes.
Lo, I come before you,
bringing MAAT to you,
having repelled evil for you.
I have not done crimes against people,
I have not mistreated cattle,
I have not sinned in the place of truth.
I have not known what should not be known,
I have not done any harm.
I did not begin a day by exacting more than my due,
my name did not reach the bark of the mighty ruler.
I have not blasphemed a god,
I have not robbed the poor.
I have not done what the god abhors,
I have not maligned a servant to his master.
I have not caused pain,
I have not caused tears.
I have not killed,
I have not ordered to kill,
I have not made anyone suffer.
I have not damaged the offerings in the temples,
I have not depleted the loaves of the gods,
I have not stolen the cakes of the dead.
I have not copulated nor defiled myself.

I have not increased nor reduced the
measure,
I have not diminished the ARURA,
I have not cheated in the fields.
I have not added to the weight of the
balance,
I have not falsified the plummet of the
scales.
I have not taken milk from the mouth of
children,
I have not deprived cattle of their
pasture.
I have not snared birds in the reeds of
the gods,
I have not caught fish in their ponds.
I have not held back water in its season,
I have not dammed a flowing stream,
I have not quenched a needed fire.
I have not neglected the days of meat
offerings,
I have not detained cattle belonging to
the god,
I have not stopped a god in his
procession.
I am pure, I am pure, I am pure, I am
pure!
I am pure as is pure that great heron in
Hnes.
I am truly the nose of the lord of breath,
who sustains all the people,
on the day of completing the eye in On,
in the second month of winter, last day,
in the presence of the lord of this land.
I have seen the completion of the eye in
On!
No evil shall befall me in this land,
in this hall of the Two Truths;
for I know the names of the gods in it,
the followers of the great god!
O wide-of-stride who comes from On: I
have not done evil.
O flame-grasper who comes from
Kheraha: I have not robbed.
O long-nosed who comes from Khmun:
I have not coveted.
O shadow-eater who comes from the
cave: I have not stolen.
O savage-faced who comes from Rostau:
I have not killed people.
O lion-twins who come from heaven: I
have not trimmed the measure.

O flint-eyed who comes from Khem: I
have not cheated.
O fiery-one who comes backward: I
have not stolen a god's property.
O bone-smasher who comes from Hnes:
I have not told lies.
O flame-thrower who comes from
Memphis: I have not seized food.
O cave-dweller who comes from the
west: I have not sulked.
O white-toothed who comes from
Lakeland: I have not trespassed.
O blood-eater who comes from the
slaughter place: I have not slain
sacred cattle.
O entrails-eater who comes from the
tribunal: I have not extorted.
O lord of MAAT who comes from Maaty:
I have not stolen bread rations.
O wanderer who comes from Bubastis: I
have not spied.
O pale one who comes from On: I have
not prattled.
O villain who comes from Anjdty: I
have contended only for my goods.
O fiend who comes from
slaughterhouse: I have not committed
adultery.
O examiner who comes from Min's
temple: I have not defiled myself.
O chief of the nobles who comes from
Imu: I have not caused fear.
O wrecker who comes from Huy: I have
not trespassed.
O disturber who comes from the
sanctuary: I have not been violent.
O child who comes from the nome of
On: I have not been deaf to MAAT.
O foreteller who comes from Wensi: I
have not quarreled.
O Bastet who comes from the shrine: I
have not winked.
O backward-faced who comes from the
pit: I have not copulated with a boy.
O flame-footed who comes from the
dusk: I have not been false.
O dark one who comes from darkness: I
have not reviled.
O peace-bringer who comes from Sais: I
have not been aggressive.

O many-faced who comes from Djefet: I
have not had a hasty heart.

O accuser who comes from Utjen: I have
not attacked and reviled a god.

O horned one who comes from Siut: I
have not made many words.

O Nefertem who comes from Memphis:
I have not sinned, I have not done
wrong.

O timeless one who comes from Djedu: I
have not made trouble.

O willful one who comes from Tjebu: I
have not waded in water.

O flowing one who comes from Nun: I
have not raised my voice.

O commander of people who comes
from his shrine: I have not cursed a
god.

O benefactor who comes from Huy: I
have not been boastful.

O Nehebkau who comes from the city: I
have not been haughty.

O high-of-head who comes from the
cave: I have not wanted more than I
had.

O captor who comes from the
graveyard: I have not cursed god in
my town.

Hail to you, gods!

I know you, I know your names.

I shall not fall in fear of you,

you shall not accuse me of crime to this
god whom you follow!

No misfortune shall befall me on your
account!

You shall speak rightly about me before
the all-lord,

for I have acted rightly in Egypt.

I have not cursed a god,

I have not been faulted.

Hail to you, gods in the hall of the Two
Truths,

who have no lies in their bodies,

who live on MAAT in On,

who feed on their rightness before
Horus in his disk.

Rescue me from Babi, who feeds on the
entrails of nobles,

on that day of the great reckoning.

Behold me, I have come to you,

without sin, without guilt, without evil,

without a witness against me,

without one whom I have wronged.

I live on MAAT, I feed on MAAT,

I have done what people speak of,

what the gods are pleased with,

I have contented a god with what he
wishes.

I have given bread to the hungry,

water to the thirsty,

clothes to the naked,

a ferryboat to the boatless.

I have given divine offerings to the
gods,

invocation offerings to the dead.

Rescue me, protect me,

do not accuse me before the great god!

I am one pure of mouth, pure of hands,

one to whom welcome is said by those
who see him;

for I have heard the words spoken by
the donkey and the cat,

in the house of the open mouthed;

I was a witness before him when he
cried out,

I saw the splitting of the ISHED tree in
Rostau.

I am one who is acquainted with the
gods,

one who knows what concerns them.

I have come here to bear witness to
MAAT,

to set the balance in right position
among the dead.

O you who are high upon your
standard,

lord of the ATEF crown,

who is given the name Lord of Breath:

rescue me from your messengers,

who inflict wounds,

who mete out punishment,

who have no compassion,

for I have done MAAT for the lord of
MAAT!

I am pure,

my front is pure,

my rear is pure,

my middle has been in the well of MAAT,

no limb of mine is unclean.

I have washed in the well of the south,

I have halted at the town of the north,

in the meadow of the grasshoppers,

where the crew of Re bathes by day and
    by night,
where the gods enjoy passing by day
    and by night.
Let him come, they say to me.
Who are you? they say to me.
What is your name? they say to me.
I am the papyrus stalk,
He-Who-Is-in-the-Moringa is my name.
Where have you passed by, they say to
    me,
I have passed by the town north of the
    Moringa.
What have you seen there?
The leg and the thigh.
What did you say to them?
I have witnessed the acclaim in the land
    of the Fenkhu.
What did they give you?
A firebrand and a . . .
What did you do with them?
I buried them on the shore of the pool
    Maaty,
at the time of the evening meal.
What did you find there on the shore of
    the pool Maaty?
A scepter of flint whose name is Breath-
    giver.
What did you do to the firebrand and
    the faience column,
when you had buried them?
I lamented over them,
I took them up,
I extinguished the fire,
I broke the column,
threw it in the pool.
Come then, enter the gate of this hall of
    the Two Truths,
for you know us.
I shall not let you enter through me,
says the beam of this gate,
unless you tell my name.
Plummet-of-the-Place-of-Truth is your
    name.
I shall not let you enter through me,
says the right leaf of this gate,
unless you tell my name.
Scale-Pan-That-Carries-MAAT is your
    name.
I shall not let you enter through me,
says the left leaf of this gate,

unless you tell my name.
Scale-Pan-of-Wine is your name.
I shall not let you pass over me,
says the threshold of this gate,
unless you tell my name.
Ox-of-Geb is your name.
I shall not open for you,
says the bolt of this gate,
unless you tell my name.
Toe-of-His-Mother is your name.
I shall not open for you,
says the bolt-clasp of this gate,
unless you tell my name.
Eye-of-Sobk-Lord-of-Bakhu is your
    name.
I shall not open for you,
I shall not let you enter by me,
says the keeper of this gate,
unless you tell my name.
Breast-of-Shu-Given-Him-to-Guard-
    Osiris is your name.
We shall not let you pass over us,
say the cross-timbers,
unless you tell our name.
Offspring-of-Renenutet is your name.
You know us, pass over us.
You shall not tread upon me,
says the floor of this hall.
Why not, since I am pure?
Because we do not know your feet,
with which you tread on us;
tell them to me.
Who-enters-before-Min is the name of
    my right foot,
WNPT-of-Nephthys is the name of my left
    foot.
Tread upon us, since you know us.
I shall not announce you,
says the guard of the hall,
unless you tell my name.
Knower-of-Hearts, Examiner-of-Bellies
    is your name.
To which god present shall I announce
    you?
Tell it to the interpreter of the Two
    Lands.
Who is the interpreter of the Two
    Lands?
It is Thoth.
Come, says Thoth.
Why have you come?

I have come here to report.
What is your condition?
I am free of all wrongdoing,
I avoided the strife of those in their day,
I am not one of them.
To whom shall I announce you?
To him whose roof is of fire,
whose walls are living cobras,
the floor of whose house is in the flood.
Who is he?
He is Osiris.
Proceed, you are announced,
the eye is your bread,
the eye is your beer,
the eye is your offering on earth,
so says he to me.

This is the way to act toward the hall of the Two Truths. A man says this speech when he is pure, clean, dressed in fresh cloths, shod in white sandals, painted with eye-paint, anointed with the finest oil of myrrh. One shall offer to him beef, fowl, incense, bread, beer, and herbs. And you make this image in drawing on a clean surface in red paint mixed with soil on which pigs and goats have not trodden.

He for whom this scroll is recited will prosper, and his children will prosper. He will be the friend of the king and his courtiers. He will receive bread, beer, and a big chunk of meat from the altar of the great god. He will not be held back at any gate of the west. He will be ushered in with the kings of Upper and Lower Egypt. He will be a follower of Osiris.

Effective a million times.

#35: Ritual of the Substitute King
(*ANET* 355–56)[2]

Certain ancient Near Eastern rituals were preventative in nature. For example, if a disaster or calamity was anticipated and forecast through magical omens, certain countermeasures could ward off the pending disaster. In such cases, a substitute animal or human effigy was identified with the person in danger, and by reciting the cultic formula, the substitute is offered to the offended deity. Tragically, the substitute was usually killed in the course of the ritual. Such practices are known from Mesopotamia as early as the beginning of the second millennium B.C. In the reading presented here from the fourteenth or thirteenth century B.C., a Hittite king is warned of a fatal omen sent by the moon-god. The substitute, a prisoner of war, is not slain but is allowed to return to his homeland, which apparently was intended to remove the offense from the Hittite homeland and free the king from the predicted disaster.[3]

[During the night the king] takes the . . . [substitutes] and goes to the [sanctuary] of the moon-god. [He presents them to the moon-god and] says: In the matter about which [I prayed] to you, listen to me, moon-god, my lord! [That omen that you] gave—if you found fault with me, *ten witness* that I have given [you] straightaway [these substitutes]. These take, [but let me go free]! They drive up to the [sanctuary] a live steer [and consecrate] it . . . The king goes up to the [sanctuary and speaks as follows: That] omen that you gave, O moon-god—if you found fault with me [and] wished to behold with your own eyes [the sinner's abasement, see, I, the king], have come in person [to your sanctuary] and have [given] you these substitutes. Consider [the substitution]! Let these die! But, let me not die! They hand [the substitutes over to the] . . . and he takes them away. [When] he has finished . . . [them], he casts *spells of deliverance over him*.

He [brings a healthy prisoner to the sanctuary]. They anoint the prisoner with the fine oil of kingship, and [he speaks] as follows: This man *is* the king. To him [have I given] a royal name. Him have I clad [in the vestments] of kingship. Him have I crowned with the diadem. Remember this: That evil omen [signifies] short years *and* short days. Pursue this substitute! The one shekel of silver, the one shekel of gold, the one mina of copper, the one mina of tin, the one mina of iron, the one mina of [lead], all this is [removed] from his [body]. The one healthy prisoner is released, and he has him taken back to his country. The king submits to the [waving ceremony], and afterward the king goes to bathe.

When it dawns, the king submits to the [waving ceremony] and afterward he performs the ritual of the house *and* the pure ritual. When it is light, the king performs the . . . ritual. When he goes away he takes a bath and consecrates one . . . sheep to the sun-god under the open sky.

Words [of] . . . he speaks as follows: Sun-god of Heaven, my lord! That omen that the moon-god gave—if he found fault with me, you accept, sun-god of Heaven and *all* you gods, these substitutes that I have given and let me go free! To *appearing before* you, I might [prefer] appearing before the sun-goddess of Arinna. [Afterward] he goes into . . . and [con-secrates one . . . sheep] to Eresh-kigal. He prays as follows: Eresh-kigal, my lady! That omen that the moon-god gave—if he found fault with me, *remember* that the gods of heaven have delivered me into your hands. Take these substitutes that I have handed over to you and let me go free! I want to see the sun-god of Heaven with mine eyes! They offer pieces of raw and cooked meat, and the king arranges for cups at his own expense.

When night comes, he consecrates one . . . sheep for the moon-god under the open sky and speaks as follows: Moon-god, my lord! That omen that you gave—if you found fault with me, *remember that* you delivered me into the hands of the gods of the nether world and Eresh-kigal. I made my peace with the gods of the nether world *and* handed over substitutes *to them*. Take those, but let me go free! To *appearing before* you I might [prefer] *appearing before* the sun-god of Heaven. The king offers pieces of raw and cooked meat and arranges for cups.

#36: Instructions for Cultic Officials and Temple Personnel
(*ANET* 207–10)[4]

A list of instructions from a Hittite king in the middle of the thirteenth century B.C. to cultic functionaries offers a wealth of information on the administration of the temple and the Hittite conceptions of human-divine relations. Punishment is corporate, meaning that retribution is not just for the offender, but for his whole family, a concept also attested in the Old Testament. Furthermore, if the offense escapes the attention of humans, the deities will execute punishment nonetheless. The concepts of ritual cleanliness and uncleanliness found here are, of course, well known from the Old Testament's pronouncements on the priesthood and cult.

Furthermore, let those who prepare the daily loaves be clean. Let them be bathed *and* [groomed], let their *body* [hair] and nails be removed. Let them be clothed in clean dresses. [While unclean], let them not prepare *the loaves*; let those who are [agreeable] to the gods' soul and person prepare them. The bakers' house in which they prepare them—let that be swept *and* scrubbed. Furthermore, let a pig or a dog not stay at the door of the place where the loaves are broken. Are the minds of men and of the gods generally different? No! With regard to the matter with which we are dealing? No! Their minds are exactly alike. When a servant is to stand before his master, he is bathed and clothed in clean *garments*; he either gives him his food, or he gives him his beverage. And because he, his master, eats *and* drinks, he is relaxed in spirit and feels one with him. But if he *the servant* is ever remiss, *if* he is inattentive, his mind is alien to him. And if a slave causes his master's anger, they will either kill him or they will injure him at his nose, his eyes *or* his ears; or [they will seize] him, his wife, his children, his brother, his sister, his in-laws, his kin whether it be a male slave or a slave-girl. They may *either* [impose the extreme penalty], *or* they may do to him nothing at all. If ever he is to die, he will not die alone; his kin will accompany him.

If then, on the other hand, anyone arouses the anger of a god, does the god take revenge on him alone? Does he not take revenge on his wife, his children, his descendants, his kin, his slaves, and slave-girls, his cattle *and* sheep together with his crop and will utterly destroy him? Be very reverent indeed to the word of a god!

Further: The festival of the month, the festival of the year, the festival of the stag, the festival of autumn, the festival of spring, the festival of thunder, the festival of HIYARASH, the festival of PUDAHASH, the festival of ISHUWASH, the festival of . . . DULASHASH, the festival of the rhyton, the festivals of the holy priest, the festivals of the Old Men, the festivals of the mothers-of-god, the festival of DAHIYASH, the festivals of the UPATI men, the festivals of PULASH, the festivals of HAHRATAR, or whatever festival else *will be celebrated* in Hattusa—if you do not celebrate them with all the cattle, sheep, loaves, beer *and* wine set *before the gods*, and if you, the god's priests, make a deal with those who give all that, you can be sure that the gods will notice what is amiss.

Or if you ever take [sacrifices that have been] set [before the gods] and do not carry them right to the gods themselves, *if* you withhold *it* from them, keep *it* in your houses, and your wives, children *or* servants consume it, *if* you give it to a relative or some UBARU befriended with you who happens to visit *you*, if you give it to him and take it away from the god and do not carry it right to him, *or if you give it to him* in several portions—you will be held responsible for that matter of dividing. Do not divide it. He who divides it, shall be killed; there shall be no recourse for him.

Every bit of the loaves, the beer *and* the wine keep in the temple. Let no one appropriate for himself a sacrificial loaf of the god *or* a thin loaf. Let no one pour out beer *or* wine from the cup. Devote every bit to the god. Furthermore, in the presence of the god speak for yourselves *these* words: Whoever has taken from your divine loaves *or* from the libation bowl, may the god, my lord, [punish] him; may he hold this man's house responsible for it! If you [wish] to eat and to drink . . . on that day, eat and drink. If you cannot finish it, keep on eating *and* drinking [for] three days. But your wives, your children *and* your servants must in no circumstances . . . [cross] the threshold of the gods. But an UBARU who may come to see someone is allowed to enter the house of the god and he may also cross the threshold of the king. So let that man *whom he is visiting* conduct him up *to the temple* and let him eat *and* drink. But if it is [a foreigner], if it is not a Hittite man, and he [approaches] the gods, [he shall be killed]. And he who conducts him *into the temple*, it makes him liable of the death penalty too.

If an ox *or* a sheep is driven up to the god as food, and you appropriate for yourselves either a fattened ox or a fattened sheep and substitute a lean one that you have slaughtered, and *if* you either consume that or put it into your pen, or put it under the yoke, or *if* you put the sheep into your fold or kill it for yourselves, and *if* you see fit [to give it away] or to turn it over to another man, of *if* you accept a price for it and thus [take it away from] the god and withhold it from *his* mouth, *if* you take it for yourselves or give it to another man and speak as follows: Since he is a god, he will not say anything, and will not do anything to us—just think how the man reacts who sees his *choice* morsel snatched away from before his eyes! The will of the gods is strong. It does not make haste to seize, but when it seizes, it does not let go *again*. Now be very reverent of the will of the gods.

Further: Whatever silver, gold, garments or bronze implements of the gods you hold, you are *merely their* caretakers. You have no right to the silver, gold, garments, *and* bronze implements of the gods, and none whatsoever to the things that are in the gods' houses. They belong to the god alone. Be very careful and let no temple official have silver *or* gold. Let him not carry it on his own body, and let him not make it into an ornament for his wife *or* his children. But if they give him silver, gold, garments, *and* bronze implements as a gift from the palace, let them be specified: So-and-so, the king has given it to him. How much its weight is, let also be set down. Furthermore let it be set down thus: At such-and-such a festival have they given it to him. Let also the witnesses be set down at the end: When they gave it to him, so-and-so and so-and-so were present. Furthermore let him not leave it in his house; let him offer it for sale. But when he sells it, let him not sell it in a secret place; let the Hittite lords be present and look on. Let what *anyone* buys be listed on a tablet and let them seal it. And when the king comes up to Hattusa, let him take it *the tablet* up to the palace and let them seal it. If he puts them up for sale on his own, he is liable to the death penalty. He who does not put up for sale silver, gold, garments, *or* implements of bronze in the same way *as here described*, also he who receives it and hides it and does not bring it to the king's court, both of them are liable to the death penalty, they shall both be killed. They are [disagreeable] to the gods. There shall in no circumstances be recourse for them.

Further: You who are temple officials, if you do not celebrate the festivals at the time proper for the festivals and *if* you celebrate the festival of spring in the autumn, or *if*—when in the course of time a festival is about to be celebrated—he who is to perform it comes to you, the priests, the anointed, the mothers-of-god, [and] to the temple officials and embraces your knees *saying*: The harvest is before me, or arranging for *my* marriage, or a journey, or some other business. Do me a favor and let me finish that business first. But when that business of mine is finished, I shall perform the festival as prescribed—do not yield to a man's whim, let him not [take precedence] *of the gods*. You must not make a deal of the gods' pleasure. Should with you a man [take precedence] *of the gods* and should you make a deal for yourselves, the gods will seek to take revenge on you in the future. They will hold a grudge against you, yourselves, your wives, your children *and* your servants. So act only according to the pleasure of the gods! And you will eat bread, drink water, and establish a family. But do not act according to the pleasure of a man. Do not sell the death penalty, but do not buy the death penalty either.

Further: You who are temple officials, be very careful with respect to the precinct. At nightfall promptly go to be in *the temple*; eat *and* drink, and if the desire for a woman [overcomes] anyone, let him sleep with a woman. But as long as . . . let him [stay] and let [everyone] promptly come up to spend the night in the temple. Whoever is a temple official, all high priests, minor priests, anointed or whoever else is allowed to cross the threshold of the gods, let *them* not fail to spend the night in the temple one by one. Furthermore, there shall be watchmen employed by night who shall patrol all night through. Outside the enclosure guards shall watch, inside the temples shall the temple officials patrol all night through and they shall not sleep. Night by night one of the high priests shall be in charge of the patrols. Furthermore, someone of those who are priests shall be in charge of the gate of the temple and guard the temple. In his own house no one *of these* shall spend the night with his wife. Whomsoever they will find down in his house, it will be a capital offense for him. Guard the temple very carefully and do not sleep. *Responsibility for* the precinct shall be divided among yourselves. He who commits an offense with respect to the precinct shall be killed; he shall not be pardoned.

If anyone has some *official* duty to perform in Hattusa, and *either* a priest *or* an anointed is to admit people who are accompanied by guards, he will admit those too. If a guard is assigned to anyone, he may also enter the enclosure. He must not speak thus: I am guarding the house of my god, but I shall not go in there. If there is some talk of enmity, *namely* that someone will undertake to defile Hattusa and *the guards* at the outer wall do not recognize him, but the temple officials recognize him inside, the guard shall definitely go after him. *In* such *situation the* guard must not fail to spend the night with his god. If he fails however, in case they do not kill him, they shall humiliate him. Naked—there shall be no garment on his body—he shall bring three times water from the Labarnas's cistern to the house of his god. Such shall be his humiliation.

Further: O priests, anointed, mothers-of-gods *and* temple officials! Some [troublemaker] may rise in the temple or another sacred building. If he rises in the temple and causes a quarrel and thereby interferes with a festival, they shall interfere with him. Let him celebrate that festival with the usual expenditure of sheep, bread *and* beer, he must not even omit the thin loaf. Whoever fails *to provide* it and does not celebrate a fully set festival, it shall be a great offense for him and he shall make up for the festival. So be very careful with a quarrel.

Further: Be very careful with the matter of fire. If there is a festival in the temple, guard the fire carefully. When night falls, quench well with water whatever fire remains on the hearth. But if there is any flame in isolated spots and *also* dry wood, *if* he who is to quench it becomes criminally negligent in the temple—even if only the temple is destroyed, but Hattusa and the king's property is not destroyed—he who commits the crime will perish together with his descendants. Of those who are in the temple not one is to be spared; together with their descendants they shall perish. So for your own good be very careful in the matter of fire.

Further: You who are kitchen servants of all the gods, cupbearers, tablemen, cooks, bakers, *or* vintners, be very careful with respect to the gods' mood. Spend much reverent care upon the gods' sacrificial loaves *and* libation bowls. The place where the bread is broken shall be swept *and* scrubbed; *the regulations concerning* the threshold shall be enforced for pigs and dogs. As to yourselves, you shall be bathed and dressed in clean garments. Furthermore, your *body* hair and your nails shall be removed. Let the mood of the gods not befall you. If a pig *or* a dog somehow approaches the implements of wood or bitumen that you have, and the kitchen servant does not discard it, but gives the god to eat from an unclean *vessel*, to such a man the gods will give dung *and* urine to eat *and* to drink. Whoever is going to sleep with a woman, he shall go to that woman in the same condition in which he performs a rite for the gods and gives the god his portion to eat and to drink. Furthermore, [at] . . . , as soon as the sun is up, he shall at once take a bath; and in the morning, at the time when the gods eat, he shall promptly be present. But, if he omits *to do so*, it will be a sin for him. Whoever sleeps with a woman, if his superior *or* his chief constrains *him*, he shall say so. If he himself does not dare tell him, he shall tell his fellow servant and shall bathe anyway. But if he knowingly postpones it and without having bathed approaches the gods' sacrificial loaves *and* libation bowl in an unclean condition, or *if* his fellow servant knows about him—namely that he placed himself first—but nevertheless conceals it, *if* afterward it becomes known, they are liable to the capital penalty; both of them shall be killed.

[Further: You who are the plowmen of the gods] . . . The young animals that you, the plowmen, are supposed to have ready, have them promptly ready at the correct time. Before a man has eaten from them, carry them promptly to the presence of the gods; let the gods not wait for them. If you delay them, you commit a sin. They will consult the oracles about you, and just as the gods, your lords, direct, so they will do to you. They will fine you an ox and ten sheep and will pacify the mind of the gods.

Further: If you plant grain, and if the priest does not send you a man to plant the seed, you shall manage by yourselves. Should you plant much, but tell the priest *that* it *was* little, or should the gods' field be thriving, but the field of the plowmen be barren and you call the gods' field yours, but your field that of the god, or should you when you store the grain declare one half, but conceal the other half and should you proceed to divide it afterward among yourselves and should it afterward become known—you may get away with appropriating it from a man, but you cannot appropriate it from a god—you will commit a sin. They will take all the grain away from you and put it in the magazines of the gods.

Further: You who hold the plow-oxen of [the gods], if you sell a plow-ox, or kill it and consume it, *if* you appropriate it for yourselves *while it belongs* to the god *saying*: It died from emaciation, or it broke *its legs*, or it ran away, or the bull gored it—and consume it yourselves, and it afterward becomes known, you will replace that ox. If however it does not become known, you will go before the god. If you are acquitted, *it is due to* your patron god; if you are convicted, it is considered a capital sin for you.

Further: You who are the gods' cowherds *and* the gods' shepherds, if there is a rite for any god at the time of bearing young and you are supposed to have ready for him either a calf, a lamb, a kid or [choice animals], do not delay them! Have them ready at the right time; do not let the gods wait for them. Before a man eats of the young animals, bring it promptly to the gods. Or if there is a festival of the cup for any god, *even* while they repair the cup, do not allow it to lapse; celebrate it for him. If you do not bring the young animals promptly to the gods, but eat first of them yourselves or send them to your superiors, but it afterward becomes known, it is considered a capital sin for you. If it does not become known—at whatever time you will bring them, you will bring them before the god with these words: If we have given this young animal to ourselves first, or have given it to our superiors, or to our wives, our children or to anyone else, we have offended the gods' feelings. Then you will drink dry the drinking vessel of the god of life. If you are found innocent, *it is due to* your patron god; but if you are found guilty, you will perish together with your wives *and* your children.

Further: If you ever make a selection *of animals* and they drive them up to the gods, your lords, the cowherd and the shepherd shall go with that selection. In the same condition in which they are selected from the pen *and* the fold, shall they bring them to the gods. On the road they must not exchange them. But if any cowherd or shepherd does wrong on the road, exchanges either a fattened ox or a fattened sheep, or makes a deal or kills it and they eat it up, and put in its place an emaciated *animal*, and it become known, it is considered a capital sin for them; they have taken the gods' choice morsel. But if it does not become known, whenever they arrive they shall take the rhyton of the god of life from the cult stand, and while doing so they shall declare as follows: If we have for ourselves withheld from the mouth of the gods their *choice* morsel, and have given it to ourselves, or *if* we have sold it for ourselves, or if we have exchanged it, made a deal and substituted in its place an emaciated *animal*, then do you, O god, pursue us together with our wives *and* our children on account of your own *choice* morsel!

#37: Dagan Festival of Emar
(Hallo and Younger, *Context of Scripture*, 1:435–36)

An important Syrian ritual has come to light in recent decades from the northwest Mesopotamian city of Emar.[5] Of several ritual texts found at Emar, the so-called ZUKRU festival is perhaps the most interesting to students of the Old Testament. The ZUKRU is the earliest Syrian example of an autumnal New Year festival, evoking comparisons with the Israelite feasts of unleavened bread and booths (unlike the Babylonian AKITU festival during the spring; see reading 38). Essentially, the ZUKRU marks a new beginning in which the city of Emar is redevoted to its deity, Dagan. The festival observes a true sabbatical

year, since the whole seventh year was set apart for the festival, reminiscent of Israel's sabbatical year (Leviticus 25:1–7). Also of interest in the reading presented here is Dagan's passage between upright stones outside the city, which appears to reestablish his rule over the city.

During the next year, in the first month, on the fourteenth day, they distribute the enclosed lambs to the gods.

On the next day, the fifteenth or Shaggar-*day*, they bring out Dagan lord of the firstborn along with all the gods and the SHASHABEYANATU spirits in procession to the Gate of the Upright Stones.

Dagan's face is covered for his departure.

They give to the gods the offerings as prescribed on the tablet.

They bring out in procession Dagan the very father and Shaggar on the same day.

Also, the Shaggar-*day* breads for all Emar go back up.

Just before evening, Dagan passes between the upright stones.

They cover his face.

In the Battle Gate they perform the rites just as for the consecration day.

The breads and the meat that were before the gods go back up into the town.

On the sixth day they distribute the enclosed lambs to the gods, just as *mentioned* previously.

On the seventh day Dagan, along with all the gods and the SHASHABEYANATU spirits, goes out in procession, his face covered.

They give the ritual requirements to the gods just as for the day *mentioned* previously.

All the meat and breads, everything that they eat, from the [seven] days and from between the upright stones they take up and [place] in return.

Nothing goes back up into the midst of the town.

After the fire, just [before evening] . . .

They uncover Dagan's face.

The wagon of Dagan passes between the upright stones.

He proceeds to Ninurta, [whom they have] mount the wagon with him].

They perform the rites just as for the day *mentioned* previously.

Reconstructed gate of Ishtar from Babylon. (Bildarchiv Preussischer Kulturbesitz)

#38: Temple Program for the New Year Festival at Babylon
(*ANET* 331–34)

"ENUMA ELISH" (reading 6) was recited annually during a twelve-day ritual in ancient Babylonia around the time of the vernal equinox. This New Year festival (also known as the AKITU festival, a name that apparently was given to rural festivals in southern Mesopotamia since the third millennium) was the high point of the religious calendar. The reading presented here prescribes the rituals involved in this festival, including the cleansing of the temple and the king's role in "taking the hand of Bel" (Marduk). Later, the king kneels before the deity and proclaims that he has not sinned by neglecting the sacred rites or by allowing Babylon to fall. The king also receives a slap across the face, which is expiatory only if it brings tears.

On the second day of the month Nisannu, two hours of the night *remaining*, the URIGALLU priest shall arise and wash with river water. He shall enter into the presence of the god Bel, and he shall . . . a linen GADALU in front of Bel. He shall recite the following prayer.

O Bel, who has no equal when angry,
O Bel, excellent king, lord of the
   countries,
who makes the great gods friendly,
O Bel, who fells the mighty with his
   glance,
lord of the kings, light of humankind,
   who divides the portions—
O Bel, your dwelling is the city of
   Babylon, your tiara is the *neighboring*
   city of Borsippa,
broad heaven is the totality of your liver.
O Bel, with your eyes you see all things,
[with] your oracles you [verify] the
   oracles,
[with] your glance you hand down the
   law.
[With] your . . . you . . . the mighty;
when you look *at them*, you grant them
   mercy;
you show them the light, *and* they speak
   of your valor.
Lord of the countries, light of the IGIGI
   gods *who* bless—
who *does not speak* of you, does not
   speak of your valor?
Who does not speak of your glory, does
   not glorify your sovereignty?
Lord of the countries, who dwells in the
   temple Eudul, who grasps the hand
   of the fallen,
grant mercy to your city, Babylon!
Turn your face to the temple Esagil,
   your house!
Establish the liberty of the people of
   Babylon, your subordinates.

Colophon: Twenty-one lines *of writing*: secrets of the temple Esagil. [Whoever reveres] the god Bel shall show *them* to nobody except the URIGALLU priest of the temple Ekua.

[After] he speaks the recitation, he shall [open the gate]. The ERIBBITI priests [shall arise] and perform their rites, in the traditional manner, [before] the deities Bel and Beltiya. [The KALU priests and the] singers *shall do* likewise.

(gap)

. . . he shall place . . . ; a seal . . . in the tiara of the god Anu . . . of the second day, upon . . . he shall place . . . before them. Three times he shall speak . . .

The evil enemies . . . who in their strength . . . this that in . . . of the exorcism . . . because the enemy and the bandit . . . the great lord, Marduk . . . has uttered a curse that cannot be altered . . . has decreed a fate that cannot be withdrawn . . . who . . . the god Bel, my lord; who . . . the lord of the countries, who . . . the city of Babylon. In the middle of the earth . . . who . . . the temple Eudul, the purification of . . . like heaven and earth . . . who extracts . . . the temples of . . . the forgetting of their rites . . . who overwhelms . . . the people dwelling in . . . the maidservants . . . of the city Babylon . . . who . . . the temple Eudul, he bound *all* of you . . . *all* of you dwell.

(gap)

On the [third] day of the month Nisannu, [at . . . o'clock, the URIGALLU priest] shall arise [and] wash with [. . . He shall speak the following] prayer to the god Bel.

(gap)

He shall open the doors. [All the ERIBBITI priests] shall enter and perform [their rites in the traditional manner. The KALU priests and the singers shall do likewise].

(gap)

When it is three hours after sunrise, [he shall call] a metalworker and give him precious stones and gold [from] the treasury of the god Marduk to make two images for *the ceremonies of* the sixth day *of Nisannu*. He shall call a woodworker and give him *some* cedar and tamarisk *pieces*. He shall call a goldsmith and give him *some* gold. From the third day *of the month Nisannu* to the sixth day, *pieces of meat* from *the slaughtered sheep offered* before the god Bel *are to be distributed as follows*: the *tail* to the metalworker, the breast to the goldsmith, the thigh to the woodworker, the ribs to the weaver. These *pieces of meat* from *the slaughtered sheep offered* before the god Bel shall be delivered to the URIGALLU priest for the artisans.

Those two images *that the artisans are to make* shall be seven finger-*widths* high. One *shall be made* of cedar, one of tamarisk. [Four] DUSHU stones shall be mounted in settings of gold weighing [four] shekels. [One image] shall hold in its left hand a snake *made* of cedar, raising its right [hand] to the god Nabu. The second *image* shall hold in its [left hand] a scorpion, raising its right hand [to the god] Nabu. They shall be clothed in red garments, [bound] in the middle [with] a palm [branch]. Until the sixth day *of the month Nisannu*, [they shall be placed] in the house of the god Madan. [Food] *from* the tray of the god Madan shall be presented to them. On the sixth day *of the month* when the god Nabu reaches the temple Ehursagtila, the slaughterer . . . shall strike off their heads. Then, a [fire] having been started in the presence of the god Nabu, they shall be thrown into it.

On the fourth day of the month Nisannu, three-and-one-third hours of the night *remaining*, the URIGALLU priest shall arise and wash with river water. A linen GADALU he shall . . . in front of the god Bel and the goddess Beltiya. He shall recite the following prayer, while lifting his hand, to the god Bel.

Powerful master of the IGIGI gods,
    exalted among the great gods,
lord of the world, king of the gods,
    divine Marduk, who establishes the
    plan,
important, elevated, exalted, superior,
who holds kingship, grasps lordship,
bright light, god Marduk, who dwells in
    the temple Eudul,
. . . who sweeps the enemy's land,

  (gap)

Who . . . heaven, heaps up the earth,
who measures the waters of the sea,
    cultivates the fields,
who dwells in the temple Eudul; lord of
    Babylon, exalted Marduk,
who decrees the fates of all the gods,
who turns over the pure scepter to the
    king who reveres him—
I am the URIGALLU priest of the temple
    Ekua, who [blesses] you.
To your city, Babylon, grant release!

To Esaggil, your temple, grant mercy!
At your exalted command, O lord of the
    great gods,
let light be set before the people of
    Babylon.

He shall *then* withdraw from the presence of the god Bel and recite the following prayer to the goddess Beltiya.

Powerful, goddess, *most* exalted of the
    female divinities,
Sarpanitu, who shines brilliantly *among*
    the stars, who dwells in the temple
    Eudul,
. . . of the goddesses, whose garment is
    bright light,
who . . . heaven, heaps up the earth,
Sarpanitu, whose position is exalted,
bright, Beltiya, sublime and elevated—
there is none like her among the female
    divinities—
who brings complaints, who defends,
who impoverishes the rich, who causes
    the poor to become wealthy,
who fells the enemy who does not fear
    her divinity,
who releases the prisoner, grasps the
    hand of the fallen—
[bless] the slave who [blesses] you!
Decree the destiny for the king who
    reveres you!
Grant life to the people of Babylon, who
    are your subordinates,
defend them in the presence of Marduk,
    king of the gods!
May *the people* speak your praise,
    magnify your lordship,
speak of your heroism, exalt your name.
Grant mercy to the servant who blesses
    you,
take his hand *when he is* in great
    difficulty and need!
Present him with life when he is sick
    and in pain,
so that he may constantly walk in
    happiness and joy,
speaking of your heroism to all people.

He shall *then* go out to the Exalted Courtyard, turn to the north and bless the temple

Esagil three times with the blessing: Iku-star, Esagil, image of heaven and earth. He shall *then* open the doors. All the ERIBBITI priests shall enter and perform their rites in the traditional manner. The KALU priests and the singers *shall do* likewise.

When this is done, [and after] the second meal of the late afternoon, the URIGALLU priest of the temple Ekua shall recite *while lifting his hand* to the god Bel the *composition entitled* "ENUMA ELISH." While he recites "ENUMA ELISH" to the god Bel, the front of the tiara of the god Anu and the resting place of the god Enlil shall be covered.

On the fifth day of the month Nisannu, four hours of the night *remaining*, the URIGALLU priest shall arise and wash with water from the Tigris and Euphrates. [He shall enter into the presence of the god Bel, and] he shall . . . a linen GAGALU in front of the god Bel and the goddess Beltiya. He shall recite the following prayer [to Bel].

My lord, is he not my lord?
My lord, . . . is not his name My Lord?
my lord, . . . my lord, king of the
  countries,
my lord, . . . my lord, . . .
Is it not my lord who gives, my lord
  who . . . ?
My lord, . . . my lord, . . .
My lord, . . . my lord, . . .
My lord, . . . my lord, who dwells in the
  temple Eudul,
My lord, . . . my lord, . . .
My lord, . . . my lord, who gives,
My lord, . . . my lord, who dwells in the
  chapel,
My lord, . . . my lord, he is my lord.
God of heaven and earth, who decrees
  the fates—my lord, be calm!
The star Musirkeshda, who carries the
  royal scepter and circle, my lord—my
  lord, be calm!
The Eridu star, the possessor of wisdom,
  my lord—my lord, be calm!
Asari, who grants the gift of cultivation,
  my lord—my lord, be calm!
Planet Jupiter, who carries the [sign] for
  all, my lord—my lord, be calm!

Planet Mercury, who causes it to rain,
  my lord—my lord, be calm!
Planet Saturn, star of justice and
  righteousness, my lord—my lord, be
  calm!
Planet Mars, fierce flame, my lord—my
  lord, be calm!
The star Sirius, who measures the
  waters of the sea, my lord—my lord,
  be calm!
The star Shupa, lord of the Enlil gods,
  my lord—my lord, be calm!
The star Nenegar, who was self-created,
  my lord—my lord, be calm!
The star Numushda, who causes the
  rains to [continue], my lord—my
  lord, be calm!
The [Sting]-of-the-Scorpion star, who . . .
  the breast of the ocean, my lord—my
  lord, be calm!
Sun, light of the world, my lord—my
  lord, be calm!
Moon, who brings the darkness, my
  lord—my lord, be calm!
My lord is my god, my lord is my lord.
  Who, except for you, is lord?

To the goddess he shall recite the following prayer.

My [merciful] lady—my lady, be calm!
My lady, who does not become angry,
  who is calm,
my lady, who gives, my lady, who is so
  very good,
my lady, . . . my lady, who is so very
  good,
the [calm] lady, who does not become
  angry, my lady, who confers [gifts],
my lady, *who receives* prayer, my lady,
  who confers [gifts],
Damkianna, mistress of heaven and
  earth, whose name is My Lady,
planet Venus, who shines brilliantly
  among the stars, whose name is My
  Lady,
the star Ban, who fells the mighty,
  whose name is My Lady.
The star Uz, who views heaven, whose
  name is My Lady,

the star Hegala, the star of abundance,
  whose name is My Lady,
the star Baltesha, the star of
  [sensuousness], whose name is My
  Lady,
the star Margidda, the bond of heaven,
  whose name is My Lady,
the star Eru, who creates sperm, whose
  name is My Lady,
the star Ninmah, who makes a gift of
  life, whose name is My Lady,
My lady, her name is My Lady. Is not
  her name My Lady?

After the recitation has been recited, he shall open the doors. All the ERIBBITI priests shall *then* enter and perform their rites in the traditional manner. The KALU priests and the singers *shall do* likewise.

When it is two hours after sunrise, after the trays of the god Bel and the goddess Beltiya have been set, he shall call a MASHMASHU priest to purify the temple and sprinkle water, *taken from* a cistern of the Tigris and a cistern of the Euphrates, on the temple. He shall beat the kettledrum inside the temple. He shall have a censer and a torch brought into the temple. [He] shall [remain] in the courtyard; he shall not enter the sanctuary of the deities Bel and Beltiya. When the purification of the temple is completed, he shall enter the temple Ezida, into the sanctuary of the god Nabu, with censer, torch, and EGUBBU vessel to purify the temple, and he shall sprinkle water *from* the Tigris and Euphrates cisterns on the sanctuary. He shall smear all the doors of the sanctuary with cedar [resin]. In the court of the sanctuary, he shall place a silver censer, upon which he shall mix aromatic ingredients and cypress. He shall call a slaughterer to decapitate a ram, the body of which the MASHMASHU priest shall use in performing the KUPPURU ritual for the temple. He shall recite the incantations for exorcising the temple. He shall purify the whole sanctuary, including its environs, and shall remove the censer. The MASHMASHU priest shall lift up the body of the aforementioned ram and proceed to the river. Facing west, he shall throw the body of the ram into the river. He shall *then* go out into the open country. The slaughterer shall do the

same thing with the ram's head. The MASH-MASHU priest and the slaughterer shall go out into the open country. As long as the god Nabu is in Babylon, they shall not enter Babylon, but stay in the open country from the fifth to the twelfth day *of the month Nisannu*. The URIGALLU priest of the temple Ekua shall not view the purification of the temple. If he does view *it*, he is no *longer* pure. After the purification of the temple, when it is three-and-one-third hours after sunrise, the URIGALLU priest of the temple Ekua shall go out and call all the artisans. They shall bring forth the Golden Heaven from the treasury of the god Marduk and [use it to] cover the temple Ezida, the sanctuary of the god Nabu, from *its* . . . to the foundation of the temple. The URIGALLU priest and the artisans shall recite the following [loud] recital.

They purify the temple,
the god Marduk from Eridu, who dwells
  in the temple Eudul,
the god Kusug . . . ,
the deity Ningirim, who listens to
  prayers,
the god Marduk purifies the temple,
the god Kusug draws the plans,
the deity Ningirim casts the spell.
Go forth, evil that happens to be in this
  temple!
May the god Bel kill you, evil demon!
Wherever you are, be suppressed!
All the artisans shall *then* go out to the
  gate.

. . . [hours] . . . the day, the URIGALLU priest [shall enter] into the presence of the god Bel, and shall . . . [in front of Bel]. He shall [prepare] the golden tray, placing upon it [roasted] meat, . . . twelve of the usual [loaves], a gold . . . filled with salt, a gold . . . filled with honey, . . . four gold dishes. He shall place a gold censer . . . in front of the tray; aromatic ingredients and cypress . . . He shall make a libation of wine . . . He shall recite the following.

[Marduk], exalted among the gods,
[who dwells in the temple Esagil], who
  creates the laws,

[who] . . . to the great gods,
. . . I praise your heroism.
[May] your heart [be sympathetic] to
whoever seizes your hands.
[In Esizkur], the temple of prayer,
[in] . . . , your place, may he raise up his
head.

After he recites the [recitation], he shall clear the tray. He shall summon all the artisans and shall turn the whole tray over to them to bring to the god Nabu. The artisans shall take it, and in . . . they shall go. When Nabu arrives [at] . . . , they shall . . . it to Nabu. [When] they have set the tray before the god Nabu, they shall lift up the [loaves] *that are on* the tray as soon as Nabu [leaves] the ship called Iddahedu, and then on the tray . . . They shall bring water *for washing* the king's hands and then shall accompany him [to the temple Esagil]. The artisans shall go out to the gate. When *the king* reaches [the presence of the god Bel], the URIGALLU priest shall leave *the sanctuary* and take away the scepter, the circle, and the sword [from the king]. He shall bring them [before the god Bel] and place them [on] a chair. He shall leave *the sanctuary* and strike the king's cheek. He shall place the . . . behind him. He shall accompany *the king* into the presence of the god Bel . . . he shall drag *him by* the ears and make him bow down to the ground . . . The king shall speak the following *only* once: I did [not] sin, lord of the countries. I was not neglectful *of the requirements* of your godship. [I did not] destroy Babylon; I did not command its overthrow [I did not]

. . . the temple Esagil, I did not forget its rites. [I did not] rain blows on the cheek of a subordinate . . . I did [not] humiliate them. [I watched out] for Babylon; I did not smash its walls . . . Have no fear . . . that the god Bel . . . The god Bel [will listen to] your prayer . . . he will magnify your lordship . . . he will exalt your kingship . . . On the day of the ESHESHU festival, do . . . in the festival of the Opening of the Gate, purify [your] hands . . . day and night . . . [The god Bel], whose city is Babylon . . . , whose temple is Esagil . . . whose dependents are the people of Babylon . . . The god Bel will bless you . . . forever. He will destroy your enemy, fell your adversary. After *the* URIGALLU *priest* says *this*, the king shall regain his [composure] . . . The scepter, circle, and sword [shall be restored] to the king. He shall strike the king's cheek. If, when [he strikes] the king's cheek, the tears flow, *it means that* the god Bel is friendly; if no tears appear, the god Bel is angry: the enemy will rise up and bring about his downfall.

When *these things* have been done, at [sunset], the URIGALLU priest shall tie together forty reeds—each three cubits long, uncut, unbroken, straight—using a palm branch as the bond. A hole shall be dug in the Exalted Courtyard and he shall put *the bundle into it.* He shall put *in it* honey, cream, first-quality oil . . . He shall . . . a white bull [before the hole]. The king shall [set all this afire] with a burning reed. The king [and the URIGALLU priest shall recite] the following recitation.

O divine bull, brilliant light that [lights up the darkness].

Part

2

Historical Books

---

8 Royal Records from Mesopotamia

The nations of Mesopotamia produced numerous inscriptions detailing the king's military exploits and building projects. These documents invite comparison and contrast with the Old Testament historical books, which have yielded striking similarities with history-writing in the ancient Near East. In general, the historiography preserved in the Old Testament is of a type rarely produced elsewhere in the ancient world.[1] This is true partly because Israel's historical sources were focused on the nation as a whole, in contradistinction to Mesopotamian sources, which were devoted to the activities of the king. Only in Israel—where nation took precedence over king—could true historiography take place.[2]

#39: Tiglath-pileser I
(Grayson, *Assyrian Royal Inscriptions*, 2.5–20)

An inscription preserving campaign reports from the reign of King Tiglath-pileser I of Assyria (1114–1076 B.C.) represents a new literary genre (royal annals) that was used by many of his successors.[3] The reading presented here is of interest to Old Testament scholars because it is the first of many such royal annals recently compared to Joshua 9–12.[4]

God Ashur, great lord, who properly administers all the gods, granter of scepter and crown, founder of sovereignty; god Enlil, lord, king of all the Anunnaku gods, father of the gods, lord of the lands; god Sin, wise one, lord of the lunar disk, lofty divine crescent; god Shamash, judge of heaven *and* underworld, who espies the enemy's treachery, who exposes the wicked; god Adad, hero, who storms over hostile regions, mountains, *and* seas; god Ninurta, valiant one, slayer of criminal and foe, fulfiller of hearts' desires; goddess Ishtar, foremost among the gods, mistress of tumult, who adorns battles.

Great gods, managers of heaven *and* underworld, whose attack means conflict and strife, who make great the sovereignty of Tiglath-pileser, beloved prince, your select one, attentive shepherd, whom you chose in the steadfastness of your hearts; upon him you set the exalted crown, you grandly established him for sovereignty over the land of the god Enlil, to him you granted leadership, supremacy, *and* valor, you pronounced forever his destiny of dominion as powerful and *the destiny* of his priestly progeny for service in Ehursagkurkurra.

Tiglath-pileser, strong king, unrivaled king of the universe, king of the four quarters, king of all princes, lord of lords, chief herdsman, king of kings, attentive purification priest, to whom by command of the god Shamash the holy scepter was given and who had complete authority over the people, subjects of the god Enlil, faithful shepherd, whose name was called over the princes, exalted bishop, whose weapons the god Ashur has sharpened and whose name he has pronounced eternally for control of the four quarters, capturer of distant districts to borders above and below, radiant day whose brilliance overwhelms the regions, splendid flame that covers the hostile land like a rain storm and, by the command of the god Enlil, having no rival defeats the enemy of the god Ashur.

The god Ashur *and* the great gods who magnify my sovereignty, who granted as my lot power and strength, commanded me to extend the border of their land. They placed in my hands their mighty weapons, deluge in battle. I gained control over lands, mountains, cult centers, and princes who were hostile to Ashur and I subdued their districts. I vied with sixty crowned heads and achieved victory over them in battle. I have neither rival in strife nor equal in conflict. I added territory to Assyria *and* people to its population. I extended the border of my land and ruled over all their lands.

In my accession year: twenty thousand MUSHKU with their five kings, who had held for fifty years the lands Alzu and Puru-lumzu—bearers of tribute and tithe to the god Ashur my lord—the MUSHKU, whom no king had ever repelled, being confident of their strength they came down *and* captured the land Kadmuhu. With the support of the god Ashur, my lord, I put my chariotry and army in readiness *and*, not bothering about the rear guard, I traversed the rough terrain of Mount Kashiyari. I fought with their twenty thousand men-at-arms and five kings in the land Kadmuhu. I brought about their defeat. Like a storm demon I piled up the corpses of their warriors on the battlefield *and* made their blood flow into the hollows and plains of the mountains. I cut off their heads *and* stacked them like grain piles around their cities. I brought out their booty, property, *and* possessions without number. I took the remaining six thousand of their troops who had fled from my weapons *and* submitted to me and regarded them as people of my land.

At that time I marched to the unsubmissive land Kadmuhu, which had withheld tribute and impost from the god Ashur, my lord. I conquered the entire land of Kadmuhu. I brought out their booty, property, *and* possessions. Their cities I burnt, razed, *and* destroyed. The remainder of the *inhabitants of the* land Kadmuhu, who had fled from my weapons *and* crossed over to the city Shereshu, which is on the opposite bank of the Tigris, made that city their stronghold. Taking my chariots and warriors I hacked through the rough mountain range and difficult paths with copper picks and made a good way for the passage of my chariots and troops. I crossed the Tigris *and* conquered their fortified city, Shereshu. I laid out like grain heaps *the corpses of* their men-at-arms in the mountains. I made their blood flow in the Tigris and the plains of the mountains. At that

time I laid low like sheep with the army of the land Kadmuhu the army of the Paphu, which had come to the aid and assistance of the land Kadmuhu. I built up mounds with the corpses of their men-at-arms on mountain ledges. I allowed the River Name to carry the bodies of their warriors out to the Tigris. I captured in battle their king, Kili-Teshub son of Kali-Teshub, who is called Errupi. I carried off his wives, his natural sons, his clan, one hundred eighty copper kettles, five bronze bathtubs, together with the *people's* gods, gold and silver, the best of their property. I brought out their booty *and* possessions. I burnt, razed, *and* destroyed that city and its palace.

With regard to the city Urratinash, their stronghold situated in the land Panaru, the terror, fear, and splendor of the god Ashur my lord overwhelmed them. To save their lives they took their gods and flew like birds to ledges on high mountains. Taking my chariotry and army I crossed the Tigris. Shadi-Teshub son of Hattuhu, king of the city Urratinash, submitted to me in his own land in order to avoid conquest. I took his natural sons and his family as hostages. He brought to me as tribute and tax sixty copper kettles, bronze bathtubs, and large bronze mugs, together with one hundred twenty men, cattle, and sheep. I accepted his *tribute* and spared his life. I imposed upon him forever the heavy yoke of my dominion. I completely conquered the extensive land Kadmuhu and subdued it at my feet.

At that time I donated to the god Ashur one bronze mug *and* one bronze bathtub from the booty and tribute of the land Kadmuhu. I gave to the god Adad, who loves me, sixty copper kettles together with their gods.

With the onslaught of my fierce weapons by means of which Ashur, the lord, gave me strength and authority I took with thirty of my chariots escorting my aggressive *personnel carriers*, my warriors trained for successful combat. I marched to the land Ishdish *where* rebellious *and* unsubmissive people *lived*. Riding in my chariot when the way was smooth and going by foot when the way was rough, I passed through the rough terrain of mighty mountains. In Mount Aruma, a difficult area that was impassable for my chariots, I abandoned my chariotry. Taking the lead of my warriors I climbed victoriously with the aggressiveness of a viper over the perilous mountain ledges. I destroyed the land Ishdish *so that it looked* like ruin hills *created by* the deluge. Their warriors I laid low in battle like sheep. I carried off their booty, possessions, and property. I burned all their cities. I imposed upon them *the obligation to provide* hostages, tribute, and taxes.

Tiglath-pileser, valiant man, opener of remote regions in the mountains, subduer of the unsubmissive, overwhelmer of all fierce *enemies*:

I subdued the rebellious and unsubmissive Shubaru. I imposed the heavy yoke of my dominion upon the lands Alzu and Purulumzu, which had abandoned *the practice of paying* tribute and tax. Annually they send tribute and tax into my presence at my city Ashur. As soon as with my valor, by means of which the god Ashur *my* lord had placed in my hand the strong weapon that subdues the unsubmissive, he commanded me to extend the border of his land, four thousand KASKU *and* URUMU, unsubmissive troops of the Hittites—who had seized by force the cities of the land Shubartu, which were vassals of the god Ashur my lord—heard of my coming to the land Shubartu. The splendor of my valor overwhelmed them. Fearing battle they submitted to me. I took them together with their property and one hundred twenty chariots *and* harnessed horses. I regarded them as people of my land.

With my valorous onslaught I marched a second time to the land Kadmuhu. I conquered all their cities *and* carried off their booty, possessions, and property. I burnt, razed, *and* destroyed their cities. Now the remainder of their troops, which had taken fright at my fierce weapons and had been cowering in the face of my strong and belligerent attack, took to secure heights in rough mountainous terrain in order to save their lives. I climbed up after them to the peaks of high mountains and perilous mountain ledges where a man could not walk. They waged war, combat, and battle with me *and* I brought about their defeat. Like a storm demon I piled up the corpses of their warriors on mountain ledges *and* made their blood flow into the hollows and plains of the mountains. I brought down their booty, possessions, and property from the secure heights of the mountains. *Thus* I became lord of the entire land of Kadmuhu and added *it* to the borders of my land.

Tiglath-pileser, strong king, snare for the unsubmissive, overwhelmer in battle with criminals:

With the exalted strength of the god Ashur, my lord, the god Ashur, *my* lord commanded me to march to the land Haria and the army of the extensive Paphu in high mountains where no other king had ever gone. Putting my chariotry and army in readiness I took a rugged route between Mount Etnu and Mount Aya. In the high mountains, which *cut* like the blade of a dagger and which were impassable for my chariots, I put the chariots on *the soldiers'* necks *and thereby* passed through the difficult mountain range. All of the Paphu, their extensive army, joined together and aggressively they took up a position to wage war, combat, and battle in Mount Azu. I fought with them in rough mountainous terrain *and* brought about their defeat. I built up mounds with the bodies of their warriors in the plains of the mountain *and* made the blood of their warriors flow into the hollows and plains of the mountain. I stormed the cities that were on mountain ledges *and* conquered twenty-five cities of the land Haria, which lies at the foot of mounts Aya, Shuira, Etnu, Shezu, Shelgu, Arzanibiu, Urusu, and Anitku. I carried off their booty, possessions, and property. I burnt, razed, *and* destroyed their cities.

The land Adaush was frightened by my strong belligerent attack and abandoned their territory. They flew like birds to ledges on high mountains. *But* the splendor of Ashur, my lord, overwhelmed them and they came back down and submitted to me. I imposed upon them tribute and impost.

I destroyed the lands Saraush *and* Ammaush, which from ancient times had not known submission, *so that they looked* like ruin hills *created by* the deluge. I fought with their army in Mount Aruma and brought about their defeat. I laid out like grain heaps the corpses of their men-at-arms. I conquered their cities, took their gods, and brought out their booty, possessions, *and* property, I burnt, razed, *and* destroyed their cities *and* turned them into ruin hills. I imposed the heavy yoke of my dominion upon them *and* made them vassals of Ashur, my lord.

I conquered the rebellious and unsubmissive lands of Isua *and* Daria. I imposed upon them tribute and impost *and* made them vassals of the god Ashur, my lord.

With my prowess, with which I conquered enemies, I took my chariotry and army *and* crossed the Lower Zab. I conquered the lands Murattash *and* Saradaush, which are within the rough terrain of mounts Asaniu *and* Atuma. I butchered their troops like sheep. I conquered their fortified city Murattash within the first third of the day. I brought out their gods, their possessions, their property, sixty copper kettles, thirty talents of copper ore, the *outstanding property* of their palace, their booty. I burnt, razed, *and* destroyed that city.

At that time I gave that copper to the god Adad, great lord, the god who loves me.

With the mighty power of the god Ashur, my lord, I marched to the land Sugu of the land Habhu, *people* unsubmissive to the god Ashur my lord. I fought on foot with six thousand of their troops—the lands Himu, Luhu, Arirgu, Alamun, Nimnu, and all of the extensive Paphu—*I fought* with all those lands in Mount Hirihu, rough terrain that *cut* like the blade of a dagger. I brought about their defeat. I built up mounds with the *corpses of* their men-at-arms on mountain ledges *and* with the blood of their warriors I dyed Mount Hirihu red like red wool. I conquered the entire land of Sugu. I brought out twenty-five of their gods, their booty, their possessions, *and* their property. I burnt, razed, *and* destroyed all of their cities. The remainder of their troops submitted to me *and* I had mercy on them. I imposed upon them tribute and impost *and* regarded them as vassals of the god Ashur, my lord.

At that time I donated the twenty-five gods of those lands, my own booty that I had taken, to adorn the temple of the goddess Ninlil, beloved chief spouse of the god Ashur, my lord, *the temple of* the gods An *and* Adad, the *temple of* the Assyrian Ishtar, the temples of my city, Ashur, and the goddesses of my land.

Tiglath-pileser, strong king, conqueror of enemy regions, rival of all kings:

At that time, with the exalted might of the god Ashur, my lord, with the firm approval *through divination* of the god Shamash, the warrior, with the support of the great gods with which I have ruled properly in the four quarters and have no rival in battle nor equal in conflict, at the command of the god Ashur, *my* lord, I marched to the lands of distant kings, on the shore of the Upper Sea, which had not known submission. I pushed through rugged paths and perilous passes, the interior of which no king had previously known, blocked trails *and* unopened remote regions. Mounts Elama, Amadanu, Elhish, Sherabeli, Tarhuna, Terkahuli, Kisra, Tarhanabe, Elula, Hashtarae, Shahishara, Ubera, Miliadruni, Shulianzi, Nubanashe, and Sheshe, sixteen mighty mountains—*I rode* in my chariot over smooth terrain *and* I hacked out the rough terrain with copper picks. I cut down URUMU trees that grow in the mountains, *thereby* constructed good bridges for the passage of my army, *and* crossed the Euphrates. The king of the land Tummu, the king of the land Tunubu, the king of the land Tualu, the king of the land Dardaru, the king of the land Uzula, the king of the land Unzamunu, the king of the land Andiabu, the king of the land Piladarnu, the king of the land Adurginu, the king of the land Kulibarzinu, the king of the land Shinibirnu, the king of the land Himua, the king of the land Paiteru, the king of the land Uiram, the king of the land Shururia, the king of the land Abaenu, the king of the land Adaenu, the king of the land Kirinu, the king of the land Albaya, the king of the land Ugina, the king of the land Nazabia, the king of the land Abarsiunu, the king of the land Dayenu, altogether twenty-three kings of the lands Nairi combined their chariotry and army in their lands *and* advanced to wage war and combat. With the onslaught of my fierce weapons I approached them *and* destroyed their extensive army like a storm of the god Adad. I laid out like grain heaps the corpses of their warriors on the open country, the plains of the mountains, and the environs of their cities. I seized in battle one hundred twenty of their chariots with equipment. Sixty kings of the lands Nairi, including those who had come to their aid, I chased at arrowpoint as far as the Upper Sea. I conquered their great cult centers *and* brought out their booty, possessions, *and* property. I burnt, razed, *and* destroyed their cities *and* turned them into ruin hills. I brought back extensive herds of horses, mules, *and* donkeys—the livestock of their pastures—without number. I captured all of the kings of the lands Nairi alive. I had mercy on those kings and spared their lives. I released them from their bonds and fetters in the presence of the god Shamash, my lord, and made them swear by my great gods an oath of eternal vassaldom. I took their natural, royal, sons as hostages. I imposed upon them a tribute of twelve hundred horses *and* two thousand cattle. I allowed them to return to their lands.

I brought Seni, king of the land Dayenu, who had not been submissive to the god Ashur my lord, in bonds and fetters to my city Ashur. I had mercy on him and let him leave my city Ashur alive in order to proclaim the glory of the great gods. *Thus* I became lord of the complete extensive lands Nairi. Indeed all their kings I subdued at my feet.

In the course of that campaign I marched to the rebellious and unsubmissive city Milidia of the land Hanigalbat. Frightened by my strong belligerent attack they submitted to me and I had mercy on them. I did not storm that city *but* I took hostages. I imposed upon them as uninterrupted annual tribute one homer of lead ore.

Tiglath-pileser, daring *and* furious flame, the deluge in battle:

With the support of the god Ashur, my lord, I took my chariots and warriors *and* set off for the desert. I marched against the AHLAMU Arameans, enemies of the god Ashur, my lord. I plundered from the edge of the land Suhu to the city Carchemish of the land Hatti in a single day. I massacred them *and* carried back their booty, possessions, and goods without number. The rest of their troops, who were frightened by the fierce weapons of the god Ashur, my lord, crossed the Euphrates. I crossed the Euphrates after them in rafts *made*

of inflated goatskins. I conquered six of their cities at the foot of Mount Beshri, burnt, razed, *and* destroyed *them, and* brought their booty, possessions, and goods to my city Ashur.

Tiglath-pileser, who treads upon dangerous people, who lays low the unsubmissive, pacifier of all the rebellious:

The god Ashur, the lord, commanded me to conquer the land Musri and I took the way between mounts Elamuni, Tala, and Harusa. I conquered all the land Musri *and* laid low their warriors. I burnt, razed, *and* destroyed the cities. The troops of the Qumanu came to the aid of the land Musri. I fought with them in the mountains, *and* brought about their defeat. I confined them to one city, the city Arinu, which is at the foot of Mount Aisa. They submitted to me *and* I spared that city. I imposed upon them hostages, tribute, *and* more.

At that time all the Qumanu, who had agreed to assist the land Musri, mustered their entire territories and took up a position to do battle and conflict. With the onslaught of my fierce weapons I fought with their twenty thousand extensive troops at Mount Tala *and* brought about their defeat. I broke up their mighty force *and* pursued them in their retreat as far as Mount Harusa, which is before the land Musri. I spread out the corpses of their warriors on mountain ledges like *slaughtered* sheep *and* made their blood flow into the hollow and plains of the mountains. I conquered their great cult centers, burnt, razed, *and* destroyed *them* and turned *them* into ruin hills.

I overwhelmed the city Hunusu, their fortified city, *so that it looked* like a ruin hill *created by* the deluge. Violently I fought with their mighty army in city and mountain *and* brought about their defeat. I laid low their men-at-arms in the mountains like sheep. Like lambs I cut off their heads *and* made their blood flow into the hollows and plains of the mountains. *Thus* I conquered that city. I took their gods *and* brought out their possessions *and* property. I burnt the city. The three great walls that were constructed with baked brick and the entire city I razed, destroyed, turned into a ruin hill and strewed SIPU stones over it. I made bronze lightning bolts *and* inscribed on them *a description of* the conquest of the lands that with my god, my lord, I conquered *and a warning* not to occupy that city and not to rebuild its wall. On that *site* I built a house of baked brick and put inside those bronze lightning bolts.

With the support of the god Ashur, my lord, I took my chariotry and warriors *and* surrounded the city Kipshuna, their royal city. The king of the Qumanu was frightened of my strong and belligerent attack and submitted to me. I spared his life. I ordered him to destroy his great wall and towers of baked brick. He destroyed from top to bottom and turned it into a ruin hill. He deported *and I* received from him three hundred families, rebels in his midst who were not submissive to the god Ashur, my lord. I took hostages from him. I imposed upon him a tribute and demand that was larger than before. I entirely subdued the extensive Qumanu at my feet.

Altogether I conquered forty-two lands and their rulers from the other side of the Lower Zab in distant mountainous regions to the other side of the Euphrates, the Hittites, and the Upper Sea in the west—from my accession year to my fifth year of reign. I subdued them to one authority, took hostages from them, *and* imposed upon them tribute and conditions.

This is apart from the numerous foreign campaigns that do not appear in the *account of* my victories *and* upon which I pursued my enemies by chariot in favorable terrain and on foot in rough terrain. I prevented the enemies from setting foot in my land.

Tiglath-pileser, valiant man, armed with the unrivaled bow, expert in the hunt:

The gods Ninurta and Palil gave me their fierce weapons and their exalted bow for my lordly arms. By the command of the god Ninurta, who loves me, I slew four extraordinarily strong wild virile bulls in the desert, in the land Mittani, and at the city Araziqu, which is before the land Hatti—*I slew them* with my strong bow, iron arrow heads, and sharp arrows. I brought their hides and horns to my city Ashur.

I killed ten strong bull elephants in the land Harran and the region of the River Habur *and* four live elephants I captured. I brought the hides and tusks *of the dead elephants* with the live elephants to my city Ashur.

By the command of the god Ninurta, who loves me, I killed on foot one hundred twenty lions with my wildly vigorous assault. In addition, eight hundred lions I felled from my *light* chariot. I have brought down every kind of wild beast and winged bird of the heavens whenever I have shot an arrow.

After I had gained complete dominion over the enemies of the god Ashur, I rebuilt *and* completed the dilapidated *portions of* the temple of the Assyrian Ishtar, my mistress, the temple of the god Amurru, the temple of the god Bel-labira, the temple of the ten gods, the temples of the gods of my city Ashur. I put in place the entrances to their temples *and* brought the great gods, my lords, inside. *Thus* did I please their great divinity. I rebuilt *and* completed the palaces, the royal residences of the great cult centers in the *various* districts of my land that since the time of my forefathers during hard years had been abandoned and had fallen into ruin and decay. I repaired the weakened fortifications of my land. I caused plows to be hitched up all over Assyria and *thereby* piled up more grain than my forefathers. I formed herds of horses, oxen, *and* donkeys from the booty I took when I gained dominion over lands with the support of the god Ashur, my lord. In addition I got control of *and* formed herds of NAYALU deer, AYALU deer, gazelles, *and* ibex that the gods Ashur and Ninurta, the gods who love me, had given me in the course of the hunt in high mountain ranges. I numbered them like flocks of sheep. I sacrificed yearly to the god Ashur, my lord, the young born to them as voluntary offerings together with my pure sacrifices.

I took cedar, boxtree, *and* Kanish oak from the lands over which I had gained dominion—such trees that none among previous kings, my forefathers, had ever planted—and I planted *them* in the orchards of my land. I took rare orchard fruit that is not found in my land *and with them* filled the orchards of Assyria.

I had in harness for the forces of my land more chariots and teams of horses than ever before. To Assyria I added land and to its people I added people. I brought contentment to my people *and* provided them with a secure abode.

Tiglath-pileser, exalted prince, the one whom the gods Ashur and Ninurta have continually guided wherever he wished *to go* and who pursued each and every one of the enemies of the god Ashur and laid low all the rebellious; son of Ashur-resha-ishi I, strong king, conqueror of enemy lands, subduer of all fierce *enemies*; grandson of Mutakkil-Nusku, whom the god Ashur the great lord chose through the selection of his steadfast heart and firmly appointed to the shepherdship of Assyria; legitimate heir of Ashur-dan I, bearer of the holy scepter, commander of the subjects of the god Enlil, the one whose deeds and offerings are pleasing to the great gods, and who lived to a ripe old age; offspring of Ninurta-apil-ekur, martial sovereign, loved one of the god Ashur, whose wings were spread like an eagle's over his land and faithfully he tended the people of Assyria:

At that time the temple of the gods An and Adad, the great gods, my lords, which Shamshi-Adad III, viceregent of Ashur, son of Ishme-Dagan II *who was* also viceregent of the god Ashur had previously built, *after* 641 years had passed it had become dilapidated and King Ashur-dan I of Assyria, son of Ninurta-apil-Ekur *who was* also king of Assyria, tore down that temple but did not rebuild *it* and for sixty years its foundation has not been relaid.

In my accession year the gods An and Adad, the great gods my lords who love my priesthood, commanded me to rebuild their shrine. I made bricks. I delineated its area, dug down to the bottom of its foundation pit, *and* laid its foundation upon bedrock. I piled up that entire area with bricks like an oven, making it fifty layers of brick deep. I laid thereon the stone foundation of the temple of the gods An and Adad. I rebuilt it from top to bottom and made it bigger than before. I constructed two large ziggurats that were appropriate for their great divinity. I planned *and* laboriously rebuilt *and* completed the pure temple, the holy shrine, their joyful abode, their happy dwelling that stands out like the stars of heaven and that

represents the choicest skills of the building trade. Its interior I decorated like the interior of heaven. I decorated its walls as splendidly as the brilliance of rising stars. I raised its tower-gates and its ziggurats to the sky and made fast its parapets with baked brick. I installed inside a pipe *suitable for the conduct* of the rites of their great divinity. I brought the gods An and Adad, the great gods, inside *and* set them on their exalted thrones. *Thus* did I please their great divinity.

The HAMRU temple of the god Adad—which Shamshi-Adad III, viceregent of Ashur, son of Ishme-Dagan II *who was* also viceregent of the god Ashur, had built—was dilapidated and in ruins. I delineated its site *and* rebuilt it from top to bottom with baked brick. I adorned it and made it stronger than before. Inside I offered pure sacrifices to the god Adad, my lord.

At that time I transported obsidian, HALTU stone, and *hematite* from the mountains of the lands Nairi, which I conquered with the support of the god Ashur my lord. I deposited *them* in the HAMRU temple of the god Adad, my lord, forever.

Because I made plans without ceasing and was not slack in the work *but* quickly completed the pure temple, the exalted shrine, for the abode of the gods An and Adad, the great gods my lords, and *thereby* pleased their great divinity: May the gods An and Adad faithfully have mercy upon me, may they love my prayers, may they heed my fervent petitions, may they grant abundant rain and extraordinarily rich years during my reign; may they lead me about safely in battle and strife; may they subdue at my feet all enemy lands, rebellious mountain regions, and rulers hostile to me; may they pronounce a favorable blessing over me and my priestly progeny; and may they firmly place my priesthood in the presence of the god Ashur and their great divinity forever like a mountain.

I wrote on my stelas and clay inscriptions my heroic victories, my successful battles, *and* the suppression of the enemies *and* foes of the god Ashur that the gods An and Adad granted me. I deposited *them* in the temple of the gods An and Adad, the great gods my lords, forever. In addition, the stelas of

Shamshi-Adad III my forefather I anointed with oil, made sacrifices, *and* returned them to their places.

In the future, in days to come, may a later prince, when the temple of the gods An and Adad the great gods my lords and those ziggurats become old and dilapidated, restore their weakened *portions*. May he anoint with oil my stelas and clay inscriptions, make sacrifices, *and* return *them* to their places. His name let him write with mine. *Then* like me may the gods An and Adad, the great gods, guide him in joy and success.

He who breaks *or* erases my stelas and inscriptions, throws *them* into water, burns *them*, covers *them* with earth, secretly stores *them* in a taboo house where there is no visibility, *who* erases my inscribed name and writes his *own* name, or *who* conceives of anything injurious and puts it into effect to the disadvantage of my stelas:

May the gods An and Adad, the great gods my lords, glare at him angrily and inflict upon him an evil curse. May they overthrow his sovereignty. May they tear out the foundations of his royal throne. May they terminate his noble line. May they smash his weapons, bring about the defeat of his army, and make him sit in bondage before his enemies. May the god Adad strike his land with terrible lightning *and* inflict his land with distress, famine, want, *and* plague. May he command that he not live one day longer. May he destroy his name *and* his seed from the land.

Month of Kuzallu, twenty-ninth day, eponym of Ina-iliya-allak, chief cupbearer.

#40: Shalmaneser III
(Grayson, *Assyrian Rulers of the Early First Millennium*, 148–51)[5]

Found in Nimrud, one of the ancient capital cities of Assyria, an alabaster monolith over six-and-a-half-feet tall is known as the "Black Obelisk." Inscribed on all four sides with an account of the campaigns of Shalmaneser III (858–824 B.C.), the obelisk has twenty rectangular panels that correspond to the inscription and illustrate payment of tribute by five conquered territories. This inscription is of interest for students of the Old Testament because of its mention of King Jehu and its depiction of Israelites in long fringed dresses, covered with a fringed robe. The reading pre-sented here is from the annotations accompanying the reliefs.

I received tribute from Sua, the Gilzanean: silver, gold, tin, bronze casseroles, the staffs of the king's hand, horses, *and* two-humped camels.

I received tribute from Jehu of the house of Omri: silver, gold, a gold bowl, a gold tureen, gold vessels, gold pails, tin, the staffs of the king's hand, *and* spears.

I received tribute from Egypt: two-humped camels, a water buffalo, a *rhinoceros*, an ante-

Scenes on the Black Obelisk of Shalmaneser III show King Jehu of Israel bowing before Shalmaneser. (© Copyright The British Museum)

lope, female elephants, female monkeys, *and* apes.

I received tribute from Marduk-apla-utsur, the Suhean: silver, gold, gold pails, ivory, spears, byssus, garments with multicolored trim, and linen *garments*.

I received tribute from Qarparunda, the Patinean: silver, gold, tin, bronze compound, bronze utensils, ivory, *and* ebony.

#41: Tiglath-pileser III
(Thomas, *Documents from Old Testament Times*, 54–55)[6]

Tiglath-pileser III (744–727 B.C.) was the brilliant military and political innovator who officially ushered in the period of Assyria's greatest imperial strength. He reconquered most of the nations of Syria-Palestine and changed the previous policy of tribute-collecting military raids to a policy of war as permanent conquest. The reading presented here from his annals is of interest because it mentions Menahem of Israel. Azriau of Yaudi has been taken by some to be King Azariah of Judah, but this interpretation is disputed.[7] In other annalistic texts, Tiglath-pileser claimed to have marched past the "borders of Israel" down the Phoenician coast through Philistia to Gaza.

In the course of my expedition *I received* the tribute of . . . [Azriau] of Yaudi like . . . Azriau of Yaudi in . . . without number, reaching to the sky, [exceedingly great] . . . with eyes like those that *look* from heaven . . . by infantry attack . . . he heard of [the approaching] massed [forces] of Ashur and was afraid . . . I smashed down, destroyed and [burned with fire] . . . they had taken away [for Azriau] and strengthened it . . . very difficult . . . was barred and high . . . was situated and its exit . . . I deepened . . . I surrounded his trusty troops, to . . . [his soldiers] I made to do forced laborers' work and . . . his great . . . like a pot [I shattered] . . . Azriau . . . as my royal palace . . . tribute like what . . . the city [Kullani] his ally . . . the cities Usnu, Siannu, Simirra, [and Kashpuna], which are by the sea, together with the cities up to Mount Saue, a mountain that abuts on the Lebanon range: Mount Baal-Sapuna as far as the Amanus mountains, the mountain of the TASHKARINU tree; the whole of the Saue territory, the districts of Kar-Addu, the town of

Hatarikka, the district of the town of Nuqudina, Mount Hasu together with towns around it, the town of Ara and the villages on both sides of them, together with the villages round about them. Mount Sarbua, the whole of the hill country, the towns of Ashani, Iadabi, Mount Iaraqu *and* the whole of its hilly territory, the towns . . . , Ellitarbi, Zitanu, as far as Attini, . . . , Bumame: nineteen areas belonging to Hamath, together with the villages around them that are on the coast of the Mediterranean Sea, which they had by sin and folly snatched away from Azriau, I restored to the territory of Assyria. I set my own official as district governor over them. 30,300 persons [I removed] from their cities and settled in the district of Ku . . . ; 1,223 persons I settled in the district of Ulluba . . . the tribute of Kushtashpi of Kummuh, Rezin of Damascus, Menaham of Samaria, [Hiram] of Tyre, Sibitti-bi'ili of Byblos, Urikki of Cilicia, Pisiris of Carchemish, I'ni-ilu of Hamath, Panammu of Sam'al, Tarhulara of Gurgum, Sulumal of Melidda, Dadi-ilu of Kaska, Uassurme of Tabal, Ushhitti of Tuna, Urballa of Tuhana, Tuhamme of Ishtunda, Urimme of Hurikna, Queen Zabibe of Arabia; gold, silver, tin, iron, elephant hide, ivory, embroidered garments, linen garments, blue-dyed cloth, purple-dyed cloth, ebony, walnut wood, everything precious, treasure *fit for* royalty, prepared *sheepskins* whose wool was dyed purple, wild birds whose outspread wings were dyed purple, horses, mules, large and small cattle, male camels, female camels with their foals I received.

#42: Sargon II
(Thomas, *Documents from Old Testament Times*, 59–61)[8]

Second Kings 17:6 states that the northern kingdom of Israel fell to "the king of Assyria." The implication of the context (17:3) is that this was Shalmaneser V (726–722 B.C.), son and successor of Tiglath-pileser III. Sargon II (721–705 B.C.), however, claimed in his ostentatious annals that he conquered Israel in his accession year. While Sargon may have been general of the Assyrian forces and thus participated jointly with Shalmaneser V in the capture of Samaria, it is also possible that Sargon simply commandeered the claim in order to enhance his propagandistic annals.

At the beginning [of my rule . . . the city of the Samarians] I [besieged and conquered] . . . who let me achieve my victory . . . carried off prisoner 27,290 of the people who dwelled in it; from among them I equipped fifty chariots for my royal army units . . . the city of Samaria] I restored and made it more habitable than before. [I brought into it] people of the countries conquered by my own hands. [My official I set over them as district governor and] imposed upon them tribute as on an Assyrian *city* . . . I made to mix with each other; the market price . . .

[The governor of Samaria] who had consorted with the king who opposed me not to do service and not to bring tribute . . . and they did battle. I clashed with them in the power of the great gods, my lords, and counted as spoil 27,290 people together with their chariots . . . and the gods in whom they trusted. From among them I equipped two hundred chariots for my royal army units, while the rest of them I made to take *up their lot* within Assyria. I restored the city of Samaria and made *it* more habitable than before. I brought into it people from the countries conquered by my own hands. My official I set over them as district governor and reckoned them as people of Assyria itself.

I surrounded and captured the city of Samaria; 27,290 of the people who dwelled in it I took away as prisoners. From among them I equipped fifty chariots and made the rest of them take up [their allotted] positions. I set over them my official and imposed on them tribute of the former king. King Hanunu of Gaza and Sib'e, commander-in-chief of Egypt, advanced to Rapihu to make a direct attack and to battle with me. I defeated them. Sib'e fled, taking fright on hearing the din of my weapons, and disappeared. I personally captured King Hanunu of Gaza. I received tribute from Pir'u of Musuru, Queen Samsi of Arabia, and from It'amar the Sabean; gold dust, horses and camels.

In the second year of my reign, [Ilubi'di of Hamath] . . . a vast [army] he collected in the town of Qarqar and the oath [of fidelity he

forget . . . and made Arpad, Simarra Damascus and Samaria to revolt against me] . . .

(gap)

He made [an agreement] and Sib'e called out his [army], being his ally, and advanced to make a direct and close battle with me. By decree of the god Ashur, my lord, I inflicted a defeat upon *Hanunu and Sib'e*, and Sib'e, like a shepherd robbed of his sheep, fled alone and disappeared. I seized on Hanunu with my own hand and brought him in fetters to my city of Ashur. [The city of Rapihu] I destroyed, demolished and burned. I took away 9,033 people together with their numerous possessions.

#43: Sennacherib
(Thomas, *Documents from Old Testament Times*, 67)[9]

Sennacherib (704–681 B.C.), son and successor of Sargon II, captured many Judean cities and besieged Jerusalem, forcing Hezekiah to pay tribute to the Assyrians. Although there are historical questions about Sennacherib's raid into Syria-Palestine in 701 B.C.,[10] the biblical and Assyrian sources are in agreement that the mighty Assyrian monarch was not able to capture Jerusalem. Hezekiah, heeding the advice of Isaiah, refused to surrender the city, and the biblical account describes the miraculous, if mysterious, defeat of the Assyrian army and the untimely death of Sennacherib (2 Kings 18–19; Isaiah 36–37). The reading presented here is from the final edition of Sennacherib's annals and is known as the "Taylor Prism," now housed in the British Museum. It describes the event in the most positive light possible, without claiming to have successfully taken the city.

But as for Hezekiah, the Jew, who did not bow in submission to my yoke, forty-six of his strong walled towns and innumerable smaller villages in their neighborhood I besieged and conquered by stamping down earth-ramps and then by bringing up battering rams, by the assault of foot soldiers, by breaches, tunneling, and field operations. I made to come out from them 200,150 people, young and old, male and female, innumerable horses, mules, donkeys, camels, large and small cattle, and counted them as the

Sennacherib's prism, on which he records his account of battle with Hezekiah. (Courtesy of the Oriental Institute of the University of Chicago)

spoils of war. He himself I shut up like a caged bird within Jerusalem, his royal city. I put watchposts strictly around it and turned back to his disaster any who went out of its city gate. His towns that I had despoiled I cut off from his land, giving them to King Mitinti of

Ashdod, King Padi of Ekron, and King Sillibel of Gaza and so reduced his land. Moreover, I fixed upon him an increase in the amount to be given as KATRE presents for my lordship, in addition to the former tribute, to be given annually. As for Hezekiah, the awful splendor of my lordship overwhelmed him, and the irregular and regular troops that he had brought in to strengthen Jerusalem, his royal city, and had obtained for his protection, together with thirty talents of gold, three hundred talents of silver, precious stones, antimony, large blocks of red stone, ivory *inlaid* couches, ivory armchairs, elephant hide, elephant tusks, ebony wood, boxwood, all kinds of valuable treasures, as well as his daughters, concubines, male and female musicians he sent me later to Nineveh, my lordly city. He sent a personal messenger to deliver the tribute and make a slavish obeisance.

#44: Cyrus Cylinder
(Thomas, *Documents from Old Testament Times*, 92–94)[11]

> Cyrus II the Persian (538–530 B.C.) officially brought the Neo-Babylonian Empire to an end and became the founder of the Achemenid dynasty in Persia. The inscription presented in this reading describes not only his victory over Babylon, but his policy of tolerance toward conquered peoples and the reconstruction of their religious sanctuaries. Cyrus's decrees to this effect are paralleled in the Hebrew text of Ezra 1:2–4 and 2 Chronicles 36:23 and the Aramaic decree in Ezra 6:1–5.[12]

The lord of the gods became furiously angry at their complaints and [forsook] their borders . . . The gods who dwelled amongst them left their dwellings, in anger at having brought *them* into Babylon. Marduk . . . turned *his face* to all their habitations that were in ruins and *to* the population of Sumer and Akkad, who were like men dead, and he had compassion. He scoured all the lands for a friend, seeking for the upright prince whom it would have to take his hand. He called King Cyrus of Anshan. He nominated him to be ruler over all. He made the land of Guti, all the warrior band of Manda, submit to him. The black-headed people whom *Marduk* put in *Cyrus's* power, to them *Cyrus* tried to be-

The Cyrus Cylinder, which describes Cyrus's victory over Babylon and his releasing captive peoples to return to their homelands. (© Copyright The British Museum)

have with justice and righteousness. Marduk the great lord, compassionate to his people, looked with gladness on *his* good deeds and his upright intentions. He gave orders that he go against his city Babylon. He made him take the road to Babylon and he went at his side like a friend and comrade. His vast army, whose number like the waters of a river cannot be determined, with their armor held close, moved forward beside him. He got him into his city Babylon without fighting or battle. He averted hardship to Babylon. He put an end to the power of Nabonidus the king who did not show him reverence. The entire population of Babylon, the whole of Sumer and Akkad, princes and governors, bowed to *Cyrus* and kissed his feet. They were glad that he was king. Their faces lighted up. The master by whose aid the mortally sick had been made alive, all had been preserved from ruin and . . . [For this] they praised him and honored his name. I am Cyrus, king of the world, great king, mighty king, king of Babylon, king of the land of Sumer and Akkad, king of the four quarters, son of Cambyses, great king, king of Anshan, grandson of Cyrus, great king, king of Anshan, descendant of Teispes, great king, king of Anshan, progeny of an unending royal line, whose rule Bel and Nabu cherish, whose kingship they desire for their hearts' pleasure. When I, well disposed, entered Babylon, I set up the seat of dominion in the royal palace amidst jubilation and rejoicing. Marduk the great god caused the bighearted inhabitants of Babylon to . . . me. I sought daily to worship him. My numerous troops moved about undisturbed in the midst of Babylon. I did not allow any to terrorize the land of [Sumer] and Akkad. I kept in view the needs of Babylon and all its sanctuaries to promote their well-being. The citizens of Babylon . . . I lifted their unbecoming yoke. Their dilapidated dwellings I restored. I put an end to their misfortunes. At my deeds Marduk, the great lord, rejoiced, and to me, Cyrus, the king who worshiped him, and to Cambyses, my son, the offspring of *my* loins, and to all my troops he graciously gave his blessing, and in good spirits before him we [glorified] exceedingly his high [divinity]. All the kings who sat in throne rooms, throughout the four quarters, from the Upper to the Lower Sea, those who dwelled in . . . , all the kings of the west country who dwelled in tents, brought me their heavy tribute and kissed my feet in Babylon. From . . . to the cities of Ashur and Susa, Agade, Eshnunna, the cities of Zamban, Meternu, Der, as far as the region of the land of Gutium, the holy cities beyond the Tigris whose sanctuaries had been in ruins over a long period, the gods whose abode is in the midst of them, I returned to their places and housed them in lasting abodes. I gathered together all their inhabitants and restored *to them* their dwellings. The gods of Sumer and Akkad whom Nabonidus had, to the anger of the lord of the gods, brought into Babylon, I at the bidding of Marduk, the great lord, made to dwell in peace in their habitations, delightful abodes. May all the gods whom I have placed within their sanctuaries address a daily prayer in my favor before Bel and Nabu, that my days be long, and may they say to Marduk my lord, May Cyrus the king who reveres you, and Cambyses his son . . .

9 Chronicles and Other Historiographic Lists

Like the royal records from Mesopotamia, numerous historical lists and particularly the "Babylonian Chronicle" series often shed direct light on events discussed in the Old Testament historical books. Beyond obvious synchronisms with the biblical historical books, these materials also illustrate the contrast between historiography in the ancient Near East and ancient Israel. In general, genuine historical literature is noticeably absent in the ancient Near East, as noted long ago by Leo Oppenheim.[1] The lists included here are the raw materials for history-writing. The Israelites also had such raw materials, but they moved beyond them to produce genuine historiography, with characterization, interpretive presentation of past events, multiple causal factors, etc.

#45: Sumerian King List
(Beyerlin, *Near Eastern Religious Texts*, 88–89)[2]

An early king list preserves the names of 140 rulers who ruled in southern Mesopotamia. The date of composition is a matter of considerable disagreement, but it appears to come from the early second millennium B.C.[3] In the list of rulers, a great flood that streamed over the earth serves as a turning point in the portrayal of Mesopotamian history. The preamble describes the history of Mesopotamian kingship from the time that kingship was lowered from heaven until this flood. Rulers from this antediluvian period are said to have lived for extraordinarily long periods of time; eight rulers from five cities rule for a total of 241,000 years. This section of the "Sumerian King List" has rightly been compared to the long-lived patriarchs of Genesis 5.[4]

When the kingship came down from heaven, the kingship was in Eridu. In Eridu Alulim became king and reigned for 28,800

The Sumerian King List preserves the names of 140 rulers in southern Mesopotamia. (Ashmolean Museum, Oxford)

years. Alalgar reigned for 36,000 years. Thus two kings reigned for 64,800 years. I *thus* leave Eridu on one side; its kingship was brought to Bad-tibira.

In Bad-tibira Enmenluanna reigned for 43,200 years. Enmengalanna reigned for 28,800 years. The divine Dumuzi, a shepherd, reigned for 36,000 years. *Thus* three kings reigned for 108,000 years. I *thus* leave Bad-tibira on one side; its kingship was brought to Larak.

In Larak, Ensipazianna reigned for 28,800 years. *Thus* one king reigned for 28,800 years. I *thus* leave Larak on one side; its kingship was brought to Sippar.

In Sippar Enmeduranna became king and reigned for 21,000 years. *Thus* one king reigned for 21,000 years. I *thus* leave Sippar on one side; its kingship was brought to Shuruppak.

In Shuruppak, Urbatutu became king and reigned for 18,600 years. *Thus* one king reigned for 18,600 years.

These are five cities; eight kings reigned for 241,000 years. *Then* the flood streamed over *the earth.*

#46: Old Babylonian Date Lists
(*ANET* 269–71)

In early Babylonia, each year derived its name from a noteworthy event that took place in the preceding year, a practice that Assyriologists refer to as "year-name" or "year-date" formula.[5] The list presented in this reading gives the names of the forty-three years of Hammurapi's rule as king of Babylon (1792–1750 B.C.) and helps scholars reconstruct the basic outline of the events of his reign.

year 1   Hammurapi *became* king.

year 2   He established justice in the country.

year 3   He constructed a throne for the main dais of the god Nanna (variant adds: in the temple E.KISH.SHIR.GAL) in Babylon.

year 4   The wall of *the sacred precinct* Gagia was built.

year 5   He constructed the ENKA.ASH.BAR.RA.

year 6   He constructed the SHIR of the goddess Laz.

year 7   Uruk and Isin were conquered.

year 8   The country Emutbal.

year 9   The canal *called* Hammurapi-hegal *was dug.*

year 10   Army *and* inhabitants of Malgia were crushed.

year 11   He conquered Rapiqum and Shalibi.

year 12   He constructed a throne for the goddess Sarpanit.

year 13   A copper stand for a royal statue *and* the pertinent DU.MAH.

year 14   He constructed a throne for the goddess Inanna of Babylon.

year 15   The seven statues.

year 16   He constructed the throne of the god Nabium.

year 17   He made the image of the goddess Inanna of Kibalbarru as high as the sky.

year 18   He constructed the main dais for Enlil in Babylon.

year 19   The big wall of Igi-hursag.

year 20   The year following: The wall of Igi-hursag. Also: The throne of Meri.

year 21   The wall of the town Bazu was built.

year 22   The statue of Hammurapi *as* king *granting* justice.

year 23   The APIN of the wall of Sippar.

year 24   He redug the TILIDA canal for *the benefit of the temple of* Enlil, and *also the bed of* the Euphrates.

year 25   The great wall of Sippar was built.

year 26   The great daises of gold.

year 27   He constructed the main emblem of reddish gold that is carried in front of the army, for the great gods, his helpers.

year 28   The temple E.NAM.HE (house of Abundance) of Adad in Babylon was built.

year 29   He constructed the image of the goddess Shala.

year 30   The year following, He constructed the image of Shala.

Also: The leader, beloved of Marduk, after having defeated the army that Elam—*counting* from the frontier of Marhashi, also Subartu, Gutium, Eshnunna, and Malgi—had raised in masses, through the mighty power of the great gods, reestablished/consolidated the foundations of *the empire of* Sumer and Akkad.

year 31   *Encouraged* by an oracle *given* by Anu and Enlil who are advancing in front of his army, *and* through the mighty power that the great gods had given to him, he was a match for the country of Emutbal and its king Rim-Sin, and . . . and *thus* forced Sumer and Akkad to *obey* his orders.

year 32 The hero who proclaims the triumphs of Marduk, overthrew in battle with his powerful weapon the army of Eshnunna, Subartu *and* Gutium and was a match *also* for the country Mankizum and the country along the bank of the Tigris as far as *the frontier of* the country Subartu.

year 33 He redug the canal *called* Hammurapi-*Spells*-Abundance-for-the-People, the Beloved-of-Anu-and-Enlil, *thus* he provided Nippur, Eridu, Ur, Larsa, Uruk *and* Isin with a permanent and plentiful water supply, and reorganized Sumer and Akkad from *its* confusion. Mari and Malgi he overthrew in battle and made Mari, and . . . and also several other cities of Subartu, by a friendly agreement, *listen* to his orders.

year 34 He built the temple E.TUR.KALAM.MA (Fold of the Country) for Anu, Inanna, and Nana.

year 35 Upon the command of Anu and Enlil he destroyed the walls of Mari and Malgia.

year 36 He restored the temple E.ME.TE.UR.SAG (The Pride of the Hero) and built the temple tower, the mighty abode of Zababa *and* Inanna, whose top is sky-high and *thus* he greatly increased the glamour of Zababa as well as of Inanna in a pious manner.

year 37 Through the great power of Marduk he overthrew the army of Turukku, Kakmu, and of the country Subartu.

year 38 Upon the command of Anu and Enlil—and with the splendid wisdom with which Marduk has endowed him—he . . . Eshnunna, which a flood had destroyed . . .

year 39 With the mighty power that Anu *and* Enlil have given him, he defeated all his enemies as far as the country of Subartu.

year 40 He made the temple E.MES.LAM (Temple of the spreading MES tree) as high as a mountain.

year 41 The goddess Tashmetum *who listens* to his supplication.

year 42 After the year Tashmetum.

Also: He made the great wall at the embankment of the Tigris high as a mountain, called its name Pier of Shamash, and built also the wall of Rapiqu at the embankment of the Euphrates.

year 43 As *to* Sippar, the primeval city of the sun-god Utu, he provided *it* with a wall made of piled-up earth.

#47: Weidner Chronicle
(Arnold, "Weidner Chronicle," 133–38)[6]

The rise of the chronicle genre in Mesopotamia marks the beginning of a new era of historiography in the ancient Near East.[7] The "Weidner Chronicle" comes early in the Mesopotamian tradition and is an important source for the views of the past prevalent at the close of the second millennium B.C.[8] The events described in this chronicle range from early Sumerian history to the beginning of the Old Babylonian dynasty, although the text was probably composed in the late second millennium B.C. The author was concerned only with the city of Babylon and the preservation of Marduk's cult center at Esagil. The chronicle is of little value for reconstructing early Mesopotamian history, in distinction from the historical objectivity of later Babylonian examples of this genre. Instead, the "Weidner Chronicle" is valuable because it is one of the earliest examples of this genre and sheds light on Mesopotamian views of history in general.

Say to King [Apil]-Sin, [king of Babylon], thus speaks King Damiqilishu *or Enlil-bani* of Isin:

. . . like . . . his reign. I wrote to you words of wisdom, words . . . You did not take them to heart. You did not listen or bend your ear to the instruction I gave you. You did not heed the choice advice that . . . , and you are pursuing other purposes. To do you a favor . . . , but it is not in your heart. For your own benefit, I advised you to strengthen the discipline of your army till distant days, but you did not consolidate it in your hands . . . shrines where I sought advice . . . Now I will tell you my experiences . . . acquaint yourself quickly with this!

I offered an offering to my lady Ninkarrak, mistress of E-gal-mah. I prayed to her, I took prayers to her, I spoke to her the thoughts that

I desired in my heart. Thus I said: Deliver into [my] hand the people of Sumer and Akkad . . . all the lands . . . Let them bring . . . the heavy tribute of the Upper and Lower Lands into E-gal-mah.

At dead of night, holy Gula, the exalted lady, stood before me, [heard] my words and spoke to me truthfully. She blessed me: In the APSU you will establish a base, in the subterranean ocean . . . You will lift your head to the distant heavens, . . . protection on high. Afterward, Marduk, king of the gods, who . . . all of heaven and earth, [Will] . . . the peoples of Sumer and Akkad . . . to the dominion of his city Babylon. He has hurried to the BIT APSI, to his father Ea the Craftsman, the Counselor of Heaven and Earth. Let Babylon, the city chosen in my heart, be exalted in all lands . . . , Esagil, the exalted shrine . . . to the border of all heaven and earth . . . , The lord of lords, who dwells in the shrine, from east to west . . . , May he shepherd the black-headed people like sheep . . . , Let the city be elevated. Of *all* countries . . .

Lord Nudimmud [put into effect] the words that he had said to him . . . From heaven's base to heaven's summit he honored him . . . Second, Anu and Enlil *and* the great gods, looked on him with steady favor . . . and their word *is* true . . .

Let him be the leader of the Upper and Lower Lands . . . May the great gods of heaven and earth tremble at his mighty sanctuary . . . Raise the head of Esagil, of Ekua, the palace of heaven *and* earth, like heaven . . . their hearts. May its foundation constantly to the end of time like heaven and earth be . . . By means of your offering I understood the matter that you mentioned, and [I shall grant you] life of long days . . .

Apart from my order, a decision was given, a worthy decree for . . . For the gods of that city, the great gods of heaven and earth, he [abandoned] . . . for the life of the renovation, monthly and yearly . . . to his decision . . . [no] god will go up against it and whoever's heart . . . At his command, the hostile gods are bound *and* clothed in filthy [garments] . . . whoever sins against the gods of that city, his star will not stand in heaven . . . *His* royal dominion will end, his scepter will be carried

off, his treasury will be turned into a ruin and [a waste land].

. . . the king of the entire heavens and earth *said* thus: The gods of heaven and earth . . . and the conduct of each former king, of which I hear again and again, to . . .

Akka son of Enmebaragesi . . .

Enmekiri the king of Uruk, ravaged the people . . .

The wise man, Adapa . . . he heard [in] his pure sanctuary and he cursed Enmekiri . . . I gave royal dominion over all lands to him and . . . his rites I made beautiful . . . like the writing of the heavens *constellations* and in Esagil . . . The king who administers the entire heavens and earth, the firstborn son . . .

In the reign of Puzur-Nirah king of Akshak, the freshwater fisherman of Esagil . . . They were catching fish for the meal of the lord of fish . . . the second lieutenants of the king took away the fish. The fisherman . . . When the eighth day had passed, the freshwater fisherman was catching fish . . . In the house of Ku-Baba, the alewife . . . they brought near [to Esagil] . . . At that time . . . newly for Esagil . . . Ku-Baba gave bread to the freshwater fisherman, *and* she gave water . . . he [quickly offered the food] to Esagil . . . The great lord Marduk looked kindly upon her and said as follows: So be it! He has given royal dominion of all lands entirely over to Ku-Baba. Ur-Zababa [commanded Sargon] to exchange the wine libations for Esagil to . . . But Sargon did not exchange *them. Instead* he was very attentive and he quickly offered *the fish* to Esagil . . . Marduk son of the prince of Apsu looked joyfully upon him and he gave him royal dominion over the four quarters. He acted as provisioner for Esagil. All who sat upon a throne [brought] their tribute to Babylon . . . As for him, he [neglected] the word that Bel spoke; he dug up the dust of its pit and opposite Agade he built *another* city and [he called] its name Babylon. Enlil changed what he had said, and from east to west they *his subjects* were hostile toward him. Sleeplessness set in.

Naram-Sin ravaged the people of Babylon. Twice he summoned the Gutian army against him *Naram-Sin* and [put to flight] his people as with the goad of a donkey driver. *Marduk* has given his royal dominion to the Gutian army. The Gutians, who were a disgruntled people, exhibited no divine reverence. They did not know how to set the cults and ordinances in order. Utu-hegal, the freshwater fisherman, caught a fish for donation *to Marduk* in the region of the sea edge. That fish was not offered to another god until it was offered to the great lord Marduk. *But* the Gutians took from his hand the fish, which was already boiled but not offered . . . [By] his noble decree, he denied the Gutian army the royal dominion of his land, and he gave *it* to Utu-hegal. Utu-hegal, the freshwater fisherman, laid his hands on *Marduk's* city with evil intent, but the river carried off his corpse.

To Shulgi son of Ur-Nammu *Marduk* gave royal dominion of all lands, [but] *Marduk's* cult observances he did not fulfill, his purification rites he defiled, and his sin . . .

Amar-Sin, his son, exchanged the large oxen and the *sheep* sacrifices of the New Year festival of Esagil . . . Goring by an ox was foretold for him and he died from the "bite" of his shoe.

Shu-Sin, for the well-being of his life, made Esagil like the writing of the heavens.

. . . that divine Shulgi did, Imbi-Sin his son . . . his sin . . .

. . . an earlier king, *your* predecessor . . . it is as you desire.

More than his father, Ea . . . heaven and earth . . . did not create; Anu and Ishtar . . . his exalted son, the great lord Marduk, [king] of the gods, prince of the gods . . .

His grandson Nabu, who . . . will name the king . . .

To his descendant, king Sumu-la-il, whose name Anu named . . .

To benefit yourself and . . . all of it . . .

[It will remain] in your possession until distant days . . . Tablet of Marduk-etir son of Etir-. . . of . . . ; a worshiper of Nabu. Return if lost.

#48: Sargon Chronicle
(*ANET* 266–67)[9]

Similar to the "Weidner Chronicle," the "Sargon Chronicle" narrates events from the late third millennium to the mid-second millennium B.C. Its interest in historical traditions has replaced the annalistic style to produce a genuine chronicle, a genre that would become important in later Babylonian literature. The reading presented here highlights historical figures and reports accomplishments in times of peace and war.

King Sargon of Agade rose *to power* in the era of Ishtar and had neither rival nor opponent. He spread his terror-inspiring glamour over all the countries. He crossed the Sea in the east and he, himself, conquered the country of the west, in its full extent, in the eleventh year *of his rule*. He established there a central government. He erected his stelas in the west. Their booty he ferried over on rafts. He made his court officials live *around his residence, thus covering an area* of five double-miles, and held sway over the totality of the countries, without exception.

He marched against the country of Kazalla and turned Kazalla into ruin-hills and heaps *of rubble*. He *even* destroyed *there every possible* perching place for a bird.

Afterward, in his old age, all the countries revolted against him and they besieged him in Agade. *But* Sargon made an armed party and defeated them, knocked them over, and crushed their vast army.

Later on, Subartu rose with its multitudes, but it bowed to his military might. Sargon made sedentary this nomadic society. Their possessions he brought into Agade. He took away earth from the [foundation]-pits of Babylon and he built upon it [another] Babylon beside the town of Agade. On account of the sacrilege he *thus* committed, the great lord Marduk became enraged and destroyed his people by hunger. From the east to the west he alienated *them* from him and inflicted upon [him] *as punishment* that he could not rest *in his grave*.

Naram-Sin son of Sargon marched against the town of Apishal and made a breach *in its wall to conquer it*. He personally caught King Rish-Adad of Apishal and the SUKKAL of Apishal. He *also* marched against the country Magan and personally caught King Mannudannu of Magan.

Shulgi son of Ur-Nammu took very good care of the town of Eridu, which is on the seashore, *but* he had evil intentions and he removed the property of the temple Esagila and of Babylon sacrilegiously. Bel [became angry] and his corpse . . . him.

Irra-imitti, the king, installed Bel-ibni, the gardener, on his throne as a substitute king and *Irra-imitti even* placed his own royal crown on *Bel-ibni's* head. *During the ceremonial rule of Bel-ibni* Irra-imitti died in his palace while [sipping] hot porridge, and Bel-ibni who was *still* sitting on the throne did not rise *any more,* he *thus* was elevated to *real* kingship.

Catchline: Ilishuma was king of Assyria in the time of [Sumuabu] *king of Babylon.*

King Hammurapi of Babylon called up his army and marched against King Rim-Sin of Ur. He personally conquered Ur and Larsa, he took their possessions to Babylon. The . . . of . . . he threw down, the [booty of] . . . he carried away.

King [Samsuiluna] of Babylon, son of [Hammurapi], the king, [did . . . , his army he called] up and . . . Rim-Sin . . . he marched. He personally conquered [Ur and Larsa; he caught] him alive in the palace . . . He marched [against] . . . and laid siege . . . its inhabitants . . .

(gap)

[Ilima]-ilum . . . water, he built . . . and made an attack against him . . . , their corpses [filled] the sea. For a second time, Samsuiluna rose to [attack] Ilima-ilum and [he inflicted] a defeat [upon his army].

Abishi son of Samsuiluna did . . . to defeat Ilima-ilum and he had the idea of damming up the Tigris; he actually dammed up the Tigris, but he did not [catch] Ilima-ilum.

In the time of Samsuditana, the country of Hatti [marched] against Akkad.

Ea-gamil, king of the sea country, [marched] against Elam.

After him, Ulamburiash, brother of Kashtiliash, of the country of the Kassites, called up his army and conquered the sea country. He held *thus* sway over the *entire* country.

Agum son of Kashtiliash called up his army and marched against the sea country. He conquered the town Dur-Ea. He demolished the temple E.EGARA.URU.NA of Ea in Dur-Ea.

#49: Babylonian Chronicles
(Grayson, *Assyrian and Babylonian Chronicles*, 87–104)[10]

During the Neo-Babylonian period, ancient scholars began to keep systematically precise records of historical events. The "Neo-Babylonian Chronicle" details outstanding events of each year beginning with the reign of Nabonassar (747–734 B.C.). The chronicles reflect the narrow perspective of the authors, who were concerned only with Babylonia and its political developments. But within these parameters, the authors were objective in their reporting, making this source one of the most important for reconstructing the history of the first millennium B.C. The reading presented here includes the Mesopotamian version of the biblical accounts leading to the siege and capture of Jerusalem in 586 B.C.

Chronicle 2

When he/they had sent . . . *to* Babylon, at night . . . they did battle within the city all day . . . of Sin-sharra-ishkun fled to Assyria. He appointed [officials within] the city. On the twelfth day of the month Elul the army of Assyria . . . entered Shaznaku and set fire to the temple . . . and in the month Tishri the gods of Kish went to Babylon. The [army of] Assyria went to Nippur and Nabopolassar retreated before them. [The army of Assyria] and the Nippureans followed him to Uruk, they did battle against Nabopolassar in Uruk, and retreated before Nabopolassar. In the month Iyyar the army of Assyria went down to Akkad. On the twelfth day of the month Tishri when the army of Assyria had marched against Babylon *and* the Babylonians had come out of Babylon; on that day, they did battle against the army of Assyria, inflicted a major defeat upon the army of Assyria, and plundered them. For one year there was no king in the land *of* Babylonia. On the twenty-sixth day of the month Marchesvan Nabopolassar ascended the throne in Babylon.

The accession year of Nabopolassar: In the month Adar Nabopolassar returned to Susa the gods of Susa whom the Assyrians had carried off and settled in Uruk.

The first year of Nabopolassar: On the seventeenth day of the month Nisan panic overcame the city. Shamash and the gods of Shapazzu went to Babylon. On the twenty-first day of the month Iyyar the army of Assyria entered [Sallat] *and* carried off the booty. On the twentieth day of the month Sivan/Tammuz the gods of Sippar went to Babylon. On the ninth day of the month Ab Nabopolassar and his army [marched] to [Sallat]. He did battle against Sallat but did not capture the city. *Instead* the army of Assyria arrived so he retreated before them and withdrew.

[The second year] of Nabopolassar: At the beginning of the month Elul the army of Assyria went down [to Akkad] and camped by the Banitu canal. They did [battle against Nabopolassar] but *achieved nothing* . . . and they withdrew.

[The third year]: On the eighth [day of the month] . . . Der rebelled against Assyria. On the fifteenth day of the month Tishri . . . the king of Assyria and his army went down to Akkad and . . . and took *it* into Nippur. Afterward Itti-ili . . . [heard] and stationed a garrison in Nippur . . . he went up [against] Syria and . . . against . . . he ravaged . . . and set out for Nineveh . . . who had come to do battle against him . . . [when] they saw him they bowed down before him . . . The rebel king . . . one hundred days . . . when . . . rebel.

Chronicle 3

The tenth year of Nabopolassar: In the month Iyyar he mustered the army of Akkad and marched along the bank of the Euphrates. The Suheans and the Hindaneans did not do battle against him *but* placed their tribute before him. In the month Ab the army of Assyria prepared for battle in Gablini and Nabopolassar went up against them. On the twelfth day of the month Ab he did battle against the army of Assyria and the army of Assyria retreated before him. He inflicted a major defeat upon Assyria *and* plundered them extensively. He captured the Manneans who had come to *the Assyrians'* aid and the Assyrian officers. On that same day he captured Gablini. In the month Ab the king of Akkad *and* his army went upstream to Mane, Sahiri, and Bali-hu. He plundered them, sacked them extensively, *and* abducted their gods. In the month Elul the king of Akkad and his army returned and on his way he took

the people of Hindanu and its gods to Babylon. In the month Tishri the army of Egypt and the army of Assyria went after the king of Akkad as far as Gablini but they did not overtake the king of Akkad *so* they withdrew. In the month Adar the army of Assyria and the army of Akkad did battle against one another at Madanu, *a suburb* of Arraphu, and the army of Assyria retreated before the army of Akkad. *The army of Akkad* inflicted a major defeat upon *the Assyrian army* and drove them *back* to the Zab River. They captured their chariots and horses and plundered them extensively. They took many . . . with them across the Tigris and brought *them* into Babylon.

[The eleventh year: The king] of Akkad mustered his army, marched along the bank of the Tigris, and in the month Iyyar he encamped against Baltil. [On the nth day] of the month Sivan he did battle against the city but he did not capture it. The king of Assyria mustered his army, pushed the king of Akkad back from Baltil, and marched after him as far as Takritain, a city on the bank of the Tigris. The king of Akkad stationed his army in the fortress of Takritain. The king of Assyria and his army encamped against the army of the king of Akkad, which was stationed in Takritain, and did battle against them for ten days. But *the king of Assyria* did not capture the city. *Instead* the army of the king of Akkad, which had been stationed in the fortress, inflicted a major defeat upon Assyria. The king of Assyria and his army [turned] and went home. In the month Marchesvan the Medes went down to Arraphu and . . .

The twelfth year: In the month Ab the Medes, after they *had marched* against Nineveh . . . hastened and they captured Tarbisu, a city in the district of Nineveh . . . They went along [the Tigris] and encamped against Baltil. They did battle against the city and . . . destroyed . . . They inflicted a terrible defeat upon a great people, plundered and [sacked] them. The king of Akkad] and his army, who had gone to help the Medes, did not reach the battle *in time*. The city . . . [The king of Akkad] and [Cyaxares] *the king of the Medes* met one another by the city *and* together they made an entente cordiale . . . [Cyaxares] and his army went home. The king of Akkad and his army went home.

[The thirteenth year: In the month Iyyar] the Suheans rebelled against the king of Akkad and became belligerent. [The king of Akkad] mustered his army and marched to Suhu. On the fourth day of the month Sivan he did [battle against] Rahilu, a city that is *on an island* in the middle of the Euphrates, and at that time he captured the city. He built his . . . The men who *live* on the bank of the Euphrates came down to him . . . he encamped [against] Anat *and* the siege engines [he brought over from] the western side . . . he brought the siege engines up to the wall. He did battle against the [city] and *captured it* . . . [the king of] Assyria and his army came down and . . . the king of Akkad and his army. *The king of Akkad went home.*

[The fourteenth year]: The king of Akkad mustered his army [and marched to] . . . The king of the Umman-manda [marched] toward the king of Akkad . . . they met one another. [The king] of Akkad . . . [Cyaxares] . . . brought across and they marched along the bank of the Tigris . . . [they encamped] against Nineveh. From the month Sivan until the month Ab—for three [months]—. . . they subjected the city to a heavy siege. [On the nth day] of the month Ab . . . they inflicted a major [defeat upon a great people]. At that time King Sin-sharra-ishkun of Assyria [died] . . . They carried off the vast booty of the city and the temple *and* [turned] the city into a ruin heap . . . of Assyria escaped from the enemy and . . . the king of Akkad . . . On the twentieth day of the month Elul Cyaxares and his army went home. After he had gone the king of Akkad [despatched his army and] they marched to Nasibin. Plunder and exiles . . . and they brought *the people of* Rusapu to the king of Akkad at Nineveh. [On the nth day of the] month . . . [Ashur-uballit II] ascended the throne in Harran to rule Assyria. Up until [the nth day of] the month . . . in Nineveh . . . from the twentieth day of the month . . . the king of . . . set out and in . . .

The fifteenth year: In the month [Tammuz the king] of Akkad [mustered his army and] . . . marched to Assyria . . . victoriously [he marched about] of . . . and he captured Shu

. . . , plundered it, *and* [carried off] its [vast] booty. In the [month Marchesvan] the king of Akkad took the lead of his army *personally* and [marched] against *Ruggulitu*. He did battle against the city and on the twenty-eighth day of the month Marchesvan captured it . . . [He] did not [leave] a single man *alive* . . . he went [home].

The sixteenth year: In the month Iyyar the king of Akkad mustered his army and marched to Assyria. From [the month] . . . until the month Marchesvan he marched about victoriously in Assyria. In the month Marchesvan the Umman-manda, [who] had come [to help] the king of Akkad, put their armies together and marched to Harran [against Ashur-uballit II] who had ascended the throne in Assyria. Fear of the enemy overcame Ashur-uballit II and the army of [Egypt that] had come [to help him] and they [abandoned] the city . . . they crossed. The king of Akkad reached Harran and . . . he captured the city. He carried off the vast booty of the city and the temple. In the month Adar the king of Akkad left their . . . He went home. The Umman-manda, who had come to help the king of Akkad, withdrew.

The seventeenth year: In the month Tammuz King Ashur-uballit II of Assyria, the large army of Egypt . . . crossed the *Euphrates* River and marched against Harran to conquer *it* . . . they [captured] *it*. They defeated the garrison that the king of Akkad had stationed inside. When they had defeated *it* they encamped against Harran. Until the month Elul they did battle against the city but *achieved nothing. However* they did not withdraw. The king of Akkad went to help his army and . . . he went up [to] Izalla and the numerous cities in the mountains . . . he set fire to their . . . At that time the army of . . . [marched] as far as the district of Urartu. In the land . . . they plundered their . . . The garrison that the king of . . . [had stationed in it set out]. They went up to . . . The king of Akkad went home.

In the [eighteenth year: In the month Elul] the king of Akkad mustered his army . . . Let [the one who] loves Nabu and Marduk keep *this tablet* and not let *it* stray into *other* hands.

Chronicle 4

The eighteenth year of Nabopolassar: In the month Elul the king of Akkad mustered his army and following the bank of the Tigris he went up to the mountain of Bit-Hanunya in the district of Urartu. He set fire to the cities *and* plundered them extensively. In the month Tebet the king of Akkad went home.

The nineteenth year: In the month Sivan the king of Akkad mustered his army and Nebuchadnezzar II, his eldest son *and* the crown prince, mustered his army. They marched to the mountains of Za... The king of Akkad left the prince and his army there while he returned to Babylon in the month Tammuz. After he had gone Nebuchadnezzar II did battle against the [fortresses], captured them, [set them on fire], *and* plundered the mountains extensively. He conquered all of the mountains as far as the district of [Urartu. In the month] Elul the prince returned to Babylon. In the month Tishri the king of Akkad mustered his army and marched [to] Kimuhu, which is on the bank of the Euphrates. He crossed the river, did battle against the city, and in the month Kislev he captured the city. He sacked it *and* stationed a garrison of his in it. In the month Shebat he went home.

The twentieth year: The army of Egypt marched against the garrison at Kimuhu, which the king of Akkad had stationed inside. They laid siege to the city for four months, captured it, *and* defeated the garrison of the king of Akkad. In the month Tishri the king of Akkad mustered his army, marched along the bank of the Euphrates, and pitched camp in Quramatu, which is on the bank of the Euphrates. He had his army cross the Euphrates and they captured Shunadiru, Elammu, and Dahammu, cities of Syria, *and* plundered them. In the month Shebat the king of Akkad went home. The army of Egypt, which was in Carchemish, crossed the Euphrates and marched against the army of Akkad, which was camped in Quramatu. They pushed the army of Akkad back so that they withdrew.

The twenty-first year: The king of Akkad stayed home *while* Nebuchadnezzar II, his eldest son *and* the crown prince, mustered the army of Akkad.

Chronicle 5

[The twenty-first year]: The king of Akkad stayed home *while* Nebuchadnezzar II, his eldest son *and* the crown prince, mustered [the army of Akkad]. He took his army's lead and marched to Carchemish, which is on the bank of the Euphrates. He crossed the river [to encounter the army of Egypt], which was encamped at Carchemish... They did battle together. The army of Egypt retreated before him. He inflicted a [defeat] upon them *and* finished them off completely. In the district of Hamath the army of Akkad overtook the remainder of the army of [Egypt that] managed to escape [from] the defeat and that was not overcome. *The army of Akkad* inflicted a defeat upon them *so that* a single *Egyptian* man [did not return] home. At that time Nebuchadnezzar II conquered all of [Hamath].

For twenty-one years Nabopolassar ruled Babylon. On the eighth day of the month Ab he died. In the month Elul Nebuchadnezzar II returned to Babylon and on the first day of the month Elul he ascended the royal throne in Babylon.

In *his* accession year Nebuchadnezzar II returned to Hattu. Until the month Shebat he marched about victoriously in Hattu. In the month Shebat he took the vast booty of Hattu to Babylon. In the month Nisan he took the hand of Bel and the son of Bel *and* celebrated the AKITU festival.

The first year of Nebuchadnezzar II: In the month Sivan he mustered his army and marched to Hattu. Until the month Kislev he marched about victoriously in Hattu. All the kings of Hattu came into his presence and he received their vast tribute. He marched to *Ashkelon* and in the month Kislev he captured it, seized its king, plundered [and sacked] it. He turned the city into a ruin heap. In the month Shebat he marched away and [returned] to [Babylon].

The [second year]: In the month Iyyar the king of Akkad strengthened his large army and [marched to Hattu]. He encamped... large siege towers he moved [across... from the month] Iyyar until the month . . . *he marched about victoriously in Hattu.*

(gap)

[The third year: In the month . . . , on] the thirteenth [day] Nabu-shumu-lishir . . . [In the month . . . the king of Akkad] mustered his army and [marched] to Hattu . . . He brought the vast [booty] of Hattu into Akkad . . .

The fourth year: The king of Akkad mustered his army and marched to Hattu. [He marched about victoriously] in Hattu. In the month Kislev he took his army's lead and marched to Egypt. *When* the king of Egypt heard *the news* he [mustered] his army. They fought one another in the battlefield and both sides suffered severe losses. The king of Akkad and his army turned and [went back] to Babylon.

The fifth year: The king of Akkad stayed home *and* refitted his numerous horses and chariotry.

The sixth year: In the month Kislev the king of Akkad mustered his army and marched to Hattu. He despatched his army from Hattu and they went off to the desert. They plundered extensively the possessions, animals, and gods of the numerous Arabs. In the month Adar the king went home.

The seventh year: In the month Kislev the king of Akkad mustered his army and marched to Hattu. He encamped against the city of Judah and on the second day of the month Adar he captured the city *and* seized *its* king. A king of his own choice he appointed in the city *and* taking the vast tribute he brought it into Babylon.

The eighth year: In the month Tebet the king of Akkad [marched] toward Hattu as far as Carchemish . . . In the month Shebat [the king went] home.

The ninth year: [In the month . . . the king of Akkad] and [his] army [marched] along the bank of the Tigris . . . The king of . . . The king of [Akkad] . . . He encamped on the bank

of the Tigris. [There was] a distance of one day's march between them. [The king] of [Elam] took fright and fear overcame him so he [went] home.

The tenth [year: The king of Akkad] stayed home. From the month Kislev until the month Tebet [there was] a rebellion in Akkad . . . he put his large [army] to the sword *and* conquered his foe . . . He marched [to] Hattu. The kings and . . . [came] and [he received] their vast booty. He returned to [Babylon.

The eleventh year]: In the month Kislev the king of Akkad [mustered his] army and marched [to Hattu].

Chronicle 6

The third year: [On the nth day of the month] . . . King Appuashu of Pirindu mustered his [large] army and set out to plunder and sack Syria. Neriglissar mustered his army and marched to Hume to oppose him. Before his *arrival* Appuashu placed the army and cavalry that he had organized in a mountain valley in ambush. *When* Neriglissar reached them he inflicted a defeat upon them *and* conquered the large army. He captured his army and numerous horses. He pursued Appuashu for a distance of fifteen double-hours of marching through difficult mountains, where men must walk in single file, as far as Ura, his royal city. *He captured* him, seized Ura, and sacked it. When he had marched for a distance of six double-hours of marching through rough mountains and difficult passes, from Ura to Kirshi—his forefathers' royal city—he captured Kirshi, the mighty city, his royal metropolis. He burnt its wall, its palace, and its people. Pitusu, a mountain that is in the midst of the ocean, and six thousand combat troops who were stationed in it he captured by means of boats. He destroyed their city and captured their people. In that same year he started fires from the pass of Sallune to the border of Lydia. Appuashu fled so he did not capture him. In the month Adar the king of Akkad went home.

10 Non-Hebrew Monumental Inscriptions

In addition to royal records and chronographic materials from Mesopotamia, texts from elsewhere in the ancient Near East also have direct bearing on Israelite historical literature. Written in the languages used by Israel's neighbors—Egyptian, Phoenician, Moabite, Aramaic—these texts were preserved on monuments (stone stelas or statues) that commemorate the deeds or acts of a king. The readings presented here are of interest for Old Testament studies because they contain some specific mention of Israel (or a historical figure from Israel) or provide a cultural parallel with ancient Israel.

#50: Merneptah Stela
(Lichtheim, *Ancient Egyptian Literature*, 2.77)[1]

One of the last kings of Egypt's once powerful nineteenth dynasty was Merneptah (1212–1202 B.C.). Sometime around 1208 B.C., he commemorated a victory against all his enemies, especially Libyans who had joined with various Sea Peoples and marched into the Delta. Several hymns of victory are preserved on a black granite stela, variously known as the "Merneptah Stela" or the "Israel Stela." Near the end of this long inscription is a section that memorializes what is apparently a separate campaign against Egypt's traditional enemies in Syria-Palestine. Included in the list of conquered groups is the earliest known extrabiblical reference to Israel. Of particular interest to Old Testament studies is a grammatical sign that marks this name not as a city-state or a foreign country but as a people group. Scholars often use this text to demonstrate that in the late thirteenth century B.C. Israel was present in Syria-Palestine as a people, but not yet viewed by the Egyptians as an established political state.

The princes are prostrate saying:
Shalom!

Not one of the Nine Bows lifts his head:
Tjehenu is vanquished, Khatti at peace,
Canaan is captive with all woe.
Ashkelon is conquered, Gezer seized,
Yanoam made nonexistent;
Israel is wasted, bare of seed,
Khor is become a widow for Egypt.
All who roamed have been subdued
by the king of Upper and Lower Egypt,
    Banere-meramun,
son of Re, Merneptah, content with
    MAAT,
given life like Re every day.

#51: Mesha Stela
(Gibson, *Textbook of Syrian Semitic Inscriptions*, 1.75–77)[2]

In 1868, a German missionary learned of the existence of a three-and-a-half-foot tall black basalt stela in Dibon, Jordan. The stone contained thirty-four lines of ancient alphabetic script, with no discernible difference from the Paleo-Hebrew script. News of the find spread, and in the ensuing years competition to acquire the stone from the local Bedouin grew fierce between the Germans and the French, exacerbated by the political climate created by the Franco-Prussian War (1870–71). Out of resentment (and perhaps financial motivation), the Bedouin shattered the stone and distributed it among the local tribal leaders. Fortunately, a French scholar had made a facsimile impression, called a "squeeze," of the inscription prior to its destruction. Almost two-thirds of the stone was eventually retrieved, and, with the help of the squeeze, the entire stela was reconstructed and has been on display in the Louvre since 1875. King Mesha of Moab set up this stela around 830 B.C. to commemorate the construction of a sanctuary and to express gratitude to Chemosh, the god of Moab, for victories over Israel. The inscription has particular importance as a source related to Israel's

The Merneptah Stela contains a reference to Israel as a people group in Syria-Palestine in the thirteenth century B.C. (Zev Radovan)

Omride dynasty and the conflict between Moab and Israel recorded in 2 Kings 3.[3]

I am Mesha son of Chemosh-yat, king of Moab, the Dibonite. My father was king over Moab for thirty years, and I became king after my father. I built this high place for Chemosh in Qarhoh, a high place of salvation, because he delivered me from all assaults, and because he let me see my desire upon all my adversaries. King Omri of Israel had oppressed Moab many days, for Chemosh was angry with his land. His son succeeded him, and he too said, I will oppress Moab. In my days he said it; but I saw my desire upon him and his house, and Israel perished utterly forever. Omri had taken possession of the land of Medeba, and dwelled there his days and much of his son's days, forty years; but Chemosh dwelled in it in my days.

I rebuilt Baal-meon, and I made a reservoir in it; and I rebuilt Kiriathaim. Then the men of Gad had settled in the land of Ataroth from of old, and the king of Israel had fortified Ataroth for himself; but I fought against the town and took it; and I slew all the inhabitants of the town, a spectacle for Chemosh and Moab. I brought back from there the lion figure of David, and dragged it before Chemosh at Kerioth; and I settled in it the men of [Sharon] and the men of [Meharit]. Next Chemosh said to me, Go take Nebo from Israel. So I went by night, and fought against it from break of dawn till noon; and I took it and slew all in it, seven thousand men and women, both natives and aliens, and female slaves; for I had devoted it to Ashtar-Chemosh. I took from thence the vessels of YHWH and dragged them before Chemosh. Then the king of Israel had fortified Jahaz, and he occupied it while warring against me; but Chemosh drove him out before me. I took from Moab two hundred men, his whole division, and I led it up against Jahaz and captured it, annexing it to Dibon.

I carried out repairs at Qarhoh on the parkland walls as well as the walls of the acropolis; and I repaired its gates and repaired its towers; and I repaired the king's residence, and I made banks for the reservoir at the spring inside the town. But there was no cistern inside the town at Qarhoh; so I said to all the people: Each of you make for yourselves a cistern in his house. I had the ditches dug for Qarhoh with Israelite prisoners. I carried out repairs at Aroer, and I mended the highway at the Arnon. I rebuilt Beth-bamoth, for it had been destroyed; and I rebuilt Bezer, for it was in ruins, with fifty men of Dibon, because all Dibon had become subject *to me.*

So did I become king *over* hundreds in the towns that I annexed to the land. Then I rebuilt Medeba also, and Beth-diblathaim. And as for Beth Baal-meon, I led *my shepherds* up there *in order to tend the* sheep of the district. Then in Horonaim there had settled[4] . . . and Chemosh said to me: Go down, fight against Horonaim. So I went down *and fought against the town and took it,* and Chemosh *dwelled*

there in my days. As for . . . , from there . . . So did I.

#52: Karatepe Inscription
(Gibson, *Textbook of Syrian Semitic Inscriptions*, 3.47–55)[5]

The longest Phoenician inscription we have to date is from Karatepe, Turkey, where an eighth-century B.C. inscription was found. Three copies of the Phoenician text were preserved, two on city gates and one on the base of a statue of Baal. Also preserved on the gates were copies of the text in hieroglyphic Luwian, making this one of the longest bilingual inscriptions available. The text is a first-person account of Azatiwada, perhaps a king or prince in Cilicia in southeastern Turkey. In addition to the historical information it provides, the inscription is of interest because it contains titles and literary formulas used in the Old Testament, particularly curses and blessings.

I am Azatiwada, blessed by Baal, servant of Baal, whom King Awarku of the Danunians made powerful. Baal made me a father and a mother to the Danunians. I revived the Danunians. I extended the land of the plain of Adana from the rising of the sun to its setting. And in my days the Danunians had everything *that was* good, and plenty *of grain,* and fine food; and I filled the granaries of Pahar. And I acquired horse upon horse, and shield upon shield, and army upon army, by the grace of Baal and the gods. And I shattered dissenters, and I drove out every evildoer who was in the land. And I put the house of my lord into good order; and I acted kindly toward the scion of my lord, and I set him on his father's throne. And I made peace with every king, and indeed every king treated me as a father because of my righteousness, and because of my wisdom, and because of my goodness of heart. And I built strong fortresses in all the remote areas on the borders, in the places where there were wicked men, leaders of gangs, not one of whom had been a subject of the house of Mopsos; but I Azatiwada placed them under my feet. And I built fortresses in these places so that the Danunians might dwell in them with their minds at peace. And I subdued strong lands at the rising of the sun, which none of the kings who were before me had been able to subdue; but

I Azatiwada subdued them. I brought them down; I settled them on the edge of my borders at the setting of the sun; and I settled Danunians *up* there. So in my days they were on all the borders of the plain of Adana from the rising of the sun to its setting, even in the places that were formerly dreaded *and* where a man was afraid to walk on a road—but in my days a woman could walk by herself with *her* spindles, by the grace of Baal and the gods. And throughout my days the Danunians and the whole plain of Adana had plenty *of grain*, and fine food, and a gracious life, and peace of mind. And I rebuilt this city, and I called its name Azatiwadaya; for Baal and Resheph of the he-goats had commissioned me to build it. And I rebuilt it by the grace of Baal, and by the grace or Resheph of the he-goats, with plenty *of grain*, and with fine food, and with gracious living, and with peace of mind, so that it might be a protection for the plain of Adana and for the house of Mopsos; for in my days the land of the plain of Adana had plenty *of grain* and fine food; and the Danunians never had night in my days. So I rebuilt this city; I called its name Azatiwadaya; I made Baal KRNTRYSH dwell in it. Now let people bring a sacrifice for all the images, the yearly sacrifice of one ox, and at plowing [time] one sheep, and at harvest time one sheep! And may Baal KRNTRYSH bless Azatiwada with life and health and powerful strength above every king! May Baal KRNTRYSH and all the gods of the city give to Azatiwada length of days, and many years, and a pleasant old age, and powerful strength above every king! And may this city be owner of plenty *of grain* and new wine; and may this people who dwell in her be owners of oxen, and owners of sheep, and owners of plenty *of grain* and new wine; and may they bear many *children*, and as they grow many become powerful, and as they grow many serve Azatiwada and the house of Mopsos, by the grace of Baal and the gods! Now, if a king among kings, or a prince among princes, or any man who is a man of renown, effaces the name Azatiwada from this gate and puts up his own name, or more than that, covets this city and pulls down this gate that Azatiwada made, and makes another gate for it and puts

his own name on it, whether it is out of covetousness or whether it is out of hatred and malice that he pulls down this gate—then let Baal-shamem and El-Creator-of-Earth and the eternal sun and the whole generation of the sons of the gods efface that kingdom and that king and that man who is a man of renown! Only may the name Azatiwada last forever like the name of the sun and the moon! . . . and the Danunians never had night in my days. So I rebuilt this city, and I gave it the name Azatiwadaya, and I made this god Baal KRNTRYSH dwell *in it*. So may Baal KRNTRYSH bless Azatiwada with life and with health, and with powerful strength above every king! May Baal KRNTRYSH give to Azatiwada length of days, and many years, and a pleasant old age, and powerful strength above every king! And the sacrifice that [a man shall bring for] all the images of this god is this: the [yearly] sacrifice of [one] ox, [and] at plowing time [one sheep, and] at harvest time one sheep. And may this city be owner of plenty *of grain* and new wine; and may this people who dwell in her be owners of oxen, and owners of sheep, and owners of plenty *of grain* [and] new wine; and may they bear many *children*, and as they grow many become powerful, and as they grow many serve Azatiwada and the house of Mopsos, by the grace of Baal and by the grace of the gods! Now, if a king among kings, or a prince among princes, or any man who is a man of renown, gives orders for the name Azatiwada to be effaced from the statue of this god, and puts up his own name, or more than that, if he covets this city and says, I will make another statue and put my own name on it, and the statue of the god that Azatiwada made, *that of* Baal KRNTRYSH, that is at the king's entrance into . . . [Only may the name] Azatiwada last forever like the name of the sun and the moon!

#53: Stela of Zakkur
(Gibson, *Textbook of Syrian Semitic Inscriptions*, 2.9–13)[6]

A monument set up by King Zakkur, ruler of two adjacent territories (Hamath and Lu'ash), was discovered in four broken and badly damaged pieces in 1903. This Aramaic inscription commemorates Zakkur's victories over Ben-Hadad (or, in Aramaic,

Bar-Hadad) son of Hazael, king of Syria. The text is significant for at least two reasons: (1) it sheds light on the historical situation in Syria-Palestine during the late ninth and early eighth centuries B.C.—particularly, details about Israel's conflicts with Syria during this period—and (2) along with others like it, it illustrates how ancient Syro-Palestinian first-person royal inscriptions could have been transposed into third-person narratives like those in the Bible.[7] (See also reading 84.)

The stela, which King Zakkur of Hamath and Lu'ash set up for Ilwer, [his lord]. I am King Zakkur of Hamath and Lu'ash. A pious man was I, and Baal-shamayn [delivered] me, and stood with me; and Baal-shamayn made me king in Hadrach. Then Bar-Hadad son of Hazael, king of Aram, organized against me an alliance of [sixteen] kings—Bar-Hadad and his army, Bargush and his army, the [king] of Kue and his army, the king of Umq and his army, the king of Gurgum and his army, the king of Sam'al and his army, the king of Melitene and his army, [the king of . . . and his army, the king of . . . and his army], and seven [others] together with their armies. All these kings laid siege to Hadrach; they put up a rampart higher than the wall of Hadrach, and dug a trench deeper than its moat. But I lifted up my hands to Baal-shamayn, and Baal-shamayn answered me, and Baal-shamayn [spoke] to me through seers and messengers; and Baal-shamayn [said to me]: Fear not, because it was I who made you king, [and I shall stand] with you, and I shall deliver you from all [these kings who] have forced a siege upon you. Then [Baal-shamayn] said to me: *Destroyed shall be* all these kings who forced [a siege upon you] . . . and this rampart that [they put up] *shall be cast down* . . . Hadrach . . . for rider and horse . . . its king in its midst. I *then* [rebuilt] Hadrach, and I added [to it] a whole circle of [strongholds]; and I established it *once more* as my kingdom, and established it as [my land. I built all] these strongholds throughout my whole territory, and I built temples for gods throughout my whole [land]. Then I rebuilt . . . [and I rebuilt] Afis; and [I gave a resting place to the gods] in the tem-

The Tel Dan Inscription provides a ninth century B.C. extrabiblical reference to the "house of David." (Tel Dan Excavation, Hebrew Union College, Jerusalem. Photo: Zev Radovan.)

ple of [Ilwer in Afis]; and I have set up this stela before [Ilwer], and [written] thereon the story of my achievements. Now, whoever effaces the story [of the achievements] of King Zakkur of Hamath and Lu'ash from this stela, and whoever removes this stela from Ilwer's [presence], and drags it away [from its place], or whoever sends [his son] . . . , let Baal-shamayn and Ilwer and . . . and Shemesh and Sahar and . . . and the gods of heaven [and the gods] of earth and the Baal of . . . [execute] the man and [his son and his whole] stock. [But forever let] the name Zakkur and the name [of his house endure].

#54: Tel Dan Inscription
(Biran and Naveh, "Tel Dan Inscription," 13)[8]

In 1993 and 1994, excavations conducted by Hebrew Union College at the northern city of Dan retrieved three fragments from a large basalt monument that had been broken in antiquity. Preserved on the monument was an Old Aramaic inscription from the mid-ninth century B.C. The name of the king who left this monument at Dan is not known, but he was likely an Aramean ruler, possibly the king of Damascus and perhaps Hazael, who came to power around 842 B.C. The inscription may refer to the deaths of King Jehoram of Israel and King Ahaziah of Judah (2 Kings 8:28–29; 9:14–29). If so, Hazael either gave himself credit for their deaths or considered Jehu his agent.[9] Due to the fragmentary nature of the text, a continuous translation is not possible, but the reading presented here shows the probable mention of Jehoram and Ahaziah, as well as the important first extrabiblical mention of the "house of David."

My father went up [against him when] he fought at . . . And my father lay down, he went to his [ancestors]. And the king of Israel entered previously in my father's land. [And] Hadad made me king. And Hadad went in front of me, [and] I departed from [the] seven . . . of my kingdom, and I slew [seventy kings], who harnessed [thousands of chariots] and thousands of horsemen. [I killed Jehoram] son of [Ahab] king of Israel, and *I* killed [Ahaziahu] son of [Jehoram king] of the house of David. And I set [their towns into ruins and turned] their land into [desolation].

11 Letters

The monumental and chronographic literature from the ancient Near East usually highlights the events of kings or preeminent political leaders, often in exaggerated, propagandistic fashion. By contrast, letters from the ancient world often provide realistic snapshots of individuals, sometimes royal, but sometimes common citizenry. The letters presented here illustrate how political or social events on the international stage affect the lives of specific individuals. Such letters, of which there are many hundreds, are also important for the light they shed on colloquial speech patterns and vocabulary in the ancient Near East.

#55: El-Amarna
(Moran, *Amarna Letters*, 326–32)[1]

By the fourteenth century B.C., a provincial dialect of Babylonia had developed in northwestern Mesopotamia and become the lingua franca of the ancient world. Its use by scribes in Syria, Anatolia, Cyprus, Canaan, and even Egypt is illustrated by the famous Amarna Letters discovered in 1887. The majority of the 382 cuneiform documents found at el-Amarna are letters, and most of them were sent from vassal kings in Syria and Canaan to Pharaoh Amenhotep III (approximately 1390–1352 B.C.) and Pharaoh Akhenaten (approximately 1352–1338 B.C.). The letters reveal a Syria-Palestine torn by Habiru/Apiru invaders and by mutual distrust among the independent city-state governors, who slander each other in order to gain the upper hand with the Egyptians. The letters frequently appeal to the Egyptian rulers to provide military help against invaders or other local rulers. This valuable collection of letters appears to describe the situation just before the events of the books of Joshua and Judges. The three letters presented here are from Abdi-Heba, the governor of Jerusalem.

Amarna Letter 286

Say [to] the king, my lord: Message of Abdi-Heba, your servant. I fall at the feet of my lord, the king, seven times and seven times. What have I done to the king, my lord? They denounce me: I am slandered before the king, my lord: Abdi-Heba has rebelled against the king, his lord. Seeing that, as far as I am concerned, neither my father nor my mother put me in this place, but the strong arm of the king brought me into my father's house, why should I of all people commit a crime against the king, my lord? As truly as the king, my lord, lives, I say to the commissioner of the king, [my] lord: Why do you love the Apiru but hate the mayors? Accordingly, I am slandered before the king, my lord. Because I say: Lost are the lands of the king, my lord, accordingly I am slandered before the king, my lord. May the king, my lord, know that *though* the king, my lord, stationed a garrison *here*, Enhamu has taken [it all] away . . . [Now], O king my lord, [there is no] garrison, [and so] may the king provide for his land. May the king [provide] for his land! All the [lands] of the king, my lord, have deserted. Ili-Milku has caused the loss of all the land of the king, and so may the king, my lord, provide for his land. For my part, I say: I would go in to the king, my lord, and visit the king, my lord, but the war against me is severe, and so I am not able to go in to the king, my lord. And may it seem good in the sight of the king, [and] may he send a garrison so I may go in and visit the king, my lord. *In truth*, the king, my lord, lives: whenever the commissioners have come out, I would say *to them*: Lost are the lands of the king, but they did not listen to me. Lost are all the mayors; there is not a mayor remaining to the king, my lord. Pray the king turn his attention to the archers so that archers of the king, my lord, come forth. The king has no lands. *The* Apiru has plundered all the lands of the king. If there are archers this year, the lands of the king, my lord, will remain. [To] the scribe of the king, my lord: Message of Abdi-Heba, your [servant]. Present eloquent words to the king, my lord. Lost are all the lands of the king, my lord.

Amarna Letter 287

[Say to the king, my] lord: [Message of Abdi]-Heba, [your] servant. [I fall at the feet] of my lord seven [times and seven times. Consider] *the entire* affair. [Milkilu and Tagi brought troops] into [Qiltu] *against me.* [Consider] the deed that they did [to your servant]. Arrows . . . they brought into [Qiltu]. May the [king] know *that* all the lands are [at] peace *with one another,* but I am at war. May the king provide for his land. Consider the lands of Gazru, Ashqaluna, and [Lakisi]. They have given them food, oil, and any other requirement. So may the king provide for archers and send the archers against men that commit crimes against the king, my lord. If this year there are archers, then the lands and the mayors will belong to the king, my lord. But if there are no archers, then the [king] will have neither lands nor mayors. Consider Jerusalem! This neither my father nor [my] mother gave to me. The [strong] hand: *the arm* [of the king] gave it to me. Consider the deed! This is the deed of Milkilu and the deed of the sons of Lab'ayu, who have given the land of the king to the Apiru. Consider, O king, my lord! *I am in the right!* With regard to the Kashites, may the king make inquiry of the commissioners. Although the house is well fortified, they attempted a very serious crime. They took their tools, and *I had to seek shelter by a support* for the roof. [And so if] he is going to send [troops] into [Jerusalem], let them come with [a garrison for] *regular service.* May the king provide for them; [all] of the land *might be in dire straits* on their account. May the king inquire about [them. Let there be] much food, much oil, much clothing, until Pauru, the commissioner of the king, comes up to Jerusalem. Gone is Addaya together with the garrison of soldiers [that] the king [provided]. May the king know *that* Addaya [said] to me: [Behold], he has dismissed me. Do not abandon it, [and] send this [year] a

The Tel of ancient Lachish, where the Lachish Ostraca (number 56) were found. (Jim Yancey)

garrison, and send right here the commissioner of the king. I sent [as gifts] to the king, my lord, . . . prisoners, five thousand . . . , [and] *eight porters* for the caravans of the [king, my lord], but they have been taken in the countryside: SHA-DE-E of Ayyaluna. May the king, my lord, know *that* I am unable to send a caravan to the king, my lord. For your information! As the king has placed his name in Jerusalem forever, he cannot abandon it—the land of Jerusalem.

Say to the scribe of the king, my lord: Message of Abdi-Heba, your servant. I fall at *your* feet. I am your servant. Present eloquent words to the king, my lord: I am soldier of the king. I *am always yours.*

And please make the Kashites responsible for the evil deed. I was almost killed by the Kashites [in] my own house. May the king [make an inquiry] in [their] regard. [May the king], my lord, [provide] for [them. Seven times] and seven times may the king, my lord, [provide] for me.

Amarna Letter 288

Say [to] the king, my lord, [my sun]: Message of Abdi-Heba, your servant. I fall at the feet of the king, my lord, seven times and seven times. Behold, the king, my lord, has placed his name at the rising of the sun and at the setting of the sun. It is, therefore, impious what they have done to me. Behold, I am not a mayor; I am a soldier of the king, my lord. Behold, I am a *friend* of the king and a tribute bearer of the king. It was neither my father nor my mother, but the strong arm of the king that placed me in the house of [my father] . . . came to me . . . I gave over [to his charge] ten slaves. Shuta, the commissioner of the king, [came to] me; I gave over to Shuta's charge twenty-one girls, [eighty] prisoners, as a gift for the king, my lord. May the king give thought to his land; the land of the king is lost. *All of it has attacked* me. I am at war as far as the land of Sheru and as far as Ginti-kirmil. All the mayors are at peace, but I am at war. I am treated like an Apiru, and I do not visit the king, my lord, since I am at war. I am situated like a ship in the midst of the sea. The strong hand of the king took the land of Nahrima and the land of Kasi, but

now the Apiru have taken the very cities of the king. Not a single mayor remains to the king, my lord; all are lost. Behold, Turbazu was slain in the city gate of Silu. The king did nothing. Behold, servants who were joined to the Apiru *smote* Zimredda of Lakisu, and Yap-tih-Hadda was slain in the city gate of Silu. The king did nothing. [Why] has he not called them to account? May the king [provide] for [his land] and may he [see] to it that archers [come out] to [his] land. If there are no archers this year, all the lands of the king, my lord, are lost. They have not reported to the king that the lands of the king, my lord, are lost and all the mayors lost. If there are no archers this year, may the king send a commissioner to fetch me, me along with my brothers, and then we will die near the king, our lord. [To] the scribe of the king, my lord: [Message] of Abdi-Heba, *your* servant. [I fall at your feet]. Present [the words that I have] offered to [the king, my lord]: I am your servant and] your son.

#56: Lachish Ostraca
(Smelik, *Writings from Ancient Israel*, 120–25)[2]

Approximately midway between Jerusalem and Gaza lay the ancient city of Lachish. This strategic position meant that Lachish was one of the last lines of defense for the kingdom of Judah. Lachish was captured by Sennacherib near the end of the eighth century B.C. and again by Nebuchadnezzar during his campaign of 588–586 B.C. Archeologists discovered twenty-two Hebrew letters written on ostraca dating from this latter episode. The letters in which the addressee is named are all to Yaosh, whom we may presume to have been a high military official in Lachish. Ostracon 3 contains the name of its sender, Hoshaiah, who commanded a military post under Yaosh's jurisdiction. It is possible that all the letters were from Hoshaiah and that these letters therefore comprise a Hoshaiah "file."[3] Ostracon 3 is particularly interesting because of the reference to an unnamed prophet. Ostracon 4 contains a fascinating reference to the smoke signals used during military campaigns (Judges 20:38, 40; Jeremiah 6:1).

Lachish Ostracon 2

To my lord Yaosh. May YHWH let my lord hear tidings of peace, right now, right now!

Who is your servant—a dog, that my lord remembers his [servant]? May YHWH *make* my [lord] *remember* a matter that you do not know *any more*.

Lachish Ostracon 3

Your servant Hoshaiah sends *a message* to [report to] my [lord Yaosh]. May YHWH let my lord hear tidings of peace and [tidings of good fortune].

And now, please open *the eyes* of your servant about the letter that *my lord* sent to your servant yesterday evening. For the heart of your servant has been sick since your sending *of the letter* to your servant and because my lord says: You do not know how to read a letter! As YHWH lives, if ever someone has tried to read a letter for me! And also every letter that comes to me—when I have read it I can repeat it [later] down to the last detail.

And it has been reported to your servant, saying: The commander of the army Coniah son of Elnathan has come down to go to Egypt. And as regards Hodujah son of Ahijah and his men, he has sent *a message* to take *them* from here.

As to the letter of Tobiah, the servant of the king, which came to Shallum son of Yada from the prophet, saying: Take care!—your [servant] has sent it to my lord.

Lachish Ostracon 4

May YHWH let my lord hear right now tidings of good fortune! And now, in accordance with everything about which my lord sent *a message*, so has your servant done. I have written in the *column of the papyrus* in accordance with everything about which [my lord] sent *a message* [to] me. And as regards *the message that* my lord sent concerning the matter at Beth-harafid: there is no one there.

And Semachiah—Shemaiah has taken him and made him go up to the city. And your servant—I [cannot] send the [witness at once] from here, but only in the course of tomorrow morning.

And let him know that we ourselves are watching the smoke signals from Lachish according to all the signals that my lord gives, for we cannot see Azekah.

#57: Arad Ostraca
(Gibson, *Textbook of Syrian Semitic Inscriptions*, 1.53)[4]

As Lachish played a strategic military role due to its geographic location, so Arad was crucial because of its location twenty miles east-northeast

Ancient Arad boasted a temple with a large altar and a holy of holies. (Bryan Beyer)

of Beersheba, along the highway from central Judah to Edom and protecting the southern frontier of the kingdom. During the period leading up to and including the Babylonian campaign in Judah, Arad was a regional military and administrative center, and Edomite forces became more threatening as the kingdom began to crumble (Obadiah 10–14; Ezekiel 25:12). Archeologists discovered numerous inscriptions, including eighteen Hebrew letters to Eliashib, apparently the commandant of the fortress. Many of the letters are requests for wine, oil, or flour, which leads to the assumption that Eliashib was responsible for procuring rations for his military personnel. The letter presented here is of interest because it mentions "the house of YHWH," which likely refers to Solomon's Temple in Jerusalem.

To my lord Eliashib
may YHWH ask
for your peace. And now—
give to Shemariah
. . . And to the Kerosite
give . . . And touching
the matter about which you
instructed me—all is well.
He is staying in the house
of YHWH.

#58: Yavneh Yam Inscription

(Smelik, *Writings from Ancient Israel*, 96)[5]

In 1960, archeologists discovered six fragments of an ostracon in the remains of a fortress near Yavneh Yam, south of Tel Aviv–Jaffa. The inscription contains the appeal of a farm worker to the governor of the district. The worker's garment has been confiscated on the grounds that he has not met his daily quota of grain, even though he has witnesses who will testify that he has met his quota. The worker appeals to the governor for the return of his garment. Recently, the nature of the inscription as a letter has been questioned, and it may be better to view it as an extrajudicial petition for justice, without the customary letter formulas and other features common to letters.[6] On the basis of epigraphy and biblical and social parallels, most scholars believe the text was composed in the late seventh century B.C.

Let my lord, the governor, hear the
   word of his servant!
Your servant is a reaper.
Your servant was in Hazar Asam
and your servant reaped
and he finished
and he has stored *the grain* during these
   days
before stopping.
When your [servant] had finished the
   harvest,
and had stored *the grain* during these
   days,
Hoshaiah came, the son of Shobai,
and he took the garment of your
   servant,
when I had finished my harvest.
It *is already now some* days *since* he took
   the garment of your servant.
And all my companions can bear
   witness for me
—they who reaped with me in the heat
   of the [harvest]—
yes, my companions can bear witness
   for me.
Amen! I am innocent of any [guilt.
Do give back] my garment,
so that I may be vindicated!
It is incumbent upon the governor to
   give [back the garment] of [his
   servant!
And show pity] on him!
[And you should hear] the [word] of
   your [servant]
and you should not *be silent*!

12 Other Hebrew Inscriptions

In addition to Hebrew letters (readings 56–58), several Hebrew inscriptions are of interest to readers of the Old Testament.

#59: Gezer Calendar
(Gibson, *Textbook of Syrian Semitic Inscriptions*, 1.2)[1]

In 1908, archeologists found a limestone tablet at Gezer, inscribed with seven lines of archaic script. Scholarly consensus about the language and shape of the letters led to an astonishing tenth-century B.C. date for the inscription. This little inscription—containing a list of the annual farming cycle, beginning in late summer—probably illustrates the earliest precursor of the Hebrew in our Old Testament, and scholars sometimes refer to it as the oldest Hebrew inscription. Since the limestone shows signs of erasures, it is often assumed that the "Gezer Calendar" was a school exercise tablet.

Months of vintage and olive harvest;
    months of
sowing; months of spring pasture;
month of flax pulling;
month of barley harvest;
month of wheat harvest and measuring;
months of pruning;
month of summer fruit.
Margin: Abijah.

#60: Siloam Tunnel Inscription
(McCarter, *Ancient Inscriptions*, 114)[2]

The Bible credits Hezekiah (715–686 B.C.) with diverting the waters of the Gihon Spring into the city of Jerusalem (2 Kings 20:20; 2 Chronicles 32:30). The context of this event is the impending invasion of Sennacherib's armies, and Hezekiah was presumably preparing for the siege (2 Chronicles 32:2–5). In 1880, boys swimming near the southwestern end of the tunnel found a now famous inscription. The "Siloam Tunnel Inscription" describes how two teams of workers started at opposite ends and dug toward each other until they met near the source of the Gihon. The completion of the tunnel was a remarkable engineering achievement by ancient standards. The inscription commemorates the event by describing the excitement of the workers when they finally heard each other's axes through the soft limestone. A recent attempt to redate the inscription to the much later Hasmonean period has not met with acceptance on the part of the learned community.[3]

. . . the breakthrough. And this was the manner of the breakthrough: While [the stone-

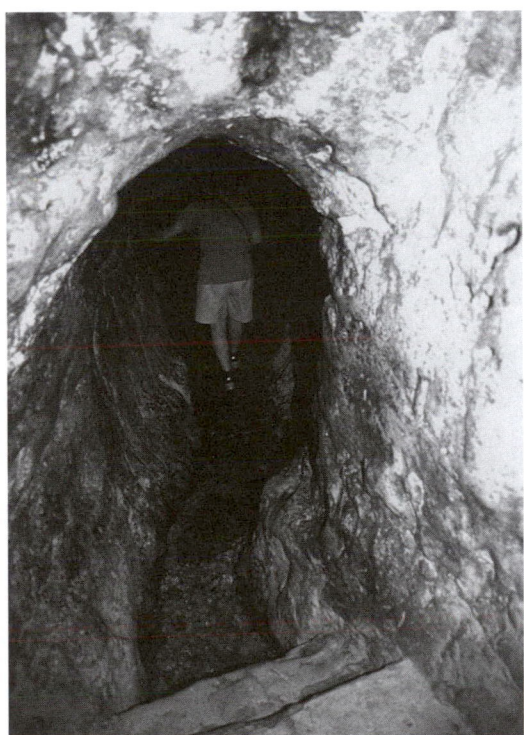

Students going through Hezekiah's Tunnel. The Siloam Inscription was discovered near the end of the tunnel. (Jim Yancey)

cutters were] still [wielding] the ax, each man toward his fellow, and while there were still three cubits to be [cut through, they heard] the sound of each man calling to his fellow, for there was a *seam* in the rock to the right [and the left]. And on the day of the break-through the stonecutters struck each man toward his fellow, ax against ax, and the waters flowed from the source to the pool, for twelve hundred cubits. And one hundred cubits was the height of the rock above the head of the stonecutters.

#61: Samaria Ostraca
(*ANET* 321)[4]

> Excavations at the city of Samaria in 1910 led to the discovery of sixty-three ostraca, most of which are dated receipts for goods shipped into the city, usually oil or wine. Most of the texts are dated to the reign of an unnamed king, usually thought to have been Jeroboam II (793–753 B.C.). Although at first glance, these little texts may not seem important, their very number makes them interesting for the study of early Hebrew epigraphy, and they present a great opportunity for the study of Israelite personal names, geographical names, and the economic structure of the northern kingdom. The texts may also have religious significance since they contain many Baal-type personal names (notice the name Abi-Baal in ostracon 2). The degree to which these receipts can be used to measure the extent of Baal worship in ancient Israel is, however, in question.

Samaria Ostracon 1

In the tenth year. To Shamaryau from Beeryam, a jar of old wine. Pega *son of* Elisha, two; Uzza *son of* . . . , one; Eliba, one; Baala *son of* Elisha, one; Jedaiah, one.

Samaria Ostracon 2

In the tenth year. To Gaddiyau from Azzo. Abi-Baal, two; Ahaz, two; Sheba, one; Merib-Baal, one.

Samaria Ostracon 18

In the tenth year. From Hazeroth to Gaddiyau. A jar of fine oil.

Samaria Ostracon 30

In the fifteenth year. From Shemida to Hilez *son of* Gaddiyau. Gera *son of* Hanniab.

Samaria Ostracon 55

In the tenth year. *From the* vineyard of Yehau-Eli. A jar of fine oil.

An Order for Barley from Samaria

Baruch *son of* [Shallum] . . .
O Baruch . . . pay attention and [give to . . . son of] Yimnah barley *to the amount of* two [measures].

#62: Blessings from Kuntillet Ajrud
(Hess, "Yahweh and His Asherah?" 21, 22, 24)[5]

> Kuntillet Ajrud, a site approximately forty miles south-southwest of Kadesh-Barnea, has yielded small inscriptions containing various blessings. Since their discovery in the 1970s, these short eighth-century B.C. blessing-inscriptions have generated an enormous amount of debate among Old Testament scholars and have forced reconsideration of the role that Asherah, the Canaanite fertility goddess, may have played in Israelite religion.[6] The word translated "Asherata" may also be "his Asherah"—that is, YHWH's Asherah." But since the texts are actually graffiti inscribed on walls and doorposts, it would be unwise to come to a conclusion that Israel was polytheistic on the basis of these texts. Furthermore, Kuntillet Ajrud is far from Jerusalem and central Judah and can hardly be taken as typical of Israelite religion in the eighth century. Moreover, the vast majority of inscriptional evidence from the Judean heartland supports the biblical picture of Israelite religion.

I bless you by YHWH of Samaria and by Asherata.

I bless you by YHWH of Teman and by Asherata.
May he *bless* you and keep you and be with my lord.

Whatever he requests from a man may it be favored . . .
let YHWH give him according to his heart *desire*.

Part
3

Poetic Books

---

13 Wisdom Literature

Mesopotamian and Egyptian wisdom literature, like the wisdom literature of the Bible, addresses many different aspects of life.[1] Many texts wrestle with questions of ultimate justice, such as, "Why do bad things happen to good people?" Others give instruction regarding interpersonal relationships. Although the Bible condemns the religious practices of pagan nations, it respects sages among such nations (1 Kings 4:29–34).

#63: Man and His God
(*ANET* 589–91)[2]

Archeological excavations at the ancient city of Nippur resulted in the discovery of "Man and His God," a work written in the Sumerian language about 2000 B.C. during the final glory years of Sumerian civilization. The writer struggles with the difficult trials he is experiencing and questions whether his god has abandoned him. In the end, his god restores him to favor. Because it addresses the theme of why the righteous suffer, this story has been called the "Sumerian Job," although no direct connection exists with the biblical Book of Job.

Let a man utter constantly the
    exaltedness of his god,
let the young man praise artlessly the
    words of his god,
let the inhabitant of the straightforward
    land [moan],
in the house [of song] let him [interpret]
    . . . to his woman friend and man
    friend,
soothe [his heart],
bring forth . . . , utter . . . ,
[measure out] . . . ,
let this lament soothe the heart of his
    god,

for a man without a god would not
    obtain food.

(gap)

I am a young man, a discerning one, *yet*
    who [respects] me [prospers] not,
my righteous word has been turned into
    a lie,
the man of deceit has covered me *with*
    the south wind, I *am forced to* serve
    him,
who [respects] me not has shamed me
    before you.
You have doled out to me suffering ever
    anew,
I entered the house, heavy is the spirit,
I, the young man, went out to the street,
    oppressed is the heart,
with me, the [valiant], my righteous
    shepherd has become angry, has
    looked upon me inimically,
my herdsman has sought out evil forces
    against me who am not *his* enemy,
my companion says not a true word to
    me,
my friend gives the lie to my righteous
    word.
The man of deceit has [conspired]
    against me,
and you, my god, do not thwart him,
you carry off my understanding,
the wicked has [conspired] against me
angered you, stormed about, planned
    evil.
I, the wise, why am I bound to the
    ignorant youths?
I, the discerning, why am I counted
    among the ignorant?
Food is all about, *yet* my food is hunger,
on the day shares were allotted to all,
    my allotted share was suffering.

(gap)

Lo, let not my mother who bore me
 cease my lament before you,
let not my sister [utter] the happy song
 and chant,
let her utter tearfully my misfortunes
 before you,
let my wife voice [mournfully] my
 suffering,
let the expert singer bemoan my bitter
 fate.
My god, the day shines bright over the
 land, for me the day is black,
the bright day, the good day has . . . like
 the . . . ,
tears, lament, anguish, and depression
 are lodged within me,
suffering overwhelms me like one who
 does *nothing but* weep,
the demon of fate in its hand . . . me,
 carries off my breath of life,
the malignant sickness demon [bathes]
 in my body,
the bitterness of my path, the [evil] of
 [my] . . .

(gap)

My god, you who are my father who
 begot me, [lift up] my face,
[like] an innocent cow, in [pity] . . . the
 groan,
how long will you neglect me, leave me
 unprotected?
Like an ox . . .
How long will you leave me unguided?
They say—the sages—a word righteous
 and straightforward:
Never has a sinless child been born to its
 mother,
. . . a sinless [workman] has not existed
 from of old.
My god, the . . . of destruction that I
 have . . . against you,
the . . . of . . . that I have prepared before
 you,
let them not . . . the man, the [wise];
 utter, *my god*, [words of grace] upon
 him,
when the day is not *yet* [bright], in my
 . . . , in my . . . , make me walk before
 you,

my impure *and* my lackluster . . .—
 [touch] their . . . ,
[utter words of grace] upon [him] whom
 you . . . on the day of wrath,
whom you . . . [on] the day . . .—
 pronounce joy [upon] him.
My god, now that you have [shown] me
 my sins . . . ,
in the gate of . . . , I would speak . . . ,
I, the young man, would [confess] my
 sins before you.
May you [rain] upon the assembly . . .
 like a cloud,
may you . . . [in] your [chamber] my
 groaning [mother] . . . ,
me, the [valiant], may you . . . [in
 wisdom my] groaning . . .

(gap)

The man—his bitter weeping was heard
 by his god,
when the lamentation and wailing that
 filled him had soothed the heart of
 his god for the young man,
the righteous words, the artless words
 uttered by him, his god accepted,
the words that the young [man]
 prayerfully confessed,
[pleased] the . . . , the flesh of his god,
 and his god withdrew his hand from
 the evil word,
. . . which oppresses the heart, . . . he
 embraces,
the encompassing sickness demon,
 which had spread wide its wings, he
 [swept away],
the . . . , which had smitten him like a
 . . . , he dissipated,
the *demon of* fate, who had been placed
 there in [accordance] with his
 [sentence], he turned [aside],
he turned the [young man's] suffering
 into joy,
set by him the . . . [good] . . . spirit *as a*
 watch *and* guardian,
gave him . . . the tutelary deity of
 friendly countenance.
[The man uttered] constantly the
 exaltedness of his god.

#64: LUDLUL BEL NEMEQI
(*ANET* 596–600)[3]

The words LUDLUL BEL NEMEQI mean "I will praise the lord of wisdom" and comprise the beginning of a piece of ancient wisdom literature sometimes called the "Babylonian Job." The text dates to the mid- to late first millennium B.C. The hero, Shubshi-meshre-Shakkan, describes how the gods and his friends all abandoned him and how all attempts to placate the gods only made his circumstances worse. Finally, he receives a promise that the gods will restore him, and they do under the leadership of Marduk, head of the Babylonian pantheon.

I will praise the lord of wisdom, the
  [deliberative] god,
who lays hold of the night, but frees the
  day,
Marduk, the lord of wisdom, the
  [deliberative] god,
who lays hold of the night, but frees the
  day,
whose fury surrounds him like a storm
  wind,
but whose breeze is as pleasant as a
  morning zephyr,
whose anger is irresistible, whose rage is
  a devastating flood,
but whose heart is merciful, whose
  mind forgiving,
the . . . of whose hands the heavens
  cannot hold back,
but whose gentle hand sustains the
  dying,
Marduk, the . . . of whose hands the
  heavens cannot hold back,
but whose gentle hand sustains the
  dying.

  (*gap*)

My god has forsaken me and
  [disappeared],
my goddess has cut me off and stayed
  removed from me.
The benevolent spirit who was *always*
  beside [me] has departed,
my protective spirit has flown away and
  seeks someone else.
My dignity had been taken away, my
  manly good looks jeopardized,

my pride has been cut off, my protection
  has skipped off.
Terrifying omens have been brought
  upon me,
I was put out of my house and
  wandered about outside.
The omens concerning me are confused,
  daily there [is inflammation].
I cannot stop going to the diviner and
  dream interpreter.
What is said in the street portends ill for
  me.
When I lie down at night my dream is
  terrifying.

  (*gap*)

Although I was a respectable man, I
  have become a slave.
To my [many relations] I have become
  like a recluse.
If I walk the street, fingers are pointed at
  me;
if I enter the palace, eyes blink.
My own town looks on me as an enemy;
even my land is savage and hostile.
My friend has become a stranger,
my companion has become an evil
  person and a demon.
In his rage my comrade denounces me,
constantly my associate [furbishes] his
  weapons.
My close friend has brought my life into
  danger;
my slave has publicly cursed me in the
  assembly.
. . . the crowd has defamed me.
When someone who knows me sees me,
  he [passes by on the other side].
My family treats me as if I were not
  related to them,
the grave is ready for anyone who
  speaks well of me,
but he who speaks ill of me is promoted.
The one who slanders me has the god's
  help;
the . . . who says "god have mercy"
  when death is imminent
without delay becomes well through his
  protective god.
I have no one to go at my side, nor have
  I found anyone understanding.

(gap)

I called to my god, but he did not show
    his face,
I prayed to my goddess, but she did not
    raise her head.
Even the diviner with his divination
    could not make a prediction,
and the interpreter of dreams with his
    libation could not elucidate my case.
I sought the favor of the ZAQIQU spirit,
    but he would not enlighten me;
the exorcist with his ritual could not
    appease the divine wrath against me.
What strange conditions everywhere!
When I look behind *me*, there is
    persecution, trouble.

(gap)

For myself, I gave attention to
    supplication and prayer:
my prayer was discretion, sacrifice my
    rule.
The day for worshiping the god was a
    joy to my heart;
the day of the goddess's procession was
    profit and gain to me.
The king's blessing—that was my joy,
and the accompanying music became a
    delight for me.
I had my land keep the god's rites,
and brought my people to value the
    goddess's name.
I made the praise for the king like a
    god's,
and taught the people respect for the
    palace.
I wish I knew that these things would be
    pleasing to one's god!
What is good for oneself may be offense
    to one's god,
what in one's own heart seems
    despicable may be proper to one's
    god.
Who can know the will of the gods in
    heaven?
Who can understand the plans of the
    underworld gods?
Where have humans learned the way of
    a god?
He who was alive yesterday is dead
    today.

One moment he is worried, the next he
    is boisterous.
One moment he is singing a joyful song,
a moment later he wails like a
    professional mourner.
Their condition changes *as quickly as*
    opening and shutting *the eyes.*

(gap)

My house has become my prison.
My arms are powerless—my own flesh
    is a manacle,
my feet are fallen flat—my own person
    is a fetter.
My afflictions are grievous, my wound
    is severe.
A whip full of needles has struck me,
the goad that pricked me was covered
    with barbs.
All day long the tormentor torments
    [me],
and at night he does not let me breathe
    easily for a minute.
Through twisting my joints are parted,
my limbs are splayed and knocked
    apart.
I spent the night in my dung like an ox,
and wallowed in my excrement like a
    sheep.
My symptoms are beyond the exorcist,
and my omens have confused the
    diviner.
The exorcist could not diagnose the
    nature of my sickness,
nor could the diviner set a time limit on
    my illness.
My god has not come to the rescue nor
    taken me by the hand;
my goddess has not shown pity on me
    nor gone by my side.
My grave was waiting, and my funerary
    paraphernalia ready,
before I was even dead lamentation for
    me was finished.

(gap)

A third time I had a dream,
and in the dream I had at night
a remarkable young woman of shining
    countenance,
. . . , equal to a god.

A queen of the peoples . . .
She entered and [sat down] . . .
She spoke my deliverance . . .
Fear not, she said, I [will . . . you].
. . . [had] a dream . . .
She said: Be delivered from your very
    wretched state,
whoever has had a vision during the
    night.
In the dream Urnindinlugga . . .
A bearded young man wearing a head
    covering,
an exorcist, carrying a *cuneiform* tablet,
Marduk has sent me.
To Shubshi-meshre-Shakkan I have
    brought prosperity,
from Marduk's pure hands I have
    brought prosperity.
Marduk had entrusted me into the hands
    of my ministrant.
[In] waking hours he sent a message
and showed his favorable sign to my
    people.
In the . . . sickness . . .
My illness was quickly over and [my]
    . . . broken.
After the mind of my lord had quieted
and the heart of merciful Marduk
    rejoiced,
[after he had] received my prayers . . .
To whom turning is pleasant . . .

    (gap)

[He brought] near his spell that binds
    . . .

[He drove] away the evil wind to the
    horizon,
to the surface of the underworld he took
    [the headache,
he sent] down the evil cough to its
    Apsu,
the irresistible demon he returned [to]
    Ekur,
he overthrew the LAMASHTU demon,
    sending her off to the mountain,
he sent the chills to the flowing water
    and the sea.
He tore up the root of weakness as if it
    were a plant.
Troubled sleep, the *continual* sleepiness

he took far away like smoke with which
    the heavens get filled.

    (gap)

The Babylonians saw how [Marduk]
    restores to health,
and all mouths proclaim [his] greatness:
Who would have thought that he would
    see his sun?
Who would have thought that he would
    walk along his street?
Who but Marduk could have restored
    the dying to life?
Apart from Sarpanitum, which goddess
    could have granted life?
Marduk can even restore to life someone
    already in the grave,
Sarpanitum knows how to save from
    destruction.
Wherever the earth is laid, and the
    heavens are extended,
wherever the sun-god shines, and the
    fire god blazes,
wherever water flows and winds blow,
creatures whose clay Aruru took in her
    fingers,
those endowed with life, who walk
    about,
humanity, all of it, gives praise to
    Marduk!

#65: Babylonian Theodicy
(*ANET* 601–4)[4]

Composed about 1000 B.C., the "Babylonian Theodicy" is an acrostic poem, having twenty-seven stanzas of eleven lines each. The acrostic reads "I, Saggil-kinam-ubbib, the incantation priest, am an adorer of the god and the king." The work is a dialogue between a sufferer and his friend. The sufferer complains about his lot in life, while the friend attempts to defend the conventional thinking of the day regarding suffering in the world.

Sufferer

O sage . . . come, [let] me tell you.
. . . [let] me inform you.
. . . you,
I . . . , who suffered greatly, will not
    cease to reverence you.

Where is the wise man of your caliber?
Where is the scholar who can rival you?
Where is the counselor to whom I can
relate my trouble?
I am finished. Anguish has come upon
me.
When I was still a child, fate took my
father;
my mother who bore me went to the
Land of No Return.
My father and mother left me without
anyone to be my guardian.

Friend

Respected friend, what you say is sad.
Dear friend, you have let your [mind]
dwell on evil.
You have made your good sense like
that of an incompetent person;
you have changed your beaming face to
scowls.
Our fathers do indeed give up and go
the way of death.
It is an old saying that they cross the
river Hubur.
When you look upon all of humankind
. . . it is not . . . that has made the
impoverished firstborn rich.
Who prefers as a favorite the rich man?
He who looks to his god has a protective
spirit;
the humble man who fears his goddess
accumulates wealth.

Sufferer

My friend, your mind is a spring whose
depth has not been found,
the high swell of the sea, which does not
subside.
I will ask you a question; listen to what I
say.
Pay attention for a moment; hear my
words.
My body is . . . hunger is my fear;
my success has vanished, my [stability]
has gone.
My strength is weakened, my prosperity
has ended,
moaning and trouble have darkened my
features.

The grain of my fields is far from
satisfying [me],
beer, the people's sustenance, is far from
[being enough for me].
Can a life of happiness be assured? I
wish I knew how!

Friend

What I say is restrained . . .
But you . . . your reason contrarily.
You make [your] . . . diffuse and
irrational,
you [turn] your select . . . blind.
As to your persistent unending desire
for . . .
[The former] security . . . [is] . . . by
prayers.
The appeased goddess returns with . . .
. . . without setting things aright, takes
pity on . . .
Ever seek the [correct standards] of
justice.
Your . . . , the mighty one, will show
kindness,
. . . will grant mercy.

Sufferer

Your mind is the north wind, a pleasant
breeze for the people.
Dearest friend, your advice is good.
Just one word would I put before you.
Those who do not seek the god go the
way of prosperity,
while those who pray to the goddess
become destitute and impoverished.
In my youth I tried to find the will of my
god;
with prostration and prayer I sought my
goddess.
But I was pulling a yoke in a useless
labor.
My god decreed poverty instead of
wealth *for me*.
A cripple does better than I, a dullard
keeps ahead of me.
The rogue has been promoted, but I
have been brought low.

Friend

My just, knowledgeable friend, your
thoughts are perverse.
You have now forsaken justice and
[blaspheme] against your god's plans.
In your mind you think of disregarding
the divine ordinances.
. . . the sound rules of *your* goddess.
The clever plans of the god [are] . . . like
the center of heaven,
the decrees of the goddess are not . . .
. . . humanity has learned well.
Their ideas . . . to humankind;
to grasp the way of a goddess . . .
Their reason is close at hand.

Sufferer

I have looked around in the world, but
things are turned around.
The god does not impede the way of
even a demon.
A father tows a boat along the canal,
while his son lies in bed.
The eldest son makes his way like a lion,
the second son is happy to be a mule
driver.
The heir goes about along the streets
like a [peddler],
the younger son *has enough* that he can
give food to the destitute.
What has it profited me that I have
bowed down to my god?
I must bow even to a person who is
lower than I,
the rich and opulent treat me, as a
youngest brother, with contempt.

Friend

O wise one, O learned one, who masters
knowledge,
your heart has become hardened and
you accuse the god wrongly.
The mind of the god, like the center of
the heavens, is remote;
knowledge of it is very difficult; people
cannot know it.
Among all the creatures whom Aruru
formed
[why] should the oldest offspring be so
. . . ?

In the case of a cow, the first calf is a
runt,
the later offspring is twice as big.
A first child is born a weakling,
but the second is called a mighty
warrior.
Although it is possible to find out what
the will of the god is, people do not
know how to do it.

Sufferer

Pay attention, my friend, understand
my clever ideas,
heed my carefully chosen words.
People extol the word of a strong man
who has learned to kill
but bring down the powerless who has
done no wrong.
They confirm *the position of* the wicked
for whom what should be an
abomination is considered right
yet drive off the honest man who heeds
the will of his god.
They fill the [storehouse] of the
oppressor with gold,
but empty the larder of the beggar of its
provisions.
They support the powerful, whose . . . is
guilt,
but destroy the weak and trample the
powerless.
And as for me, an insignificant person, a
prominent person persecutes me.

Friend

Narru, king of the gods, who created
humankind,
and majestic Zulummar, who pinched
off the clay for them,
and goddess Mami, the queen who
fashioned them,
gave twisted speech to the human race.
With lies, and not truth, they endowed
them forever.
Solemnly they speak favorably of a rich
man,
He is a king, they say; riches should be
his,
but they treat a poor man like a thief,

they have only bad to say of him and
plot his murder,
making him suffer every evil like a
criminal, because he has no . . .
Terrifyingly they bring him to his end,
and extinguish him like glowing
coals.

Sufferer

You are kind, my friend; behold my
trouble,
help me; look on my distress; know it.
I, though humble, wise, and a suppliant,
have not seen help or aid even for a
moment.
I have gone about the square of my city
unobtrusively,
my voice was not raised, my speech was
kept low.
I did not raise my head, but looked at
the ground,
I did not worship even as a slave in the
company of my associates.
May the god who has abandoned me
give help,
may the goddess who has [forsaken me]
show mercy,
the shepherd, the sun of the people,
pastures *his flock* as a god should.

#66: Instruction of Ptahhotep
(*ANET* 412–14)

The "Instruction of Ptahhotep" comes from Egypt and appears to date to the late third millennium B.C., although the earliest manuscripts date several centuries later. The text describes Ptahhotep as an important official under Pharaoh Isesi of Egypt's fifth dynasty. After a prologue in which Ptahhotep laments his old age and requests that his son stand in his place before pharaoh, Ptahhotep then proceeds to instruct his son about the laws of life and interpersonal relationships.

The instruction of the mayor and vizier Ptahhotep, under the majesty of the king of Upper and Lower Egypt: Izezi, living forever and ever. The mayor and vizier Ptahhotep says:

O sovereign, my lord! Oldness has come; old age has descended. Feebleness has arrived; dotage is coming anew. The heart sleeps wearily every day. The eyes are weak, the ears are deaf, the strength is disappearing because of weariness of heart, and the mouth is silent and cannot speak. The heart is forgetful and cannot recall yesterday. The bone suffers old age. Good is become evil. All taste is gone. What old age does to men is evil in every respect. The nose is stopped up and cannot breathe. *Simply* to stand up or to sit down is difficult.

Let a command be issued to this servant to make a staff of old age, that my son may be made to stand in my place. Then may I speak to him the words of them that listen and the ideas of the ancestors, of them that hearkened to the gods. Then shall the like be done for you, that strife may be banished from the people and the Two Banks may serve you.

Then the majesty of this god said:

Egyptian Civilization was noted for its artistry and wisdom. (Copyright Erich Lessing/Art Resource, N.Y.)

Teach him first about speaking. Then he may set an example for the children of officials. May obedience enter into him, and all heart's poise. Speak to him. There is no one born wise.

The beginning of the expression of good speech, spoken by the hereditary prince and count, god's father and god's beloved, eldest son of the king, of his body, the mayor and vizier, Ptahhotep, in instructing the ignorant about wisdom and about the rules for good speech, as of advantage to him who will hearken and of disadvantage to him who may neglect them.

Then he said to his son:

Let not your heart be puffed up because of your knowledge; be not confident because you are a wise man. Take counsel with the ignorant as well as the wise. The *full* limits of skill cannot be attained, and there is no skilled man equipped to his *full* advantage. Good speech is more hidden than the emerald, but it may be found with maidservants at the grindstones . . .

If you are a leader commanding the affairs of the multitude, seek out for yourself every beneficial deed, until it may be that your *own* affairs are without wrong. Justice is great, and its appropriateness is lasting; it has not been disturbed since the time of him who made it, *whereas* there is punishment for him who passes over its laws. It is the *right* path before him who knows nothing. Wrongdoing has never brought its undertaking into port. *It may be that* it is fraud that gains riches, *but* the strength of justice is that it lasts, and a man may say: It is the property of my father . . .

If you are one of those sitting at the table of one greater than yourself, take what he may give, when it is set before your nose. You should gaze at what is before you. Do not pierce him with many stares, *for such* an aggression against him is an abomination to the KA. Let your face be cast down until he addresses you, and you should speak *only* when he addresses you. Laugh after he laughs, and it will be very pleasing to his heart and what you may do will be pleasing to the heart. No one can know what is in the heart.

As for the great man when he is at meals, his purposes conform to the dictates of his KA.

He will give to the one whom he favors. The great man gives to [the man whom he can reach,] *but* it is the KA that lengthens out his arms. The eating of bread is under the planning of god—it is *only* a fool who would [complain of] it.

(gap)

If you are a poor fellow, following a man of distinction, one of good standing with the god, know not his former insignificance. You should not be puffed up against him because of what you knew of him formerly. Show regard for him in conformance with what has accrued to him—property does not come of itself. It is their law for him who wishes them. [As for him who oversteps, he is feared]. It is god who makes *a man's* quality, and he defends him *even* while he is asleep . . .

If you are a man of standing and found a household and produce a son who is pleasing to god, if he is correct and inclines toward your ways and listens to your instruction, while his manners in your house are fitting, and if he takes care of your property as it should be, seek out for him every useful action. He is your son, whom your KA engendered for you. You should not cut your heart off from him.

But a man's seed *often* creates enmity. If he goes astray and transgresses your plans and does not carry out your instruction, *so that* his manners in your household are wretched, and he rebels against all that you say, while his mouth [runs on] in the *most* wretched talk, *quite* [apart from his experience], while he possesses nothing, you should cast him off: he is not your son at all. He was not really born to you. *Thus* you enslave him entirely according to his *own* speech . . . He is one whom god has condemned in the *very* womb . . .

If you are one to whom petition is made, be calm as you listen to the petitioner's speech. Do not rebuff him before he has swept out his body or before he has said that for which he came. A petitioner likes attention to his words better than the fulfilling of that for which he came. He is rejoicing thereat more than any *other* petitioner, *even* before what has been heard has come to pass. As for him who plays the rebuffer of a petitioner, men say: Now why is he doing it? It is not *necessary* that everything about which he has petitioned [should] come to pass, *but* a good hearing is a soothing of the heart.

(*gap*)

If you are a man of standing, you should found your household and love your wife at home as is fitting. Fill her belly; clothe her back. Ointment is the prescription for her body. Make her heart glad as long as you live. She is a profitable field for her lord. You should not contend with her at law, and keep her far from gaining control . . . Her eye is her stormwind. Let her heart be soothed through what may accrue to you; it means keeping her long in your house . . .

(*gap*)

If a son accepts what his father says, no project of his miscarries. He whom you instruct as your obedient son, who will stand well in the heart of the official, his speech is guided with respect to what has been said to him, one regarded as obedient . . . *But* the [induction] of him who does not listen miscarries. The wise man rises early in the morning to establish himself, *but* the fool rises early in the morning *only* to [agitate] himself.

As for the fool who does not listen, he cannot do anything. He regards knowledge as ignorance and profit as loss. He does everything blameworthy, so that one finds fault with him every day. He lives on that through which he should die, and guilt is his food. His character therefrom [is told] as something known to the officials: dying while alive every day . . .

An obedient son is a follower of Horus. It goes well with him when he hears. When he becomes old and reaches a venerable state, he converses in the same way to his children, by renewing the instruction of his father. Every man is [as] *well* [instructed as he acts]. If he converses with *his* children, then they will speak *to* their children.

#67: Instruction of Merikare
(*ANET* 414–18)[5]

The oldest manuscripts of the "Instruction of Merikare" come from the mid-second millennium

B.C., although the original Egyptian text dates from the late third millennium B.C., probably a century or two after the "Instruction of Ptah-hotep." The beginning of the text is broken, but appears to come from Merikare's father,[6] who instructs his son how to serve as an effective ruler.

[The beginning of the instruction that the king of Upper and Lower Egypt: . . . made] for his son, King Merikare . . .

. . . [If] you [find a man who] . . . , whose adherents are many in total, . . . and he is gracious in the sight of his partisans, . . . and he is [excitable], a talker—remove him, kill [him], wipe out his name, [destroy] his faction, banish the memory of him and of his adherents who love him.

The contentious man is a disturbance to citizens: he produces two factions among the youth. If you find that the citizens adhere to him . . . , denounce him in the presence of the court, and remove [him]. He also is a traitor. A talker is an [exciter] of a city. [Divert] the multitude and suppress its heat . . .

(*gap*)

Be a craftsman in speech, *so that* you may be strong, *for* the tongue is a sword to [a man], and speech is more valorous than any fighting. No one can circumvent the skillful of heart . . . They who know his wisdom do not attack him, and no [misfortune] occurs where he is. Truth comes to him *fully* brewed, in accordance with the sayings of the ancestors.

Copy your fathers and your ancestors . . . Behold, their words remain in writing. Open, that you may read and copy *their* wisdom. *Thus* the skilled man becomes [learned].

Be not evil: patience is good. Make your memorial to last through the love of you . . . God will be praised as *your* reward, . . . praises because of your goodness and prayers for your health . . .

Respect the nobles and make your people to prosper. Establish your boundaries and your [frontier patrol]. It is good to act for the future. Respect a life of attentiveness, for mere [credulity] will *lead* to wretchedness . . . He who is covetous when other men possess is a fool, *because* [life] upon earth passes by, it has no length. Happy is he who [is without] sin in it. *Even* a million men may be of no avail to the lord of the Two Lands . . .

(*gap*)

May you speak justice in your *own* house, *that* the great ones who are on earth may fear you. Uprightness of heart is fitting for the lord. It is the forepart of the house that inspires respect in the back.

Do justice while you endure upon earth. Quiet the weeper; do not oppress the widow; supplant no man in the property of his father; and impair no officials at their [posts]. Be on your guard against punishing wrongfully. Do not slaughter: it is not of advantage to you. *But* you should punish with beatings and with arrests; this land will be *firmly* grounded thereby—except *for* the rebel, when his plans are discovered, for the god knows the treacherous of heart, and the god condemns his sins in blood . . . Do not kill a man when you know his good qualities, one with whom you once did sing the writings. He who reads in the SIPU book . . . god, free-moving of foot in difficult places, *his* soul comes to the place that it knows. It does not miss the ways of yesterday. No magic can oppose it, *but* it reaches those who will give it water.

(*gap*)

Do not distinguish the son of a man from a poor man, *but* take to yourself a man because of the work of his hands. Every skilled work should be practiced according to the . . . of the lord of a strong arm. Protect your frontier and build your [fortresses], *for* troops are of advantage to their lord.

Make monuments . . . for the god. That is what makes to live the name of him who does it. A man should do what is of advantage to his soul: the monthly service of the priest, putting on the white sandals, visiting the temple, revealing the mysteries, having access to the shrine, and eating bread in the temple. Make the offering table flourish, increase the loaves, and add to the daily offerings. It is an advantage to him who does it.

(*gap*)

It is a goodly office, the kingship. It has no son and no brother, made to endure on its monuments. *But* it is one *king* who promotes another. A man works for him [who] was before him, through a desire that what *he* has done may be maintained by someone else coming after him.

(*gap*)

More acceptable is the character of one upright of heart than the ox of the evildoer. Act for the god, that he may act similarly for you, with oblations that make the offering table flourish and with a carved inscription—that is what bears witness to your name. The god is aware of him who acts for him.

Well directed are men, the cattle of the god. He made heaven and earth according to their desire, and he repelled the water monster. He made the breath of life *for* their nostrils. They who have issued from his body are his images. He arises in heaven according to their desire. He made for them plants, animals, fowl, and fish to feed them. He slew his enemies and injured *even* his *own* children because they thought of making rebellion. He makes the light of day according to their desire, and he [sails by] in order to see them.

You should do nothing harmful [with regard to me, who has given] all the laws concerning the king. [Open] your face, that you may be raised as a man. You shall reach me, without having an accuser. Do not kill a single one that comes close to you, when you have shown him favor: the god knows him. He who prospers on earth is one of them, and they who follow the king are gods. Give the love of yourself to the whole world; a good character is a remembrance . . . [It has been] said *to* you: May the time of the sufferer be destroyed! by those who are in the back of the house of King Khety, in contrast to its [situation] today.

Behold, I have spoken to you the profitable matters of my *very* belly. May you act on what is established before your face.

#68: Instruction of Any
(*ANET* 420–21)[7]

The "Instruction of Any" dates from the mid-second millennium B.C., most likely from Egypt's eighteenth dynasty.[8] It takes the father-son approach common in the Book of Proverbs (2:1; 3:1; 4:1) and in other similar Egyptian literature. In contrast to other Egyptian works, however, the father is a lower official, and thus the advice is probably intended more for a middle-class audience. The text is also unusual for its time in that it records the son's hesitancy to heed his father's counsel.

Take to yourself a wife while you are *still* a youth, that she may produce a son for you. Beget [him] for yourself while you are *still* young. Teach him to be a man. A man whose people are many is happy; [he is] saluted *respectfully* with regard to his children.

Celebrate the feast of your god and repeat it at its season. God is angry at them who disregard him. Have witnesses attending when you make offering [at] the first time of [doing] it. If someone comes to [require your examination], have them set on papyrus your goings-down at this time . . . Singing, dancing, and incense are his food, and to receive prostrations is his property *right*. The god will magnify the name of him who [does it] . . .

. . . Be on your guard against a woman from abroad, who is not known in her *own* town. Do not [stare at] her when she passes by. Do not know her carnally: she is a deep water, whose windings one knows not, a woman who is far away from her husband. I am sleek, she says to you every day. She has no witnesses when she waits to ensnare you. It is a great crime *worthy* of death, when one hears of it . . .

Do not talk a lot. Be silent, and you will be happy. Do not be garrulous. The dwelling of god, its abomination is clamor. Pray with a loving heart, all the words of which are hidden, and he will do what you need, he will hear what you say, and he will accept your offering . . .

(gap)

. . . You should not express your *whole* heart to the stranger, to let him discover your speech against you. If a [passing] remark issuing from your mouth is hasty and [it is] repeated, you will make enemies. A man may fall to ruin because of his tongue . . . The belly of a man is wider than a storehouse, and it is full of every *kind of* response. You should choose the good and say them, while the bad are shut up in your belly . . .

. . . Make offering to your god, and beware of sins against him. You should not inquire about his [affairs]. Be not *too* free with him during his procession. Do not approach him *too closely* to carry him. You should not [disturb the veil]; beware of [exposing what it shelters]. Let your eye have regard to the nature of his anger, and prostrate yourself in his name. He shows *his* power in a million forms. *Only* they are magnified whom he magnifies. The god of this land is the sun that is on the horizon, and *only* his images are upon earth. If incense be given as their daily food, the lord of appearances will be established.

Double the food that you give to your mother, and carry her as she carried *you*. She had a heavy load in you, but she did not leave it to me. You were born after your months, *but* she was still yoked *with you, for* her breast was in your mouth for three years, [continuously]. Although your filth was disgusting, *her* heart was not [disgusted], saying: What can I do? She put you into school when you were taught to write, and she continued on [your behalf] every day, with bread and beer in her house.

When you are a young man and take to yourself a wife and are settled in your house, set your eye on how your mother gave birth to you and all *her* bringing you up as well. Do not let her blame you, nor may she *have to* raise her hands to the god, nor may he *have to* hear her cries.

(gap)

. . . You should not supervise *too closely* your wife in her *own* house, when you know that she is efficient. Do not say to her: Where is it? Fetch *it* for us! when she has put *it* in the *most* useful place. Let your eye have regard, while you are silent, that you may recognize her abilities. How happy it is when your hand is with her! Many are here who do not know what a man should do to stop dissension in his house . . . Every [man] who is settled in a house should hold the hasty heart firm. You should not pursue after a woman; do not let her steal away your heart.

#69: Instruction of Amenemope
(*ANET* 421–24)[9]

Although manuscripts of the "Instruction of Amenemope" date to the first millennium B.C., scholars generally agree that the original composition comes from about 1200 B.C.[10] Many note a literary relationship with Proverbs 22–23, although they disagree over the extent of that relationship.[11] The "Instruction of Amenemope" also demonstrates a shift in Egyptian thinking. Humility, integrity, and moral character are rewards in and of themselves, and happiness no longer lies in power and in an abundance of possessions.

The beginning of the teaching of life, the testimony for prosperity, all precepts for interaction with elders, the rules for courtiers, to know how to return an answer to him who said it, and to direct a report to one who has sent him, in order to direct him to the ways of life, to make him prosper upon earth, let his heart go down into its shrine, steer him away from evil, and to rescue him from the mouth of the rabble, revered in the mouth of the people; made by the overseer of the soil, one experienced in his office, the seed of a scribe of Egypt, the overseer of grains who regulates the measure and manages the [yield of grain] for his lord, who registers islands and newly appearing lands in the great name of his majesty, [who] establishes landmarks at the boundaries of the arable land, who protects the king by his records, and who makes the land register of Egypt; the scribe who sets up the divine offerings for all the gods and gives land titles to the common people; the overseer of grains [and provider] of foods, who [transports magazines] with grain, the truly silent one in Abydos of the Thinite Nome, the triumphant one of Akhmim, possessor of a tomb on the west of Panopolis, possessor of a grave in Abydos, Amen-em-Opet son of Ka-nakht, the triumphant one of Abydos; *for* his son, the smallest of his children, the littlest of his adherents, the privy councilor of Min Ka-mutef, the water pourer of Wen-nofer, who installs Horus upon the throne of his father, . . . [examiner] of the god's mother, inspector of the black cattle of the terrace of Min, who protects Min in his shrine, Hor-em-maa-kheru being his right name, the child of a notable of Akhmim and son of the sistrum player of Shu and Tefnut and chief choir leader of Horus, Ta-Usert.

Chapter 1

He says: Give your ears, hear what is said,
give your heart to understand them.
To put them in your heart is worth while,
but it is damaging to him who neglects them.
Let them rest in the casket of your belly,
that they may be a [key] in your heart.
At a time when there is a whirlwind of words,
they shall be a mooring stake [for] your tongue.
If you spend your time while this is in your heart,
you will find it a success;
you will find my words a treasury of life,
and your body will prosper upon earth.

Chapter 6

Do not carry off the landmark at the boundaries of the arable land,
nor disturb the position of the measuring cord;
be not greedy after a cubit of land,
nor encroach upon the boundaries of a widow . . .
Guard against encroaching upon the boundaries of the fields,
lest a terror carry you off.
One satisfies god with the will of the lord,
who determines the boundaries of the arable land . . .
Plow in the fields, that you may find your needs,
that you may receive bread of your own threshing floor.
Better is a measure that the god gives you
than five thousand *taken* illegally.
They do not spend a day *in* the granary or barn;
they make no provisions for the beer jar.

The completion of a moment is their
    lifetime in the storehouse;
at daybreak they are sunk *from sight*.
Better is poverty in the hand of the god
than riches in a storehouse;
better is bread, when the heart is happy,
than riches with sorrow.

Chapter 7

Cast not your heart away in pursuit of
    riches,
for there is no ignoring Fate and
    Fortune.
Place not your heart upon externals,
for every man belongs to his *appointed*
    hour.
Do not strain to seek an excess,
when your needs are safe for you.
If riches are brought to you by robbery,
they will not spend the night with you;
at daybreak they are not in your house:
their places may be seen, but they are
    not.
The ground has opened its mouth . . .
    that it might swallow them up,
and might sink them into the
    underworld.
Or they have made themselves a great
    breach of their *own* size
and are sunken down into the
    underworld.
Or they have made themselves wings
    like geese
and are flown away to the heavens.
Rejoice not yourself *over* riches *gained* by
    robbery,
nor mourn because of poverty.
If an archer [in the van] advances *too far*,
then his [squad] abandons him.
The ship of the covetous is left *in* the
    mud,
while the boat of the silent man *has* a
    fair breeze.
You should make prayer to the Aten
    when he rises,
saying: Give me prosperity and health.
He will give you your needs for this life,
and you will be safe from terror.

Chapter 9

Do not associate to yourself the heated
    man,
nor visit him for conversation.
Preserve your tongue from answering
    your superior,
and guard yourself against reviling him.
Do not make him cast his speech to
    lasso you,
nor make *too* free with your answer.
You should discuss an answer *only*
    [with] a man of your *own* size,
and guard yourself against plunging
    headlong into it.
Swifter is speech when the heart is hurt
than wind of the [headwaters] . . .
Do not leap to hold to such a one,
lest a terror carry you off.

Chapter 11

Be not greedy for the property of a poor
    man,
nor hunger for his bread.
As for the property of a poor man, it *is* a
    blocking to the throat,
it makes a [vomiting] to the gullet.
If he has [obtained] it by false oaths,
his heart is perverted by his belly . . .
The mouthful of bread *too* great you
    swallow and vomit up,
and are emptied of your good.

Chapter 13

Do not confuse a man with a pen upon
    papyrus—
the abomination of the god.
Do not bear witness with false words,
nor [support] another person *thus* with
    your tongue.
Do not take an accounting of him who
    has nothing,
nor falsify your pen.
If you find a large debt against a poor
    man,
make it into three parts,
forgive two, and let one stand.
You will find it like the ways of life;
you will lie down and sleep *soundly*; in
    the morning
you will find it *again* like good news.

Better is praise as one who loves men
than riches in a storehouse;
better is bread, when the heart is happy,
than riches with sorrow.

Chapter 18

Do not spend the night fearful of the
morrow.
At daybreak what is the morrow like?
Man knows not what the morrow is like.
God is *always* in his success,
whereas man is in his failure;
one thing are the words that men say,
another is what the god does.
Say not: I have no wrongdoing,
nor *yet* strain to seek quarreling.
As for wrongdoing, it belongs to the
god;
it is sealed with his finger.
There is no success in the hand of the
god,
but there is no failure before him.
If he pushes himself to seek success,
in the completion of a moment he
damages it.
Be steadfast in your heart, make firm
your breast.
Steer not with your tongue *alone*.
If the tongue of a man *be* the rudder of a
boat,
the all-lord is its pilot.

Chapter 20

Do not confuse a man in the law court,
nor [divert] the righteous man.
Give not your attention *only* to him
clothed in white,
nor give consideration to him that is
unkempt.
Do not accept the bribe of a powerful
man,
nor oppress for him the disabled.
Justice is the great reward of god;
he gives it to whom he will . . .
Do not falsify the [income] on the
records,
nor damage the plans of god.
Do not discover for your own self the
will of god,
without *reference to* Fate and Fortune.

Chapter 23

Do not eat bread before a noble,
nor lay on your mouth at first.
If you are satisfied with false chewings,
they are a pastime for your spittle.
Look at the cup that is before you,
and let it serve your needs.
As a noble is great in his office,
he is as a well abounds *in the drawing of
water*.

Chapter 25

Do not laugh at a blind man nor tease a
dwarf
nor injure the affairs of the lame.
Do not tease a man who is in the hand
of the god,
nor be fierce of face against him if he
errs.
For man is clay and straw,
and the god is his builder.
He is tearing down and building up
every day.
He makes a thousand poor men as he
wishes,
or he makes a thousand men as
[overseers],
when he is in his hour of life.
How joyful is he who reaches the west,
when he is safe in the hand of the god.

Chapter 28

Do not [recognize] a widow if you catch
her in the fields,
nor fail to be [indulgent] to her reply.
Do not neglect a stranger *with* your oil
jar,
that it be doubled before your brethren.
God desires respect for the poor
more than the honoring of the exalted.

#70: Words of Ahiqar
(*ANET* 427–30)

An Aramaic composition with an Assyrian flavor
dates from the sixth–fifth centuries B.C. and was
discovered among the papyri at the Egyptian city
of Elephantine. The "Words of Ahiqar" describe
the life of Ahiqar, an official in the Assyrian court,
whose adopted nephew falsely accused him of
treason. The executioner secretly spared Ahiqar's

life, and the king later restored Ahiqar to prominence. Many of Ahiqar's words of wisdom contain similar themes to the Book of Proverbs.[12]

Then King [Esarhaddon] of Assyria [answered] and said: [Do you, Nabusumiskun one] of my father's officers, who [ate] of my father's bread, seek [the old man Ahiqar] wherever you may find [and kill him]. Otherwise this old man [Ahiqar] is a wise scribe [and counselor of all Assyria], and is liable to corrupt the land against us. Then, when [the king of Assyria had spoken thus], he appointed with him two other men to see how [it would turn out]. So this officer [Nabusumiskun went away] riding on a [swift horse, and those men] with him. Then, after three more days, [he and the others] who were with him [sighted me] as I was walking among the vineyards. [Now when this] officer [Nabusumiskun beheld me] he straightway rent his mantle and moaned: [Are you] the wise scribe and man of good counsel, who [was a righteous] man [and by] whose counsel and words all of Assyria was guided? [Extinguished be] [the lamp of your son whom you brought] up, whom you set up at the gate of the palace. He has ruined you, and an [evil] return [is it. Then], I, Ahiqar, was afraid. I answered and said to [that officer Nabusumiskun: Am] I [not] the same Ahiqar who once saved you from an undeserved death? [When Sennacherib], the father of this King Esarhaddon, sought to [kill you, then] I brought you to my house. There I sustained you as a man deals with his brother, having hidden you from him and having said: I killed him—until at a [later] time and after many days I brought you before King Sennacherib and cleared you of offenses before him and he did you no evil. Moreover, Sennacherib was well pleased with me for having kept you alive and not having killed you. Now do you do to me even as I did to you. Don't kill me. Take me to your house until other times. King Esarhaddon is merciful as any man. In the end he will remember me and wish for my advice. Then you will [present] me to him and he will spare me alive. Then the officer Nabusumiskun [answered] and said: Fear not, my [lord] Ahiqar, father of all Assyria, by whose counsel King Sennacherib

and *all* the host of Assyria *were guided*! Then the officer Nabusumiskun said to his companions, those two men that were with him: [Do you listen and pay attention] to me while I tell you [my] plan, and a [very] good plan it is. [So those [men answered] and said [to him: Tell] us, O officer Nabusumiskun, [whatever you will, and we shall listen to] you. The [officer] Nabusumiskun then spoke and said to them: Listen to me. This is [Ahiqar]. He [is] a great man [and a bearer of the seal] of [King] Esarhaddon, and the whole army of [Assyria] was guided by his counsel and words. Let us not kill him [undeservedly]. I will give you [a] eunuch [slave] of mine. Let him be slain [between these] two mountains instead of this Ahiqar. [When it is reported, and] the king [sends] other men [after] us to see the body of this Ahiqar, then [they'll see the body] of [this] eunuch slave of mine. In the end [King] Esarhaddon [will remember Ahiqar and desire his advice] and he will [regret etc.].

(gap)

Withhold not your son from the rod, else you will not be able to save [him from wickedness]. If I smite you, my son, you will not die, but if I leave you to your own heart [you will not live]. A blow for a bondman, a [rebuke] for a bondwoman, and for all your slaves [discipline. One who] buys a [runaway] slave [or] a thievish handmaid [squanders his fortune] and [disgraces] the name of his father and his offspring with the reputation of his wantonness. . . . Two things [that] are meet, and the third pleasing to Shamash: one who [drinks] wine and gives it to drink, one who guards wisdom, and one who hears a word and does not tell. Behold that is dear [to] Shamash. But he who drinks wine and does not [give it to drink], and one whose wisdom goes astray, [and] . . . is seen . . . [Wisdom] . . .

To gods also she is dear. [For all time] the kingdom is [hers]. In [heaven] is she established, for the lord of holy ones has exalted [her. My son, chatter] not overmuch so that you speak out [every word that] comes to your mind; for men's *eyes* and ears are everywhere *trained* [upon] your mouth. Beware lest it be [your] [undoing]. More than all watchfulness watch your mouth, and [over] what [you hear] harden your heart. For a word is a bird: once released no man can [recapture it]. First [count] [the secrets of] your mouth; then bring out your [words] by number. For the [instruction] of a mouth is stronger than the [instruction] of war. Treat not lightly the word of a king: let it be healing for your [flesh]. Soft is the utterance of a king; *yet* it is sharper and stronger than a [two]-edged knife. Look before you: a hard look [on the face] of a [king] *means*: Delay not! His wrath is swift as lightning: do you take heed unto yourself that he [display it] not against your [utterances] and you perish [before] your time. [The wrath] of a king, if you be commanded, is a burning fire. Obey [it] at once. . .

I have lifted sand, and I have carried salt; but there is naught that is heavier than [grief]. I have lifted bruised straw, and I have taken up bran; but there is naught that is lighter than a sojourner. War troubles calm waters between good [friends]. If a man be small and grow great, his words [soar] above him. For the opening of his mouth is an [utterance] of gods, and if he be beloved of gods they will put something good in his mouth to say. Many are [the stars of heaven whose] names no man knows. By the same token, no man knows humankind.

(gap)

[If] you [are needy], my son, borrow corn and wheat that you may eat and be sated and give to your children with you. Take not a heavy loan from an evil man. [Moreover, if] you take a loan, give no rest to yourself until [you repay the loan. A loan] is sweet as . . . , but its repayment is grief. My [son, hearken not] with your ears to [a lying man]. For a man's charm is his truthfulness; his repulsiveness, the lies of his lips. [At first] a throne [is set up] for the liar, but in the [end they find] out his lies and spit in his face. A liar's neck is cut like a . . . virgin that [is hidden] from sight, like a man who causes misfortune that does not proceed from god. [Despise not]

what is in your lot, nor covet a wealth that is denied you. [Multiply not] riches and make not great your heart. [Whosoever takes no pride] in the names of his father and mother, may the [sun] not shine [upon him]; for he is a wicked man.

(gap)

If you would be [exalted], my son, [humble yourself before god], who humbles an [exalted] man and [exalts a lowly man]. What [men's] lips curse, god does [not] curse . . . God shall twist the twister's mouth and tear out [his] tongue. Let not good [eyes] be darkened, nor [good] ears [be stopped, and let a good mouth love] the truth and speak it. A man of [becoming] conduct whose heart is good is like a mighty [city] that is [situated] upon a [mountain]. There is [none that can bring him down. Except] a man [dwell] with god, how can he be guarded by his own refuge? . . . , But he with whom god is, who [can cast] him down? . . . A man [knows not] what is in his fellow's heart. So when a good man [sees] a [wicked] man [let him beware of him]. Let him [not] join with him on a journey or be a [neighbor] to him—a good man [with a bad man]. The [bramble] sent to [the] pomegranate tree [saying]: The bramble to the pomegranate: Wherefore the [multitude] of *your* thorns [to him that touches] your [fruit]? . . . The [pomegranate tree] answered and said to the bramble: You are all thorns to him that touches you. All that come in contact with a righteous man are on his side. [A city] of wicked men shall on a gusty day be pulled apart, and in . . . its gates be brought low; for the spoil [of the righteous are they]. Mine eyes that I lifted up unto you and my heart that I gave you in wisdom [you have scorned, and you have] brought my name into [disgrace]. If the wicked man seize the corners of your garment, leave it in his hand. Then approach Shamash: he will take his and give it to you.

14 Love Poems

The biblical Song of Songs presents an extended love poem.[1] Although Mesopotamian literature provides some parallels to this book,[2] Egyptian literature provides clearer parallels.

#71: Egyptian Love Songs
(Hallo and Younger, *Context of Scripture*, 1:127–29)

Egyptian love songs from 1300–1150 B.C. bear an interesting resemblance to the biblical Song of Songs. Naturally, the poems include allusions to Egyptian deities rather than to Yahweh. Also, since the Egyptians were not shepherds (Genesis 46:34), the Egyptian poems lack the pastoral imagery so apparent in Song of Songs (1:5–7; 4:1–2; 6:2–3).[3]

Boy

If only I were the laundryman
of my sister's linen garment
even for one month!
I would be strengthened
by grasping [the clothes] that touch her
   body.
For it would be I who washed out the
   Moringa oils
that are in her kerchief.
Then I'd rub my body
with her cast-off garments,
and she . . .
[Oh I would be in] joy and delight,
my [body] vigorous!

Boy

One alone is my sister, having no peer:
more gracious than all other women.
Behold her, like Sothis rising
at the beginning of a good year:

shining, precious, white of skin,
lovely of eyes when gazing.
Sweet her lips when speaking:
she has no excess of words.
Long of neck, white of breast,
her hair true lapis lazuli.
Her arms surpass gold,
her fingers are like lotuses.
Full her hips, narrow her waist,
her thighs carry on her beauties.
Lovely of walk when she strides on the
   ground,
she has captured my heart in her
   embrace.
She makes the heads of all men
turn about when seeing her.
Fortunate is whoever embraces her—
he is like the foremost of lovers.
Her coming forth appears
like *that of* the one yonder—the unique
   one.

Girl

My brother stirs up my heart with his
   voice,
making me take ill.
Although he is among the neighbors of
   my mother's house,
I cannot go to him.
Mother is right to command me thus:
Avoid seeing him!
Yet my heart is vexed when he comes to
   mind,
for love of him has captured me.
He is senseless of heart—
and I am just like him!
He does not know my desires to
   embrace him,
or he would send word to my mother.
O brother, I am decreed for you

by the golden one.
Come to me that I may see your beauty!
May father and mother be glad!
May all people rejoice in you together,
rejoice in you, my brother!

Girl

I passed close by his house,
and found his door ajar.
My brother was standing beside his
    mother,
and with him all his kin.
Love of him captures the heart
of all who stride upon the way—
a precious youth without peer!
A brother excellent of character!
He gazed at me when I passed by,
but I exult by myself.
How joyful my heart in rejoicing,
my brother, since I *first* beheld you!
If only mother knew my heart—
she would go inside for a while.
O golden one, put that in her heart!
Then I could hurry to my brother
and kiss him before his company,
and not be ashamed because of anyone.
I would be happy to have them see
that you know me,
and I'd hold festival to my goddess.
My heart leaps up to go forth
to make me gaze on my brother tonight.

Boy

Seven whole days I have not seen my
    sister.
Illness has invaded me,
my limbs have grown heavy,
and I barely sense my own body.
Should the master physicians come to
    me,
their medicines could not ease my heart.
The priests have no *good* method,
because my illness cannot be diagnosed.
Telling me: Here she is!—that's what
    will revive me.
Her name—that's what will get me up.
The coming and going of her
    messengers—
that's what will revive my heart.
More potent than any medicine is my
    sister for me;
she is more powerful for me than the
    Compendium.
Her coming in from outside is my
    amulet.
I see her—then I become healthy.
She opens her eyes—my limbs grow
    young.
She speaks—then I become strong.
I hug her—and she drives illness from
    me.
But she has left me for seven days.

15 Hymns and Prayers

Prayer to deities played an important role in the religious experience of many ancient societies.[1] The Egyptian and Mesopotamian prayers presented here appeal to various deities. In some, the focus is praise of the deity; in others, the worshiper asks the deity for blessing or deliverance from a difficult situation.

#72: Hymn to Amon-Re
(*ANET* 365–67)[2]

> The main papyrus containing the "Hymn to Amon-Re" dates from 1550–1350 B.C., but the hymn itself may date to an earlier time.[3] Although Egypt was a polytheistic society, the text reflects a tendency of this time to centralize divine power in one god.

Adoration of Amon-Re, the bull residing in Heliopolis, chief of all gods, the good god, the beloved, who gives life to all that is warm and to all good cattle.

Hail to you, Amon-Re,
lord of the thrones of the Two Lands,
  presiding over Karnak,
bull of his mother, presiding over his
  fields!
Far-reaching of stride, presiding over
  Upper Egypt,
lord of the Madjoi and ruler of Punt,
eldest of heaven, firstborn of earth,
lord of what is, enduring in all things,
  enduring in all things.
Unique in his nature like the [fluid] of
  the gods,
the goodly bull of the Ennead, chief of
  all gods,
the lord of truth and father of the gods.
Who made humankind and created the
  beasts,

lord of what is, who created the fruit
  tree,
made herbage, and gave life to cattle.
The goodly demon whom Ptah made,
the goodly beloved youth to whom the
  gods give praise,
who made what is below and what is
  above,
who illuminates the Two Lands
and crosses the heavens in peace:
the king of Upper and Lower Egypt: Re,
  the triumphant,
chief of the Two Lands,
great of strength, lord of reverence,
the chief one, who made the entire
  earth.
More distinguished in nature than any
  other god.

  (*gap*)

Hail to you, who are in peace!
Lord of joy, terrible of appearances,
lord of the URAEUS serpent, lofty of
  plumes,
beautiful of diadem, and lofty of White
  Crown.
The gods love to see you
with the Double Crown fixed upon your
  brow.
The love of you is spread throughout
  the Two Lands,
when your rays shine forth in the eyes.
The good of the people is your arising;
the cattle grow languid when you shine.
The love of you is in the southern sky;
the sweetness of you is in the northern
  sky.
The beauty of you carries away hearts;
the love of you makes arms languid;
your beautiful form relaxes the hands;

and hearts are forgetful at the sight of
you.
You are the sole one, who made [all] that
is,
[the] solitary sole [one], who made what
exists,
from whose eyes humankind came
forth,
and upon whose mouth the gods came
into being.
He who made herbage [for] the cattle,
and the fruit tree for humankind,
who made that *on which* the fish in the
river may live,
and the birds [soaring] in the sky.
He who gives breath to what is in the
egg,
gives life to the son of the slug,
and makes that on which gnats may
live,
and worms and flies in like manner;
who supplies the needs of the mice in
their holes,

The Egyptian system of writing—known as hieroglyphics
and shown here at the top of the Rosetta Stone—was
quite different from the cuneiform writing of
Mesopotamia and Syria-Palestine. (© Copyright The
British Museum)

and gives life to flying things in every
tree.
Hail to you, who did all this!

(*gap*)

Sovereign—life, prosperity, health!—
and chief of the gods!
We praise your might, according as you
did make us.
[Let us act] for you, because you
brought us forth.
We give you thanksgiving because you
have wearied yourself with us!
Hail to you, who made all that is!
Lord of truth and father of the gods,
who made mortals and created beasts,
lord of the grain,
who made *also* the living of the beasts of
the desert.
Amon, the bull beautiful of
countenance,
the beloved in Karnak,
great of appearances in the house of the
BENBEN,
taking again the diadem in Heliopolis,
who judges the Two *Lands* in the great
broad hall,
the chief of the great Ennead.
The solitary sole one, without his peer,
presiding over Karnak,
the Heliopolitan, presiding over his
Ennead,
and living on truth every day.

(*gap*)

The gods are in joy,
the crew of Re is in satisfaction,
Heliopolis is in joy,
for the enemies of Atum are
overthrown.
Karnak is in satisfaction, Heliopolis is in
joy,
the heart of the lady of life is glad,
for the enemy of her lord is overthrown.
The gods of Babylon are in jubilation,
they who are in the shrines are
salaaming,
when they see him rich in his might.
The demon of the gods,
the righteous one, lord of Karnak,

in this your name Maker of
Righteousness;
the lord of provisions, bull of [offerings],
in this your name Amon, bull of his
mother;
maker of all humankind,
creator and maker of all that is,
in this your name Atum-Khepri.
Great falcon, festive of bosom,
beautiful of face, festive of breast,
pleasing of form, lofty of plume,
on whose brow the two URAEI [flutter].
To whom the hearts of humankind make
approach,
to whom the people turn about;
who makes festive the Two Lands with
his comings forth.
Hail to you, Amon-Re, lord of the
thrones of the Two Lands,
whose city loves his rising!

#73: Hymn to the Aten
(*ANET* 369–71)[4]

The "Hymn to the Aten" comes from the fourteenth century B.C. and is credited to Akhenaten,
teenage pharaoh of Egypt's New Kingdom. It was
found on a wall of the tomb of Ay, an Egyptian
official. The hymn exalts the doctrine of the sun-
god Aten as the one true god who created and
sustains the world and everything in it. As in the
"Hymn to Amon-Re," divine power is centralized
in one god.

Praise of Re Har-akhti, rejoicing on the horizon, in his name as Shu who is in the Aten
disc, living forever and ever; the living great
Aten who is in jubilee, lord of all that the Aten
encircles, lord of heaven, lord of earth, lord
of the house of Aten in Akhet-Aten; *and praise
of* the king of Upper and Lower Egypt, who
lives on truth, the lord of the Two Lands: Nefer-
kheperu-Re Wa-en-Re; the son of Re, who lives
on truth, the lord of diadems: Akh-en-Aten,
long in his lifetime; *and praise of* the chief wife
of the king, his beloved, the lady of the Two
Lands: Nefer-neferu-Aten Nefertiti, living,
healthy, and youthful forever and ever; *by the*
fan bearer on the right hand of the king . . .
eye. He says:

You appear beautifully on the horizon of
heaven,
you living Aten, the beginning of life!
When you are risen on the eastern
horizon,
you have filled every land with your
beauty.
You are gracious, great, glistening, and
high over every land;
your rays encompass the lands to the
limit of all that you have made:
as you are Re, you reach to the end of
them;
you subdue them *for* your beloved son.
Although you are far away, your rays
are on earth;
although you are in [their] faces, [no one
knows your] going.
When you set in the western horizon,
the land is in darkness, in the manner of
death.
They sleep in a room, with heads
wrapped up,
nor sees one eye the other.

(*gap*)

At daybreak, when you arise on the
horizon,
when you shine as the Aten by day,
you drive away the darkness and give
your rays.
The Two Lands are in festivity [every
day],
awake and standing upon *their* feet,
for you have raised them up.
Washing their bodies, taking *their*
clothing,
their arms are *raised* in praise at your
appearance.
All the world, they do their work.
All beasts are content with their
pasturage;
trees and plants are flourishing.
The birds that fly from their nests,
their wings are *stretched out* in praise to
your KA.
All beasts spring upon *their* feet.
Whatever flies and alights,
they live when you have risen *for* them.
The ships are sailing north and south as
well,

for every way is open at your
appearance.
The fish in the river dart before your
face;
your rays are in the midst of the great
green sea.
Creator of seed in women,
you who make fluid into man,
who maintains the son in the womb of
his mother,
who soothes him with what stills his
weeping,
you nurse *even* in the womb,
who gives breath to sustain all that he
has made!
When he descends from the womb to
[breathe]
on the day when he is born,
you open his mouth completely,
you supply his necessities.
When the chick in the egg speaks within
the shell,
you give him breath within it to
maintain him.
When you have made him his
fulfillment within the egg, to break it,
he comes forth from the egg to speak at
his completed *time*;
he walks upon his legs when he comes
forth from it.
How manifold it is, what you have
made!
They are hidden from the face *of man*.
O sole god, like whom there is no other!
You created the world according to your
desire,
while you were alone:
all men, cattle, and wild beasts,
whatever is on earth, going upon *its*
feet,
and what is on high, flying with its
wings.
The countries of Syria and Nubia, the
[land] of Egypt,
you set every man in his place,
you supply their necessities:
everyone has his food, and his time of
life is reckoned.
Their tongues are separate in speech,
and their natures as well;
their skins are distinguished,

as you distinguish the foreign peoples.
You make a Nile in the underworld,
you bring it forth as you desire
to maintain the people *of Egypt*
according as you made them for
yourself,
the lord of all of them, wearying *himself*
with them,
the lord of every land, rising for them,
the Aten of the day, great of majesty.
All distant foreign countries, you make
their life *also*,
for you have set a Nile in heaven,
that it may descend for them and make
waves upon the mountains,
like the great green sea,
to water their fields in their towns.

(gap)

The world came into being by your
hand,
according as you have made them.
When you have risen they live,
when you set they die.
You are lifetime your own self,
for one lives *only* through you.
Eyes are *fixed* on beauty until you set.
All work is laid aside when you set in
the west.
But when [you] rise [again,
everything is] made to flourish for the
king . . .
Since you did found the earth
and raise them up for your son,
who came forth from your body:

The king of Upper and Lower Egypt, . . .
Akhenaten, . . . and the chief wife of the king
. . . Nefertiti, living and youthful forever and
ever.

#74: Hymn to Enlil
(Beyerlin, *Near Eastern Religious Texts*, 100–101)

The Sumerian "Hymn to Enlil" dates to the Old
Babylonian period (2000–1595 B.C.). Most of the
tablet fragments containing the hymn were discovered at Nippur, the site of the Ekur, Enlil's temple. The hymn begins by describing Nippur and
the temple proceedings, but focuses on Enlil's supremacy among the gods.

Wise lord, the planner, who knows your
   will?
Endowed with strength, lord of Ekur,
born in the mountains, lord of Esharra,
storm of great might, father Enlil,
you who were brought up by
      Dingirmach, you go furiously to
      battle,
you scatter the hill country like grain,
      and mow *it* as the sickle mows
      barley!
You have taken your father's side
      against the rebellious land,
you approach as the one who destroys
      the hills,
you break the hostile lands like a reed,
make all your foes of one mind!
I am the protective wall against all
      hostile lands and the one who keeps
      them off.
You cast down the mighty, enter the
      door of heaven,
you grasp the bolt of heaven,
break open the heavenly lock,
remove the closure of heaven,
you cast down the rebellious land in
      heaps!
You do not allow the rebellious,
      uncontrollable land to rise again.
Lord, how long will you trouble the
      land that you made of one mind,
who can soften your angry heart?
The sayings of your mouth are not
      despised,
who could rebel against them?
I am the lord, the lion of the holy An,
      the hero of Sumer,
I make the fishes of the sea glad, and see
      that the birds do not fall down,
the wise countryman, who plows the
      field, Enlil, I am he.
Indeed you are the lord who has grown
      great, the hero of your father!
No enemy can escape your right hand,
nor any wicked man flee from your left
      hand.
The hostile land over which your saying
      has gone forth, you will not allow to
      rise again,
you leave no one in the rebellious land
      that you cursed.

Lord of Ekur, full of far-reaching power,
you are the first among the gods!
Chief of the Anunnaki,
lord who guides the plow, Enlil, you are
      he,
Indeed, chief of the Anunna gods,
you are the lord who guides the plow!

#75: Hymn to Shamash
(Beyerlin, *Near Eastern Religious Texts*,
102–4)[5]

The Babylonian sun-god Shamash is the focus of
"Hymn to Shamash," which dates to the late second millennium B.C.[6] Shamash was the god of
justice, and the hymn describes his careful attention to justice in this world, rewarding the person of integrity and judging those who practice
evil. The hymn gives special emphasis to fairness
in the business world.

O illuminator . . . *in* the heavens,
who makes the darkness bright . . .
      above and below,
Shamash, illuminator . . . *in* the heavens,
who makes the darkness bright . . .
      above and below!
Your beams cover . . . like a net.
You lighten the darkness of the high
      hills!
At your appearing the rulers of the gods
      rejoice,
all the IGIGI exult,
your rays constantly grasp the secret
      things,
in your constant light their traces are
      visible.
Your blinding light constantly seeks out
      . . .
the four banks of the world, like Girru
      . . .
O illuminator of the darkness, you open
      the nipples of heaven,
make the beard of light glow, the
      cornfield, the life of the land;
your rays cover the high mountains,
your glowing light fills the surface of the
      lands,
you bow over the hills to survey the
      earth,
you suspend from heaven the circle of
      the earth.

You protect all the people of the lands,
and all that Ea, king of the princes, has
   created is entrusted to you.
You shepherd all that is endowed with
   the breath of life,
you are its shepherd above and below.
Regularly and without ceasing you pass
   through the heavens,
you travel over the wide world day by
   day,
over the flood of the sea, the hills, over
   earth and heaven
you go daily without ceasing like a . . .
In the underworld you care for the
   princes of the Kubu, the Annunaki,
above, you direct the affairs of all men,
shepherd, of those below, guardian of
   the world above,
Shamash, you preserve the light of
   everything.
Again and again you cross the sea in all
   its breadth,
whose deepest foundations not *even* the
   IGIGI know.
Shamash, your blaze penetrates the
   abysses of the sea,
so that the monsters in the depths of the
   sea look on your light.
When you rise, the gods of the land
   assemble,
an angry glare lies over the land.
What is planned by the lands of many
   tongues—
you know and you recognize their way.
All humankind bows before you,
O Shamash, all the world longs for your
   light.
If a man practices usury, you destroy his
   power,
if a man acts maliciously, an end is made
   to him.
You *yourself* make the unjust judge
   discover prison,
you lay punishment on the one who
   accepts a bribe and commits injustice,
but the one who rejects a bribe and
   intercedes for the weak
is well pleasing to Shamash, and he will
   lengthen his life.
The wise judge who gives righteous
   judgments,

completes a palace and lives among the
   princes.
The one who practices deception when
   he holds the corn measure,
who lends out *corn* according to the
   middle measure *and then* requires
   back a large measure,
the curse of the people will overtake
   him before his time.
If he requires repayment before time, a
   burden will be laid on him,
his heir will not receive his possessions,
and his brothers will not *be able to* enter
   his house.
The honest merchant who lends corn
   according to the great measure, earns
   much respect,
he is well pleasing to Shamash, and will
   prolong his life.
He will found a great family, gain
   prosperity,
like the water of an ever-flowing spring
   his descendants will endure.
You loose the bonds of those who
   bowed before you,
you ever accept the prayer of those who
   constantly bless you anew.
But they praise your name with
   reverence
and worship your majesty forever.
Illuminator of the darkness, lightener of
   the gloom,
who dispels the dark and shines over
   the broad earth,
who makes the day to shine and sends
   down scorching heat on the earth at
   midday,
and so makes the broad earth glow like a
   flame,
yet shortens the days and lengthens the
   nights,
[brings] cold, frost, ice and snow.

#76: Prayer to Ishtar
(*ANET* 383–85)

The "Prayer to Ishtar" appears to date to the mid-second millennium B.C., although the oldest copies come from almost a millennium later. Ishtar played a prominent role in the Babylonian pantheon as goddess of love and war. The prayer begins with praise to Ishtar for her exalted role in the universe.

She is then implored to see the worshiper's plight and bring deliverance. Some scholars see a connection between the style of this prayer and biblical laments, but this prayer begins with praise to God while biblical laments typically begin by describing the worshiper's difficult situation.

I pray to you, O lady of ladies, goddess of goddesses.
O Ishtar, queen of all peoples, who guides humankind aright,
O Irnini, ever exalted, greatest of the IGIGI,
O most mighty of princesses, exalted is your name.
You indeed are the light of heaven and earth, O valiant daughter of Sin.
O supporter of arms, who determines battle,
O possessor of all divine power, who wears the crown of dominion,
O lady, glorious is your greatness; over all the gods it is exalted.
O star of lamentation, who causes peaceable brothers to fight,
yet who constantly gives friendship,
O mighty one, lady of battle, who suppresses the mountains,
O Gushea, the one covered with fighting and clothed with terror
you make complete judgment and decision, the ordinances of heaven and earth.
Chapels, holy places, sacred sites, and shrines pay heed to you.
Where is not your name, where is not your divine power?
Where are your likenesses not fashioned, where are your shrines not founded?
Where are you not great, where are you not exalted?
Anu, Enlil, and Ea have made you high; among the gods they have caused your dominion to be great.
They have made you high among all the IGIGI; they have made your position preeminent.
At the thought of your name heaven and earth tremble.

The gods tremble; the Anunnaki stand in awe.
To your awesome name humankind must pay heed.
For you are great and you are exalted.
All the black-headed *people and* the masses of humankind pay homage to your might.
The judgment of the people in truth and righteousness you indeed decide.
You regard the oppressed and mistreated; daily you cause them to prosper.
Your mercy! O lady of heaven and earth, shepherdess of the weary people.
Your mercy! O lady of holy Eanna the pure storehouse.
Your mercy! O lady; unwearied are your feet; swift are your knees.
Your mercy! O lady of conflict *and* of all battles.

(gap)

I have cried to you, suffering, wearied, and distressed, as your servant.
See me O my lady; accept my prayers.
Faithfully look upon me and hear my supplication.
Promise my forgiveness and let your spirit be appeased.
Pity! For my wretched body, which is full of confusion and trouble.
Pity! For my sickened heart, which is full of tears and suffering.
Pity! For my wretched intestines, *which are full of* confusion and trouble.
Pity! For my afflicted house, which [mourns bitterly].
Pity! For my feelings, which are satiated with tears and suffering.
O [exalted] Irnini, fierce lion, let your heart be at rest.
O angry wild ox, let your spirit be appeased.
Let the favor of your eyes be upon me.
With your bright features look faithfully upon me.
Drive away the evil spells of my body *and* let me see your bright light.
How long, O my lady, shall my adversaries be looking upon me,

in lying and untruth shall they plan evil against me,

shall my pursuers and those who exult over me rage against me?

How long, O my lady, shall the crippled and weak seek me out?

One has made for me long sackcloth; thus I have appeared before you.

The weak have become strong; but I am weak.

I toss about like flood water, which an evil wind makes violent.

My heart is flying; it keeps fluttering like a bird of heaven.

I mourn like a dove night and day.

I am beaten down, and so I weep bitterly.

With Oh and Alas my spirit is distressed.

I—what have I done, O my god and my goddess?

Like one who does not fear my god and my goddess I am treated.

(gap)

How long, O my lady, will you be angered so that your face is turned away?

How long, O my lady, will you be infuriated so that your spirit is enraged?

Turn your neck that you have set against me; set your face [toward] good favor.

Like the water of the opening up of a canal let your emotions be released.

Let me trample my foes like the ground; subdue my haters and cause them to crouch down under me.

Let my prayers and my supplications come to you.

Let your great mercy be upon me.

Let those who see me in the street magnify your name.

As for me, let me glorify your divinity and your might before the black-headed *people*, [saying],

Ishtar indeed is exalted; Ishtar indeed is queen;

the lady indeed is exalted; the lady indeed is queen.

Irnini, the valorous daughter of Sin, has no rival.

#77: Psalm to Marduk
(*ANET* 389–90)

The oldest extant copies of the "Psalm to Marduk" date to the mid-first millennium B.C., although scholars believe the original text dates much earlier.[7] The worshiper begins by asking Marduk, chief god of the Babylonian pantheon, why his prayers have gone unanswered. He confesses whatever sin he might have committed and asks Marduk to restore their relationship.

O lord, at your going into the temple [may your house say to you: Be appeased].

O prince, lord Marduk, at your going into the temple, may your house . . .

O great hero, lord Enbilulu at your going into the temple, may your house . . .

Be appeased, O lord; be appeased, O lord; may your house . . .

Be appeased, O lord of Babylon; may your house . . .

Be appeased, O lord of Esagila; may your house . . .

Be appeased, O lord of Ezida; may your house . . .

Be appeased, O lord of Emachtila; may your house . . .

In Esagila the house of your lordship, may your house . . .

May your city say to you: Be appeased; may your house . . .

May Babylon say to you: Be appeased; may your house . . .

May Anu the great, father of the gods, say to you: How long? *and:* Be appeased.

May the great mountain, father Enlil, *say to you:* How long? . . .

May the princess of city and house, the great mother, Ninlil, *say to you:* How long? . . .

May Ninurta, the chief son of Enlil, the exalted arm of Anu, *say to you:* How long? . . .

May Sin, the lamp of heaven and earth, *say to you:* How long? . . .

May the hero Shamash, the bearded one,
son of Ningal *say to you*: How long?
. . .

May Ea, king of the Deep, *say to you*:
How long? . . .

May Damkina, queen of the Deep, *say to you*: How long? . . .

May Sarpanitum, daughter-in-law of the
Deep *say to you*: How long? . . .

May . . . Nabu *say to you*: How long? . . .

May . . . firstborn of Urash *say to you*:
How long? . . .

May . . . Tashmetum say to you: How
long? *and*: Be appeased.

May the great princess, the lady Nana,
say to you: How long? . . .

May the lord Madana, director of the
Anunnaki, *say to you*: How long? . . .

May Baba, the gracious lady, *say to you*:
How long? . . .

May Adad, the son beloved of Anu, *say
to you*: How long? . . .

May Shala, the great wife, *say to you*:
How long? . . .

O lord, mighty one who dwells in Ekur
let your own divine spirit bring you
rest.

O you who are the hero of the gods—
may the gods of heaven and earth
cause your anger to be appeased.

Do not neglect your city, Nippur; O lord,
be appeased, may they say to you.

Do not neglect your city, Sippar; O lord,
be appeased . . .

Do not neglect Babylon, the city of your
rejoicing; O lord, be appeased . . .

Look favorably on your house; look
favorably on your city; O lord, be
appeased . . .

Look favorably on Babylon and Esagila;
O lord, be appeased . . .

The bolt of Babylon, the lock of Esagila,
the bricks of Ezida restore to their
places; O lord, be appeased, may the
gods of heaven and earth say to you.

#78: Plague Prayers of Mursilis II
(*ANET* 394–96)[8]

The "Prayers of Mursilis II" date to around
1350–1325 B.C. Mursilis became king of the Hittite Empire after his father, Suppiluliuma I, died

from some sort of plague, a plague that also
claimed the life of Mursilis's brother Arnuwanda
II. The plague continued several years into Mursilis's reign and also resulted in a great number
of deaths among the general Hittite population.
In his prayers, the king confesses his sins to the
Hittite gods, points out the restitution already
made to the gods, and asks them to remove the
effects of the plague.

Hattian storm-god, my lord, and you, Hattian gods, my lords! Mursilis, the great king,
your servant, has sent me *with the order*: Go!
To the Hattian storm-god, my lord, and to the
gods, my lords, speak as follows:

What is this that you have done? A plague
you have let into the land. Hatti land has been
cruelly afflicted by the plague. For twenty
years now men have been dying in my father's days, in my brother's days, and in mine
own since I have become the priest of the
gods. When men are dying in Hatti land like
this, the plague is in no wise over. As for me,
the agony of my heart and the anguish of my
soul I cannot endure any more.

When I celebrated festivals, I worshiped
all the gods, I never preferred one temple to
another. The matter of the plague I have laid
in prayer before all the gods making vows to
them *saying*: Listen to me, you gods, my lords!
Drive forth the plague from Hatti land! The
reason for which people are dying in Hatti
land—either let it be established by an omen,
or let me see it in a dream, or let a prophet declare it! But the gods did not listen to me and
the plague got no better in Hatti land. Hatti
land was cruelly afflicted.

The few people who were left to give sacrificial loaves and libations were dying too.
Matters again got too much for me. So I made
the anger of the gods the subject of an oracle.
I learnt of two ancient tablets. The first tablet
dealt with the offerings to the river Mala. The
old kings had regularly presented offerings
to the river Mala. But now a plague has been
rampant in Hatti land since the days of my
father, and we have never performed the offerings to the river Mala.

The second tablet concerned Kurustama.
When the Hattian storm-god had brought
people of Kurustama to the country of Egypt
and had made an agreement concerning them

with the Hattians so that they were under oath to the Hattian storm-god—although the Hattians as well as the Egyptians were under oath to the Hattian storm-god, the Hattians ignored their obligations; the Hattians promptly broke the oath of the gods. My father sent foot soldiers and charioteers who attacked the country of Amka, Egyptian territory. Again he sent troops, and again they attacked it. When the Egyptians became frightened, they asked outright for one of his sons to *take over* the kingship. But when my father gave them one of his sons, they killed him as they led him there. My father let his anger run away with him, he went to war against Egypt and attacked Egypt. He smote the foot soldiers and the charioteers of the country of Egypt. The Hattian storm-god, my lord, by his decision even then let my father prevail; he vanquished and smote the foot soldiers and the charioteers of the country of Egypt. But when they brought back to Hatti land the prisoners that they had taken, a plague broke out among the prisoners and they began to die.

When they moved the prisoners to Hatti land, these prisoners carried the plague into Hatti land. From that day on people have been dying in Hatti land. Now, when I found that tablet dealing with the country of Egypt, I made the matter the subject of an oracle of the god *and asked*: Those arrangements that were made by the Hattian storm-god—namely that the Egyptians and the Hattians as well were put under oath by the Hattian storm-god, that the Damnassaras deities were present in the temple of the Hattian storm-god, and that the Hattians promptly broke their word—has this perhaps become the cause of the anger of the Hattian storm-god, my lord? And *so* it was established.

(*gap*)

Because I humble myself and cry for mercy, hearken to me, Hattian storm-god, my lord! Let the plague stop in Hatti land!

(*gap*)

Hattian storm-god, my lord, *and* you gods, my lords! It is only too true that man is sinful. My father sinned and transgressed against the word of the Hattian storm-god, my lord.

But I have not sinned in any respect. It is only too true, however, that the father's sin falls upon the son. So, my father's sin has fallen upon me. Now, I have confessed before the Hattian storm-god, my lord, and before the gods, my lords *admitting*: It is true, we have done it. And because I have confessed my father's sin, let the soul of the Hattian storm-god, my lord, and *those* of the gods, my lords, be again pacified! Take pity on me and drive the plague out of Hatti land! Suffer not to die the few who are still left to offer sacrificial loaves and libations!

(*gap*)

See! I am praying to you, Hattian storm-god, my lord. So save my life! If indeed it is for those reasons that I have mentioned that people are dying—as soon as I set them right, let those that are still able to give sacrificial loaves and libations die no longer! If, on the other hand, people are dying for some other reason, either let me see it in a dream, or let it be found out by an oracle, or let a prophet declare it, or let all the priests find out by incubation whatever I suggest to them. Hattian storm-god, my lord, save my life! Let the gods, my lords, prove their divine power! Let someone see it in a dream! For whatever reason people are dying, let that be found out! . . . Hattian storm-god, my lord, save my life! Let this plague abate again in Hatti land!

What is this, O gods, that you have done? A plague you have let into the land. Hatti land, all of it, is dying; so no one prepares sacrificial loaves and libations for you. The plowmen who used to work the fields of the god are dead; so no one works or reaps the fields of the god at all. The grinding women who used to make the sacrificial loaves for the gods are dead; so they do not make the sacrificial loaves any longer. From whatever corral *or* sheepfold they used to select the sacrifices of sheep and cattle, the cowherds and the shepherds are dead and the corral [and the sheepfold are empty]. So it comes to pass that the sacrificial loaves *and* libations, and the offerings of animals have stopped. And you, O gods, come on this day and hold us responsible. Man has lost his wits, and there is nothing that we do aright. O gods, whatever sin you behold, either let a prophet rise and declare it, or let the sibyls or the priests learn about it by incubation, or let man see it in a dream! . . . O gods, take pity again on Hatti land!

(gap)

But now all the surrounding countries have begun to attack Hatti land. Let it again become a matter of concern to the sun-goddess of Arinna! O god, bring not your name into disrepute!

Whatever rage *or* anger the gods may feel, and whosoever may not have been reverent toward the gods, let not the good perish with the wicked! If it is one town, or one [house], or one man, O gods, let that one perish alone! Look upon Hatti land with favorable eyes, but the evil plague give to [those other] countries!

Part

4

Prophetic Books

16 Prophecies, Visions, and Apocalyptic

References to prophecy and prophets are found in many different types of ancient Near Eastern literature. In biblical prophecy, the prophets receive messages from God through various means and deliver them to their intended audiences. Careful reading of the texts presented here highlights the unique nature of biblical prophecy, although general parallels certainly exist.

#79: Mari Prophecy
(Moran, "New Evidence from Mari," 29–32, 46–48)

The ancient city of Mari (Tel Hariri) was located on the banks of the Euphrates River.[1] French archeologists excavated the site from 1933 to 1938, and the discovery of the royal palace archives produced over twenty thousand cuneiform documents, most of which date to 1800–1760 B.C. The Mari texts shed significant light on the patriarchal period in that they describe the movements of nomadic peoples in the vicinity of Mari. Some of these nomads and the citizens of Mari have names similar to those in Genesis: Abram, Ishmael, Jacob, Rebekah, and Laban, for example. The Mari texts also refer to male and female prophets or ecstatics who served a particular deity and issued pronouncements concerning the king. The reading presented here relates their messages to King Zimri-Lim of Mari. The ecstatics utter counsel to the king, but their messages lack the strong moral base so evident in the biblical prophets.[2]

Speak to my lord: Thus Shibtu your maidservant. For a report on the campaign that my lord is on, I asked a man and a woman . . . for the signs, and the word is very favorable to my lord. Similarly, with regard to Ishme-Dagan I asked the man and the woman, and the word on him is not favorable. And as to the report on him, he has been placed under the foot of my lord. Thus they *spoke*: My lord lifted the HUMASHUM to Ishme-Dagan, and *spoke* thus:

With the HUMASHUM I will beat you. Just wrestle and I will beat you in wrestling. Thus I *spoke*: Is my lord drawing near to battle? Thus they *spoke*: A battle will not be fought. Right on arriving *Ishme-Dagan's* auxiliary troops will be scattered; furthermore, they will cut off the head of Ishme-Dagan and put *it* under the foot of my lord. Thus *my lord will say*: The army of Ishme-Dagan is large, and if I [arrive], will his auxiliary troops be scattered from him? They have hemmed in my auxiliary troops. It is Dagan, Adad, Itur-Mer, and Belet-ekallim—and Adad indeed is the lord of decision!—who [march] at my lord's side. Heaven forbid that my lord should [say] this, saying: By means of arms I *must* [lay] them [low]. I am not making [them speak]. On their own they speak, on their [own] they agree. Thus they *say*: The auxiliary troops of Ishme-[Dagan] are *made up of* prisoners. With acts of treachery and deception they . . . with him. They do not accept his . . . Before my lord his army will be scattered.

#80: Neo-Assyrian Prophecies
(*ANET* 606–7)

Certain Akkadian texts from the first millennium B.C. show some similarity to biblical prophecy. The intention of these texts is, somewhat vague, for they simply list political events during a particular period. Some scholars argue that they are examples of *vaticinium ex eventu* or "prophecy written after the event." Clearly, the Akkadian prophecies differ significantly from classic biblical prophecy.

[That ruler's days will be short]. That land [will have another ruler.

A ruler will arise], he [will rule] for eighteen years. The country will live safely, the interior of the country will be happy, the people will [have abundance]. The gods will make beneficial decisions for the country, favorable winds [will blow]. The date palm and the furrow will bring in good yield. Shakkan and Nisaba will . . . in the land. There will be *favorable* rain and high water, the people of the land will observe a festival. That ruler will be killed in an uprising.

A ruler will arise, he will rule for thirteen years.

There will be an attack of Elam against Akkad, and the booty of Akkad will be carried off. The temples of the great gods will be destroyed, the defeat of Akkad will be decreed *by the gods*. There will be confusion, disturbance, and unhappy events in the land, and the reign will diminish *in power*; another man, whose name is not mentioned *as a successor* will arise, and will seize the throne as king and will put to death his officials. He will fill with the [corpses] of half the army the lowlands of Tupliash, plain and level ground, and the people of the land will experience a severe famine.

A ruler will arise, his days will be few, and he will not rule the land.

A ruler [will arise], he will rule for three years. The canals [of that land] will fill up with silt.

(gap)

[A ruler will arise, he will rule for . . . years] . . . That king [will rule] all the regions. His people will [have] abundance and . . . The regular offerings for the IGIGI gods that had ceased he will reestablish, the gods [will] . . . Favorable winds will blow, [there will be] abundance, and . . . in [the land]. Cattle [will lie down] safely in the open. The vegetation of winter [will last] through the summer, the vegetation of [summer will last through the winter]. The offspring of the domestic animals [will thrive].

A ruler will arise, he will rule for eight years.

(gap)

A ruler will arise, he [will rule] for three years. The remainder of the people [will return to their homes]. Abandoned cities will be reinhabited . . . There will be rebellions, and then . . . For Akkad [there will be] enmity . . . The rites of Ekur and of Nippur will [be transferred] to [another] country. The . . . of Enlil will [return] to Nippur. That ruler [will defeat] the land of Amurru.

A ruler will arise, he will [rule] for eight years. The temples of the gods [will be restored], at the advice [of the king] the rites of the great gods [will be restored. There will be] *favorable* rain and high water in the land. The people who have experienced evil [will experience good]. The rich will become poor, the poor will become rich . . . The one who was [rich] will stretch out his hand to the poor . . . , the mother will speak what is right to her daughter. [The elders] will sit and will give advice to the land. [Locusts will arise] and devour the land, the king will [bring] hard times upon his land.

#81: Admonitions of Ipuwer
(*ANET* 441–44)

The "Admonitions of Ipuwer," the "Prophecies of Nefertiti," and the "Report of Wen-Amon" (readings 81–83) are the closest Egyptian parallels to biblical prophecy. Some scholars, however, argue that these texts omit vital details essential to drawing a parallel.[3] Dated to about 2000 B.C., the "Admonitions of Ipuwer" describes the negative aspects of Egyptian society, calls Egypt's citizens to repent, and anticipates a coming day when a good ruler will bring this about.

[Doorkeepers] say: Let us go and plunder . . . The laundryman refuses to carry his load . . . Bird [catchers] have marshaled the battle array . . . [Men of] the Delta marshes carry shields . . . A man regards his son as his enemy . . . A man of character goes in mourning because of what has happened in the land . . . Foreigners have become people everywhere . . .

. . . Why really, the [face] is pale. The bowman is ready. Robbery is everywhere. There is no man of yesterday . . .

Why really, the Nile is in flood, *but* no one plows for himself, *because* every man says: We do not know what may happen throughout the land!

Why really, women are dried up, and none can conceive. Khnum cannot fashion *mortals* because of the state of the land.

Why really, poor men have become the possessors of treasures. He who could not make himself a pair of sandals is *now* the possessor of riches . . .

Why really, many dead are buried in the river. The stream is a tomb, and the embalming place has really become the stream.

Why really, nobles are in lamentation, while poor men have joy. Every town says: Let us banish many from us.

Why really, they who built [pyramids have become] farmers. They who were in the ship of the god are charged with forced [labor]. No one really sails north to [Byblos] today. What shall we do for cedar for our mummies? Priests were buried with their produce, and [nobles] were embalmed with the oil thereof as far away as Keftiu, *but* they come no *longer*. Gold is lacking . . . How important it *now* seems when the oasis people come carrying their festival provisions: reed mats, . . . fresh REDMET plants, . . . of birds, and . . .

Why really, laughter has disappeared, and is [no longer] made. It is wailing that pervades the land, mixed with lamentation . . .

Why really, the children of nobles are dashed against the walls. The *once* prayed-for children are *now* laid out on the high ground . . .

Why really, grain has perished on every side . . . Everybody says: There is nothing! The storehouse is stripped bare; its keeper is stretched out on the ground . . . Ah, would that I had raised my voice at that time—it might save me from the suffering in which I am!

Why really, magic is exposed. [Go spells] and [enfold spells] are made ineffectual because they are repeated by *ordinary* people.

Why really, *public* offices are open, and their reports are read. Serfs have become the owners of serfs . . .

Why really, the writings of the scribes of the mat have been removed. The grain sustenance of Egypt is *now* a come-and-get-it.

Behold now, something has been done that never happened for a long time: the king has been taken away by poor men.

Behold, he who was buried as a falcon now lies on a mere bier. What the pyramid hid has become empty.

Behold now, it has come to a point where the land is despoiled of the kingship by a few irresponsible men.

Behold now, it has come to a point where *men* rebel against the URAEUS, the . . . of Re, which makes the Two Lands peaceful.

Behold, the secret of the land, whose limits are [unknowable], is laid bare. The residence *may* be razed within an hour . . .

Behold, the [guardian]-serpent is taken from her hole. The secrets of the kings of Upper and Lower Egypt are laid bare . . .

Behold, nobles' ladies are *now* [gleaners], and nobles are in the workhouse. *But* he who never *even* slept on a [plank] is *now* the owner of a bed . . .

Behold, the owners of robes are *now* in rags. *But* he who never wove for himself is *now* the owner of fine linen . . .

Behold, he who knew not the lyre is *now* the owner of a harp. He who never sang for himself *now* praises the goddess of music . . .

Behold, the bald-headed man who had no oil has become the owner of jars of sweet myrrh.

Behold, she who had not *even* a box is *now* the owner of a [trunk]. She who looked at her face in the water is *now* the owner of a mirror . . .

Behold, the king's men [thrash around among] the cattle of the destitute . . .

Behold, the king's men [thrash around among] geese, which are presented *to* the gods instead of oxen . . .

Behold, nobles' ladies are growing hungry, *but* the king's men are sated with what they have done.

Behold, not an office is in its *proper* place, like a stampeded herd that has no herdsman.

Behold, cattle are *left* free wandering, *for* there is no one to take care of them. Every man takes for himself and brands *them* with his name . . .

Behold, he who had no grain is *now* the owner of granaries. He who had to get a loan for himself *now* issues it . . .

. . . Authority, perception, and justice are with you, *but* it is confusion that you would set throughout the land, together with the noise of contention. Behold, one thrusts against another. Men conform to what you have commanded. If three men go along a road, they are found to be two men: it is the greater number that kills the lesser. Does then the herdsman love death? So then you will command that a reply be made: It is [because] one man [loves] and another hates. [That is, their forms] are few everywhere. [This really means that you have acted] to bring such *a situation* into being, and you have spoken lies . . . All these years are civil strife. A man may be slain on his *own* roof, while he is on the watch in his boundary house. Is he brave and saves himself?—that means that he will live . . . Would that you might taste of some of the oppressions thereof! Then you would say: . . .

. . . But it is still good when the hands of men construct pyramids, when canals are dug, and when groves of trees are made for the gods.

But it is still good when men are drunken, when they drink MIYET and their hearts are happy.

But it is still good when shouting is in the mouths *of men*, when the notables of the districts are standing and watching the shouting from their houses, clothed in a cloak, purified [already and firm bellied] . . .

. . . None can be found who will stand [in their places] . . . Every man fights for his sister, and he protects his own person. Is *it* the Nubians? Then we shall make our *own* [protection]. [Fighting police] will hold off the barbarians. Is it the Libyans? Then we shall [turn away]. The Madjoi [fortunately] are with Egypt. How is it that every man kills his brother? The military classes that we marshal for ourselves have become [barbarians, beginning to destroy that from which they took their being] and to show the Asiatics the state of the land. And yet all the foreigners are afraid of [them] . . .

What Ipu-wer said, when he answered the majesty of the all-lord: . . . To be ignorant of it is something pleasant to the heart. You have done what is good in their hearts, *for* you have kept people alive [thereby]. *But still* they cover up their faces for fear of the morrow.

Once upon a time there was a man who was old [and in the presence of] his salvation, while his son was *still* a child, without understanding.

#82: Prophecies of Neferti
(*ANET* 444–46)[4]

The "Prophecies of Neferti" was apparently composed as a political document during the reign of Amenemhet I (1990–1960 B.C.).[5] Summoned to the court of King Snefru (fourth dynasty), Neferti (Nefer-rohu) proclaims words regarding Egypt's future. Although written as prophecy, the real purpose of this composition is to legitimize the monarchy of Amenemhet I against other Egyptian leadership.[6]

Now it happened that the majesty of the king of Upper and Lower Egypt: Snefru, the triumphant, was the beneficent king in this entire land. On one of these days it happened that the official council of the residence city entered into the great house—life, [prosperity], health!—to offer greeting. Then they went out, that they might offer greetings *elsewhere*, according to their daily procedure. Then his majesty—life, prosperity, health!—said to the seal bearer who was at his side: Go and bring me *back* the official council of the residence city, which has gone forth hence to offer greetings on this [day]. *Thereupon they* were ushered in to him immediately. Then they were on their bellies in the presence of his majesty a second time.

Then his majesty—life, prosperity, health!—said to them: *My* people, behold, I have caused you to be called to have you seek out for me a son of yours who is wise, or a brother of yours who is competent, or a friend of yours who has performed a good deed, one who may say to me a few fine words or choice speeches, at the hearing of which my [majesty] may be entertained.

Then they put *themselves* upon their bellies in the presence of his majesty—life, prosperity, health!—once more. Then they said before his majesty—life, prosperity, health! A great lector priest of Bastet, O sovereign, our lord, whose name is Nefer-rohu—he is a commoner valiant [with] his arm, a scribe competent with his fingers; he is a man of rank, who has more property than any peer of his. Would that he [might be permitted] to see his majesty! Then his majesty—life, prosperity, health!—said: Go and [bring] him to me!

Then he was ushered in to him immediately. Then he was on his belly in the presence of his majesty—life, prosperity, health! Then his majesty—life, prosperity, health!—said: Come, pray, Nefer-rohu, my friend, that you may say to me a few fine words or choice speeches, at the hearing of which my majesty may be entertained! Then the lector priest Nefer-rohu said: Of what has *already* happened or of what is going to happen, O sovereign—life, prosperity, health!—[my] lord. Then his majesty—life, prosperity, health!—said: Rather of what is going to happen. [If it has] taken place [by] today, [pass it by]. Then he stretched forth his hand for the box of writing equipment; then he drew forth a scroll of papyrus and a palette; thereupon he put *it* into writing.

What the lector [priest] Nefer-rohu said, that wise man of the east, he who belonged to Bastet at her appearances, that child of the Heliopolitan nome, as he brooded over what *was to* happen in the land, as he called to mind the state of the east, when the Asiatics would move about with their strong arms, would disturb the hearts [of] those who are at the harvest, and would take away the spans of cattle at the plowing. He said:

Bestir thyself, O my heart, as you bewail this land in which you did begin! To be silent is [repression]. Behold, there is something about which men speak as [terrifying], for, behold, the great man is a thing passed away *in the land* where you did begin. Be not lax; behold, it is before your face! May you rise up against what is before you, for, behold, although great men are concerned with the land, what has been done is as what is not done. [Re must begin the foundation] *of the earth over again*. The land is completely perished, *so that* no remainder exists, *so that* not *even* the black of the nail survives from what was fated.

This land is *so* damaged *that* there is no one who is concerned with it, no one who speaks, no one who weeps. How is this land? The sun disc is covered over. It will not shine *so that* people may see. No one can live when clouds cover over *the sun*. Then everybody is deaf for lack of it.

I shall speak of what is before my face; I cannot foretell what has not *yet* come.

The rivers of Egypt are empty, *so that* the water is crossed on foot. Men seek for water for the ships to sail on it. Its course is [become] a sandbank. The sandbank is [against] the flood; the place of water [is against] the [flood]—*both* the place of water [and] the sandbank. The south wind will oppose the north wind; the skies are no *longer* in a single wind. A foreign bird will be born in the marshes of the northland. It has made a nest beside men, and people have let it approach through want of it. Damaged indeed are those good things, those fish ponds, *where there were* those who clean fish, overflowing with fish and fowl. Everything good is disappeared, and the land is prostrate because of woes from that [food], the Asiatics who are throughout the land.

Foes have arisen in the east, and Asiatics have come down into Egypt . . . No protector will listen . . . Men will enter into the [fortresses]. Sleep will [be banished] from my eyes, as I spend the night wakeful. The wild beasts of the desert will drink at the rivers of Egypt and be at their ease on their banks for lack of [someone to scare them away].

(gap)

I show you the land topsy-turvy. The weak of arm is *now* the possessor of an arm. Men salute *respectfully* him who *formerly* saluted. I show you the undermost on top, turned about [in proportion to] the turning about of [my belly]. Men live in the necropolis. The poor man will make wealth . . . It is the paupers that will be eating bread, while the servants [rejoice]. The Heliopolitan nome, the birthplace of every god, will no [longer be on earth].

Then it is that a king will come, belonging to the south, Ameni the Triumphant, his name. He is the son of a woman of the land of Nubia; he is one born in Upper Egypt. He will take the [White] Crown; he will wear the Red Crown; he will unite the Two Mighty Ones; he will satisfy the two lords with what they desire. The encircler-of-the-fields *will be* in his grasp, the oar . . .

Rejoice, you people of his time! The son of a man will make his name forever and ever. They who incline toward evil and who plot rebellion have subdued their speech for fear of him. The Asiatics will fall to his sword, and the Libyans will fall to his flame. The rebels belong to his wrath, and the treacherous of heart to the awe of him. The URAEUS serpent that is on his brow stills for him the treacherous of heart.

There will be built the wall of the ruler— life, prosperity, health!—and the Asiatics will not be permitted to come down into Egypt that they might beg for water in the customary manner, in order to let their beasts drink. And justice will come into its place, while wrongdoing is [driven] out. Rejoice, he who may behold *this* and who may be in the service of the king!

The learned man will pour out water for me, when he sees what I have spoken come to pass.

It has come *to its end* in [success], by the [scribe].

#83: Report of Wen-Amon
(*ANET* 25–29)[7]

Scholars disagree as to whether the "Report of Wen-Amon" records an actual mission, but they do agree that it depicts a realistic historical situation.[8] The text describes the third decade of the reign of Ramses XI (1090–1080 B.C.), a time of great strife within Egypt. Wen-Amon, an official of the Amon temple, records his travels to Byblos to obtain lumber, describes the challenges and dangers he encountered, and mentions how a god laid hold of a young man and put him into a trance.

Year five, fourth month of the third season, day sixteen: the day on which Wen-Amon, the senior of the forecourt of the house of Amon, [lord of the thrones] of the Two Lands, set out to fetch the woodwork for the great and august bark of Amon-Re, king of the gods, which is on [the river and which is named]: User-het-Amon. On the day when I reached Tanis, the place [where Ne-su-Ba-neb]-Ded and Ta-net-Amon were, I gave them the letters of Amon-Re, king of the gods, and they had them read in their presence. And they said: Yes, I will do as Amon-Re, king of the gods, our [lord], has

said! I spent up to the fourth month of the third season in Tanis. And Ne-su-Ba-neb-Ded and Ta-net-Amon sent me off with the ship captain Mengebet, and I embarked on the great Syrian sea in the first month of the third season, day one.

I reached Dor, a town of the Tjeker, and Beder, its prince, had [fifty] loaves of bread, one jug of wine, and one leg of beef brought to me. And a man of my ship ran away and stole one [vessel] of gold, [amounting] to five DEBEN, four jars of silver, amounting to twenty DEBEN, and a sack of eleven DEBEN of silver. [Total of what] he [stole]: five DEBEN of gold and thirty-one DEBEN of silver.

I got up in the morning, and I went to the place where the prince was, and I said to him: I have been robbed in your harbor. Now you are the prince of this land, and you are its investigator who should look for my silver. Now about this silver—it belongs to Amon-Re, king of the gods, the lord of the lands; it belongs to

Mediterranean coastline near Caesarea. (Jim Yancey)

Ne-su-Ba-neb-Ded; it belongs to Heri-Hor, my lord, and the other great men of Egypt! It belongs to you; it belongs to Weret; it belongs to Mekmer; it belongs to Zakar-Baal, the prince of Byblos!

And he said to me: Whether you are important or whether you are eminent—look here, I do not recognize this accusation that you have made to me! Suppose it had been a thief who belonged to my land who went on your boat and stole your silver, I should have repaid it to you from my treasury, until they had found this thief of yours—whoever he may be. Now about the thief who robbed you—he belongs to you! He belongs to your ship! Spend a few days here visiting me, so that I may look for him.

I spent nine days moored *in* his harbor, and I went *to* call on him, and I said to him: Look, you have not found my silver. [Just let] me [go] with the ship captains and with those who go *to* sea! But he said to me: Be quiet! . . . I went out of Tyre at the break of dawn.

(gap)

And the [prince] of Byblos sent to me, saying: Get [out of my] harbor! And I sent to him, saying: Where should [I go to]? . . . If [you have a ship] to carry me, have me taken to Egypt again! So I spent twenty-nine days in his [harbor, while] he [spent] the time sending to me every day to say: Get out *of* my harbor!

Now while he was making offering to his gods, the god seized one of his youths and made him possessed. And he said to him: Bring up [the god]! Bring the messenger who is carrying him! Amon is the one who sent him out! He is the one who made him come! And while the possessed *youth* was having his frenzy on this night, I had *already* found a ship headed for Egypt and had loaded everything that I had into it. While I was watching for the darkness, thinking that when it descended I would load the god *also*, so that no other eye might see him, the harbor master came to me, saying: Wait until morning—so says the prince. So I said to him: Aren't you the one who spent the time coming to me every day to say: Get out *of* my harbor? Aren't you saying: Wait tonight in order to let the ship that I have found get away—and *then* you will come

again *to* say: Go away? So he went and told it to the prince. And the prince sent to the captain of the ship to say: Wait until morning—so says the prince!

When morning came, he sent and brought me up, but the god stayed in the tent where he was, *on* the shore of the sea. And I found him sitting *in* his upper room, with his back turned to a window, so that the waves of the great Syrian sea broke against the back of his head.

So I said to him: [May] Amon [favor you]! But he said to me: How long, up to today, since you came from the place where Amon is? So I said to him: Five months and one day up to now. And he said to me: Well, you're truthful! Where is the letter of Amon that *should be* in your hand? Where is the dispatch of the high priest of Amon that *should be* in your hand? And I told him: I gave them to Ne-su-Ba-neb-Ded and Ta-net-Amon. And he was very, very angry, and he said to me: Now see—neither letters nor dispatches are in your hand! Where is the cedar ship that Ne-su-Ba-neb-Ded gave to you? Where is its Syrian crew? Didn't he turn you over to this foreign ship captain to have him kill you and throw you into the sea? *Then* with whom would they have looked for the god? And you too—with whom would they have looked for you too? So he spoke to me.

But I said to him: Wasn't it an Egyptian ship? Now it is Egyptian crews that sail under Ne-su-Ba-neb-Ded! He has no Syrian crews. And he said to me: Aren't there twenty ships here in my harbor that are in commercial relations with Ne-su-Ba-neb-Ded? As to this Sidon, the other *place* that you have passed, aren't there fifty more ships there that are in commercial relations with Werket-El, and are drawn up to his house? And I was silent in this great time.

And he answered and said to me: On what business have you come? So I told him: I have come after the woodwork for the great and august bark of Amon-Re, king of the gods. Your father did *it*, your grandfather did *it*, and you will do it too! So I spoke to him. But he said to me: To be sure, they did it! And if you give me *something* for doing it, I will do it! Why, when my people carried out this commission, pharaoh—life, prosperity, health!—sent six ships loaded with Egyptian goods, and they unloaded them into their storehouses! You—what is it that you're bringing me—me also? And he had the journal rolls of his fathers brought, and he had them read out in my presence, and they found a thousand DEBEN of silver and all kinds of things in his scrolls.

So he said to me: If the ruler of Egypt were the lord of mine, and I were his servant also, he would not have to send silver and gold, saying: Carry out the commission of Amon! There would be no carrying of a royal gift, such as they used to do for my father. As for me—me also—I am not your servant! I am not the servant of him who sent you either! If I cry out to the Lebanon, the heavens open up, and the logs are here lying *on* the shore of the sea! Give me the sails that you have brought to carry your ships that would hold the logs for *Egypt*! Give me the ropes [that] you have brought [to lash the cedar] logs that I am to cut down to make you . . . that I shall make for you *as* the sails of your boats, and the [spars] will be *too* heavy and will break, and you will die in the middle of the sea! See, Amon made thunder in the sky when he put Seth near him. Now when Amon founded all lands, in founding them he founded first the land of Egypt, from which you come; for craftsmanship came out of it, to reach the place where I am, and learning came out of it, to reach the place where I am. What are these silly trips that they have had you make?

And I said to him: *That's* not true! What I am on are no "silly trips" at all! There is no ship upon the river that does not belong to Amon! The sea is his, and the Lebanon is his, of which you say: It is mine! It forms the [nursery] for User-het-Amon, the lord of [every] ship! Why, he spoke—Amon-Re, king of the gods—and said to Heri-Hor, my master: Send me forth! So he had me come, carrying this great god. But see, you have made this great god spend these twenty-nine days moored *in* your harbor, although you did not know *it*. Isn't he here? Isn't he the *same* as he was? You are stationed *here* to carry on the commerce of the Lebanon with Amon, its lord. As for your saying that the former kings sent silver

and gold—suppose that they had life and health; *then* they would not have had such things sent! *But* they had such things sent to your fathers in place of life and health! Now as for Amon-Re, king of the gods—he is the lord of this life and health, and he was the lord of your fathers. They spent their lifetimes making offering to Amon. And you also—you are the servant of Amon! If you say to Amon: Yes, I will do *it*! and you carry out his commission, you will live, you will be prosperous, you will be healthy, and you will be good to your entire land and your people! *But* don't wish for yourself anything belonging to Amon-Re, *king of* the gods. Why, a lion wants his own property! Have your secretary brought to me, so that I may send him to Ne-su-Ba-neb-Ded and Ta-net-Amon, the [officers] whom Amon put in the north of his land, and they will have all kinds of things sent. I shall send him to them to say: Let it be brought until I shall go back again to the south, and I shall *then* have every bit of the debt still *due to you* brought to you. So I spoke to him.

So he entrusted my letter to his messenger, and he loaded in the [keel], the bow post, the stern post, along with four other hewn timbers—seven in all—and he had them taken to Egypt. And in the first month of the second season his messenger who had gone to Egypt came back to me in Syria. And Ne-su-Ba-neb-Ded and Ta-net-Amon sent four jars and one KAKMEN of gold; five jars of silver; ten pieces of clothing in royal linen; ten KHERD of good Upper Egyptian linen; five hundred *rolls of* finished papyrus; five hundred cowhides; five hundred ropes; twenty sacks of lentils; and thirty baskets of fish. And she sent to me *personally*: five pieces of clothing in good Upper Egyptian linen; five KHERD of good Upper Egyptian linen; one sack of lentils; and five baskets of fish.

And the prince was glad, and he detailed three hundred men and three hundred cattle, and he put supervisors at their head, to have them cut down the timber. So they cut them down, and they spent the second season lying there.

In the third month of the third season they dragged them *to* the shore of the sea, and the prince came out and stood by them.

(gap)

And I went *to* the shore of the sea, to the place where the timber was lying, and I spied eleven ships belonging to the Tjeker coming in from the sea, in order to say: Arrest him! Don't let a ship of his *go* to the land of Egypt! Then I sat down and wept. And the letter scribe of the prince came out to me, and he said to me: What's the matter with you? And I said to him: Haven't you seen the birds go down to Egypt a second time? Look at them—how they travel to the cool pools! *But* how long shall I be left here! Now don't you see those who are coming again to arrest me?

So he went and told it to the prince. And the prince began to weep because of the words that were said to him, for they were painful. And he sent out to me his letter scribe, and he brought to me two jugs of wine and one ram. And he sent to me Ta-net-Not, an Egyptian singer who was with him, saying: Sing to him! Don't let his heart take on cares! And he sent to me, to say: Eat and drink! Don't let your heart take on cares, for tomorrow you shall hear whatever I have to say.

When morning came, he had his assembly summoned, and he stood in their midst, and he said to the Tjeker: What have you come *for*? And they said to him: We have come after the [blasted] ships that you are sending to Egypt with our opponents! But he said to them: I cannot arrest the messenger of Amon inside my land. Let me send him away, and you go after him to arrest him.

So he loaded me in, and he sent me away from there at the harbor of the sea. And the wind cast me on the land of Alashiya.

#84: Stela of Zakkur

(Gibson, *Textbook of Syrian Semitic Inscriptions*, 2.9–13)

The "Stela of Zakkur" appeared in chapter 10 on non-Hebrew monumental inscriptions. In addition to its value as a historical document, it also provides insight into the role of seers and prophets in Syria. Seers and prophets give the king military advice as he ponders what to do in the face of his enemy. See reading 53 for the translation.

#85: Marduk Prophecy

(Block, *Gods of the Nations*, 169–71)[9]

The "Marduk Prophecy" provides a good example of fictional autobiography.[10] The writer presents a historical record as if it is yet future to serve his propagandistic purpose. The text begins with Marduk calling the gods to listen to him as he describes how he built Babylon with all its greatness. He then depicts the sad state that befell the city when he left it. Finally, he portrays in detail Babylon's "future" when a good king arises.

O Haharnim, Hayashum,
Anum, Enlil,
Nudimmud, Ea,
Muati, Nabium.
You great gods, acknowledge my secrets!
I will gird up my loins; I will speak a
    word.
I, Marduk, the great lord,
the wanderer, the scout, who has been
    surveying the mountains,
the wanderer, the scout, who has been
    traveling the lands,
who has stalked throughout all their
    lands,
from the rising of the sun to the setting
    of the sun,
. . . I
issued the order, and went out to the
    land of Hatti.
I inquired of the Hittites.
The throne of my divinity
I erected in its midst.
During the twenty-four years that I
    spent in its midst,
the roadways of the citizens of Babylon
I established there.
Its . . . merchandise and its goods *were
    sent*
to Sippar, Nippur,
and Babylon.
[A king of Babylon] arose
and grasped [my hand].
. . . Babylon,
which . . . was at peace,
the market of Babylon was favorable.
The crown of my divinity
the image . . .
water, rain . . .
three days . . .

The crown of my divinity
and the image . . .
for my body . . .
I returned. [With reference to Babylon I
    declared]:
Bring [your tribute]
O lands [to Babylon]!

(gap)

. . . Baltil . . .
. . . The temple of Baltil . . .
Its shrine he polished like jewels.
Luxury I bestowed [on him]

(gap)

. . . year after year [I blessed him].
After I had girded *the loins* of the people
    of Enlil with him
I provided him with wings like the birds.
All the lands he filled.
I completed *my days*; I blessed the land of
    Assyria.
. . . of the fortunes I granted him.
I gave him [a certain number] measures
    of grain *and* measures of tin
I returned home. With reference to
    Babylon I declared:
Bring your tribute, O lands,
to Babylon!
I Marduk, the great lord,
I am the Master of Fates and Decrees.
Who has undertaken such a journey *as
    this*?
In the manner . . . in which I departed, so
    I have returned. I issued the order.
I went to the land of Elam,
and all the gods went *with me*. I myself
    issued the command.
The meal offering of the temples I
    terminated myself.
Sakan *the cow-god* and Nisaba *the grain-
    goddess* I sent up to heaven.
Siris *the beer-god* made the heart of the
    people sick.
The corpses of the people block the
    doorways.
Brothers consume one another.
Friends beat each other up with
    weapons.
The nobles against the poor
stretch out their hands.

The scepter becomes short. The land is
    laid low.
Usurpers trouble the land.
Lions block the way.
Dogs [roam about] and bite people.
None whom they bite recover; they die.
My days I fulfilled; my years I
    completed.
For my city, Babylon,
and Ekur-Sagila within I yearned.
I called all the goddesses.
I declared: Bring your tribute,
O lands, to Babylon!
A king of Babylon will arise.
The wondrous temple,
Ekur-Sagila, he will restore.
The plans of the heavens and the earth
he will draw in Ekur-Sagila.
Its height he will alter. Freedom from
    taxes
he will establish in my city, Babylon,
he will grasp my hand, and into my city,
    Babylon,
and in the Ekur-Sagila he will let me
    enter forever.
The *procession* ship, Matusha, he will
    restore.
Its rudder he will repair with SARIRU
    gold.
Its bow he will [plate] with PASHALLU
    metal.
Sailors, who take care of *it*,
he will cause to board it.
To the right and to the left they will be
    stationed.
The prince will experience the goodness
    of god.
The days of his reign will be long.
Ekur-Egishnugal
he will polish like jewels.
Ningal,
the temple of Sin,
with its silver and its property
and its possessions
in the doorway of the god
with Sin . . .
of Egishnugal
the entire land
this prince will be mighty and without
    rival.

The city he will rule. The dispersed he
   will gather.
Ekur-Egalmah and the other shrines
he will polish like jewels. Ningal,
Gula, Kurnunitum,
from the city of Hariddi—those
   themselves,
and the houses of the rooms of their
   delight,
he will cause to respond.
The prince will permit the land to eat his
   special crops.
His days will be long.
The shrines he will polish like jewels.
All the gods
he will cause to answer.
The scattered land he will gather
and its foundations he will establish.
The gate of heaven
will be constantly opened.
Ningirsu will rule
the rivers will bring fish.
The field will be full of produce.
The grass of winter *will endure* till
   summer.
The grass of summer *will endure* till
   winter.
The harvest of the land will succeed. The
   market will be good.
Evil will be brought to order.
Disorder will be cleared. Evil will be
   enlightened.
Clouds will constantly be present.
Brother will console brother.
A son will honor his father like a god.
A mother will . . . her daughter.
A bride will be crowned. She will honor
   her husband.
One [will find] compassion among men
   perpetually.
A young man will establish . . . his
   produce
that prince will rule all the lands.

#86: Uruk Prophecy
(Hunger and Kaufman, "New Akkadian Prophecy Text," 372–73)

Like the "Marduk Prophecy," the "Uruk Prophecy"
presents a historical record as if it is yet future. The
text records how the city of Uruk and its major

temple, Eanna, suffered under a former evil dynasty until a new and better dynasty restored it.

The king will be shut up in his palace for
several months.

[Somebody] will arise and come to rule
the devastated part of the land . . . from the
Sealand, who had ruled in Babylon.

After him a king will arise, but he will not
provide justice in the land, he will not give
the right decisions for the land. He will remove the ancient protective goddess of Uruk
from Uruk and make her dwell in Babylon;
a goddess who is not the protective goddess
of Uruk he will make dwell in her sanctuary
and devote to her people not belonging to
her. He will impose heavy tax on the people
of Uruk. He will devastate Uruk, fill the
canals with mud, and abandon the cultivated
fields.

After him a king will arise, but he will not
provide justice in the land, he will not give
the right decisions for the land. He will take
the property of Babylonia to Assyria.

After him a king will arise, but he as well
will not provide justice in the land, he will
not give the right decisions for the land. He
will subdue the world, and all the world will
tremble at the mention of his name.

But after him, a king will arise in Uruk
who will provide justice in the land and will
give the right decisions for the land. He will
establish the rites of the cult of Anu in Uruk.
He will remove the ancient protective goddess of Uruk from Babylon and let her dwell
in her own sanctuary in Uruk. The people
belonging to her he will devote to her. He
will rebuild the temples of Uruk and restore
the sanctuaries of the gods. He will renew
Uruk. The gates of Uruk he will build of lapis
lazuli. He will fill the rivers and fields with
abundant yield.

After him his son will arise as king in Uruk
and become master over the world. He will
exercise rule and kingship in Uruk and his
dynasty will be established forever. The
kings of Uruk will exercise rulership like the
gods.

17 Divination and Incantation Texts

Ancient peoples longed to discover and know the will of the gods. Divination and incantations were two attempts to do just that. Divination involved the observation and interpretation of various natural phenomena to determine what the divine realm was revealing. Incantations involved the recitation of words or spells to appease the offended deity and/or to bring about the desired result in the worshiper's life.

#87: Divination
(Hallo and Younger, *Context of Scripture*, 1:423–26)

Divination involved using various means to tap divine power and receive an indication about the will of the gods. These means included *lecanomancy* (observing oil dropped into water), *libanomancy* (observing smoke rising from a censer), and *aleuromancy* (observing flour scattered on water). Divination also included observation of natural phenomena: stars, unusual births, animal behavior, and more. *Extispicy* involved examination of the entrails of a sacrificial animal, from which the priest "read" messages from the gods that were supposedly encoded in the arrangement or abnormalities of the animal's internal organs.[1]

If there is a HAL sign at the emplacement of "the well-being" the reign of Akkad is over.

If the entire liver is anomalous—Omen of the king of Akkad regarding catastrophe.

Omen of Ibbi-Sin when Elam reduced Ur to tell and rubble.

If the "rise of the head of the bird" is dark on the left and the right there will be PITRUSTA.

When you make an extispicy and in a favorable result there is one PITRUSTU the extispicy is unfavorable; in an unfavorable result the extispicy is favorable.

If a sheep bites his right foot—raids of the enemy will be constant against my land.

If *I throw oil into water and* the oil divides itself into two—the sick person will die; for the campaign: the army will not return.

If an anomaly has no right ear—the reign of the king will come to an end; his palace will be scattered; overthrow of the elders of the city; the king will have no advisors; the mood of the land will change; the herds of the land will decrease; you will make a promise to the enemy.

If an anomaly has no left ear—the god has heard the prayer of the king, the king will take the land of his enemy, the palace of the enemy will be scattered, the enemy will have no advisors, you will decrease the herd of the enemy, he will make a promise you.

If an anomaly's right ear is cleft—that oxfold will be scattered.

If an anomaly's left ear is split—that oxfold will expand; the oxfold of the enemy will be scattered.

If an anomaly has two ears on the left and none on the right—the enemy will take your border city, your adversary will prevail over you.

If a ram's horns protrude from its forehead—that oxfold will be scattered.

If there is an eclipse of the moon in Nisannu and it is red—prosperity for the people.

If Venus wears a black tiara *it means* [Saturn] stands in front of her.

If Venus wears a white tiara *it means* [Jupiter] stands in front of her . . .

If Venus wears a green tiara *it means* Mars stands in front of her.

If Venus wears a red tiara *it means* Mercury stands in front of her.

If a city lifts its head to the heaven—that city will be abandoned

If a city's garbage pit is green—that city will be prosperous.

If there are bearded women in a city—hardship will seize the land.

If in a man's house a dog is inscribed on the wall—worry . . .

If everything for a banquet in the temple is regularly provided—the house will have regular good fortune.

If a god enters a man's house for a banquet—constant uprising and contention will be constant for the man's house.

If a man repairs a moon disk—his god [will always shepherd him] steadfastly.

If a man repairs a sun disk—his god [will always shepherd him] steadfastly.

If there is black fungus in a man's house—there will be brisk trade in the man's house; the man's house will be rich.

If there is green and red fungus in a man's house—the master of the house will die, dispersal of the man's house.

If a snake crosses from the right of a man to the left of a man—he will have a good name.

If a snake crosses from the left of a man to the right of a man—he will have a bad name.

If a white cat is seen in a man's house—*for* that land hardship will seize it.

If a black cat is seen in a man's house—that land will experience good fortune.

If a red cat is seen in a man's house—that land will be rich.

If a multicolored cat is seen in a man's house—that land will not prosper.

If a yellow cat is seen in man's house—that land will have a year of good fortune.

If a man scrapes dirt from his nose—his adversary will submit [to him].

If a man breaks a drinking vessel from which he is drinking—for three days lamentations [will befall him].

So that *the evil* not approach: he should throw its shards in the river and then [it will] not [approach him].

If a woman, her husband dies and a son of her [father-in-law marries her—that man will be rich]

If a man has sex with his brother's daughter—wherever he goes [there will be shortages].

So that *the evil* does not approach: Say thus: God, my strength! [and then it will not approach him].

If a man has sex with the daughter of his brother's daughter—[he will lay his hand] on whatever is not his; he will have profit; the family [will be rich].

If a man has sexual relations with an old woman—he will quarrel daily.

If a man divorces his first-ranking wife—unhappiness *until* the end of days, quarreling will be constant for him, his days will be short.

If in a man's house, a ghost enters the ear of the mistress of the house—mourning will take place in the man's house.

If a severed head laughs—conquest of the army . . .

If a man laughs in his sleep—he will become very sick.

If a man grinds his teeth *while sleeping*—he will experience troubles.

If a mole is very white—that man will become poor, very . . .

If a mole is very green—*ditto* . . .

If a mole is very red—he will be [rich]

If his garment hangs down and is marked with white blemishes—garment of deprivations.

If the walls of a house are dotted with very white *spots*—the master of that house will die a death of violence.

If a man *while speaking* bites his lower lip—*his word* will find acceptance.

#88: SHURPU Incantation
(Reiner, *Šurpu*, 11–12; translated from the German by Elizabeth Eremic)

Incantations involved the recitation of various formulas in an attempt to gain a deity's attention, favor, or forgiveness. A popular form of Mesopotamian incantation was SHURPU, a term that means "burning" and denoted the rite of purification practiced during the recitation of the incantation.[2]

I have called you, you gods of the night.
With you I summoned the night, the
   veiled bride.
I summoned the dusk, midnight, and
   the gray dawn of morning,

because the sorceress bewitched me,
the nightmare bound me.
They have separated my god and my
goddess from me.
I have become burdensome to him who
sees me,
I have no rest day and night.
They have filled my mouth with magic
knots,
closed up my mouth with flour,
denied me drinking water.
My jubilation is lamentation, my joy is
mourning.
Draw near, you great gods, hear my
pleas!
Give me justice, observe my walk.
I have fashioned the image of my
sorcerer and sorceress,
of my enchanter and enchantress,
have laid them at your feet and brought
my case before you.
Because she has done evil, sought after
bad things.
May she die, but may I stay alive!
May her magic, her spook, her witchery
be dissolved!
The tamarind that grew in the treetop
make me clean!
The date palm that catches up the whole
wind, unbind me!
May the MASTAKAL herb that fills the
earth make me shine!
May the pine cone full of seeds unbind
me!

#89: MAQLU Incantation
(Meier, *Die assyrische Beschwörungssammlung Maqlu*, 7–12;
translated from the German by
Elizabeth Eremic)

Along with SHURPU, another popular Mesopotamian incantation was MAQLU, a term that means
"burning." In contrast to SHURPU's emphasis on
purification, MAQLU focuses on counteracting the
evil influence of identified people—a sorcerer, for
example.[3]

May she who spoke evil magic spells
against me melt like tallow!
She who made magic, may she dissolve
like salt!

Her knots are untied, her intrigues
demolished,
all of her words fill the steppe
according to the command *that* the gods
of the night have released.
Oath. Earth, earth, yes earth!
Gilgamesh *is* the lord of your anathema:
what magic you also practice, I know it,
what magic I also practice, you do not
know it.
What sorcery also my sorceresses
practice is confused, has no one to
undo it, no unbinder!
Oath. My city Zabban, my city Zabban,
my city Zabban has two gates,
one facing the east, the second facing the
west,
one facing sunrise, the second facing
sunset.
I raise a bud from the MASTAKAL herb
upward,
to the gods of the heavens I offer up
water.
As you are, yes, you pure ones,
make me pure, even me!
[Oath. Nusku], the image of my sorcerer,
these images of my sorceress,
[the images] of my [sorcerer] and my
sorceress,
the images of my male and female
bewitcher,
[the images] of my male and female
[beguiler],
the images of my male and female
mischief makers,
[the images] of my male and female
[evil] doers,
the images of my male and female
enemy,
[the images] of my male and female
[pursuer],
the images of my male and female
accuser,
[the images] of my [male] and female
slanderer,
the images [of my male and] female
schemer,
[the images] of my [male] and female
conjurer of plans,
the images of my male [and] female
evil—

Judge [Nusku], you know them, I do not
    know them—
[the sorcery], magic, [spook], evil goings
    on,
bewitching, revolt, evil [word], love,
    hate,
pettifogging, murder, laming of the
    mouth, . . .
changing of the heart, glowing of face,
    insanity,
all that [exists, that] they turned to, have
    let themselves turn to,
these are they, these are their images:
[since they are not] standing *themselves*, I
    will lift these images up.
You, [Nusku, judge] who catches the
    evil ones and enemies, catch them,
    while I do not run aground!
Those who have fashioned my image,
    who have reproduced my visage,
who have grabbed hold of [my face],
    tied off my throat,
stabbed my chest, bent my back,
weakened [my arms], took away my
    manly strength,
spurned the heart of the [gods with me],
    weakened my strength,
shook out the strength of my arms,
    bound my knees,
filled me with lameness and weakness,
allowed me to eat [magical food],
allowed me to drink magical [water],
washed me with filthy wash [water],
rubbed me with ointment from evil
    herbs,
chose me to be one who is dead,
laid my water of life into the grave,
had god, king, lords, and princes scorn
    me.
You, O god of fire, who burns the
    sorcerer and the sorceress,
who destroys the evil shoot of the
    sorcerer and sorceress,
who runs to ground the evil ones, you
    are he.
I have called out to you: Like Samas the
    judge,

procure justice for me, make my
    decision!
With fire consume sorcerer and
    sorceress!
Gobble up my enemies, devour those
    who would do evil toward me!
May they feel your furious weather!
May they come to an end as water
    flowing through a hose!
May their fingers be cut off as by a stone
    mason!
By your exalted command that does not
    alter,
and your faithful promise, that does not
    change.
Oath. Exalted Nusku, of the branch of
    Anu,
reflection of your father, firstborn of
    Enlil,
sapling of the ocean, product of the lord
    of heaven and earth,
I have raised the torch, I have
    illuminated you, even you.
The male magician who cast a spell on
    me: take his magic and use it on him
    as he would use it on me!
The female magician who cast a spell on
    me: take her magic and use it on her
    as she would use it on me!
The sorcerer who used his sorcery on
    me: take his sorcery and use it on him
    as he has used it on me!
The sorceress who used her sorcery on
    me: take her sorcery and use it on her
    as she has used it on me!
The witch that enchanted me: take her
    enchantment and enchant her as she
    has enchanted me!
As for those who have fashioned an
    image after my likeness,
who have taken my spittle, who have
    plucked out my hair,
who have cut off the hem of my cloak,
    pulled the earth out from underneath
    me as I walked along:
the god of fire, the hero, unbind their
    oath.

18 Lamentations

The biblical Book of Lamentations mourns the destruction of Jerusalem because of Judah's sin against God and pleads with God to restore his people and rebuild the city. The Book of Psalms contains laments in which the writer bemoans his sad state, affirms his trust in God, and calls on God for deliverance (for example, Psalms 3, 4, 5, 137).[1] Israel's neighbors also had lament literature; two of the best examples are presented here.

#90: Lamentation over the Destruction of Ur
(*ANET* 455–63)[2]

The city of Ur fell to the Amorites and Elamites about 2000 B.C., marking the end of the Ur III period, the last flourishing of Sumerian glory. The laments presented here presumably appeared shortly thereafter, probably through the sponsorship of one of the Isin dynasty's early kings. The first lament describes Ninlil, wife of Ur's city-god Nanna, as she pleads before the council of the gods for the deliverance of her city. The second lament highlights the role of Nanna himself,

first pleading for his city, then abandoning the city to its decreed destruction. These laments have stylistic parallels with the biblical Book of Lamentations, although the theological purpose of Lamentations is quite different.

He has abandoned his stable, his
　　sheepfold *has been delivered* [to] the
　　wind;
the [wild ox] has abandoned his stable,
　　his sheepfold *has been delivered* [to] the
　　wind.
The lord of all the lands has abandoned
　　his stable, his sheepfold *has been
　　delivered* [to] the wind;
Enlil has abandoned . . . Nippur, his
　　sheepfold *has been delivered* [to] the
　　wind.
His wife Ninlil has abandoned *her stable*,
　　her sheepfold *has been delivered* [to]
　　the wind;
Ninlil has abandoned their house [Kiur],
　　her sheepfold *has been delivered* [to]
　　the wind.

The civilization of ancient Ur produced many great artistic and literary pieces, including this sounding box of a harp (the "standard of Ur"). (© Copyright The British Museum)

The [queen] of Kesh has [abandoned]
her stable, her sheepfold *has been
delivered* [to] the wind;
Ninmah has [abandoned] their house
Kesh, her sheepfold *has been delivered*
[to] the wind.
She who is of Isin has abandoned *her
stable*, her sheepfold *has been delivered*
[to] the wind;
Ninisinna has [abandoned] the shrine
Egalmah, her [sheepfold] *has been
delivered* [to] the wind.
The queen of Erech has abandoned *her
stable*, her [sheepfold] *has been
delivered* [to] the wind;
Inanna has abandoned their house
Erech, her sheepfold *has been delivered*
[to] the [wind].
Nanna has abandoned Ur, his sheepfold
has been delivered [to] the [wind];
Sin has abandoned Ekishnugal, [his
sheepfold] *has been delivered* [to] the
wind.
His wife Ningal has [abandoned] *her
stable*, her [sheepfold] *has been
delivered* [to] the wind.
Ningal has [abandoned] her Enunkug,
her [sheepfold] *has been delivered* [to]
the wind.
The wild ox of Eridu has abandoned *his
stable*, his sheepfold *has been delivered*
[to] the wind;
Enki has abandoned their house Eridu,
his sheepfold *has been delivered* [to] the
wind.

(gap)

O city, a bitter lament set up as your
lament;
your lament, which is bitter—O city, set
up your lament.
His righteous city that has been
destroyed—bitter is its lament;
his Ur, which has been destroyed—
bitter is its lament.
Your lament, which is bitter—O city, set
up your lament;
his Ur, which has been destroyed—
bitter is its lament.
Your lament, which is bitter—how long
will it grieve your weeping lord?

Your lament, which is bitter—how long
will grieve the weeping Nanna?
O brickwork of Ur, a bitter lament set up
as your lament;
O Ekishnugal, a bitter lament set up as
your lament;
O shrine Enunkug, a bitter lament set up
as your lament.
O Kiur, you kigallu, a bitter lament set
up as your lament;
O shrine of Nippur . . . , a bitter lament
set up as your lament;
O brickwork of the Ekur, a bitter lament
set up as your lament.

(gap)

Your lament, which is bitter—how long
will it grieve your weeping lord?
Your lament, which is bitter—how long
will it grieve the weeping Nanna?
O city of [name], you have been
destroyed;
O city of [high walls], your land has
perished.
O my city, like an innocent ewe your
lamb has been torn away from you;
O Ur, like an innocent goat your kid has
perished.

(gap)

The third song.
Ur has been given over to tears;
its antiphon.
On that day, after [the lord had been
overcome by the storm],
after, [in spite of the lady], her city had
been destroyed;
on that day, [after the lord had been
overwhelmed by the storm],
after they had [pronounced] the utter
destruction of my city;
after they had [pronounced] the utter
destruction of Ur,
after they had directed that its people be
killed—
on that day truly I abandoned not my
city;
my land truly I forsake not.
To Anu the water of my eye truly I
poured;
to Enlil I in person truly made
supplication.

Let not my city be destroyed, truly I said
unto them;
let not Ur be destroyed, truly I said unto
them;
let not its people perish, truly I said unto
them.
Truly Anu changed not this word;
truly Enlil with its "it is good; so be it"
soothed not my heart.
For the second time, when the council
had . . .
And the Anunnaki . . . [had seated
themselves],
the legs truly I . . . , the arms truly I
[stretched out],
to Anu the water of my eye truly I
poured;
to Enlil I in person truly made
supplication.
Let not my city be destroyed, truly I said
unto them;
let not Ur be destroyed, truly I said unto
them;
let not its people perish, truly I said unto
them.
Truly Anu changed not this work;
truly Enlil with its "it is good; so be it"
soothed not my heart.
The utter destruction of my city truly
they directed,
the utter destruction of Ur truly they
directed;
that its people be killed, as its fate truly
they decreed.
Me like one who has given them my . . .
Me of my city truly they [deprived];
my Ur of me truly they [deprived].
Anu changes not his command;
Enlil alters not the command that he
had issued.
The fourth song.
Her city has been destroyed; her
ordinances have become inimical;
its antiphon.
Enlil called the storm; the people groan.
The storm of overflow he carried off
from the land; the people groan.
The good storm he carried off from
Sumer; the people groan.
To the evil storm he issued directions;
the people groan.

To Kingaluda, the tender of the storm,
he entrusted it.
The storm that annihilates the land he
called; the people groan.
The evil winds he called; the people
groan.
Enlil brings Gibil to his aid.
The great storm of heaven he called; the
people groan.
The great storm howls above; the people
groan.
The land-annihilating storm roars
below; the people groan.
The evil wind, like the rushing torrent,
cannot be restrained;
the boats of the city it attacks *and*
devours,
at the base of heaven it [made the . . .
whirl]; the people groan.
In front of the storm [fires burned]; the
people groan.

(gap)

The storm ordered by Enlil in hate, the
storm that wears away the land,
covered Ur like a garment, [enveloped]
it like linen.
The fifth song.
The raging storm has attacked
unceasingly; the people groan;
its antiphon.
On that day the *good* storm was carried
off from the city; that city into ruins,
O father Nanna, that city into ruins was
made; the people groan.
On that day the *good* storm was carried
off from the land; the people groan.
Its people, not potsherds, filled its sides;
its walls were breached; the people
groan.
In its lofty gates, where they were wont
to promenade, dead bodies were
lying about;
in its boulevards, where the feasts were
celebrated, [scattered they lay].
In all its streets, where they were wont
to promenade, dead bodies were
lying about;
in its places, where the festivities of the
land took place, the people lay in
heaps.

(gap)

Ur—its weak and *its* strong perished through hunger;

mothers and fathers who did not leave their houses, were overcome by fire;

the young lying on their mothers' laps, like fish were carried off by the waters;

of the nursemaids, [pried open were their strong KIRIMMU garments];

the judgment of the land perished; the people groan.

The counsel of the land [was dissipated]; the people groan.

The mother left her daughter; the people groan.

The father turned away from his son; the people groan.

In the city the wife was abandoned, the child was abandoned, the possessions were scattered about;

the black-headed people [into their family places] . . . were carried off.

Its lady like a flying bird departed from her city;

Ningal like a flying bird departed from her city;

on all its possessions that had been accumulated in the land, a defiling hand was placed.

(gap)

The city they make into ruins; the people groan.

Its lady cries: Alas for my city; cries: Alas for my house;

Ningal cries: Alas for my city; cries: Alas for my house.

As for me, the woman, my city has been destroyed, my house too has been destroyed;

O Nanna, Ur has been destroyed, its people have been dispersed.

#91: Balaam of Deir Alla

(Hackett, *Balaam Text from Deir 'Alla*, 29–30)[3]

Discovered in 1967 in the east Jordan Valley, the Deir Alla text mentions a seer named Balaam son of Beor—apparently the same seer who blessed the Israelites as they passed through Moab (Numbers 22). This text describes how Balaam received a prophecy from the gods that reported their displeasure with events on earth.

The account of [Balaam son of Beor] who was a seer of the gods. The gods came to him in the night, and he saw a vision like an oracle of El. Then they said to [Balaam] son of Beor: Thus he will do . . . hereafter, which . . . And Balaam arose the next day . . . from . . . but he was not [able to] . . . and he wept grievously. And his people came up to him [and said to] him: Balaam son of Beor, why are you fasting and crying? And he said to them: Sit down! I will tell you what the [Shaddayyin have done]. Now, come, see the works of the gods! The gods gathered together; the Shaddayyin took their places at the assembly. And they said to [Shaddayyin] . . . : Sew up, bolt up the heavens in your cloud, ordaining darkness instead of eternal light! And put the dark . . . [seal] on your bolt, and do not remove it forever! For the swift reproaches the griffin-vulture and the voice of vultures sings out. The [stork] . . . the young of the NHS bird (?) and claws up young herons. The swallow tears at the dove and the sparrow . . . the rod, and instead of the ewes, it is the staff that is led. Hares eat [a wolf] . . . drink wine and hyenas give heed to chastisement. The whelps of the [fox] . . . laughs at the wise. And the poor woman prepares myrrh while the priestess . . . for the prince, a tattered loincloth. The respected one *now* respects *others* and the one who gave respect is *now* [respected] . . . and the deaf hear from afar . . . [and the of] a fool see visions. The constraint of fertility . . . the leopard. The piglet chases the [young of] . . . his boy, full of love . . . Why do the scion and the firepit containing foliage . . . [so that] El will be satisfied. Let him go to the house of eternity, the [house] the house where the traveler does not rise and the bridegroom does not rise, the house . . . and the worm from the tomb, from those who have arisen among human beings, and from the graves of . . . As for counsel, is it not you with whom he will take counsel; or for advice, will he not ask advice from one residing . . . ? . . . You will cover him with one garment. If you are unkind to him, he will falter. If you . . . I will put . . .

under your head. You will lie down on your eternal bed to perish . . . to themselves. The scion sighs to himself. [The scion] sighs . . . Death will take the newborn child, the suckling . . . The heart of the scion is weak for he goes to . . . to his end . . . to make known the account he spoke to his people orally, your judgment and your punishment . . . and we will not drink.

Notes

Items listed in the bibliography are referenced in the notes by author's surname and short title; see the bibliography for full publication data. All publication data for other bibliographic items are spelled out in full, with the exception of Pritchard's *Ancient Near Eastern Texts Relating to the Old Testament*, which is abbreviated *ANET*.

Chapter 1: *Creation and the Flood*

1. See also Hallo and Younger, *Context of Scripture*, 1:513–15; M. Civil, "The Sumerian Flood Story," in Lambert and Millard's *Atra-ḫasīs*, 138–45; Jacobsen, "Eridu Genesis"; *ANET* 42–44; and S. N. Kramer, "The Sumerian Deluge Myth: Reviewed and Revised," *Anatolian Studies* 33 (1983): 115–21.

2. See also Beyerlin, *Near Eastern Religious Texts*, 85–86; Jacobsen, *Harps That Once*, 181–204; and Kramer, *Sumerian Mythology*, 54–59.

3. Kramer, *History Begins at Sumer*, 141–47. But see the objections of Beyerlin, *Near Eastern Religious Texts*, 85.

4. See also Kramer, *History Begins at Sumer*, 92–95.

5. See also Hallo and Younger, *Context of Scripture*, 1:516–18; and Beyerlin, *Near Eastern Religious Texts*, 76–77.

6. Jacobsen, *Harps That Once*, 151.

7. See also Hallo and Younger, *Context of Scripture*, 1:450–53; Beyerlin, *Near Eastern Religious Texts*, 91–93; and Dalley, *Myths from Mesopotamia*, 1–38.

8. I. Kikawada and A. Quinn, *Before Abraham Was* (Nashville: Abingdon, 1985); and Walton, *Ancient Israelite Literature*, 41–42.

9. Lambert and Millard, *Atra-ḫasīs*, 31–41.

10. See also Hallo and Younger, *Context of Scripture*, 1:390–402; Dalley, *Myths from Mesopotamia*, 228–77; Beyerlin, *Near Eastern Religious Texts*, 80–84; Heidel, *Babylonian Genesis*, 18–60; Thomas, *Documents from Old Testament Times*, 5–16; and L. W. King, *The Seven Tablets of Creation* (2 vols.; London: Luzac, 1902), 1–115.

11. "ENUMA ELISH" 4.135–38 may also contain interesting parallels with Old Testament covenant-making. See D. B. Weisberg, "Loyalty and Death: Some Ancient Near Eastern Metaphors," *Maarav* 7 (1991): 262–66.

12. Jacobsen, "Battle between Marduk and Tiamat"; idem, "Religious Drama in Ancient Mesopotamia," in *Unity and Diversity: Essays in the History, Literature, and Religion of the Ancient Near East* (ed. H. Goedicke and J. J. M. Roberts; Baltimore: Johns Hopkins University Press, 1975), 75–76; and Smith, *Ugaritic Baal Cycle*, 1.110–14.

13. See also *ANET* 129–42; Hallo and Younger, *Context of Scripture*, 1:241–74; Gibson, *Canaanite Myths and Legends*, 37–81; Matthews and Benjamin, *Old Testament Parallels*, 157–68; Thomas, *Documents from Old Testament Times*, 128–33; and Smith, *Ugaritic Baal Cycle*, 1.116–361 (first two tablets).

14. See note 12 above.

15. Scholarly consensus accepts the six tablets numbered *KTU* 1.1–6 as the "Baal Cycle."

16. For the most up-to-date introduction to the "Baal Cycle," see Smith, *Ugaritic Baal Cycle*.

17. For a cautious assessment of Ugaritic and Old Testament comparisons, see Smith, *Ugaritic Baal Cycle*, 1.xxvi–xxviii.

18. See also *ANET* 3; Hallo and Younger, *Context of Scripture*, 1:7–8; and Allen, *Genesis in Egypt*, 13–14.

19. See also Hallo and Younger, *Context of Scripture*, 1:21–23; Lichtheim, *Ancient Egyptian Literature*, 1.51–57; and Allen, *Genesis in Egypt*, 42–47.

20. D. B. Redford, *Egypt, Canaan, and Israel in Ancient Times* (Princeton: Princeton University Press, 1992), 396–400.

21. See also Hallo and Younger, *Context of Scripture*, 1:61–66.

22. See also Beyerlin, *Near Eastern Religious Texts*, 152; and H. G. Güterbock, "The Song of Ullikummi: Revised Text of the Hittite Version of a Hurrian Myth," *Journal of Cuneiform Studies* 5 (1951): 135–61.

23. For discussion of the Hurrian myth cycle, see Hoffner, *Hittite Myths*, 38–40.

24. See also Hallo and Younger, *Context of Scripture*, 1:458–60; Heidel, *Gilgamesh Epic and Old Testament Parallels*; Dalley, *Myths from Mesopotamia*, 39–153; Jackson, *Epic of Gilgamesh*; A. George, *The Epic of Gilgamesh: The Babylonian Epic Poem and Other Texts in Akkadian and Sumerian* (New York: Barnes & Noble, 1999); and Thomas, *Documents from Old Testament Times*, 17–26 (tenth and eleventh tablets only).

25. T. Jacobsen, *The Treasures of Darkness: A History of Mesopotamian Religion* (New Haven: Yale University Press, 1976), 208–15; J. H. Tigay, *The Evolution of the Gilgamesh Epic* (Philadelphia: University of Pennsylvania Press, 1982); Kramer, *History Begins at Sumer*, 148–53; and D. Damrosch, *The Narrative Covenant: Transformations of Genre in the Growth of Biblical Literature* (San Francisco: Harper & Row, 1987), 88–143.

26. Lambert and Millard, *Atra-ḫasīs*, 11, 14–15.

Chapter 2: *Tower of Babel*

1. See also Jacobsen, *Harps That Once*, 289–90; Hallo and Younger, *Context of Scripture*, 1:547–50; and Beyerlin, *Near Eastern Religious Texts*, 86–87.

2. Jacobsen translates the key phrase as "bilingual Sumer"; *Harps That Once*, 289. For further discussion, see D. I. Block, "The Role of Language in Ancient Israelite Perceptions of National Identity," *Journal of Biblical Literature* 103 (1984): 335–36; and J. H. Walton, "The Mesopotamian Background of the Tower of Babel Account and Its Implications," *Bulletin for Biblical Research* 5 (1995): 174–75.

Chapter 3: *Ancestral Customs*

1. Selman, "Comparative Customs and the Patriarchal Age"; and Walton, *Ancient Israelite Literature*, 49–58.

2. See also *ANET* 220.

3. Abraham's taking a second wife is similar to the custom attested in the law code of Hammurapi; see *ANET* 172, laws 144 and 146.

4. Paying a shepherd with newborn animals is paralleled in Old Babylonian law, as preserved in the code of Hammurapi.

5. Burrows, "Complaint of Laban's Daughters."

Chapter 4: *Epic Literature*

1. See also *ANET* 119; Hallo and Younger, *Context of Scripture*, 1:461; Beyerlin, *Near Eastern Religious Texts*, 98–99; and Matthews and Benjamin, *Old Testament Parallels*, 55–56.

2. The "Autobiography of Sargon" is sometimes called the "Legend of Sargon," although there is also a Sumerian text by that name.

3. See also *ANET* 18–22; and Hallo and Younger, *Context of Scripture*, 1:77–82.

4. See also *ANET* 149–55; Hallo and Younger, *Context of Scripture*, 1:343–56; Beyerlin, *Near Eastern Religious Texts*, 225–26; Matthews and Benjamin, *Old Testament Parallels*, 85–94; Gibson, *Canaanite Myths and Legends*, 103–22; Parker, *Pre-biblical Narrative Tradition*, 99–144; and Aitken, *Aqhat Narrative*.

5. The name Danel is spelled differently than the name Daniel in the Old Testament book by that name, but is spelled the same as the wise and shadowy figure in Ezekiel 14:14 and 28:3.

6. See also *ANET* 142–49; Hallo and Younger, *Context of Scripture*, 1:333–43; Beyerlin, *Near Eastern Religious Texts*, 223–25; Matthews and Benjamin, *Old Testament Parallels*, 201–5; Gibson, *Canaanite Myths and Legends*, 82–102; Parker, *Pre-biblical Narrative Tradition*, 145–216; McCarter, *Ancient Inscriptions*, 75–76; and G. Knoppers, "Dissonance and Disaster in the Legend of Kirta," *Journal of the American Oriental Society* 114 (1994): 572–82.

Chapter 5: *Covenants and Treaties*

1. See also *ANET* 482, where "lettuce" in W. F. Albright's translation should be changed to "goat."

2. Wiseman, "Abban and Alalah"; and Hess, "Slaughter of the Animals," 57–58.

3. McCarthy, *Treaty and Covenant*, 86–94.

4. G. E. Mendenhall, *Law and Covenant in Israel and the Ancient Near East* (Pittsburgh: Biblical Colloquium, 1955), 32–34; McCarthy, *Treaty and Covenant*; and Walton, *Ancient Israelite Literature*, 95–109.

5. See also Hallo and Younger, *Context of Scripture*, 2:96–98.

6. See also *ANET* 532.

7. Hess, "Slaughter of the Animals," 61–62.

8. See also Hallo and Younger, *Context of Scripture*, 2:213–17; and *ANET* 659–60.

9. Fitzmyer, *Aramaic Inscriptions of Sefire*, 122–23.

Chapter 6: *Law Codes*

1. Strictly speaking, the technical term *code* is inappropriate for these collections, since several types of legal cases are omitted from the various lists. These lists, therefore, are not comprehensive, but are meant to cover most situations encountered in that particular culture.

2. J. J. Finkelstein, *The Ox That Gored* (Transactions of the American Philosophical Society 71.2; Philadelphia: American Philosophical Society, 1981); and Walton, *Ancient Israelite Literature*, 74–91.

3. See also Hallo and Younger, *Context of Scripture*, 2:408–10; *ANET* 523–25; and J. J. Finkelstein, "The Laws of Ur-Nammu," *Journal of Cuneiform Studies* 22 (1968): 66–82.

4. Since the middle component of this ruler's name is disputed (either Uru-ka-gina or Uru-inim-gina), we have left the name in transcription to acknowledge the uncertainty.

5. Cooper, *Sumerian and Akkadian Royal Inscriptions*, 70–74; and Kramer, *Sumerians*, 317–22.

6. See also Hallo and Younger, *Context of Scripture*, 2:410–14; *ANET* 159–61; and Boecker, *Law and the Administration of Justice*, 58–60.

7. See also Hallo and Younger, *Context of Scripture*, 2:332–35; *ANET* 161–63; and Boecker, *Law and the Administration of Justice*, 60–65.

8. See also Hallo and Younger, *Context of Scripture*, 2:335–53; *ANET* 163–80; Boecker, *Law and the Administration of Justice*, 67–133; and Driver and Miles, *Babylonian Laws*, 2.1–304.

9. The dates given for Hammurapi follow the so-called middle chronology, which has reached consensus among many Assyriologists.

10. See also Hallo and Younger, *Context of Scripture*, 2:353–60; *ANET* 180–81; and Driver and Miles, *Assyrian Laws*, 380–87.

11. See also Hallo and Younger, *Context of Scripture*, 2:106–19; and *ANET* 188–97.

12. See also Hallo and Younger, *Context of Scripture*, 2:360–61; *ANET* 197–98; and Driver and Miles, *Babylonian Laws*, 2.324–47.

Chapter 7: *Cultic Texts*

1. See also Hallo and Younger, *Context of Scripture*, 2:59–64; *ANET* 34–36; and Beyerlin, *Near Eastern Religious Texts*, 64–67.

2. See also Beyerlin, *Near Eastern Religious Texts*, 178–79.

3. Hallo and Younger, *Context of Scripture*, 1:161.

4. See also Hallo and Younger, *Context of Scripture*, 1:217–21; Beyerlin, *Near Eastern Religious Texts*, 180–84; and Sturtevant, "Hittite Text on the Duties."

5. For an introduction to Emar, see D. E. Fleming, "More Help from Syria: Introducing Emar to Biblical Studies," *Biblical Archaeologist* 58 (1995): 139–47.

Chapter 8: *Royal Records from Mesopotamia*

1. For a helpful overview of historiography, see Walton, *Ancient Israelite Literature*, 111–34. It is possible to speak of "real" history writing among the nations of the ancient Near East, although the differences between the Old Testament histories and their ancient counterparts must not be minimized. See Younger, *Ancient Conquest Accounts*, 52–53.

2. J. Van Seters, *In Search of History: Historiography in the Ancient World and the Origins of Biblical History* (New Haven: Yale University Press, 1983), 354–55.

3. H. Tadmor, "Observations on Assyrian Historiography," in *Essays on the Ancient Near East in Memory of Jacob Joel Finkelstein* (ed. M. D. Ellis; Memoirs of the Connecticut Academy of Arts and Sciences 19; Hamden, Conn.: Archon, 1977), 209.

4. See Younger, *Ancient Conquest Accounts*, 79–89, and elsewhere in Younger for other royal annals included here.

5. See also Hallo and Younger, *Context of Scripture*, 2:269–70; *ANET* 281; McCarter, *Ancient Inscriptions*, 21–22; and Luckenbill, *Ancient Records of Assyria and Babylonia*, 1.211 §§589–93.

6. See also Hallo and Younger, *Context of Scripture*, 2.284–86; *ANET* 282–83; and Luckenbill, *Ancient Records of Assyria and Babylonia*, 1.274–76 §770 and §772.

7. The reading "Azriau of Yaudi" itself is now in doubt. See Hallo and Younger, *Context of Scripture*, 2:285 n. 10.

8. See also Hallo and Younger, *Context of Scripture*, 2:296–7; *ANET* 284–85; Luckenbill, *Ancient Records of Assyria and Babylonia*, 2.2–3 §§4–5, 2.26 §55; Matthews and Benjamin, *Old Testament Parallels*, 127–29; and Lie, *Inscriptions of Sargon II*, 1.4–9.

9. See also Hallo and Younger, *Context of Scripture*, 2:302–3; *ANET* 288; Luckenbill, *Ancient Records of Assyria and Babylonia*, 2.120–21 §240; idem, *Annals of Sennacherib*, 32–34 §3.18–49; and Matthews and Benjamin, *Old Testament Parallels*, 139.

10. The most long-standing debate centers on whether Sennacherib conducted one or two campaigns into Palestine, one in 701 B.C. and another over a decade later; see most notably J. Bright, *A History of Israel* (3d ed.; Philadelphia: Westminster, 1981), 298–309; and W. H. Shea, "Sennacherib's Second Palestinian Campaign," *Journal of Biblical Literature* 104 (1985): 401–18.

11. See also Hallo and Younger, *Context of Scripture*, 2:314–16; *ANET* 315–16; Matthews and Benjamin, *Old Testament Parallels*, 147–50; and McCarter, *Ancient Inscriptions*, 27–28.

12. The claim that the "Cyrus Cylinder" offers a precise parallel with the biblical texts has to be tempered in light of recent research; see H. G. M. Williamson, "Exile and After: Historical Study," in *The Face of Old Testament Studies: A Survey of Contemporary Approaches* (ed. D. W. Baker and B. T. Arnold; Grand Rapids: Baker, 1999), 243 n. 19. The cylinder is, however, quite compatible with a positive evaluation of the biblical evidence.

Chapter 9: *Chronicles and Other Historiographic Lists*

1. Oppenheim refers specifically to Mesopotamian literature; see A. L. Oppenheim, *Ancient Mesopotamia: Portrait of a Dead Civilization* (rev. ed.; Chicago: University of Chicago Press, 1977), 19. Mesopotamian authors never developed beyond *Listenwissenschaft* ("list-science"), as illustrated by the lists and chronicles included in this chapter; see J. Goody, *The Domestication of the Savage Mind* (Cambridge: Cambridge University Press, 1977), 74–111. On the differences between Israelite and Mesopotamian historiography in general, see Arnold, "Weidner Chronicle."

2. See also *ANET* 265–66; Jacobsen, *Sumerian King List*; and McCarter, *Ancient Inscriptions*, 7–8.

3. The Sumerian king list presented here appears to have served as an apology for the post–Ur III Isin dynasty; P. Michalowski, "History as Charter: Some Observations on the Sumerian King List," *Journal of the American Oriental Society* 103 (1983): 237–48.

4. Walton, *Ancient Israelite Literature*, 127–31.

5. The Babylonian practice of naming years is distinct from Assyrian LIMMU eponym lists, which contain the name and rank of a high official for each year, sometimes including additional references to notable events.

6. See also Hallo and Younger, *Context of Scripture*, 1:468–70; and Grayson, *Assyrian and Babylonian Chronicles*, 145–51.

7. On the nature of Mesopotamian historiography and the relationship of king lists to chronicles, see Grayson, *Assyrian and Babylonian Chronicles*, 1–5.

8. On the significance of "Weidner Chronicle" for comparative research, see Arnold, "Weidner Chronicle."

9. See also Grayson, *Assyrian and Babylonian Chronicles*, 152–56.

10. See also Wiseman, *Chronicles of Chaldaean Kings*, 51–77; *ANET* 303–5 (chronicle 3 only); and Hallo and Younger, *Context of Scripture*, 1:467–68 (selected portions).

Chapter 10: *Non-Hebrew Monumental Inscriptions*

1. See also Hallo and Younger, *Context of Scripture*, 2:40–41; *ANET* 378; Thomas, *Documents from Old Testament Times*, 137–41; McCarter, *Ancient Inscriptions*, 48–50; and Matthews and Benjamin, *Old Testament Parallels*, 81–82.

2. See also Hallo and Younger, *Context of Scripture*, 2:137–38; *ANET* 320–21; Beyerlin, *Near Eastern Religious Texts*, 237–40; Thomas, *Documents from Old Testament Times*, 195–98; McCarter, *Ancient Inscriptions*, 90–92; Matthews and Benjamin, *Old Testament Parallels*, 112–14; and Smelik, *Writings from Ancient Israel*, 29–50.

3. For the discovery, interpretation, language, and historical and religious significance of the "Mesha Stela," see Dearman, *Studies in the Mesha Inscription and Moab*.

4. Recently reconstructed by André Lemaire as the following: "Now as for Horonaim, there dwelt therein the House of [Da]vid [and] (they) sa[id: . . .]." See André Lemaire, "'House of David' Restored in Moabite Inscription" *Biblical Archaeology Review* 20 (1994): 30–37, and K. A. Kitchen, "A Possible Mention of David in the Late Tenth Century B.C.E.," *Journal for the Study of the Old Testament* 76 (1997): 35–36.

5. See also Hallo and Younger, *Context of Scripture*, 2:148–50; *ANET* 653–54; Beyerlin, *Near Eastern Religious Texts*, 240–42; and Matthews and Benjamin, *Old Testament Parallels*, 115–17.

6. See also Hallo and Younger, *Context of Scripture*, 2:155; *ANET* 655–56; Beyerlin, *Near Eastern Religious Texts*, 229–32; and Thomas, *Documents from Old Testament Times*, 242–50.

7. A. R. Millard, "Israelite and Aramean History in the Light of Inscriptions," *Tyndale Bulletin* 41 (1990): 261–75.

8. See also A. Biran and J. Naveh, "An Aramaic Stele Fragment from Tel Dan," *Israel Exploration Journal* 43

(1993): 81–98; Hallo and Younger, *Context of Scripture*, 2:161–62; and B. Halpern, "The Stela from Dan: Epigraphic and Historical Considerations," *Bulletin of the American Schools of Oriental Research* 296 (1994): 63–80.

9. For discussion and other possible interpretations of the "Tel Dan Inscription," see Biran and Naveh, "Tel Dan Inscription"; and McCarter, *Ancient Inscriptions*, 87–90.

Chapter 11: *Letters*

1. See also *ANET* 487–89; Thomas, *Documents from Old Testament Times*, 38–45; and Matthews and Benjamin, *Old Testament Parallels*, 79–80.

2. See also *ANET* 322; Gibson, *Textbook of Syrian Semitic Inscriptions*, 1.37–43; Thomas, *Documents from Old Testament Times*, 214–17; and Matthews and Benjamin, *Old Testament Parallels*, 134–36.

3. Gibson, *Textbook of Syrian Semitic Inscriptions*, 1.33.

4. See also *ANET* 569; Aharoni, *Arad Inscriptions*, 35; Smelik, *Writings from Ancient Israel*, 113; and Matthews and Benjamin, *Old Testament Parallels*, 134–36.

5. See also Pardee, *Handbook of Ancient Hebrew Letters*, 15–24; *ANET* 568; Gibson, *Textbook of Syrian Semitic Inscriptions*, 1.26–30; and Matthews and Benjamin, *Old Testament Parallels*, 132–33.

6. F. W. Dobbs-Allsopp, "The Genre of the Mesad Hashavyahu Ostracon," *Bulletin of the American Schools of Oriental Research* 295 (1994): 49–55.

Chapter 12: *Other Hebrew Inscriptions*

1. See also Hallo and Younger, *Context of Scripture*, 2:222; *ANET* 320; Smelik, *Writings from Ancient Israel*, 18–28; Thomas, *Documents from Old Testament Times*, 201–3; and Matthews and Benjamin, *Old Testament Parallels*, 104–5.

2. See also Hallo and Younger, *Context of Scripture*, 2:145–46; *ANET* 321; Gibson, *Textbook of Syrian Semitic Inscriptions*, 1.22; Smelik, *Writings from Ancient Israel*, 64–71; Thomas, *Documents from Old Testament Times*, 209–11; and Matthews and Benjamin, *Old Testament Parallels*, 130–31.

3. J. Rogerson and P. R. Davies, "Was the Siloam Tunnel Built by Hezekiah?" *Biblical Archaeologist* 59 (1996): 138–49; and R. S. Hendel, "The Date of the Siloam Inscription: A Rejoinder to Rogerson and Davies," *Biblical Archaeologist* 59 (1996): 233–37.

4. See also Gibson, *Textbook of Syrian Semitic Inscriptions*, 1.5–13; Smelik, *Writings from Ancient Israel*, 51–62; and Thomas, *Documents from Old Testament Times*, 204–8.

5. See also Gogel, *Grammar of Epigraphic Hebrew*, 414–15; Hallo and Younger, *Context of Scripture*, 2:171–72; Smelik, *Writings from Ancient Israel*, 155–60.

6. For more on this discussion, see B. T. Arnold, "Religion in Ancient Israel," in *The Face of Old Testament Studies: A Survey of Contemporary Approaches* (ed. D. W. Baker and B. T. Arnold; Grand Rapids: Baker, 1999), 411–13.

Chapter 13: *Wisdom Literature*

1. Walton, *Ancient Israelite Literature*, 169–97.
2. See also Kramer, "Man and His God"; and Hallo and Younger, *Context of Scripture*, 1:485.
3. See also Hallo and Younger, *Context of Scripture*, 1:486–92.
4. See also Hallo and Younger, *Context of Scripture*, 1:492–95.
5. See also Hallo and Younger, *Context of Scripture*, 1:61–66.
6. Hallo and Younger, *Context of Scripture*, 1:61.
7. See also Hallo and Younger, *Context of Scripture*, 1:110–15.
8. Hallo and Younger, *Context of Scripture*, 1:110; and Walton, *Ancient Israelite Literature*, 173.
9. See also Hallo and Younger, *Context of Scripture*, 1:115–22.
10. Walton, *Ancient Israelite Literature*, 174; and Hallo and Younger, *Context of Scripture*, 1:115.
11. Walton, *Ancient Israelite Literature*, 192–97, presents a solid summary of the pertinent issues surrounding the date of the "Instruction of Amenemope."
12. Matthews and Benjamin, *Old Testament Parallels*, 179–83.

Chapter 14: *Love Poems*

1. Walton, *Ancient Israelite Literature*, 189–92.
2. Kramer, *Sacred Marriage Rite*; and *ANET* 637–45.
3. For a complete discussion of Egyptian love poetry, see Fox, *Song of Songs and the Ancient Egyptian Love Songs*.

Chapter 15: *Hymns and Prayers*

1. Walton, *Ancient Israelite Literature*, 135–68.
2. See also Hallo and Younger, *Context of Scripture*, 1:37–40.
3. Walton, *Ancient Israelite Literature*, 142 n. 25; and *ANET* 365.
4. See also Hallo and Younger, *Context of Scripture*, 1:44–46.
5. See also Hallo and Younger, *Context of Scripture*, 1:418–19.
6. Lambert, *Babylonian Wisdom Literature*, 122–23, provides a good summary of the issues surrounding the date of the "Hymn to Shamash."

7. Walton, *Ancient Israelite Literature*, 137.
8. See also Hallo and Younger, *Context of Scripture*, 1:156–60.

Chapter 16: *Prophecies, Visions, and Apocalyptic*

1. For a good summary of the significance of Mari, see Malamat, "Mari."
2. For an excellent discussion of Mari prophecy, see Moran, "New Evidence from Mari."
3. Walton, *Ancient Israelite Literature*, 203. See also Hallo and Younger, *Context of Scripture*, 1:89–98, 106–10, who do not categorize the "Report of Wen-Amon" as prophecy, but refer to the "Admonitions of Ipuwer" as "prophecy" (intentionally in quotation marks).
4. See also Hallo and Younger, *Context of Scripture*, 1:106–10.
5. Hallo and Younger, *Context of Scripture*, 1:106.
6. Hallo and Younger, *Context of Scripture*, 1:106–7.
7. See also Hallo and Younger, *Context of Scripture*, 1:89–93.
8. Hallo and Younger, *Context of Scripture*, 1:89.
9. See also Hallo and Younger, *Context of Scripture*, 1:480–81.
10. Longman, *Fictional Akkadian Autobiography*.

Chapter 17: *Divination and Incantation Texts*

1. Hoffner, "Ancient Views of Prophecy and Fulfillment," 258.
2. For a detailed summary of incantations, see Reiner, *Šurpu*, 1–6.
3. Reiner, *Šurpu*, 2–3.

Chapter 18: *Lamentations*

1. Walton, *Ancient Israelite Literature*, 160–63.
2. See also Hallo and Younger, *Context of Scripture*, 1:535–39.
3. See also Hoftijzer and van der Kooij, *Aramaic Texts from Deir ʿAlla*; and Hallo and Younger, *Context of Scripture*, 2:140–45.

Bibliography

Aharoni, Y. *Arad Inscriptions*. Jerusalem: Israel Exploration Society, 1981.

Aitken, K. T. *The Aqhat Narrative: A Study in the Narrative Structure and Composition of an Ugaritic Tale*. Journal of Semitic Studies Monograph 13. Manchester: University of Manchester, 1990.

Allen, J. P. *Genesis in Egypt: The Philosophy of Ancient Egyptian Creation Accounts*. Yale Egyptological Studies 2. New Haven: Yale University Press, 1988.

Arnold, B. T. "The Weidner Chronicle and the Idea of History in Israel and Mesopotamia." Pp. 129–48 in *Faith, Tradition, and History: Old Testament Historiography in Its Near Eastern Context*. Edited by A. R. Millard, J. K. Hoffmeier, and D. W. Baker. Winona Lake, Ind.: Eisenbrauns, 1994.

Beyerlin, W. (ed.). *Near Eastern Religious Texts Relating to the Old Testament*. Translated by John Bowden. Old Testament Library. Philadelphia: Westminster, 1975.

Biran, A., and J. Naveh. "The Tel Dan Inscription: A New Fragment." *Israel Exploration Journal* 45 (1995): 1–18.

Block, D. I. *The Gods of the Nations: Studies in Ancient Near Eastern National Theology*. 1st edition. Evangelical Theological Society Monograph Series 2. Jackson, Miss.: Evangelical Theological Society, 1988.

Boecker, H. J. *Law and the Administration of Justice in the Old Testament and Ancient East*. Translated by J. Moiser. Minneapolis: Augsburg, 1980.

Burrows, M. "The Complaint of Laban's Daughters." *Journal of the American Oriental Society* 57 (1937): 259–76.

Coogan, M. D. *Stories from Ancient Canaan*. Louisville: Westminster, 1978.

Cooper, J. S. *Sumerian and Akkadian Royal Inscriptions*, vol. 1: *Presargonic Inscriptions*. New Haven, Conn.: American Oriental Society, 1986.

Dalley, S. *Myths from Mesopotamia: Creation, the Flood, Gilgamesh, and Others*. Oxford: Oxford University Press, 1989.

Dearman, J. A. (ed.). *Studies in the Mesha Inscription and Moab*. Atlanta: Scholars Press, 1989.

Driver, G. R., and J. C. Miles. *The Assyrian Laws*. Oxford: Clarendon, 1935.

———. *The Babylonian Laws*, vol. 1: *Legal Commentary*; vol. 2: *Transliterated Text, Translation, Philological Notes, Glossary*. Oxford: Clarendon, 1952–55.

Faulkner, R. O. *The Ancient Egyptian Coffin Texts*. 3 volumes. Warminster, England: Aris & Phillips, 1973–78.

———. *The Ancient Egyptian Pyramid Texts*. Oxford: Clarendon, 1969.

Finkelstein, J. J. "An Old Babylonian Herding Contract and Genesis 31:38f." *Journal of the American Oriental Society* 88 (1968): 30–36.

Fitzmyer, J. A. *The Aramaic Inscriptions of Sefire*. Rome: Pontifical Biblical Institute Press, 1967.

Fox, M. V. *The Song of Songs and the Ancient Egyptian Love Songs*. Madison: University of Wisconsin Press, 1985.

Gibson, J. C. L. *Canaanite Myths and Legends*. 2d edition. Edinburgh: Clark, 1977.

———. *Textbook of Syrian Semitic Inscriptions*. 3 volumes. Oxford: Clarendon, 1971–82.

Gogel, Sandra Landis. *A Grammar of Epigraphic Hebrew*. Society of Biblical Literature Resources for Biblical Study 23. Atlanta: Scholars Press, 1998.

Grayson, A. K. *Assyrian and Babylonian Chronicles*. Texts from Cuneiform Sources 5. Locust Valley, N.Y.: Augustin, 1975.

———. *Assyrian Royal Inscriptions*. 2 volumes. Wiesbaden: Harrassowitz, 1972–76.

———. *Assyrian Rulers of the Early First Millennium B.C. (858–745 B.C.)*. Royal Inscriptions of Mesopotamia 3. Toronto: University of Toronto Press, 1996.

Hackett, J. A. *The Balaam Text from Deir 'Alla*. Chico, Calif.: Scholars Press, 1980.

Hallo, W. W., and K. L. Younger Jr. (eds.). *The Context of Scripture*, vol. 1: *Canonical Compositions from the Biblical World*. Leiden: Brill, 1997.

Heidel, A. *The Babylonian Genesis: The Story of Creation*. 2d edition. Chicago: University of Chicago Press, 1951.

———. *The Gilgamesh Epic and Old Testament Parallels*. 2d edition. Chicago: University of Chicago Press, 1949.

Held, M. "Philological Notes on the Mari Covenant Rituals." *Bulletin of the American Schools of Oriental Research* 200 (1970): 32–40.

Hess, R. S. "The Slaughter of the Animals in Genesis 15." Pp. 55–65 in *He Swore an Oath: Biblical Themes from Genesis 12–50*. Edited by R. S. Hess, P. E. Satterthwaite, and G. J. Wenham. Cambridge: Tyndale House, 1993.

———. "Yahweh and His Asherah? Epigraphic Evidence for Religious Pluralism in Old Testament Times." Pp. 11–23 in *One God, One Lord in a World of Religious Plu-*

ralism. Edited by A. D. Clarke and B. W. Winter. Cambridge: Tyndale House, 1991.

Hoffner, H. A., Jr. "Ancient Views of Prophecy and Fulfillment: Mesopotamia and Asia Minor." *Journal of the Evangelical Theological Society* 30 (1987): 257–65.

———. *Hittite Myths*. Edited by G. M. Beckman. Atlanta: Scholars Press, 1990.

Hoftijzer, J., and G. van der Kooij. *Aramaic Texts from Deir 'Alla*. Leiden: Brill, 1976.

Hunger, H., and S. A. Kaufman. "A New Akkadian Prophecy Text." *Journal of the American Oriental Society* 95 (1975): 371–75.

Jackson, D. P. *The Epic of Gilgamesh*. Wauconda, Ill.: Bolchazy-Carducci, 1992.

Jacobsen, T. "The Battle between Marduk and Tiamat." *Journal of the American Oriental Society* 88 (1968): 104–8.

———. "The Eridu Genesis." *Journal of Biblical Literature* 100 (1981): 513–29.

———. *The Harps That Once . . . : Sumerian Poetry in Translation*. New Haven: Yale University Press, 1987.

———. *The Sumerian King List*. Assyriological Studies 11. Chicago: University of Chicago Press, 1939.

Kramer, S. N. "The 'Babel of Tongues': A Sumerian Version." *Journal of the American Oriental Society* 88 (1968): 108–11. Reprinted in *"I Studied Inscriptions from before the Flood": Ancient Near Eastern, Literary, and Linguistic Approaches to Genesis 1–11*, pp. 278–82. Edited by R. S. Hess and D. T. Tsumura. Sources for Biblical and Theological Study 4. Winona Lake, Ind.: Eisenbrauns, 1994.

———. *History Begins at Sumer*. 3d edition. Philadelphia: University of Pennsylvania Press, 1981.

———. "Man and His God." Pp. 170–82 in *Wisdom in Israel and in the Ancient Near East*. Edited by M. Noth and D. W. Thomas. Vetus Testamentum Supplement 3. Leiden: Brill, 1955.

———. *The Sacred Marriage Rite*. Bloomington: Indiana University Press, 1969.

———. *Sumerian Mythology: A Study of Spiritual and Literary Achievement in the Third Millennium B.C.* Revised edition. New York: Harper & Row, 1961.

———. *The Sumerians: Their History, Culture, and Character*. Chicago: University of Chicago Press, 1963.

Lambert, W. G. *Babylonian Wisdom Literature*. Oxford: Clarendon, 1960.

Lambert, W. G., and A. R. Millard. *Atra-ḫasīs: The Babylonian Story of the Flood*. Oxford: Clarendon, 1969.

Lewis, B. *The Sargon Legend: A Study of the Akkadian Text and the Tale of the Hero Who Was Exposed at Birth*. American Schools of Oriental Research Dissertation Series 4. Cambridge: American Schools of Oriental Research, 1980.

Lichtheim, M. *Ancient Egyptian Literature: A Book of Readings*. 3 volumes. Berkeley: University of California Press, 1973–80.

Lie, A. G. *The Inscriptions of Sargon II, King of Assyria*, vol. 1: *The Annals*. Paris: Geuthner, 1929.

Longman, T., III. *Fictional Akkadian Autobiography*. Winona Lake, Ind.: Eisenbrauns, 1991.

Luckenbill, D. D. *Ancient Records of Assyria and Babylonia*. 2 volumes. Chicago: University of Chicago Press, 1926.

———. *The Annals of Sennacherib*. Chicago: University of Chicago Press, 1924.

Malamat, A. "Mari." Vol. 11 / cols. 972–89 in *Encylopaedia Judaica*. Jerusalem: Keter, 1971.

Matthews, V. H., and D. C. Benjamin. *Old Testament Parallels: Laws and Stories from the Ancient Near East*. New York: Paulist, 1991.

McCarter, P. K., Jr. *Ancient Inscriptions: Voices from the Biblical World*. Washington, D.C.: Biblical Archaeology Society, 1996.

McCarthy, D. J. *Treaty and Covenant: A Study in Form in the Ancient Oriental Documents and in the Old Testament*. Rome: Pontifical Biblical Institute Press, 1978.

Meier, G. *Die assyrische Beschwörungssammlung Maqlu*. Archiv für Orientforschung, Beiheft 2. Osnabruck: Graz, 1967.

Moran, W. L. *The Amarna Letters*. Baltimore: Johns Hopkins University Press, 1992.

———. "New Evidence from Mari on the History of Prophecy." *Biblica* 50 (1969): 15–56.

Pardee, D. *Handbook of Ancient Hebrew Letters*. Atlanta: Scholars Press, 1982.

Parker, S. B. *The Pre-biblical Narrative Tradition: Essays on the Ugaritic Poems Keret and Aqhat*. Atlanta: Scholars Press, 1989.

Parpola, S., and K. Watanabe. *Neo-Assyrian Treaties and Loyalty Oaths*. State Archives of Assyria 2. Helsinki: Helsinki University Press, 1988.

Pritchard, J. B. (ed.). *Ancient Near Eastern Texts Relating to the Old Testament*. 3d edition. Princeton: Princeton University Press, 1969.

Reiner, E. *Šurpu: A Collection of Sumerian and Akkadian Incantations*. Archiv für Orientforschung, Beiheft 11. Osnabruck: Graz, 1970.

Roth, M. T. *Law Collections from Mesopotamia and Asia Minor*. Edited by P. Michalowski. Atlanta: Scholars Press, 1995.

Selman, M. J. "Comparative Customs and the Patriarchal Age." Pp. 91–140 in *Essays on the Patriarchal Narratives*. Edited by A. R. Millard and D. J. Wiseman. Winona Lake, Ind.: Eisenbrauns, 1983.

Simpson, W. K. *The Literature of Ancient Egypt: An Anthology of Stories, Instructions, and Poetry*. New Haven: Yale University Press, 1972.

Smelik, K. A. D. *Writings from Ancient Israel: A Handbook of Historical and Religious Documents*. Translated by G. I. Davies. Edinburgh: Clark, 1991.

Smith, M. S. *The Ugaritic Baal Cycle*, vol. 1: *Introduction with Text, Translation, and Commentary of KTU 1.1–1.2*. Leiden: Brill, 1994.

Speiser, E. A. "New Kirkuk Documents Relating to Family Laws." *Annual of the American Schools of Oriental Research* 10 (1930): 1–73.

Sturtevant, E. H. "A Hittite Text on the Duties of Priests and Temple Servants." *Journal of the American Oriental Society* 54 (1934): 363–406.

Thomas, D. W. (ed.). *Documents from Old Testament Times*. London: Nelson, 1958.

Walton, J. H. *Ancient Israelite Literature in Its Cultural Context*. Grand Rapids: Zondervan, 1989.

Wiseman, D. J. "Abban and Alalah." *Journal of Cuneiform Studies* 12 (1958): 124–29.

———. *The Alalakh Tablets*. Occasional Publications of the British Institute of Archaeology at Ankara 2. London: British Institute of Archaeology at Ankara, 1953.

———. *Chronicles of Chaldaean Kings (626–556 B.C.)*. London: British Museum, 1956.

Younger, K. L., Jr. *Ancient Conquest Accounts: A Study in Ancient Near Eastern and Biblical History Writing*. Journal for the Study of the Old Testament 98. Sheffield: JSOT Press, 1990.

Scripture Index

Genesis

1   63
1:6–8   32
1:26–27   65
2:7   20, 65
5   150
11:1–9   71
12–50   72
15   96, 101
15:9–10   96
21:27   96
26:28   96
31:14–16   73
31:38–40   73
31:44   96
31:50   72
46:34   192

Exodus

2:1–10   75
20–24   96, 97
21–23   112
21:15   112
21:22–25   112
21:28–32   112

Leviticus

17–26   112

24:19–20   112
25:1–7   127

Numbers

22   225

Deuteronomy

12–26   112
19:21   112
26:13–15   118

Joshua

9–12   137
24   96, 97

Judges

20:38   168
20:40   168

2 Samuel

9–20   88

1 Kings

1–2   88
4:29–34   175

2 Kings

3   161
8:28–29   165
9:14–29   165
17:3   145
17:6   145
18–19   146
20:20   171

2 Chronicles

32:2–5   171
32:30   171
36:23   147

Ezra

1:2–4   147
6:1–5   147

Psalms

3   222
4   222
5   222
8   19
19   19
104   19
137   222

Proverbs

2:1   185
3:1   185
4:1   185
22–23   187

Song of Songs

1:5–7   192
4:1–2   192
6:2–3   192

Isaiah

36–37   146

Jeremiah

6:1   168
34:18–20   96, 101

Ezekiel

14:14   228 n. 5
25:12   170
28:3   228 n. 5

Obadiah

10–14   170

Acknowledgments

W. L. Moran, "New Evidence from Mari on the History of Prophecy." *Biblica* (Editrice Pontificio Istituto Biblico, Roma, 1969).

Princeton University Press

J. B. Pritchard, ed., *Ancient Near Eastern Texts Relating to the Old Testament.* Copyright © 1950, 1955, 1969 renewed 1978 by Princeton University Press. Reprinted by permission of Princeton University Press.

SCM Press

W. Beyerlin, ed., *Near Eastern Religious Texts Relating to the Old Testament,* translated by John Bowden, Old Testament Library (1975). Used by permission of SCM Press.

Semitic Museum, Harvard University

J. A. Hackett, *The Balaam Text from Deir 'Alla* (1980). Reprinted by permission of the Semitic Museum, Harvard University.

Society of Biblical Literature

H. A. Hoffner Jr., *Hittite Myths,* edited by G. M. Beckman (1990). Reprinted by permission of the Society of Biblical Literature.

M. T. Roth, *Law Collections from Mesopotamia and Asia Minor,* edited by P. Michalowski (1995). Reprinted by permission of the Society of Biblical Literature.

T & T Clark

K. A. D. Smelik, *Writings from Ancient Israel: A Handbook of Historical and Religious Documents,* translated by G. I. Davies (1991).

Thomas Nelson

D. W. Thomas, ed., *Documents from Old Testament Times* (1958).

Toronto University Press

A. K. Grayson, *Assyrian Rulers of the Early First Millennium B.C. (858–745 B.C.)* (1996). Reprinted by permission of Toronto University Press.

Tyndale House

R. S. Hess, "Yahweh and His Asherah? Epigraphic Evidence for Religious Pluralism in Old Testament Times," in *One God, One Lord in a World of Religious Pluralism* (1991).

University of California Press

M. Lichtheim, *Ancient Egyptian Literature: A Book of Readings* (1973–80).

Westminster John Knox Press

M. D. Coogan, *Stories from Ancient Canaan.* ©1978 The Westminster Press. Used by permission of Westminster John Knox Press.

W. Beyerlin, ed., *Near Eastern Religious Texts Relating to the Old Testament,* translated by John Bowden, Old Testament Library (1975). Used by permission of Westminster John Knox Press.

Yale University Press

T. Jacobsen, *The Harps That Once . . . : Sumerian Poetry in Translation* (1987).

The authors and publisher have made every effort to ascertain the copyright status of every reading in this book. Any failure to give proper credit that is brought to the publisher's attention will be amended in subsequent printings of the book.

Subject Index